A smile spreads across my face when I catch a glimpse of wildflowers blooming by the side of the road. "Ah... So pretty!" Yeah, I know. I'm getting old.

— Yoshiyuki Nishi

Yoshiyuki Nishi was born in Tokyo. Two of his favorite manga series are *Dragon Ball* and the robot-cat comedy *Doraemon*. His latest series, *Muhyo & Roji's Bureau of Supernatural Investigation*, debuted in Japan's *Akamaru Jump* magazine in 2004 and went on to be serialized in *Weekly Shonen Jump*.

MUHYO & ROJI'S

BUREAU OF SUPERNATURAL INVESTIGATION

VOL. 13
The SHONEN JUMP Manga Edition

STORY AND ART BY
YOSHIYUKI NISHI

Translation & Adaptation/Alexander O. Smith
Touch-up Art & Lettering/Brian Bilter
Design/Yukiko Whitley
Editor/Amy Yu

VP, Production/Alvin Lu
VP, Publishing Licensing/Rika Inouye
VP, Sales & Product Marketing/Gonzalo Ferreyra
VP, Creative/Linda Espinosa
Publisher/Hyoe Narita

MUHYO TO ROZY NO MAHORITSU SODAN JIMUSHO © 2004
by Yoshiyuki Nishi. All rights reserved. First published in
Japan in 2004 by SHUEISHA Inc., Tokyo. English translation
rights arranged by SHUEISHA Inc. The stories, characters and
incidents mentioned in this publication are entirely fictional.

Printed in the U.S.A.

Published by VIZ Media, LLC
P.O. Box 77010
San Francisco, CA 94107

SHONEN JUMP Manga Edition
10 9 8 7 6 5 4 3 2 1
First printing, October 2009

THE WORLD'S
MOST POPULAR MANGA

www.viz.com   www.shonenjump.com

SHONEN JUMP MANGA EDITION

Muhyo & Roji's Bureau of Supernatural Investigation BSI

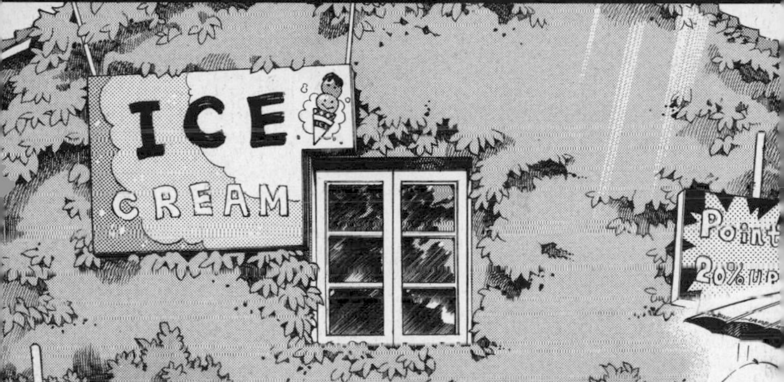
ICE CREAM
Point 20%UP
ICE
open

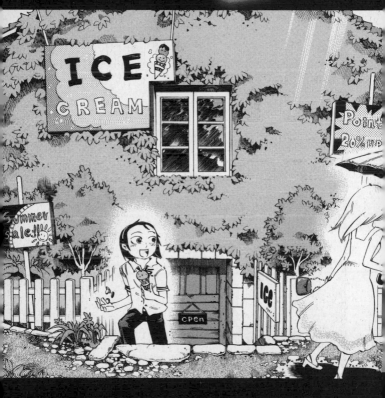

Vol. 13 A New Book of Magic Law

Story & Art by Yoshiyuki Nishi

Dramatis Personae

Jiro Kusano (Roji)

Assistant at Muhyo's office, recently promoted from the lowest rank of "Second Clerk" to that of (provisional) "First Clerk." Roji has a gentle heart and has been known to freak out in the presence of spirits. Lately, he has been devoting himself to the study of magic law so that he can pull his own weight someday.

Toru Muhyo (Muhyo)

Young, genius magic law practitioner with the highest rank of "Executor." Always calm and collected (though sometimes considered cold), Muhyo possesses a strong sense of justice and even has a kind side. Sleeps a lot to recover from the exhaustion caused by his practice.

Harumi Busujima

Executor and one of the only practitioners in the world capable of "remote magic law."

Yu Abiko (Biko)

Muhyo's classmate and an Artificer. Makes seals, pens, magic law books and other accoutrements of magic law.

Yoichi Himukai (Yoichi)

Judge and Muhyo's former classmate. Expert practitioner of all magic law except execution.

Page Klaus

Chief Investigator for the Magic Law Association, Yoichi's boss, and Muhyo and Enchu's former instructor.

Rio Kurotori (Rio)

Charismatic Artificer who turned traitor when the Magic Law Association stood by and let her mother die.

Soratsugu Madoka (Enchu)

Muhyo's former classmate and Executor-hopeful until one event turned him onto the traitor's path.

Nana Takenouchi (Nana)

High school student, spirit medium and amateur photographer. Working as an assistant photographic investigator.

Bobby

Low-level haunt and former Magic Law School (M.L.S.) student. Wants to ascend to Heaven.

Umekichi Sasanoha

First clerk and Busujima's assistant. In his true envoy form, he is called *Unryuso*. "Umekichi" is his human-form alias.

Lili & Maril Mathias

Twin siblings world-renowned for their research in magic law.

Reiko Imai

Brave Judge who joined Muhyo and gang during the fight against Face-Ripper Sophie.

Ginji Sugakiya

Upperclassman at M.L.S. Boasts the rank of Assistant Judge even though he is still enrolled in school.

Hanao Ebisu (Ebisu)

Judge and assistant to Goryo. Fired once, but has since been reinstated.

Daranimaru Goryo (Goryo)

Executor and rival to Muhyo. When Ark captured him, it was Muhyo who came to the rescue.

Ivy Cortlaw

Member of the forbidden magic law group known as Ark. A powerful Ghostmaster, she has the ability to create and control ghosts.

The Story

Magic law is a newly established practice for judging and punishing the increasing crimes committed by spirits; those who use it are called "practitioners."

Not only do Muhyo and the gang succeed in rescuing Judge Imai and Rio from the clutches of Ark, but it is revealed that Teeki himself orchestrated Rio's traitorous turn to forbidden magic law. At Biko's urging, Rio is welcomed back into the Association. Meanwhile, Page learns from Isabi that the Writ of Passage—the key to defeating Teeki—can be found somewhere in the M.L.S.! Page calls off the assault on Ark's Wailing Vale headquarters and sends Muhyo's team undercover into the M.L.S instead... But it doesn't take long for Ark assassin Ghostmaster Ivy to arrive. Now she's releasing the very haunts that the Association has kept under lock and key!

Teeki

Dangerous entity marked as a traitor to the Magic Law Association for 800 years.

Isabi

Forbidden magic law practitioner who made himself an envoy to obtain eternal life. Sole possessor of means to kill Teeki.

Muhyo & Roji's
Bureau of Supernatural Investigation
BSI

CONTENTS

13

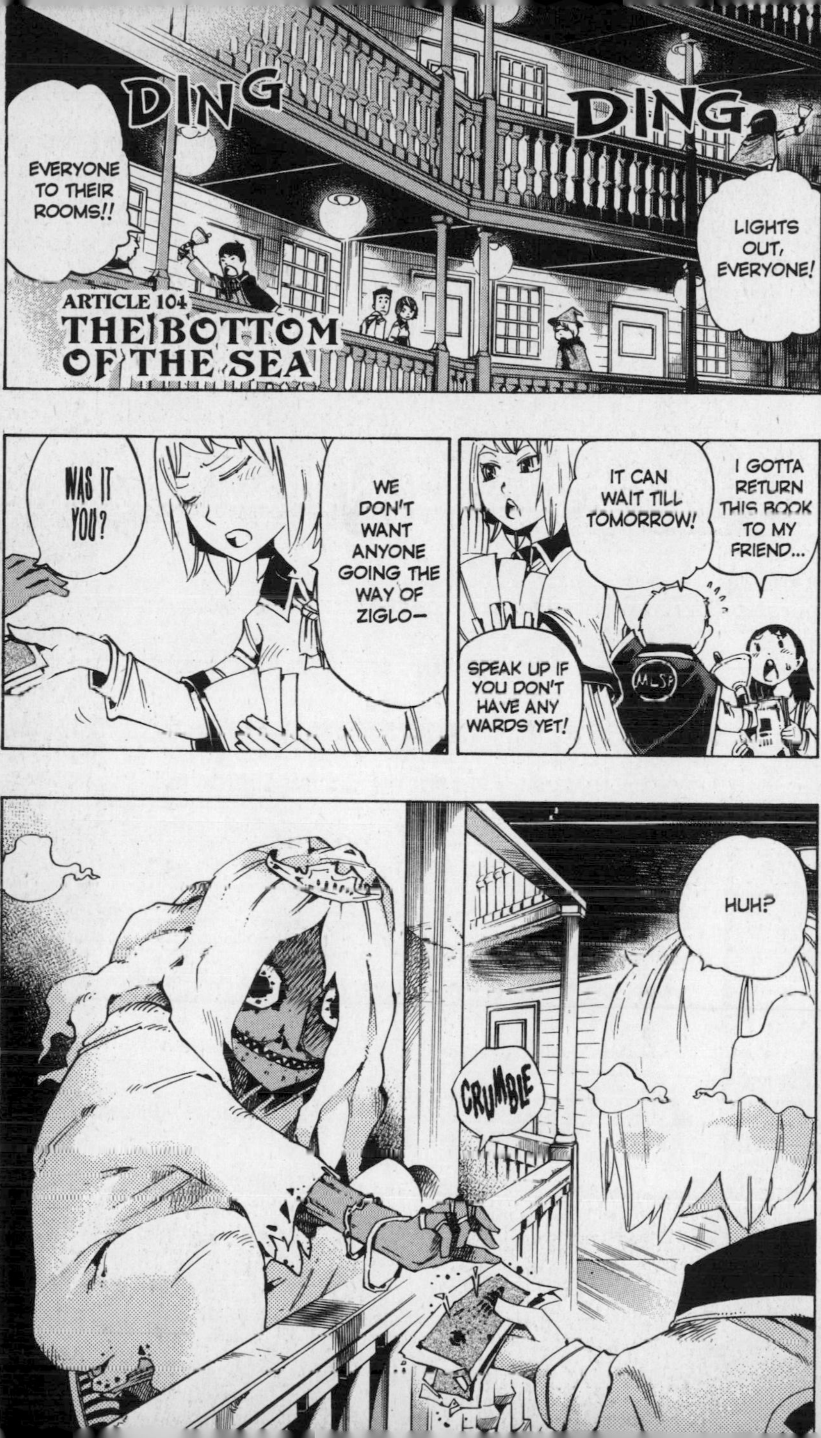
DING
LIGHTS OUT, EVERYONE!
DING
EVERYONE TO THEIR ROOMS!!
ARTICLE 104
THE BOTTOM OF THE SEA
I GOTTA RETURN THIS BOOK TO MY FRIEND...
IT CAN WAIT TILL TOMORROW!
SPEAK UP IF YOU DON'T HAVE ANY WARDS YET!
WE DON'T WANT ANYONE GOING THE WAY OF ZIGLO—
WAS IT YOU?
HUH?
CRUMBLE

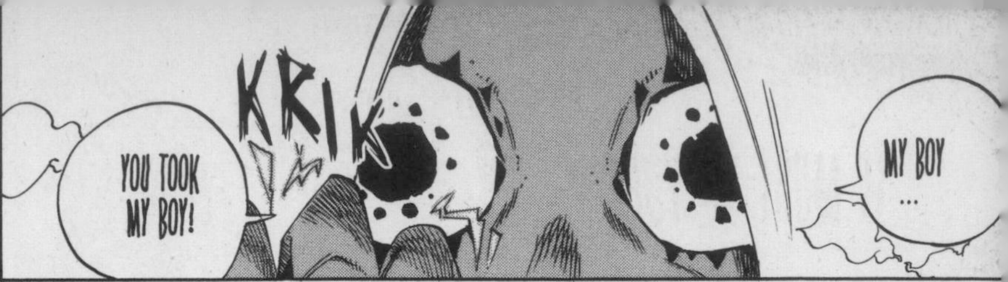
MY BOY
...
KRIK
YOU TOOK
MY BOY!

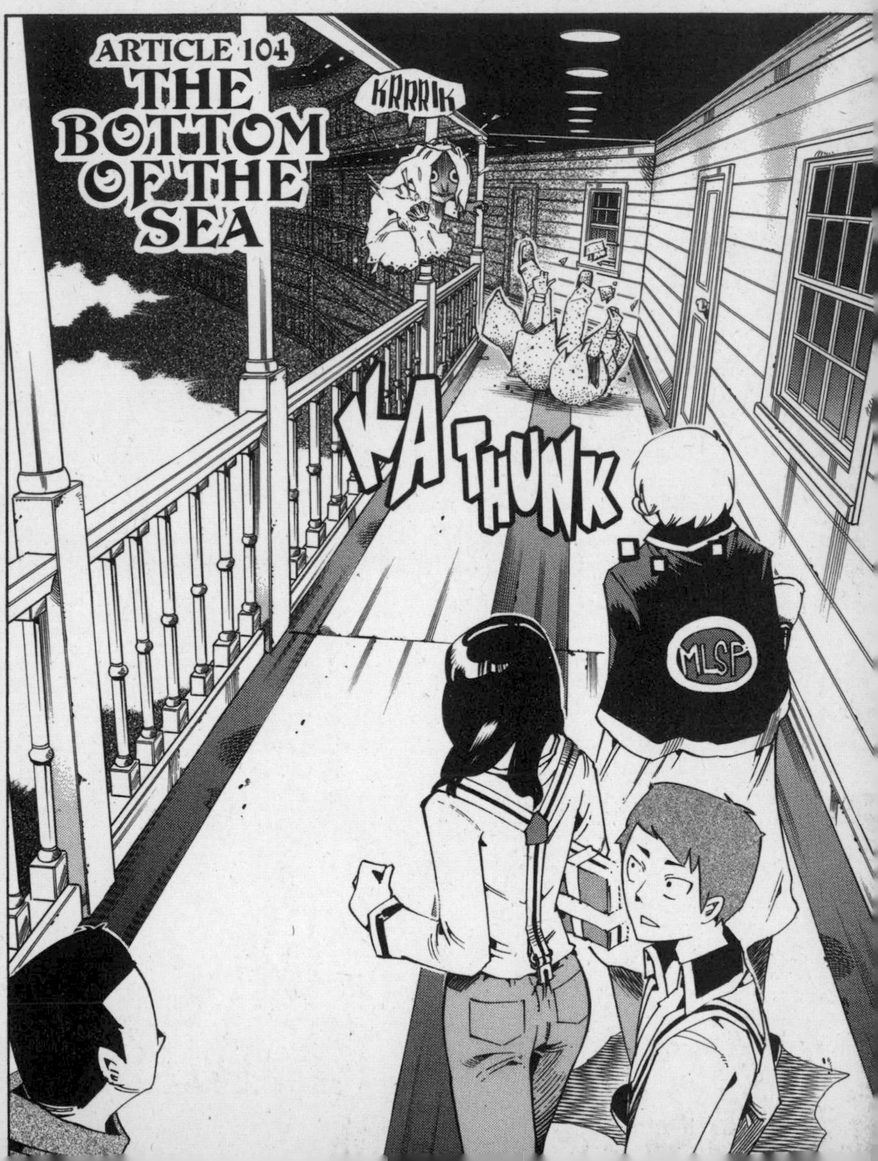
ARTICLE 104
THE BOTTOM OF THE SEA
KRRRIK
KA THUNK
MLSP

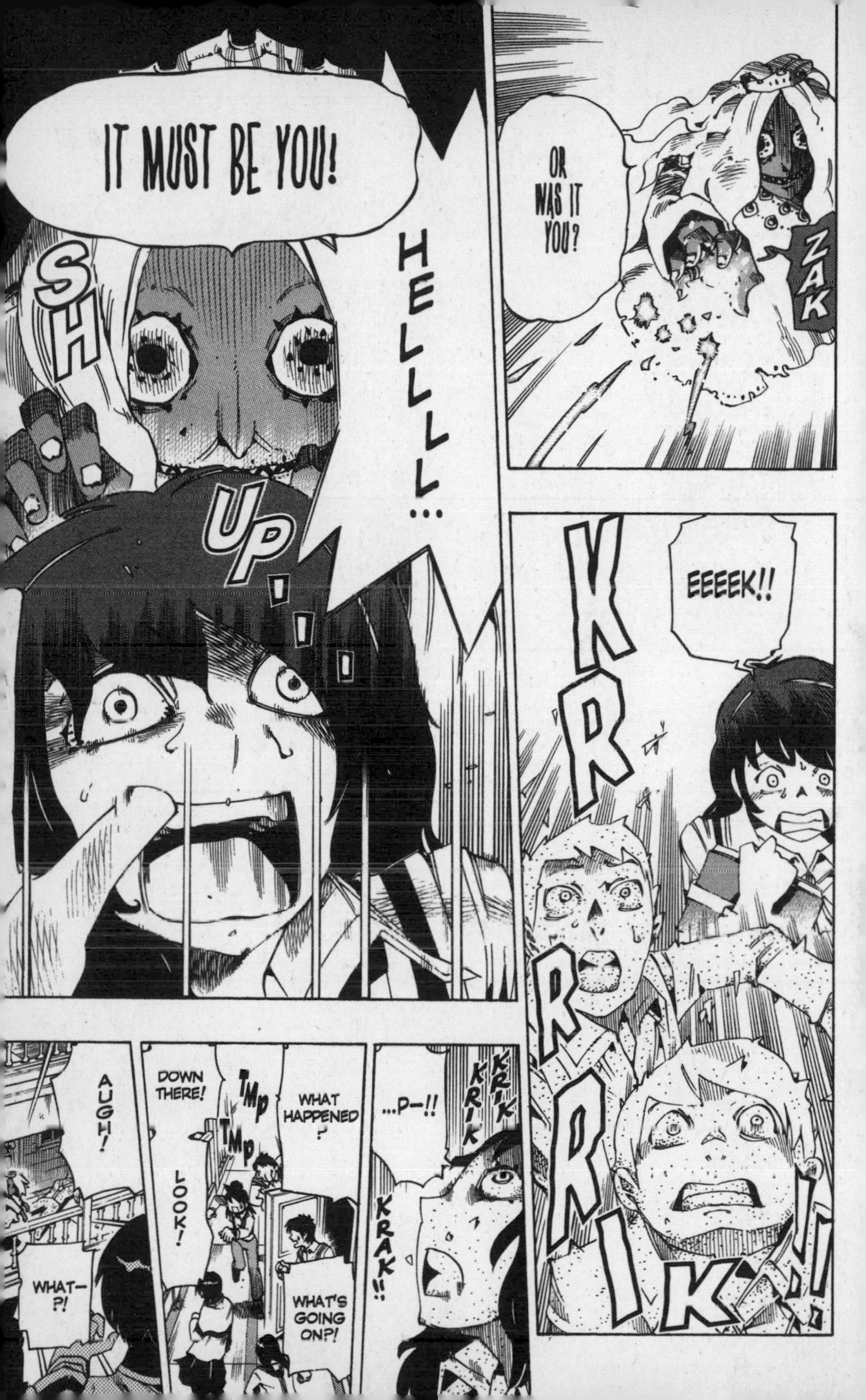

OR WAS IT YOU?
ZAK
IT MUST BE YOU!
SH
HELLLL...
UP!!!
EEEEK!!
KRRRIK!!
KRIK KRIK
KRAK!!
...P–!!
WHAT HAPPENED?
DOWN THERE!
TMP TMP
LOOK!
WHAT'S GOING ON?!
AUGH!
WHAT–?!

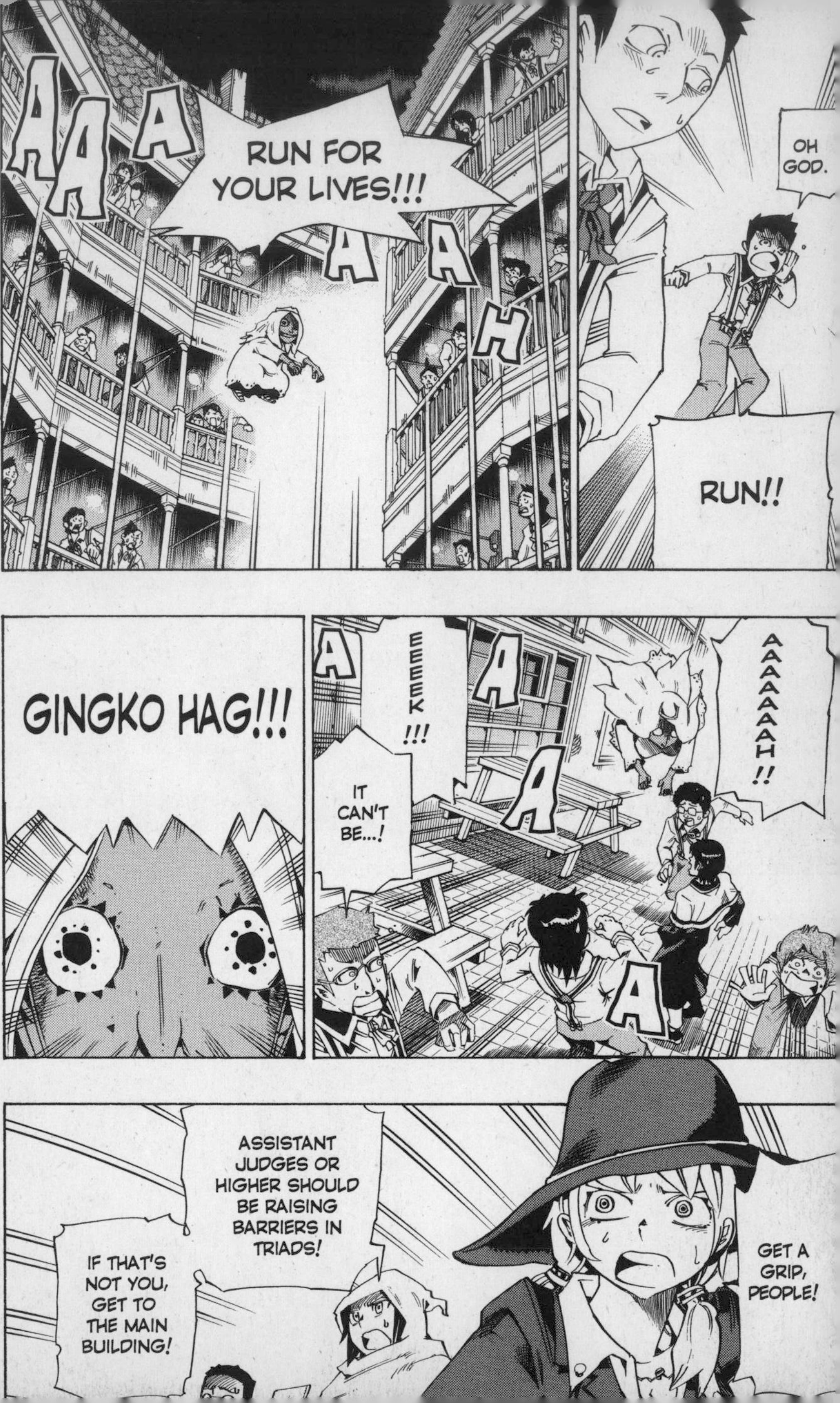
OH GOD.
RUN!!
RUN FOR YOUR LIVES!!!
AAAAAAH
AAAAAAH!!
EEEK!!!
IT CAN'T BE...!
AAAA
GINGKO HAG!!!
GET A GRIP, PEOPLE!
ASSISTANT JUDGES OR HIGHER SHOULD BE RAISING BARRIERS IN TRIADS!
IF THAT'S NOT YOU, GET TO THE MAIN BUILDING!

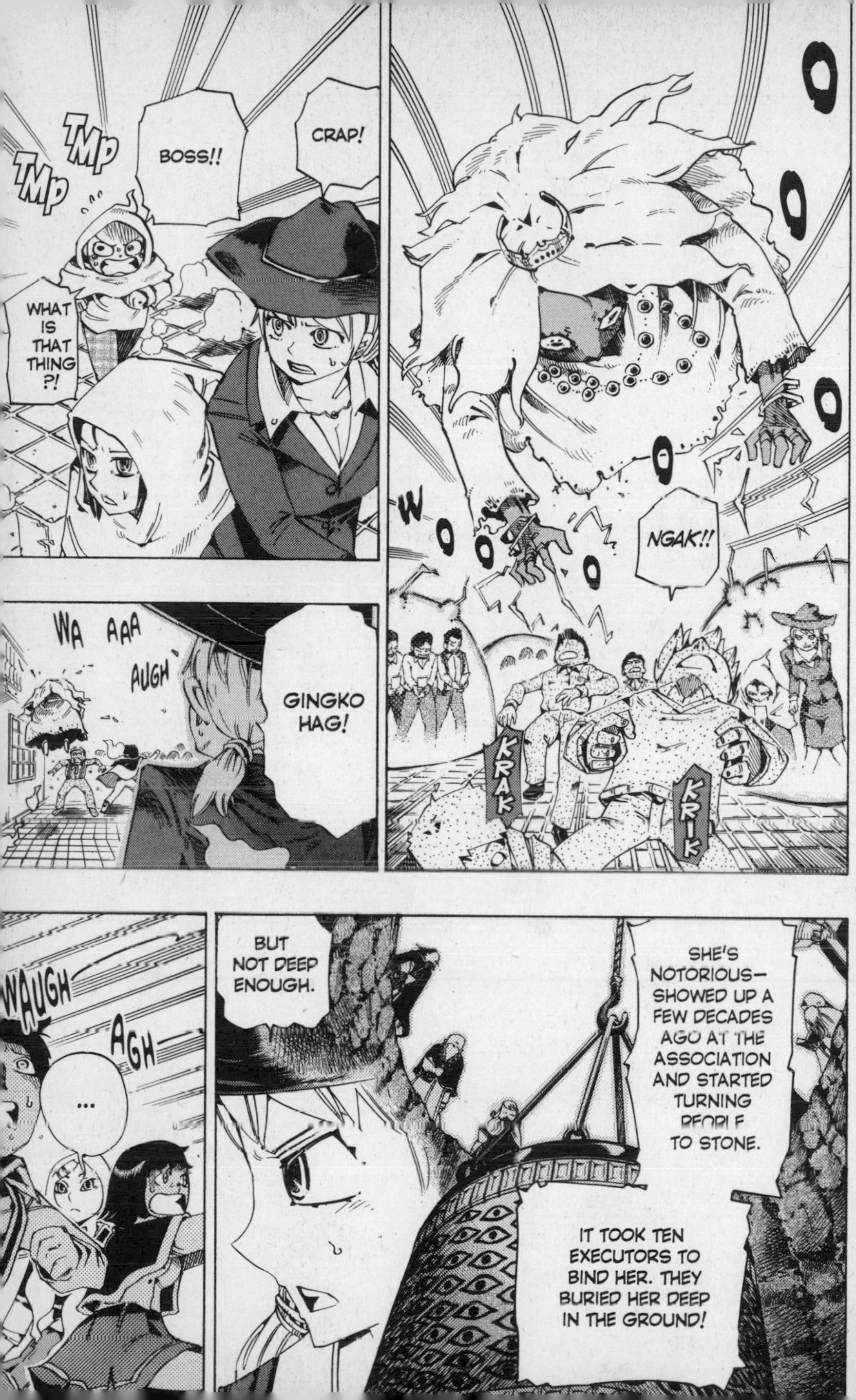
WOOOOOOO
NGAK!!
KRAK
KRIK
CRAP!
BOSS!!
TMP
TMP
WHAT IS THAT THING?!
GINGKO HAG!
WA AAA AUGH
SHE'S NOTORIOUS—SHOWED UP A FEW DECADES AGO AT THE ASSOCIATION AND STARTED TURNING PEOPLE TO STONE.
IT TOOK TEN EXECUTORS TO BIND HER. THEY BURIED HER DEEP IN THE GROUND!
BUT NOT DEEP ENOUGH.
WAUGH
AGH
...

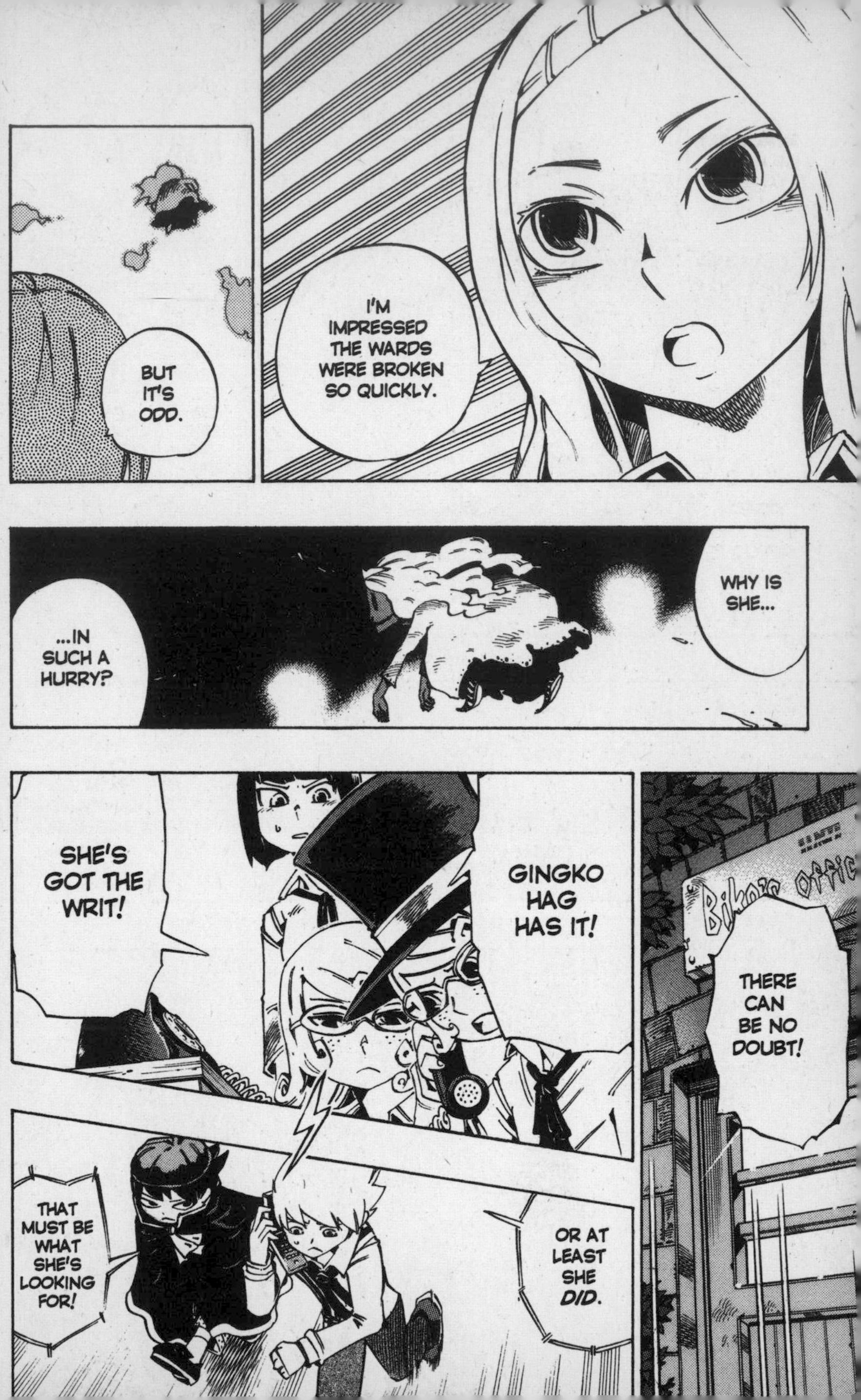
I'M IMPRESSED THE WARDS WERE BROKEN SO QUICKLY.
BUT IT'S ODD.
WHY IS SHE...
...IN SUCH A HURRY?
THERE CAN BE NO DOUBT!
GINGKO HAG HAS IT!
SHE'S GOT THE WRIT!
OR AT LEAST SHE *DID*.
THAT MUST BE WHAT SHE'S LOOKING FOR!

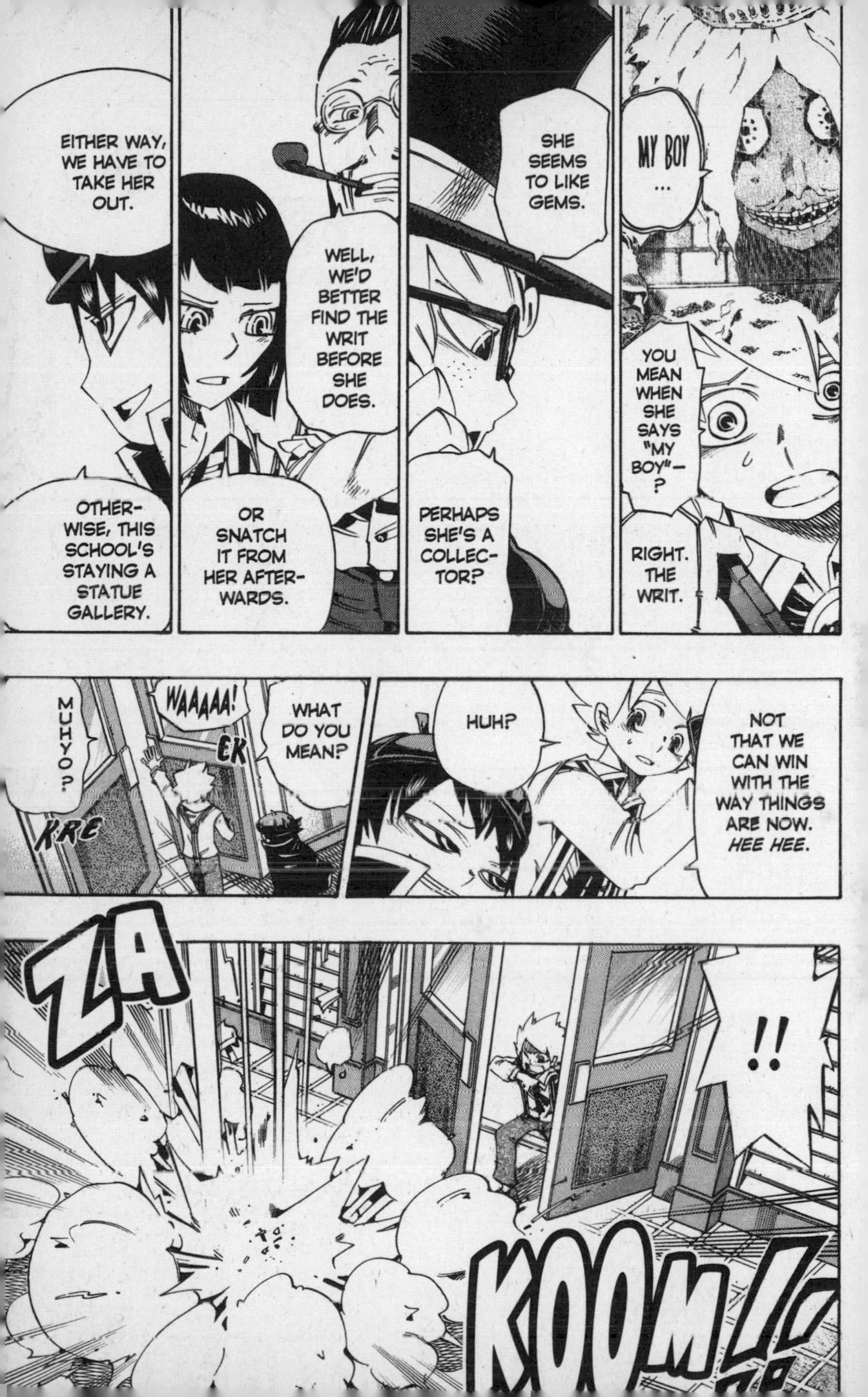
MY BOY ...
YOU MEAN WHEN SHE SAYS "MY BOY"— ?
RIGHT. THE WRIT.
SHE SEEMS TO LIKE GEMS.
PERHAPS SHE'S A COLLECTOR?
WELL, WE'D BETTER FIND THE WRIT BEFORE SHE DOES.
OR SNATCH IT FROM HER AFTER-WARDS.
EITHER WAY, WE HAVE TO TAKE HER OUT.
OTHER-WISE, THIS SCHOOL'S STAYING A STATUE GALLERY.
NOT THAT WE CAN WIN WITH THE WAY THINGS ARE NOW. *HEE HEE.*
HUH?
WHAT DO YOU MEAN?
WAAAAA!
EK
MUHYO?
KRE
!!
ZA
KOOM!!

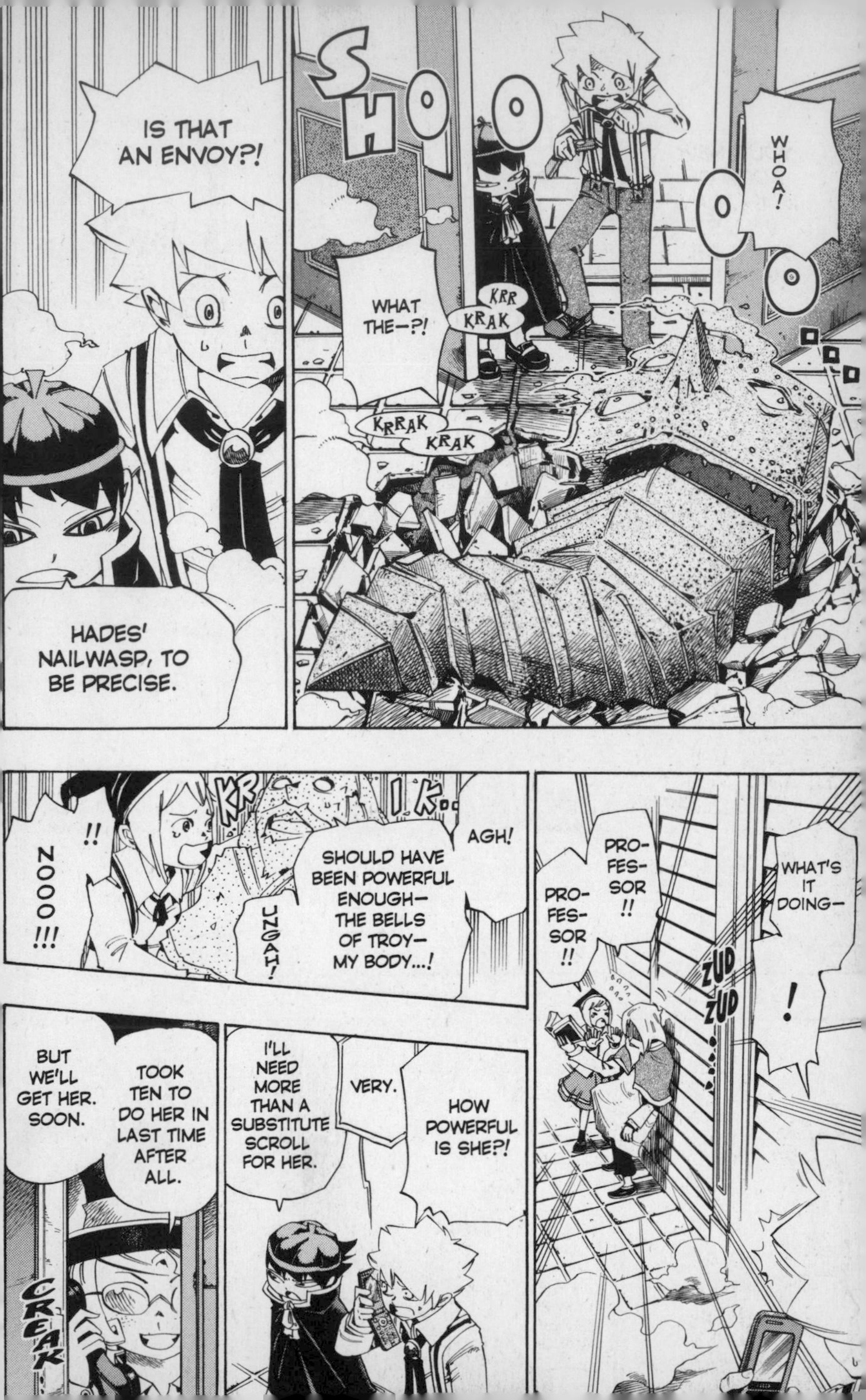
SHOOOOOO
WHOA!
WHAT THE—?!
KRR KRAK
KRRAK KRAK
IS THAT AN ENVOY?!
HADES' NAILWASP, TO BE PRECISE.
WHAT'S IT DOING—
PRO-FES-SOR!!
PRO-FES-SOR!!
ZUD ZUD
!
KRIK
AGH!
SHOULD HAVE BEEN POWERFUL ENOUGH— THE BELLS OF TROY— MY BODY...!
UNGAH!
!!
NOOO!!!
HOW POWERFUL IS SHE?!
VERY.
I'LL NEED MORE THAN A SUBSTITUTE SCROLL FOR HER.
TOOK TEN TO DO HER IN LAST TIME AFTER ALL.
BUT WE'LL GET HER. SOON.
CREAK

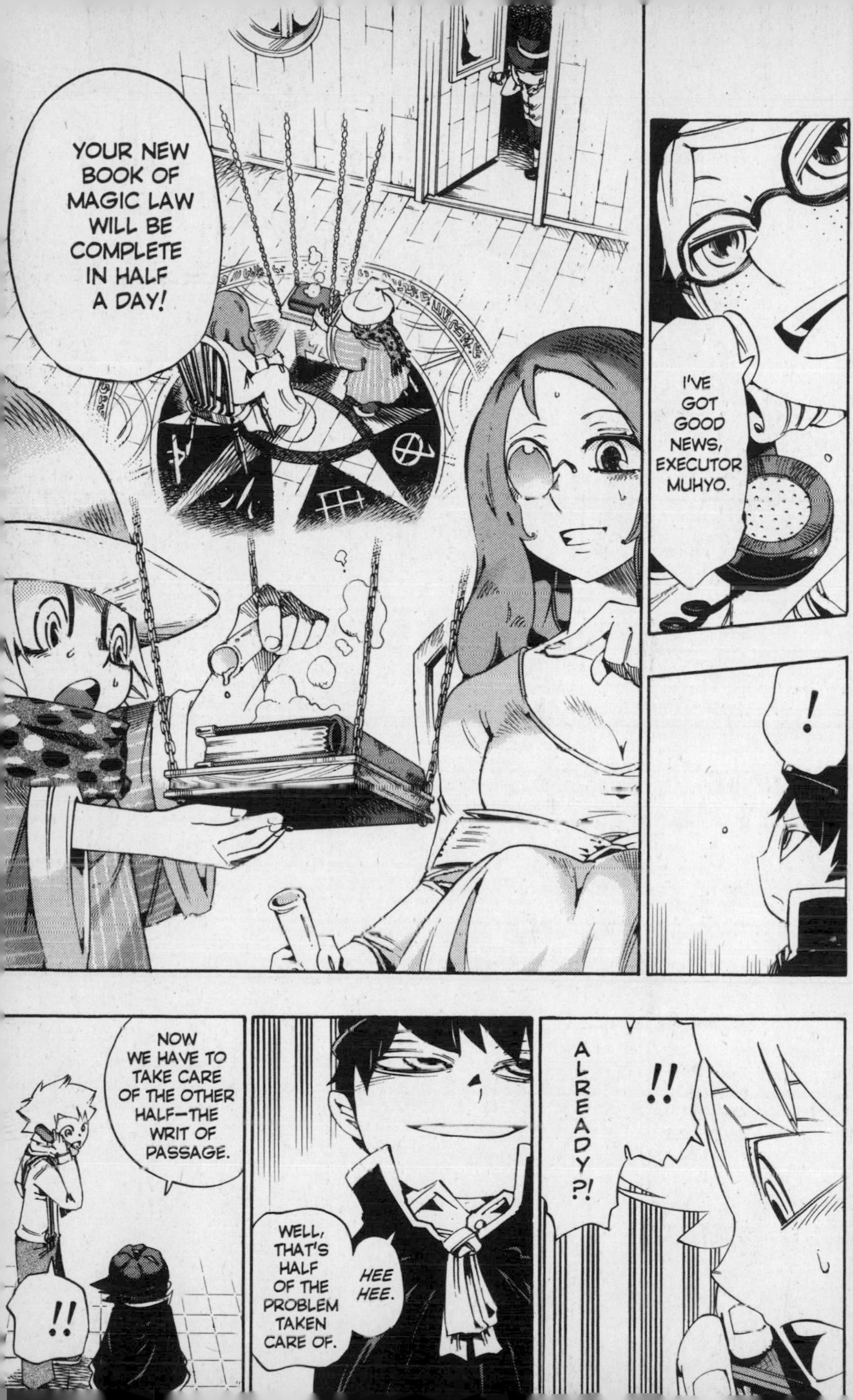
I'VE GOT GOOD NEWS, EXECUTOR MUHYO.
!
YOUR NEW BOOK OF MAGIC LAW WILL BE COMPLETE IN HALF A DAY!
ALREADY?!
!!
WELL, THAT'S HALF OF THE PROBLEM TAKEN CARE OF.
HEE HEE.
NOW WE HAVE TO TAKE CARE OF THE OTHER HALF—THE WRIT OF PASSAGE.
!!

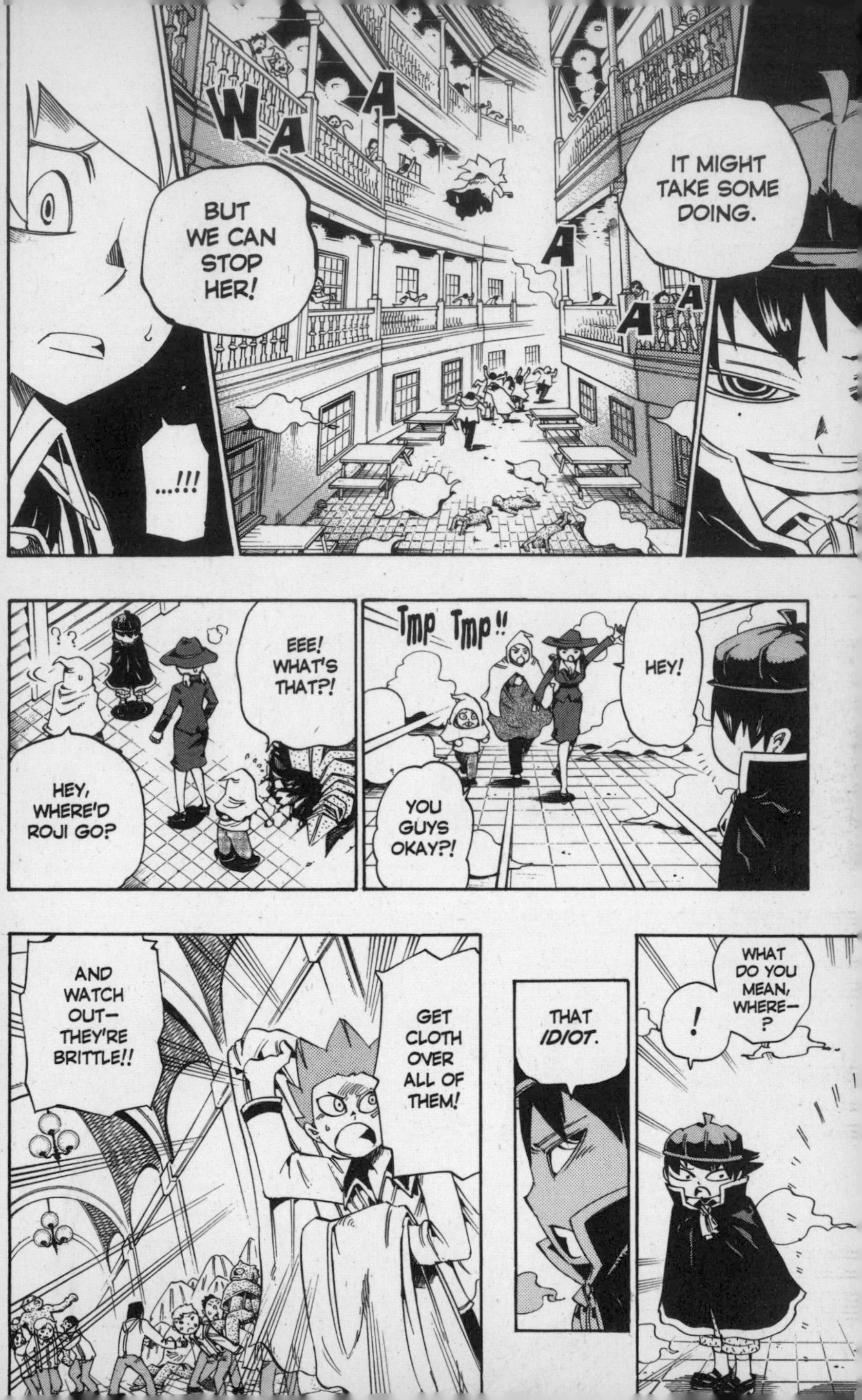
IT MIGHT TAKE SOME DOING.
WA A A A A
BUT WE CAN STOP HER!
...!!!
Tmp Tmp!!
HEY!
YOU GUYS OKAY?!
EEE! WHAT'S THAT?!
HEY, WHERE'D ROJI GO?
WHAT DO YOU MEAN, WHERE—?
!
THAT *IDIOT*.
GET CLOTH OVER ALL OF THEM!
AND WATCH OUT—THEY'RE BRITTLE!!

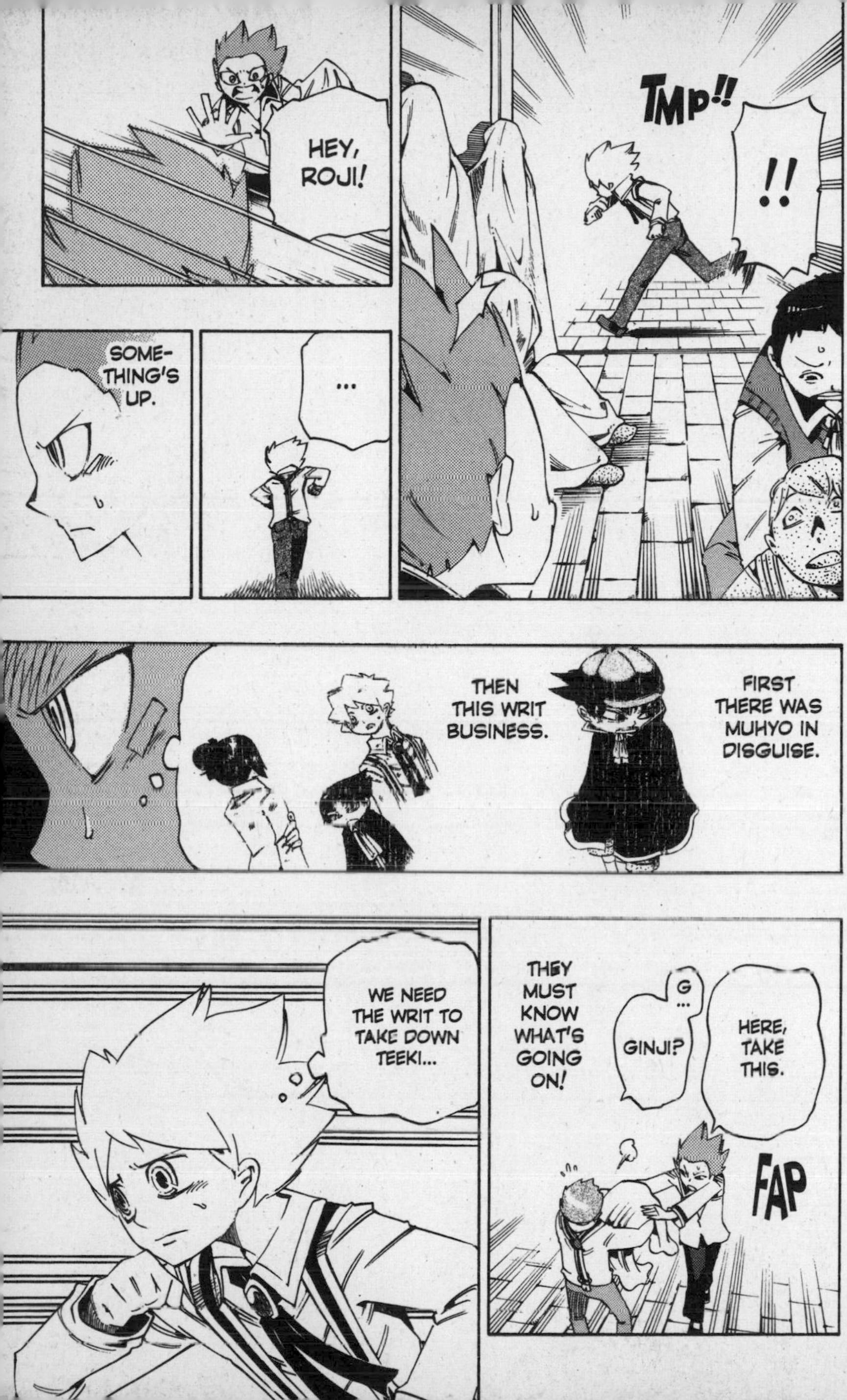
TMP!!
!!
HEY, ROJI!
...
SOME-THING'S UP.
FIRST THERE WAS MUHYO IN DISGUISE.
THEN THIS WRIT BUSINESS.
HERE, TAKE THIS.
G...
GINJI?
FAP
THEY MUST KNOW WHAT'S GOING ON!
WE NEED THE WRIT TO TAKE DOWN TEEKI...

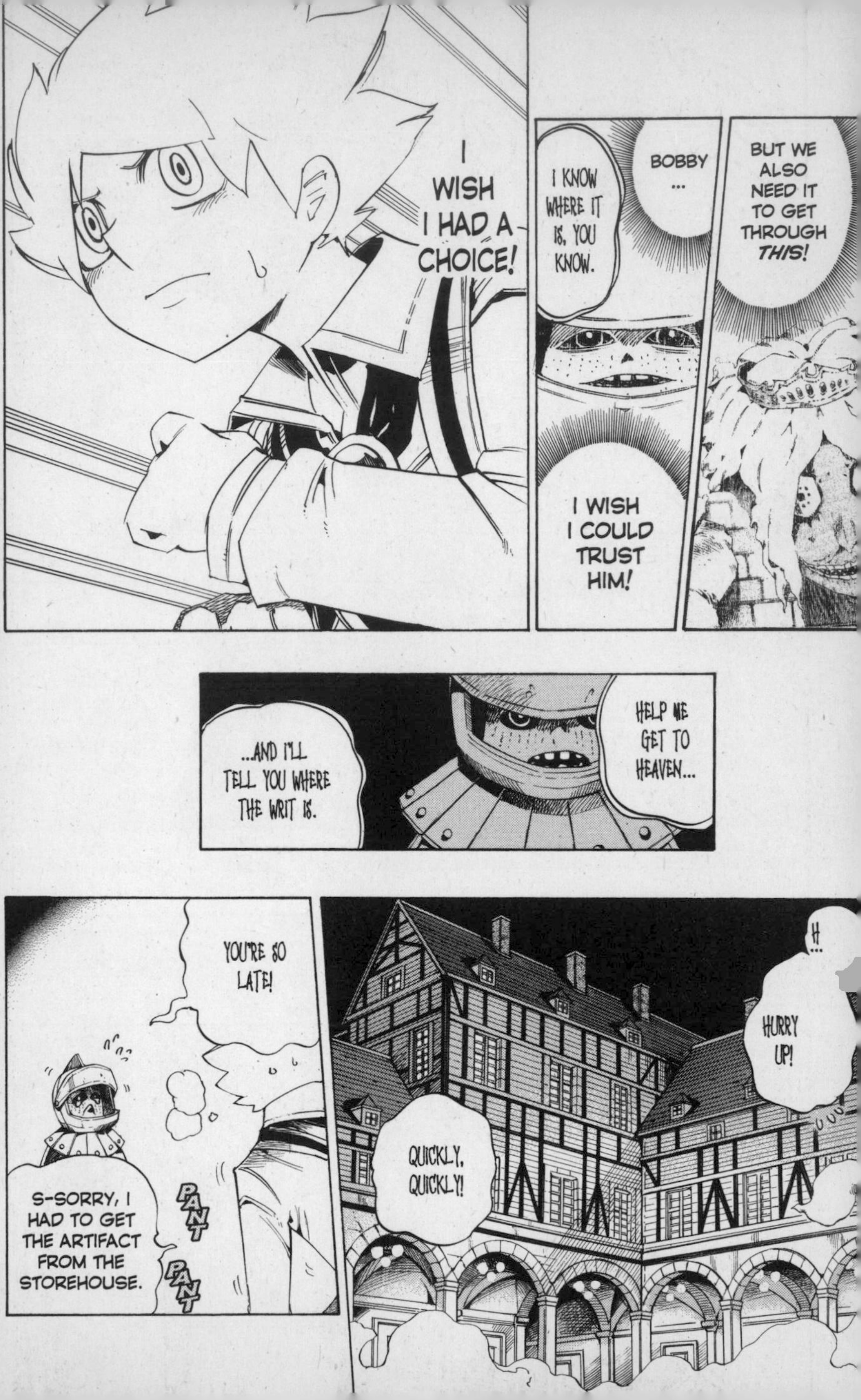
BUT WE ALSO NEED IT TO GET THROUGH *THIS*!
BOBBY...
I KNOW WHERE IT IS, YOU KNOW.
I WISH I COULD TRUST HIM!
I WISH I HAD A CHOICE!
HELP ME GET TO HEAVEN...
...AND I'LL TELL YOU WHERE THE WRIT IS.
H...
HURRY UP!
QUICKLY, QUICKLY!
YOU'RE SO LATE!
S-SORRY, I HAD TO GET THE ARTIFACT FROM THE STOREHOUSE.
PANT
PANT

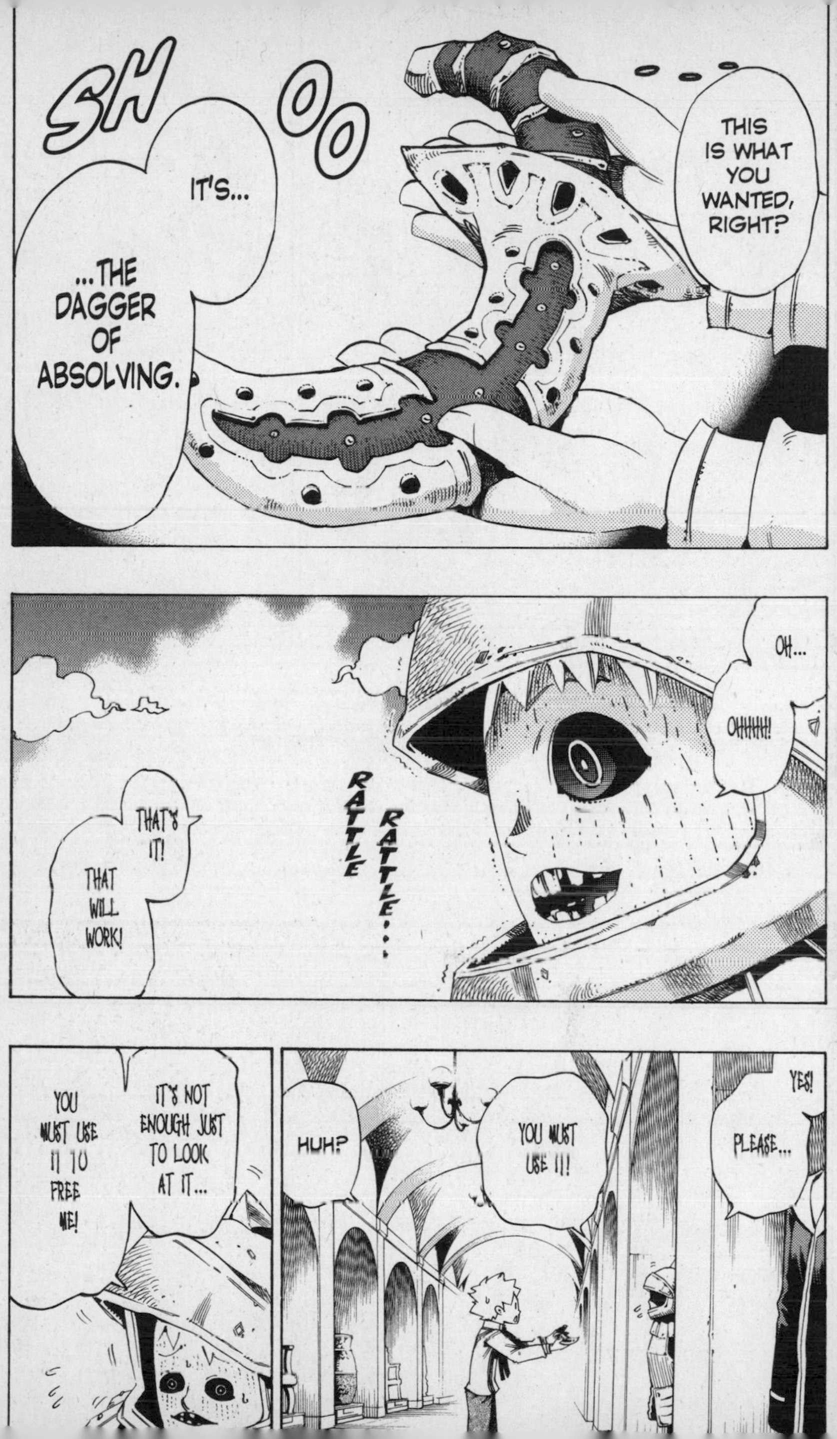
THIS IS WHAT YOU WANTED, RIGHT?
SHOO
IT'S...
...THE DAGGER OF ABSOLVING.
OH... OHHHH!
RATTLE RATTLE...
THAT'S IT!
THAT WILL WORK!
YES!
PLEASE...
YOU MUST USE IT!
HUH?
IT'S NOT ENOUGH JUST TO LOOK AT IT...
YOU MUST USE IT TO FREE ME!

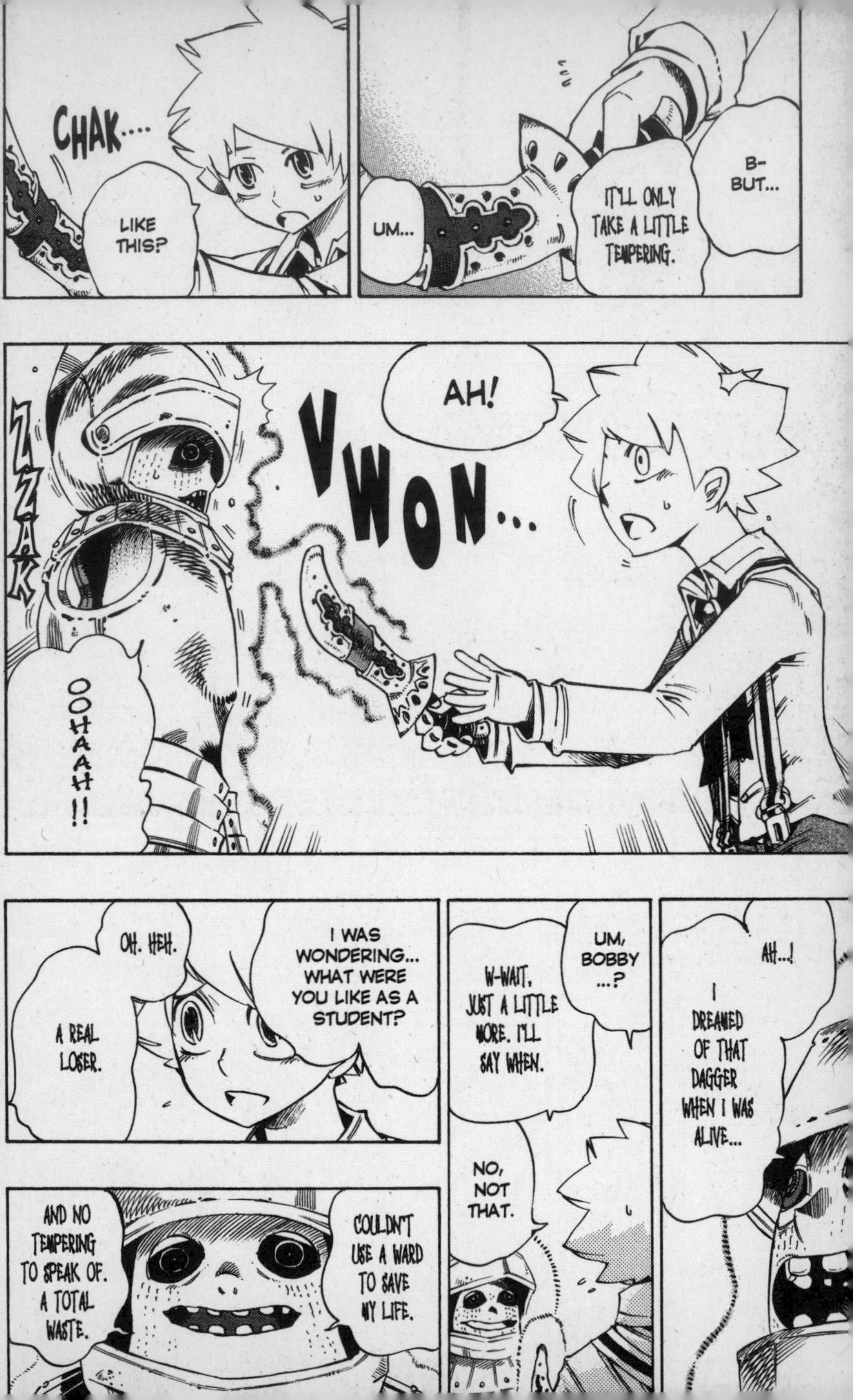

B-BUT...
IT'LL ONLY TAKE A LITTLE TEMPERING.
UM...
CHAK....
LIKE THIS?
AH!
VWON...
ZZAK
OOHAAAH!!
AH...!
I DREAMED OF THAT DAGGER WHEN I WAS ALIVE...
UM, BOBBY ...?
W-WAIT, JUST A LITTLE MORE. I'LL SAY WHEN.
NO, NOT THAT.
I WAS WONDERING... WHAT WERE YOU LIKE AS A STUDENT?
OH. HEH.
A REAL LOSER.
COULDN'T USE A WARD TO SAVE MY LIFE.
AND NO TEMPERING TO SPEAK OF. A TOTAL WASTE.

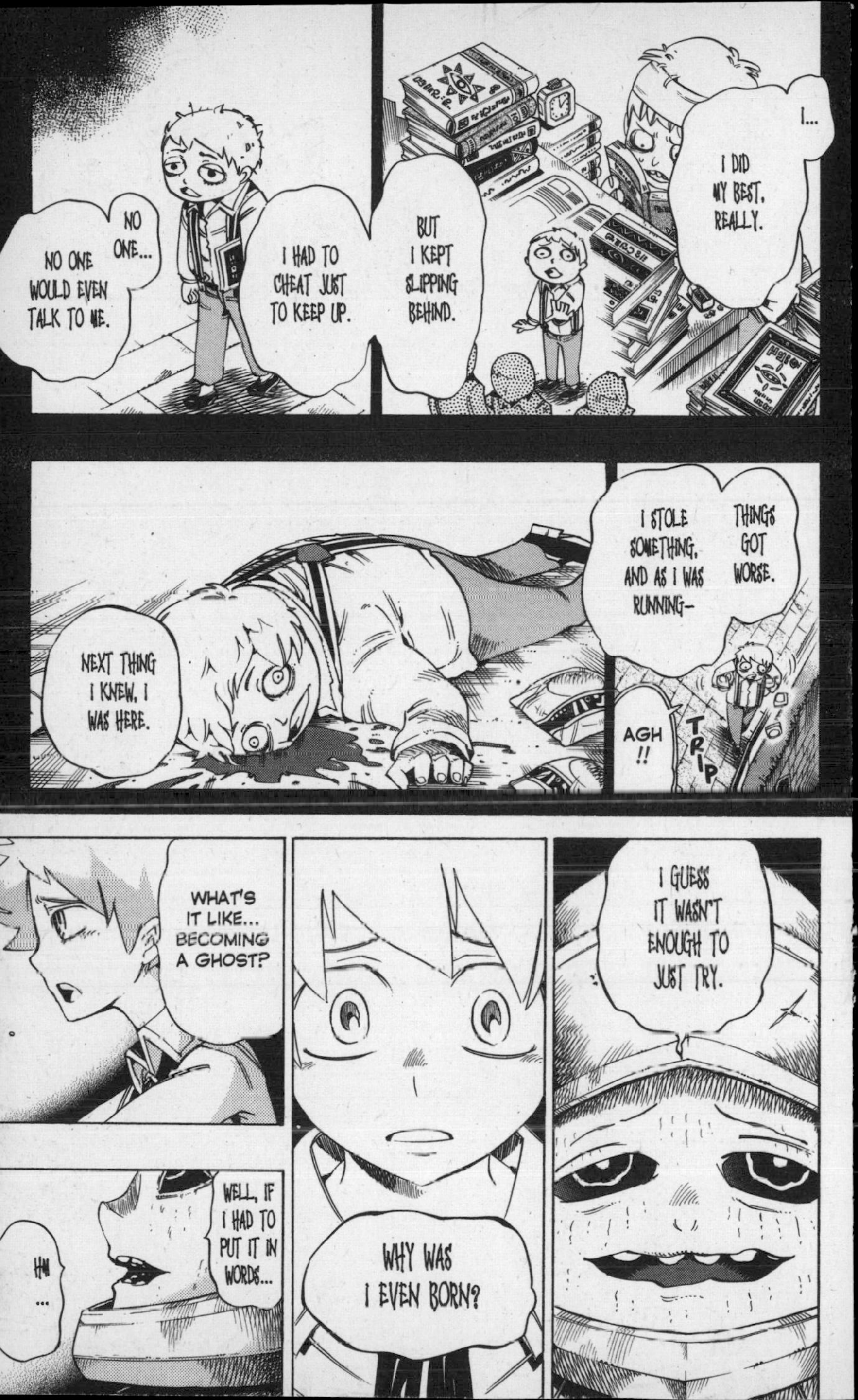

I...
I DID MY BEST, REALLY.
BUT I KEPT SLIPPING BEHIND.
I HAD TO CHEAT JUST TO KEEP UP.
NO ONE...
NO ONE WOULD EVEN TALK TO ME.
THINGS GOT WORSE.
I STOLE SOMETHING, AND AS I WAS RUNNING—
TRIP
AGH !!
NEXT THING I KNEW, I WAS HERE.
I GUESS IT WASN'T ENOUGH TO JUST TRY.
WHY WAS I EVEN BORN?
WHAT'S IT LIKE... BECOMING A GHOST?
WELL, IF I HAD TO PUT IT IN WORDS...
HM ...

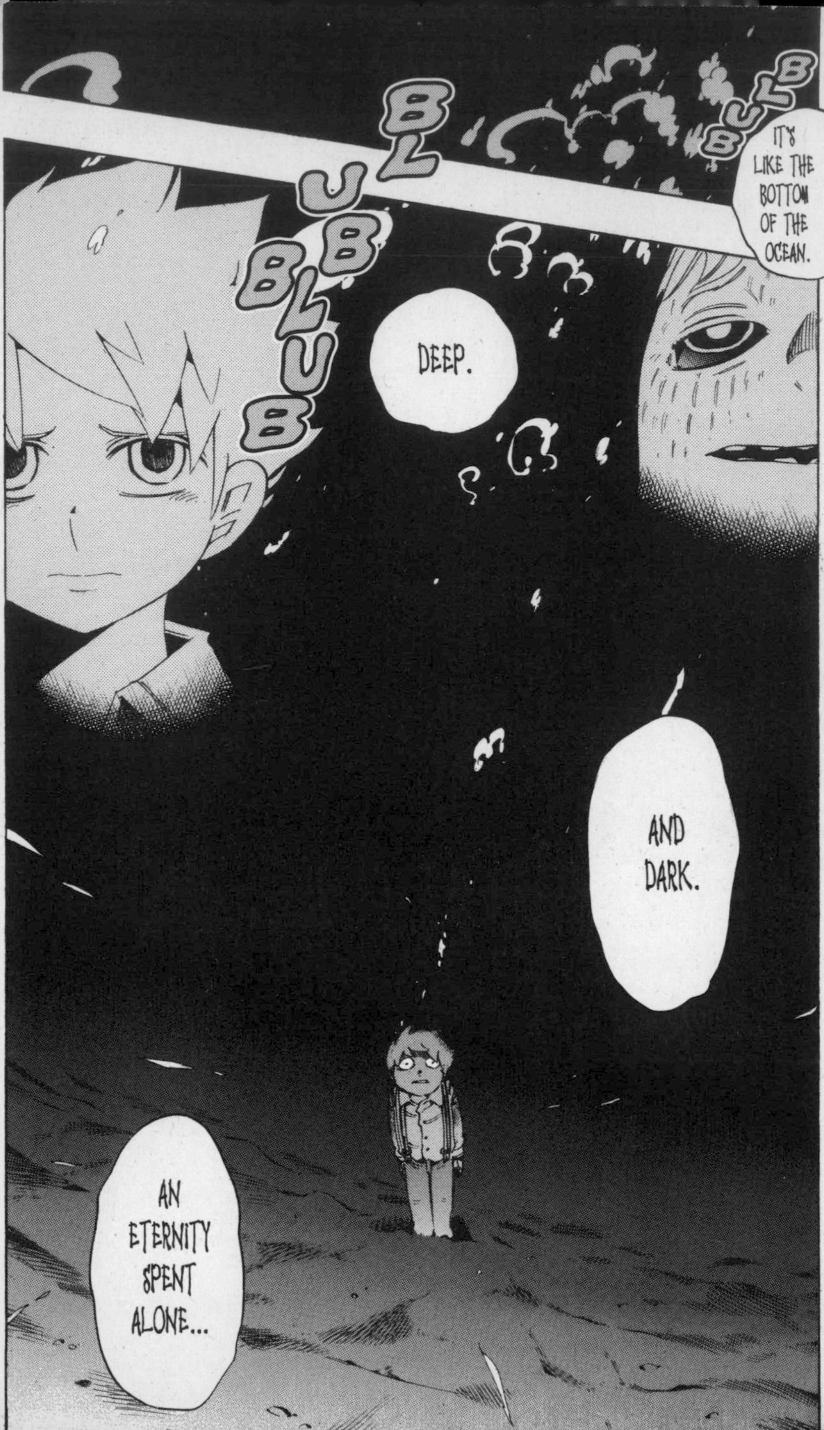
BLUB
IT'S LIKE THE BOTTOM OF THE OCEAN.
BLUB BLUB
DEEP.
AND DARK.
AN ETERNITY SPENT ALONE...

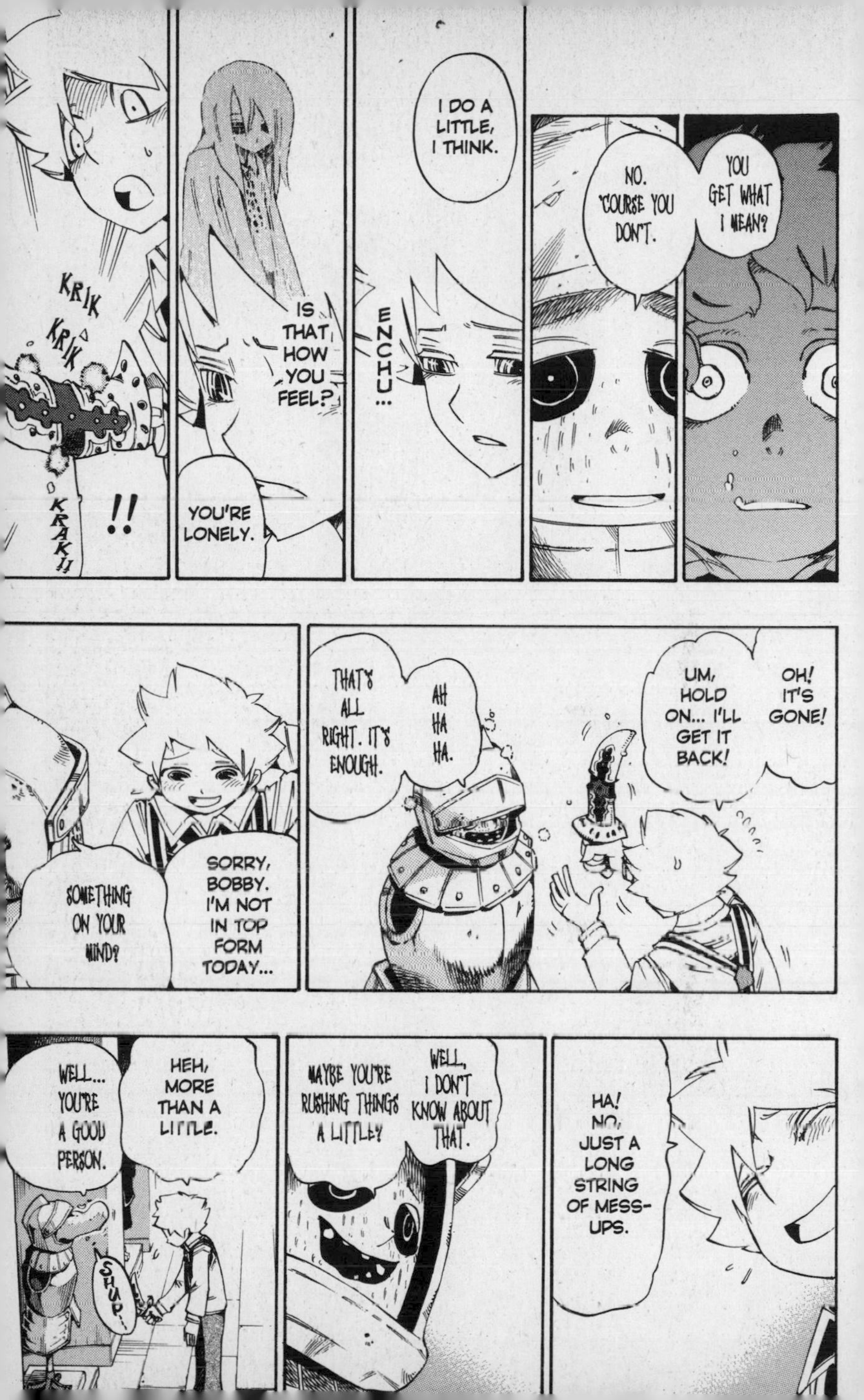
YOU GET WHAT I MEAN?
NO. 'COURSE YOU DON'T.
I DO A LITTLE, I THINK.
ENCHU...
IS THAT HOW YOU FEEL?
YOU'RE LONELY.
KRIK KRIK
KRAK!!
!!
OH! IT'S GONE!
UM, HOLD ON... I'LL GET IT BACK!
AH HA HA.
THAT'S ALL RIGHT. IT'S ENOUGH.
SORRY, BOBBY. I'M NOT IN TOP FORM TODAY...
SOMETHING ON YOUR MIND?
HA! NO, JUST A LONG STRING OF MESS-UPS.
WELL, I DON'T KNOW ABOUT THAT.
MAYBE YOU'RE RUSHING THINGS A LITTLE?
HEH, MORE THAN A LITTLE.
WELL... YOU'RE A GOOD PERSON.
SHUP...

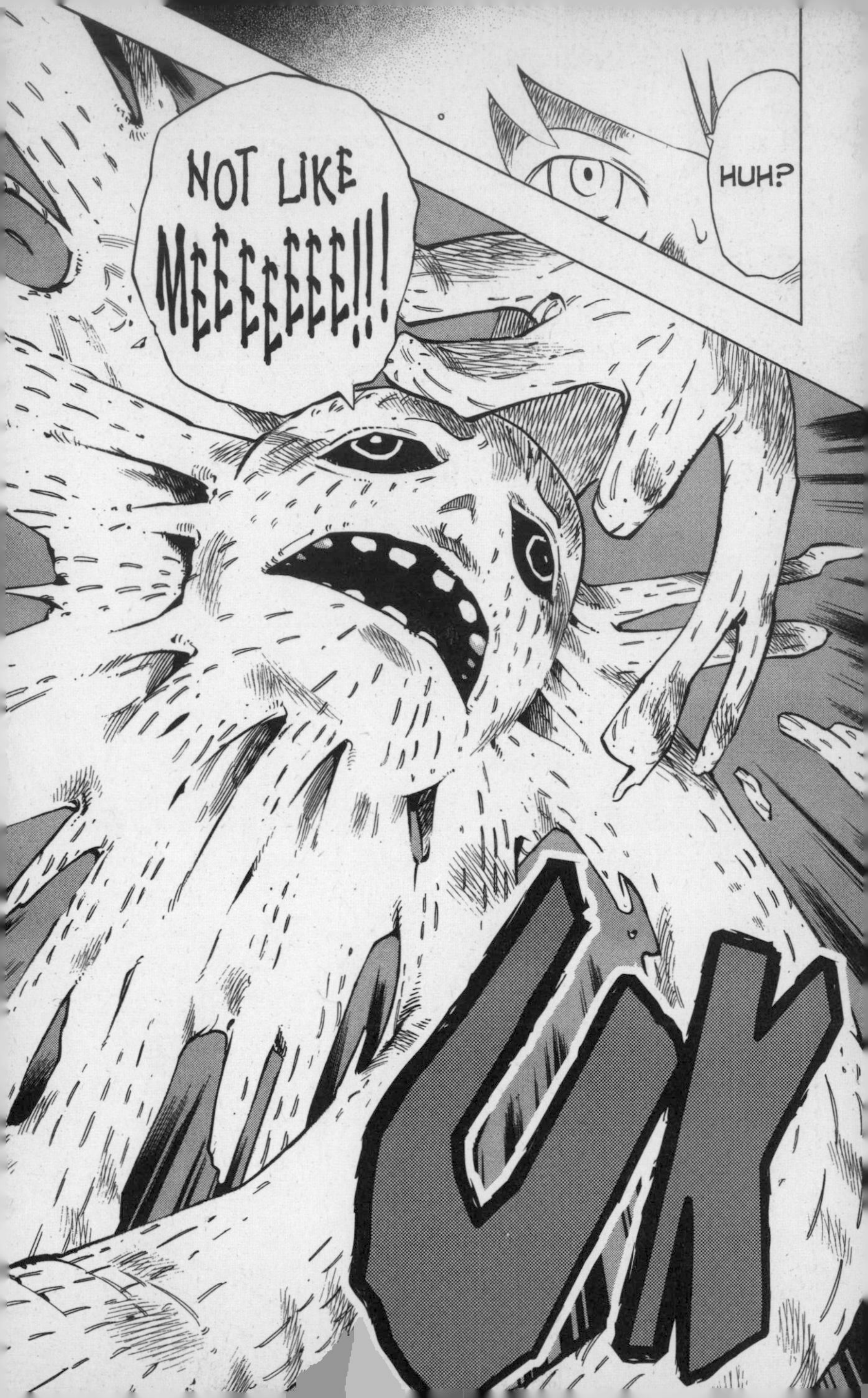
HUH?
NOT LIKE MEEEEEEE!!!

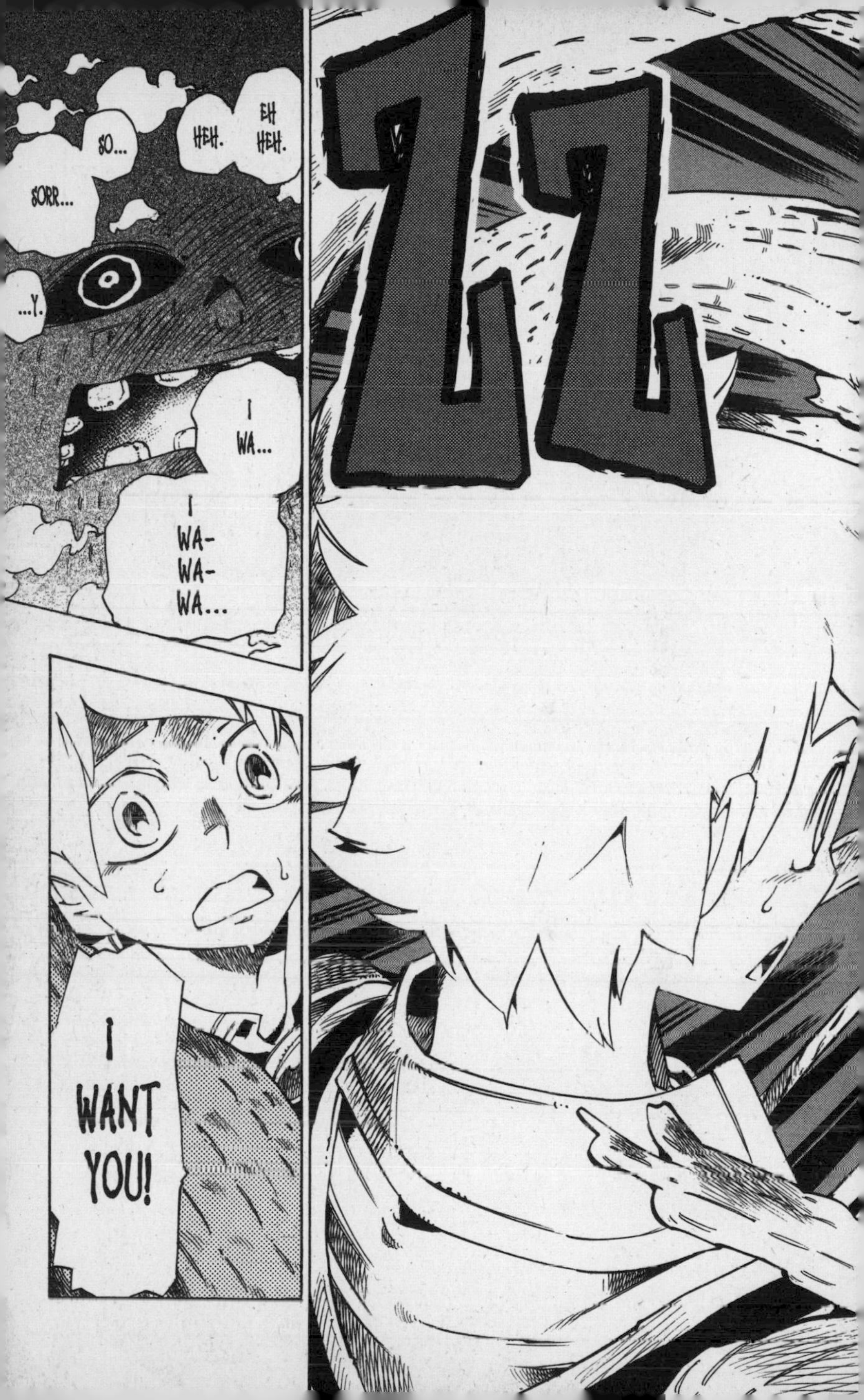
ZZ
EH HEH.
HEH.
SO...
SORR...
...Y.
I WA...
I WA-WA-WA...
I WANT YOU!

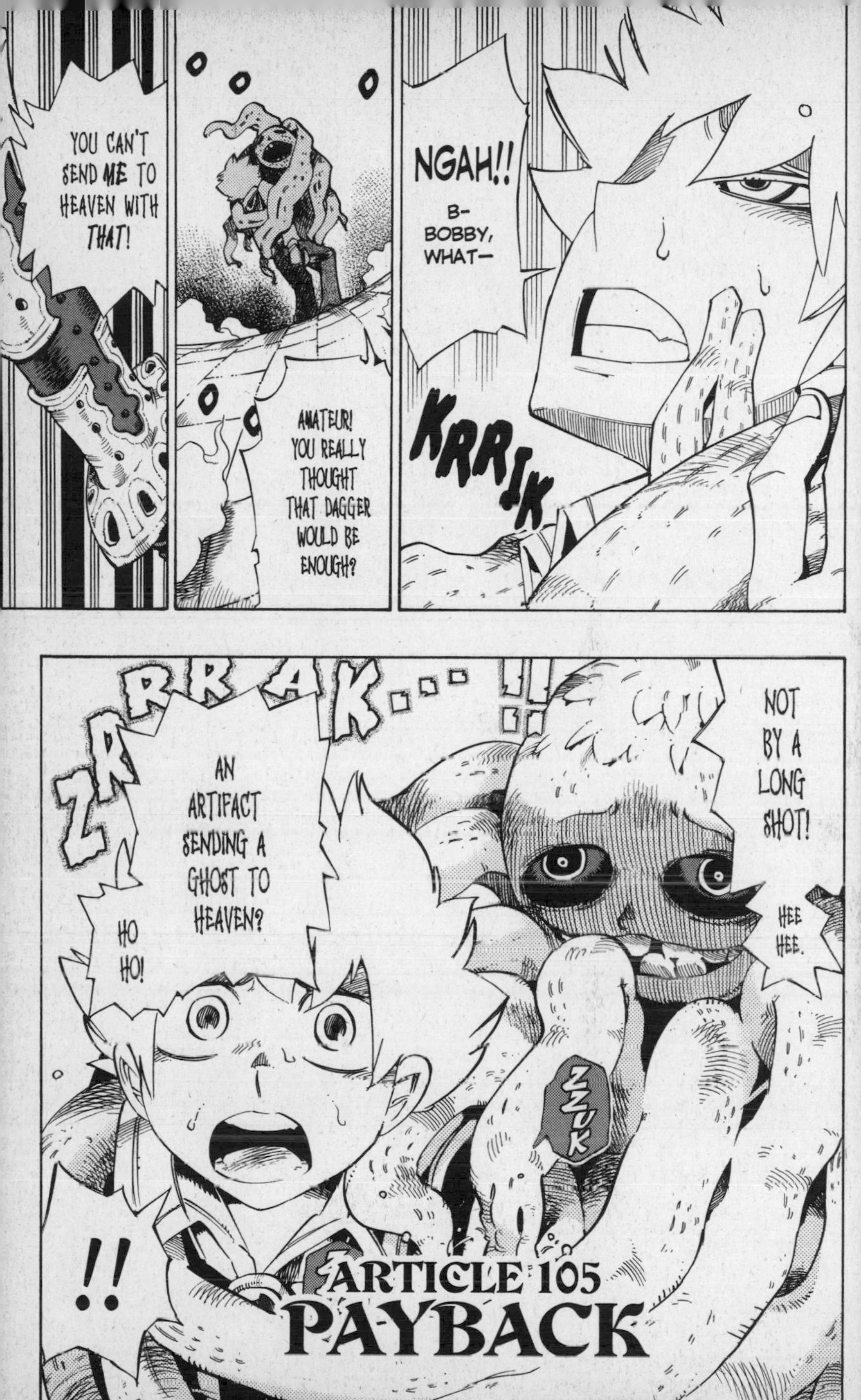
NGAH!!
B-BOBBY, WHAT—
KRRIK
AMATEUR! YOU REALLY THOUGHT THAT DAGGER WOULD BE ENOUGH?
YOU CAN'T SEND ME TO HEAVEN WITH THAT!
NOT BY A LONG SHOT!
HEE HEE.
ZARRAK...!!
AN ARTIFACT SENDING A GHOST TO HEAVEN?
HO HO!
ZZUK
!!

ARTICLE 105
PAYBACK

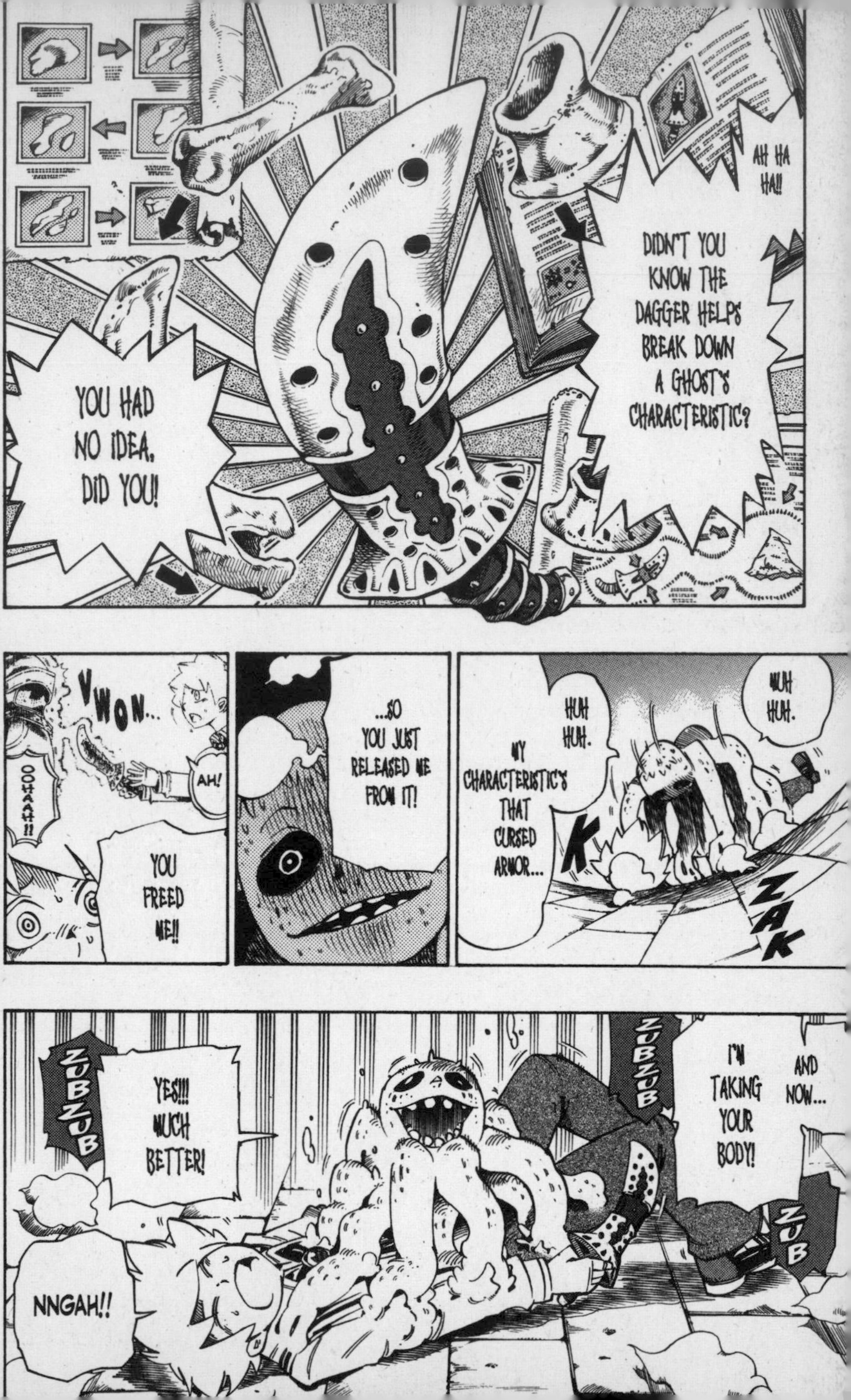
AH HA HA!!
DIDN'T YOU KNOW THE DAGGER HELPS BREAK DOWN A GHOST'S CHARACTERISTIC?
YOU HAD NO IDEA, DID YOU!
HUH HUH.
HUH HUH.
MY CHARACTERISTIC'S THAT CURSED ARMOR...
K
ZAK
...SO YOU JUST RELEASED ME FROM IT!
VWON...
AH!
OOHAAAH!!
YOU FREED ME!!
AND NOW...
I'M TAKING YOUR BODY!
ZUBZUB
ZUB
YES!!! MUCH BETTER!
ZUBZUB
NNGAH!!

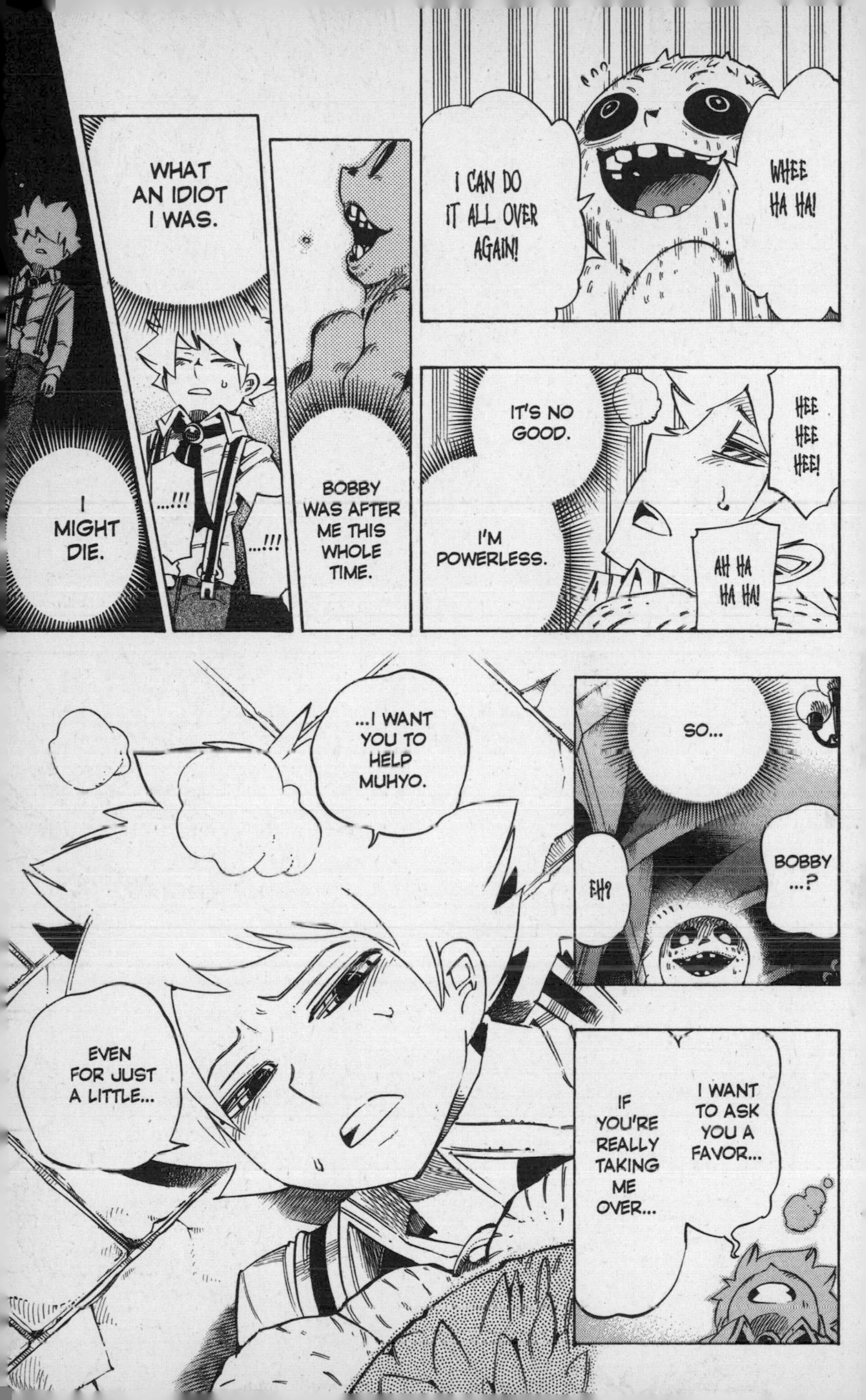
WHEE HA HA!
I CAN DO IT ALL OVER AGAIN!
HEE HEE HEE!
IT'S NO GOOD.
AH HA HA HA!
I'M POWERLESS.
BOBBY WAS AFTER ME THIS WHOLE TIME.
WHAT AN IDIOT I WAS.
...!!!
...!!!
I MIGHT DIE.
SO...
BOBBY ...?
EH?
I WANT TO ASK YOU A FAVOR...
IF YOU'RE REALLY TAKING ME OVER...
...I WANT YOU TO HELP MUHYO.
EVEN FOR JUST A LITTLE...

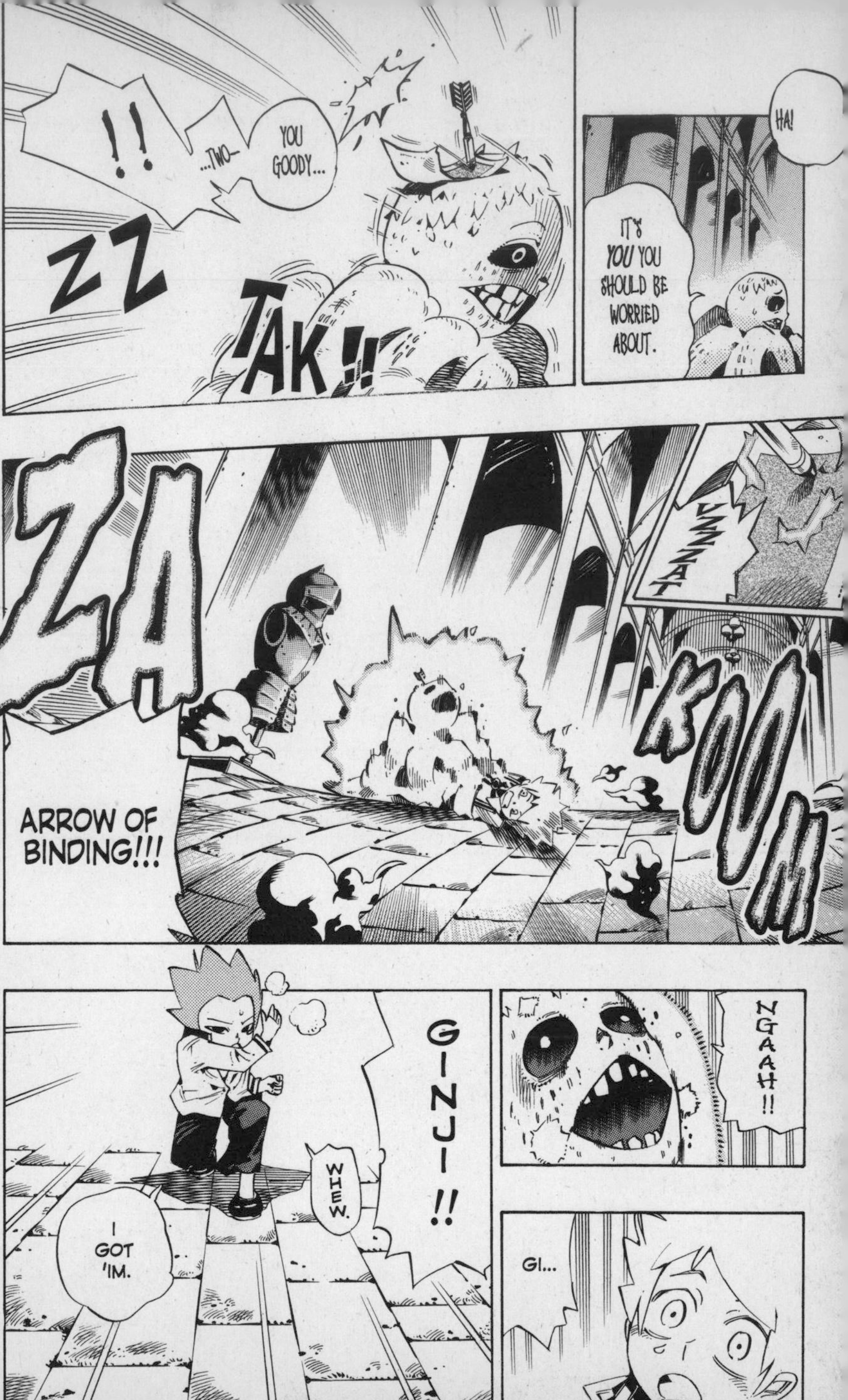
HA!
IT'S YOU YOU SHOULD BE WORRIED ABOUT.
YOU GOODY...
...TWO—
!!
ZZ
TAK!!
UZZZAT
KOOOM
ZA
ARROW OF BINDING!!!
NGAAH!!
GI...
GINJI!!
WHEW.
I GOT 'IM.

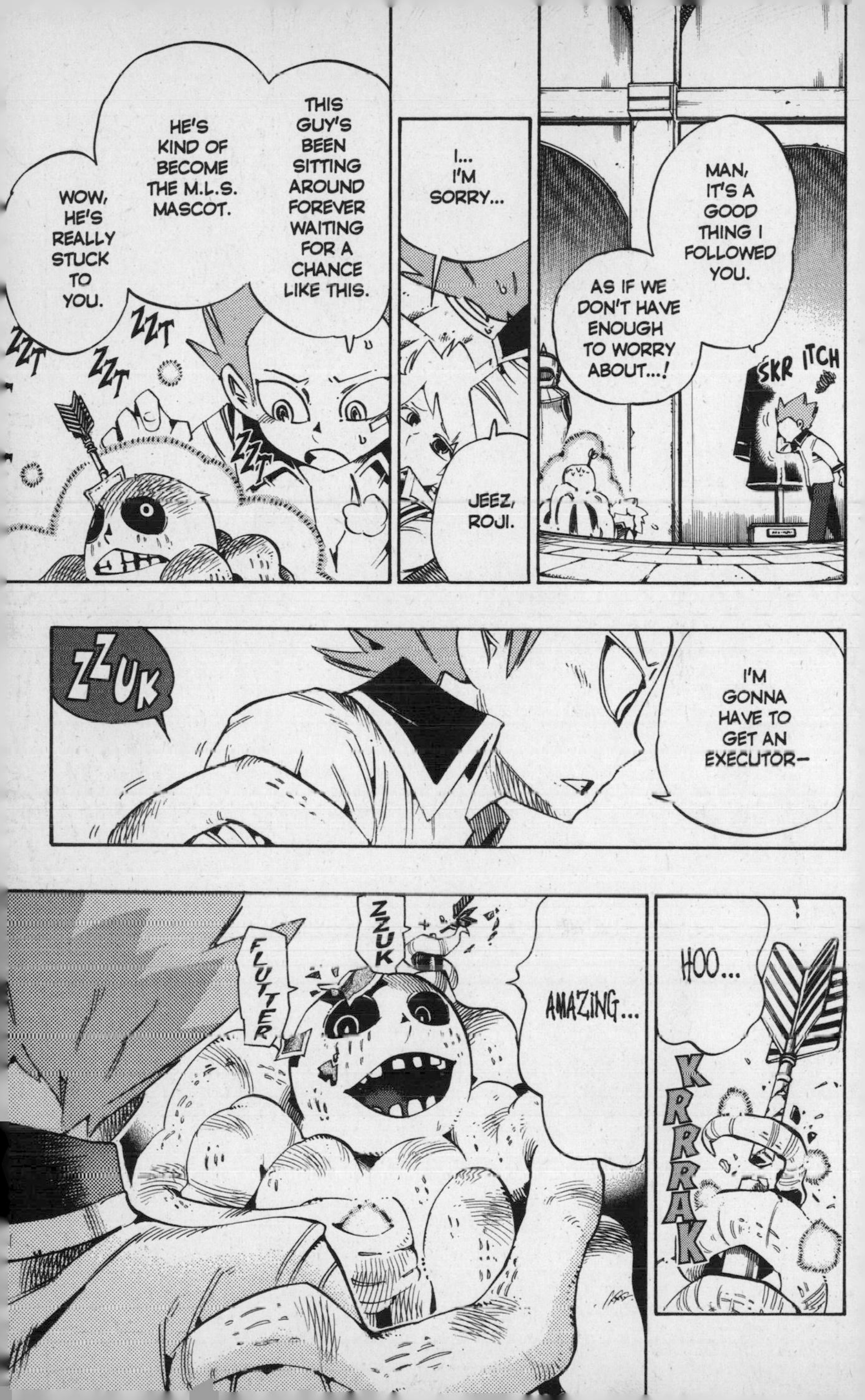
MAN, IT'S A GOOD THING I FOLLOWED YOU.
AS IF WE DON'T HAVE ENOUGH TO WORRY ABOUT...!
SKR ITCH
I... I'M SORRY...
JEEZ, ROJI.
THIS GUY'S BEEN SITTING AROUND FOREVER WAITING FOR A CHANCE LIKE THIS.
HE'S KIND OF BECOME THE M.L.S. MASCOT.
WOW, HE'S REALLY STUCK TO YOU.
ZZT
ZZT
ZZT
ZZT
I'M GONNA HAVE TO GET AN EXECUTOR—
ZZUK
HOO...
KRRRAK
AMAZING...
ZZUK
FLUTTER

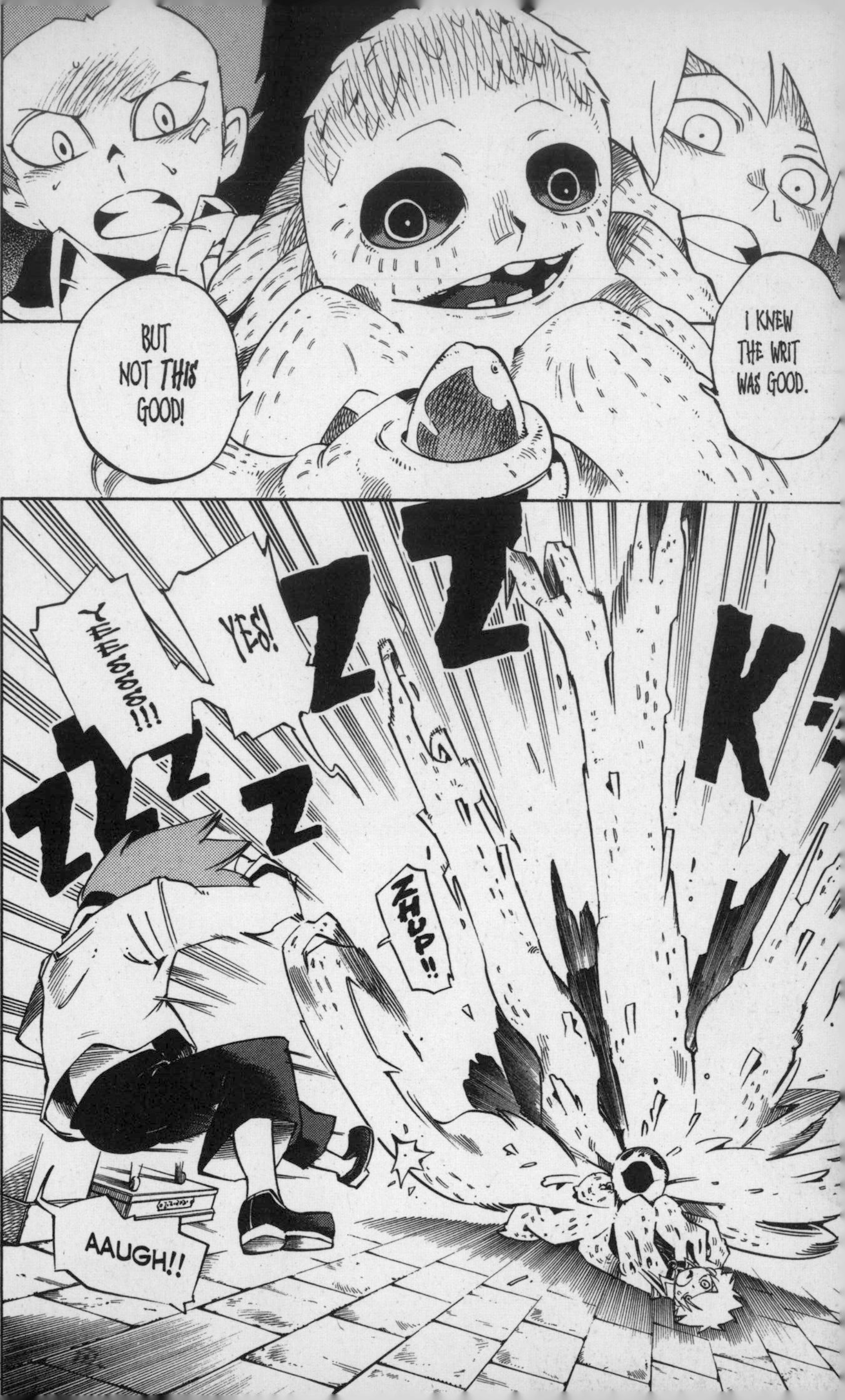
I KNEW THE WRIT WAS GOOD.
BUT NOT THIS GOOD!
ZZ
K
YES!
YEEOOOW!!!
ZZZ Z
ZHUP!!
AAUGH!!

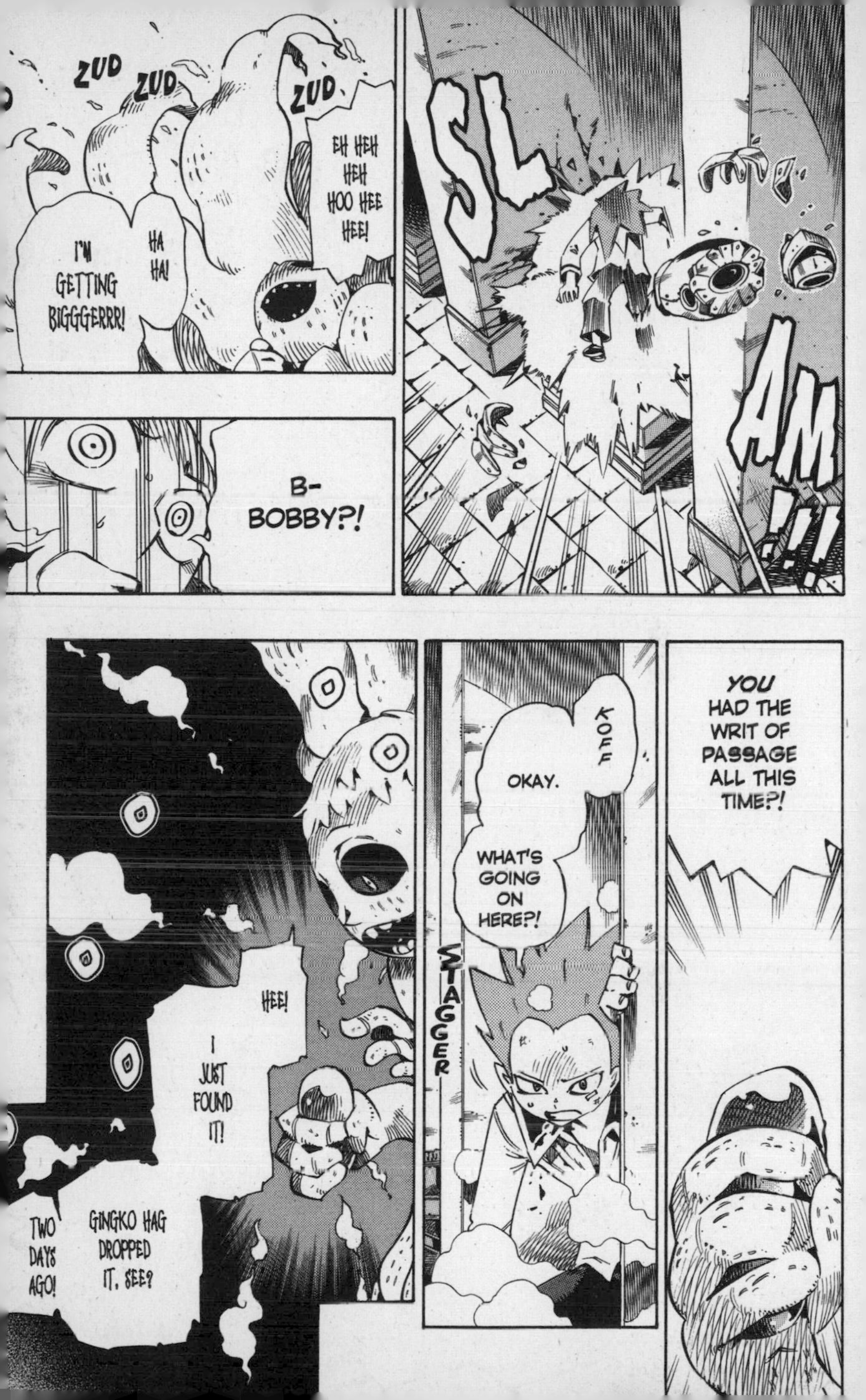
SLAM!!!
ZUD
EH HEH HEH HOO HEE HEE!
ZUD
ZUD
HA HA!
I'M GETTING BIGGGERRR!
B-BOBBY?!
YOU HAD THE WRIT OF PASSAGE ALL THIS TIME?!
KOFF
OKAY.
WHAT'S GOING ON HERE?!
STAGGER
HEE!
I JUST FOUND IT!
GINGKO HAG DROPPED IT, SEE?
TWO DAYS AGO!

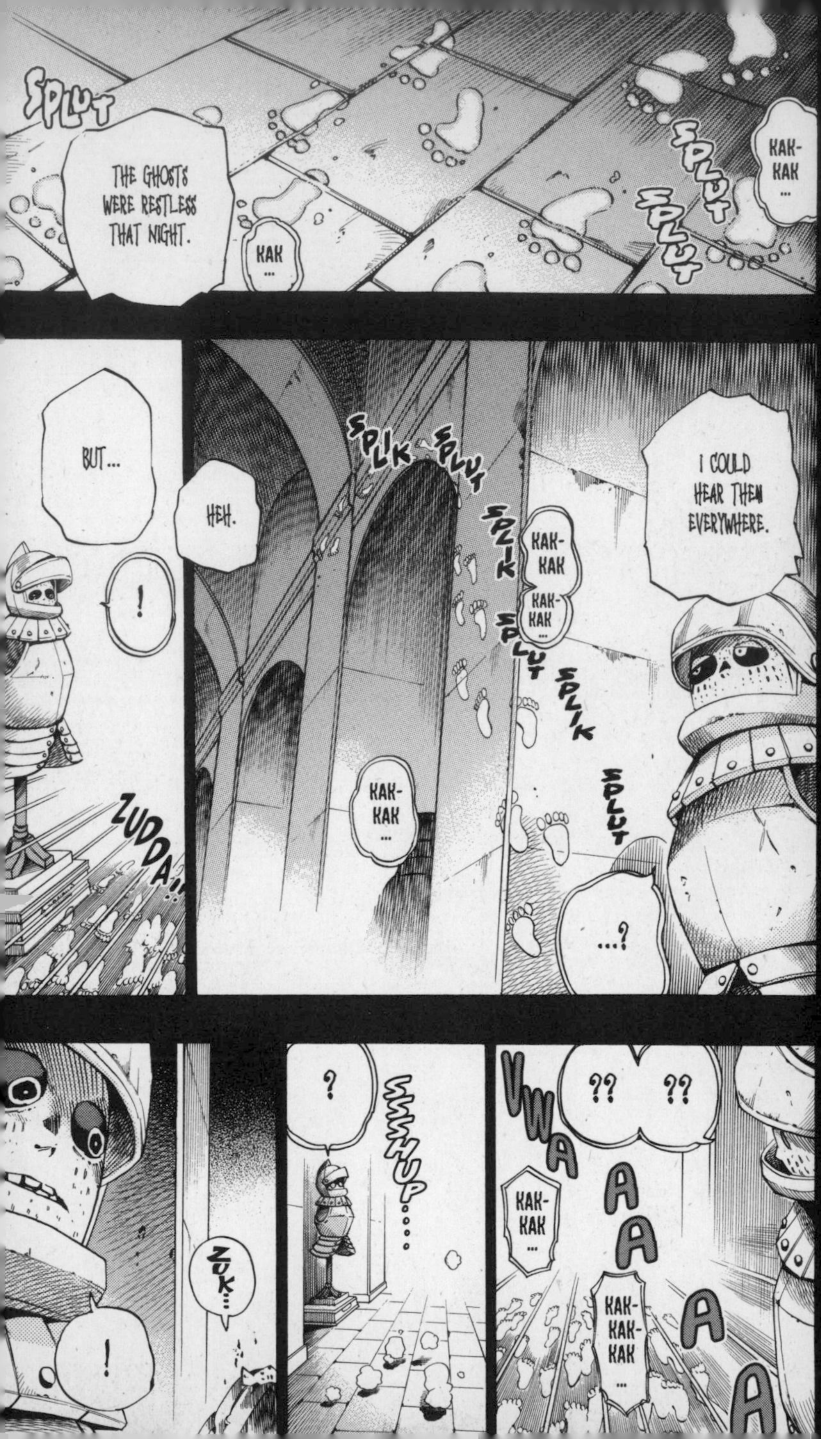
KAK-KAK...
SPLUT
SPLUT
SPLUT
THE GHOSTS WERE RESTLESS THAT NIGHT.
KAK...
I COULD HEAR THEM EVERYWHERE.
SPLIK
SPLUT
...?
SPLIK
SPLUT
SPLIK
KAK-KAK
KAK-KAK...
SPLUT
KAK-KAK...
BUT...
HEH.
!
ZUDDA!!
?? ??
VWAAAAAA
KAK-KAK...
KAK-KAK-KAK...
?
SSSHUP....
ZUK...
!

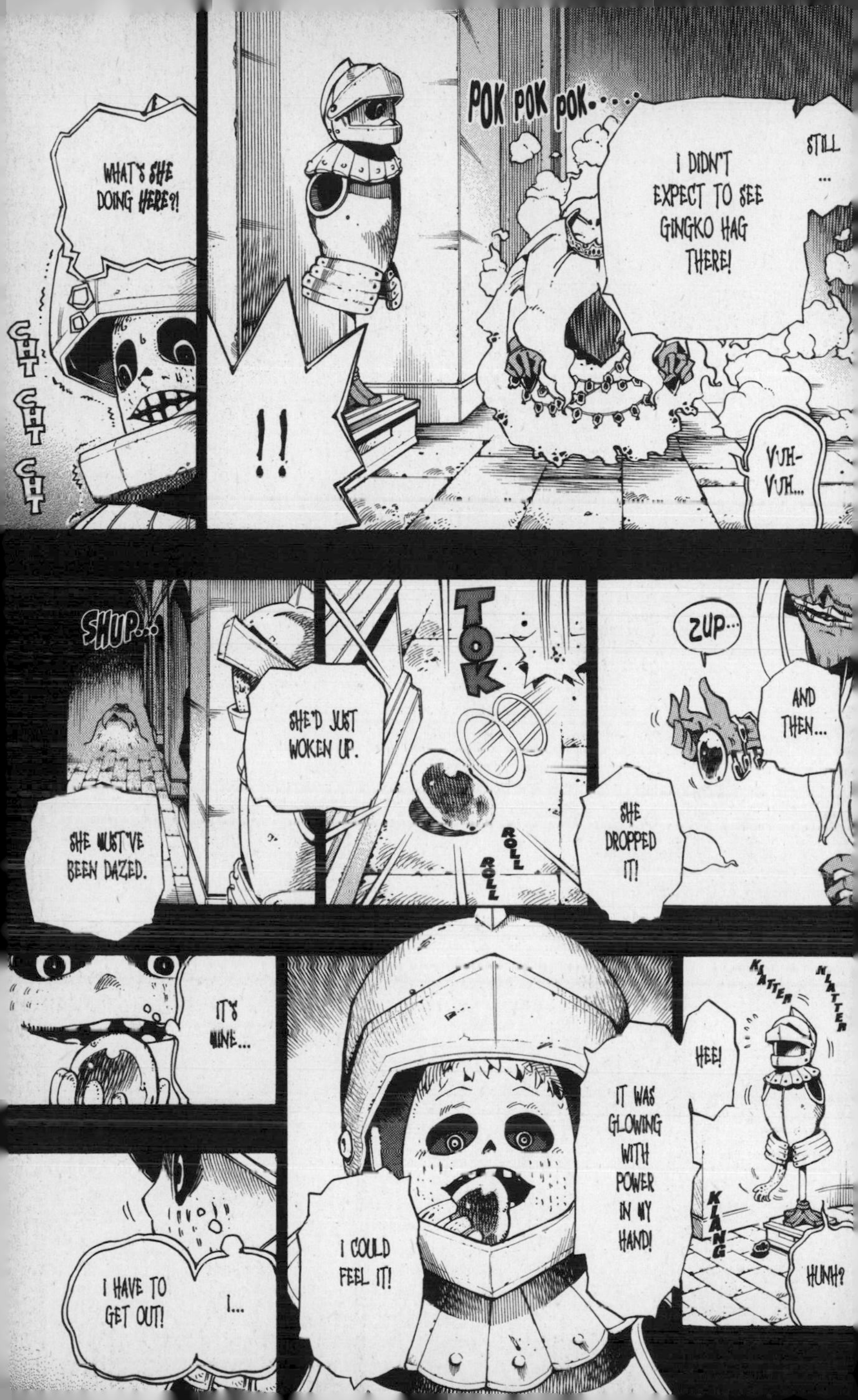
POK POK POK....
STILL...
I DIDN'T EXPECT TO SEE GINGKO HAG THERE!
VUH-VUH...
!!
WHAT'S SHE DOING HERE?!
CHT CHT CHT
ZUP...
AND THEN...
SHE DROPPED IT!
TOK
ROLL ROLL
SHE'D JUST WOKEN UP.
SHUP...
SHE MUST'VE BEEN DAZED.
KLATTER KLATTER
HEE!
KLANG
HUNH?
IT WAS GLOWING WITH POWER IN MY HAND!
I COULD FEEL IT!
IT'S MINE...
I...
I HAVE TO GET OUT!

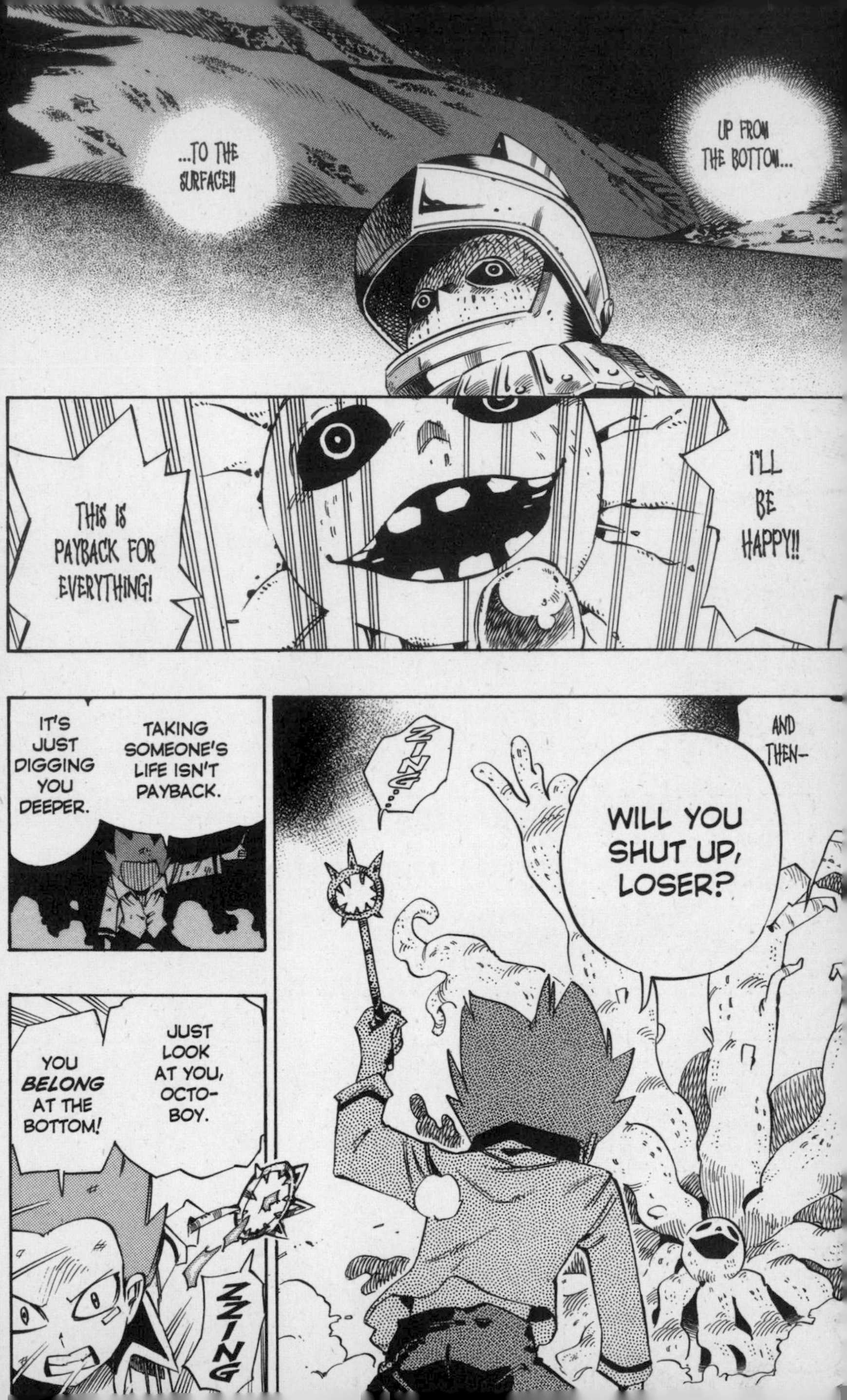
UP FROM THE BOTTOM...
...TO THE SURFACE!!
I'LL BE HAPPY!!
THIS IS PAYBACK FOR EVERYTHING!
AND THEN-
ZING...
WILL YOU SHUT UP, LOSER?
TAKING SOMEONE'S LIFE ISN'T PAYBACK.
IT'S JUST DIGGING YOU DEEPER.
JUST LOOK AT YOU, OCTO-BOY.
YOU *BELONG* AT THE BOTTOM!
ZZING

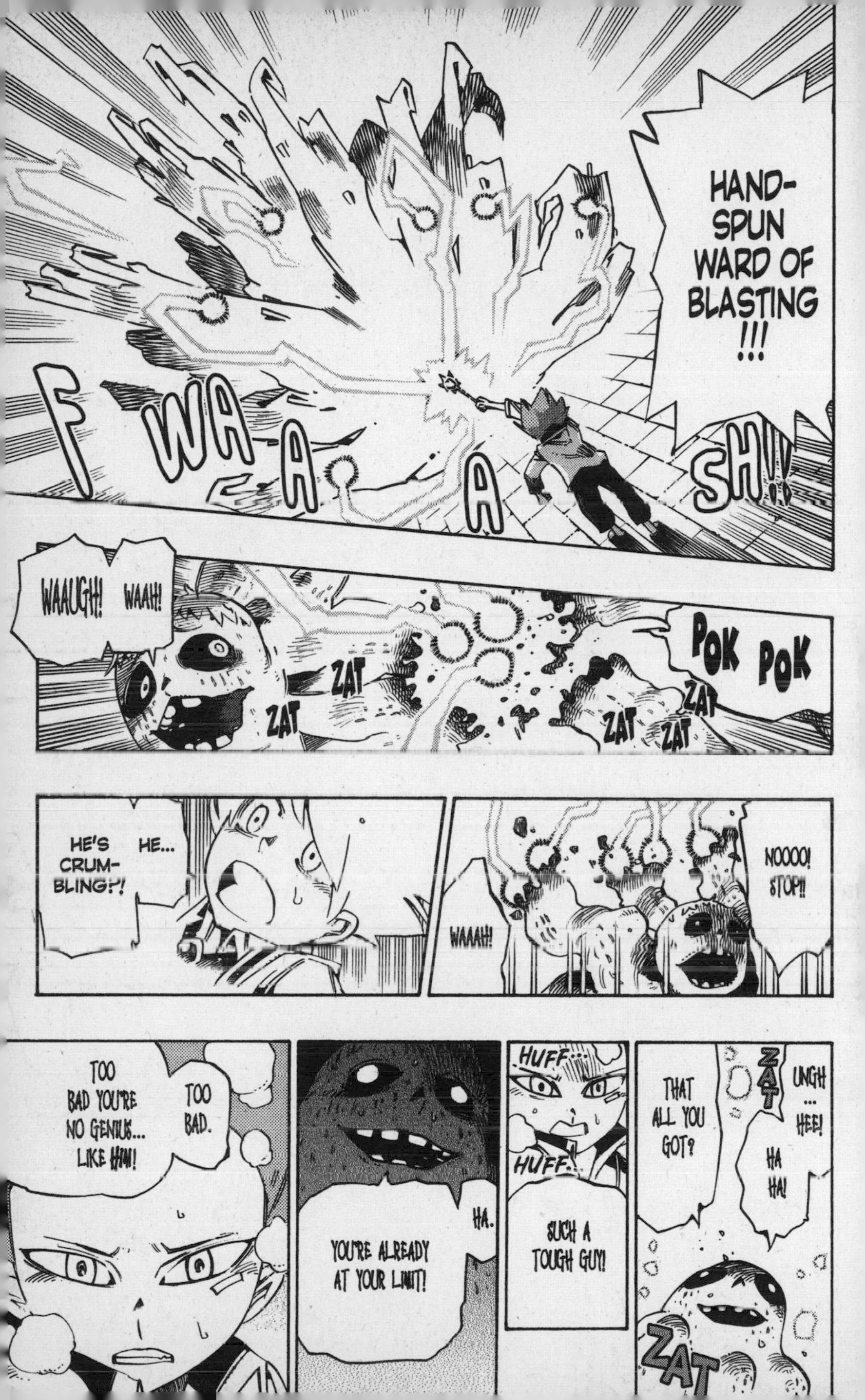
HAND-SPUN WARD OF BLASTING!!!
FWAAASH!!
POK POK
ZAT ZAT ZAT
WAAH!
WAAUGH!
ZAT ZAT
NOOOO! STOP!!
WAAAH!
HE...
HE'S CRUMBLING?!
UNGH... HEE!
HA HA!
ZAT
THAT ALL YOU GOT?
ZAT
HUFF...
HUFF...
SUCH A TOUGH GUY!
HA.
YOU'RE ALREADY AT YOUR LIMIT!
TOO BAD.
TOO BAD YOU'RE NO GENIUS... LIKE HIM!

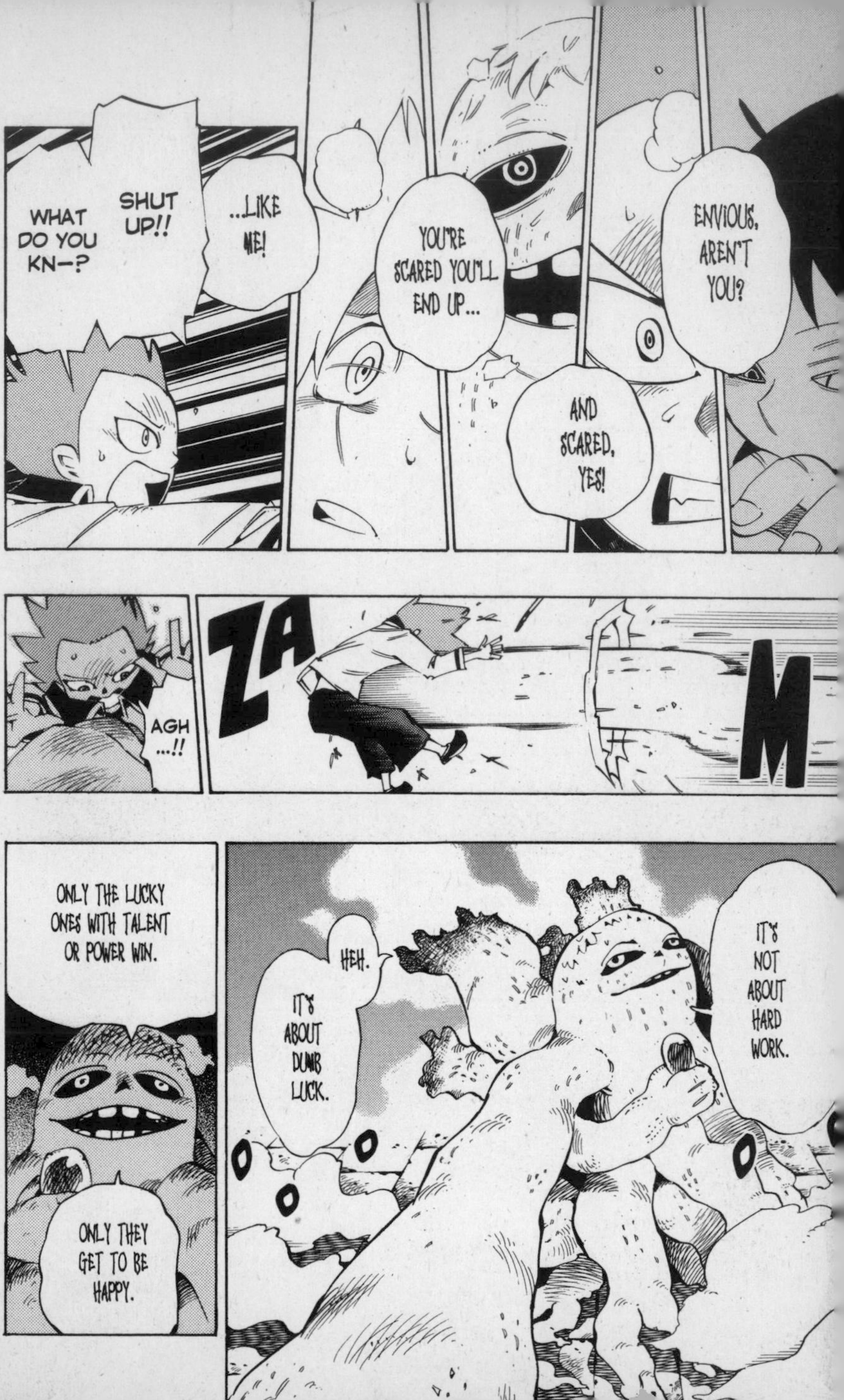
ENVIOUS, AREN'T YOU?
AND SCARED, YES!
YOU'RE SCARED YOU'LL END UP...
...LIKE ME!
SHUT UP!!
WHAT DO YOU KN—?
ZAM
AGH ...!!
IT'S NOT ABOUT HARD WORK.
HEH.
IT'S ABOUT DUMB LUCK.
ONLY THE LUCKY ONES WITH TALENT OR POWER WIN.
ONLY THEY GET TO BE HAPPY.

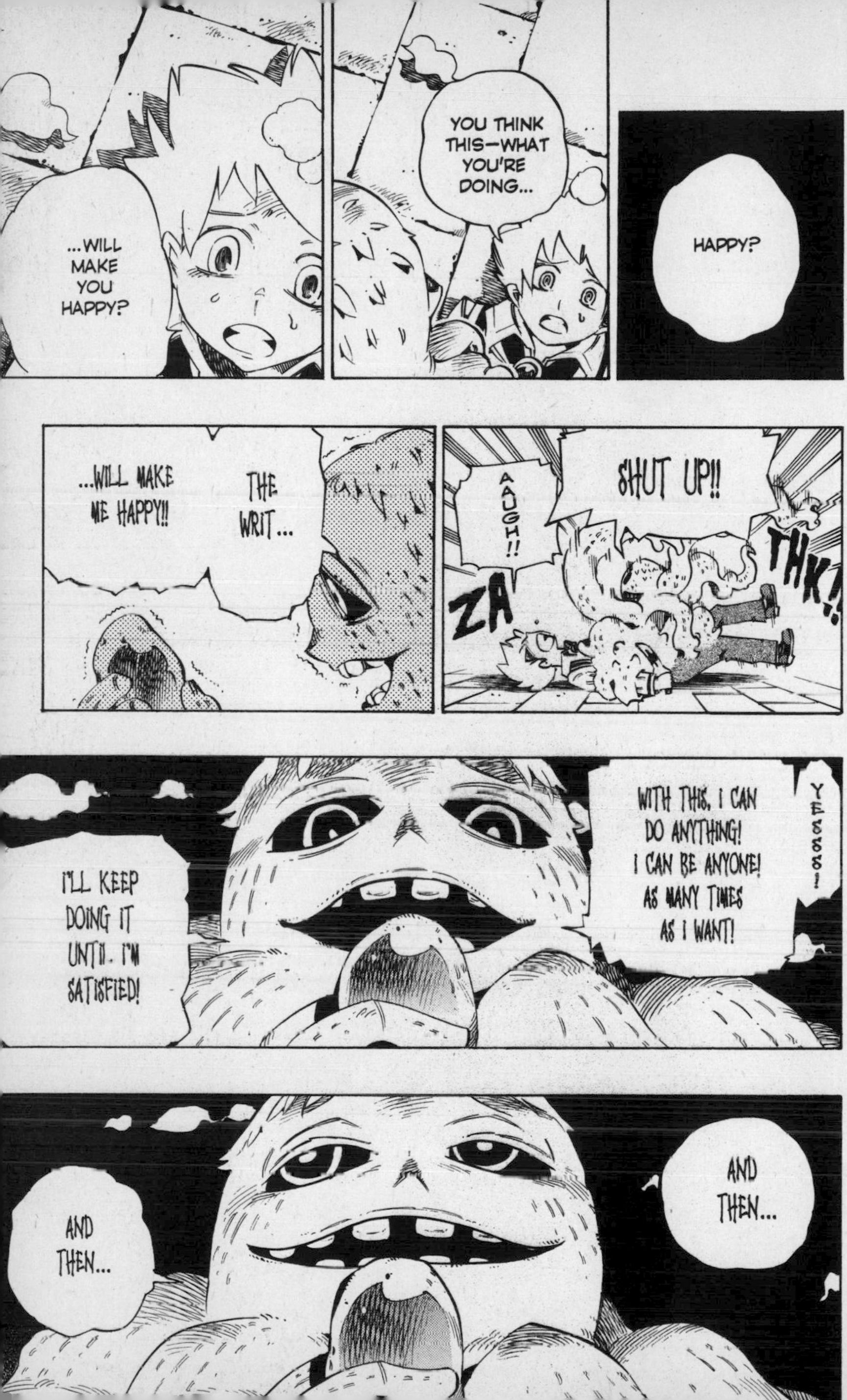
HAPPY?
YOU THINK THIS—WHAT YOU'RE DOING...
...WILL MAKE YOU HAPPY?
SHUT UP!!
AAUGH!!
THK!!
ZA
THE WRIT...
...WILL MAKE ME HAPPY!!
YESSS!
WITH THIS, I CAN DO ANYTHING! I CAN BE ANYONE! AS MANY TIMES AS I WANT!
I'LL KEEP DOING IT UNTIL I'M SATISFIED!
AND THEN...
AND THEN...

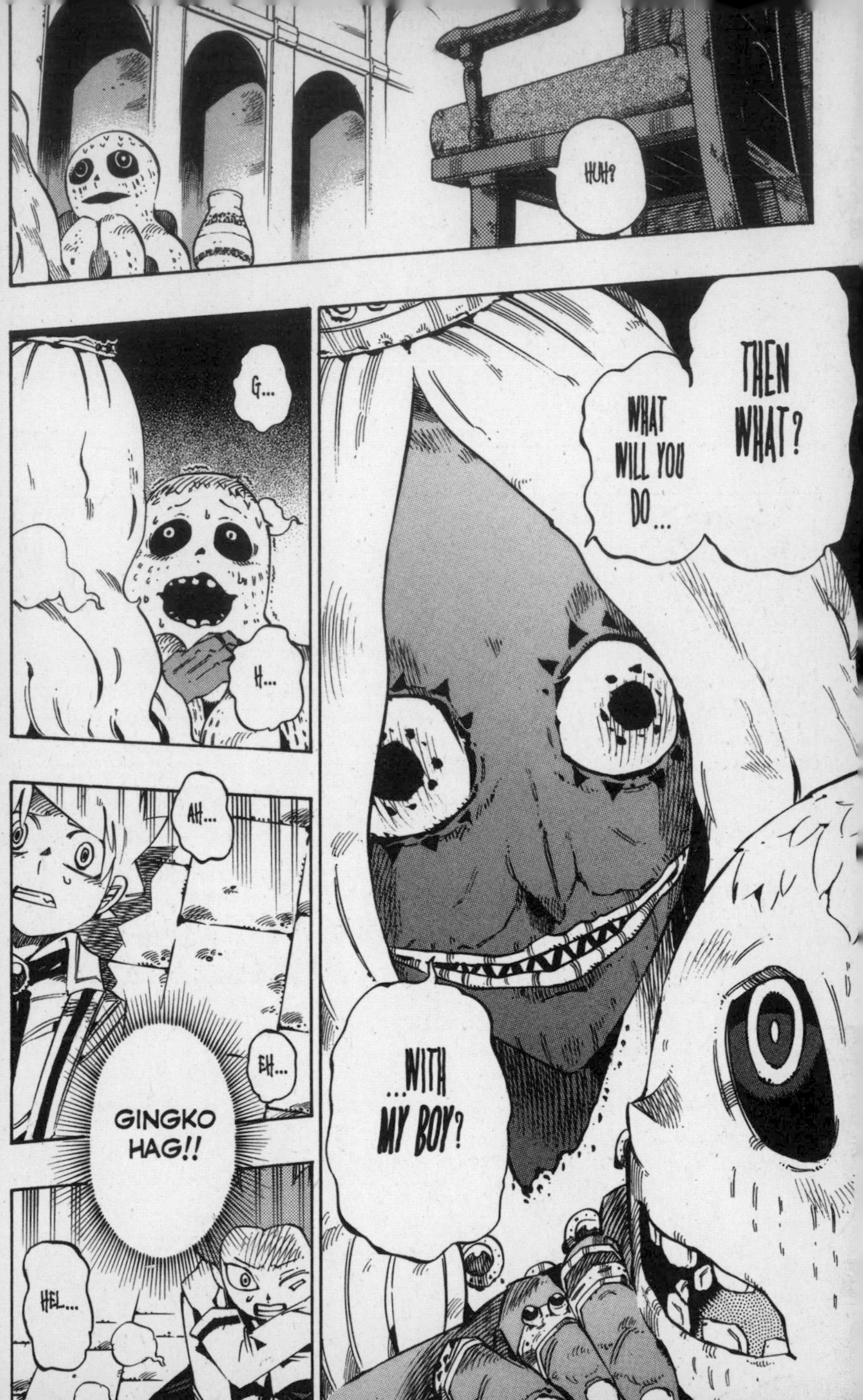
HUH?
THEN WHAT?
WHAT WILL YOU DO...
...WITH MY BOY?
G...
H...
AH...
EH...
GINGKO HAG!!
HEL...

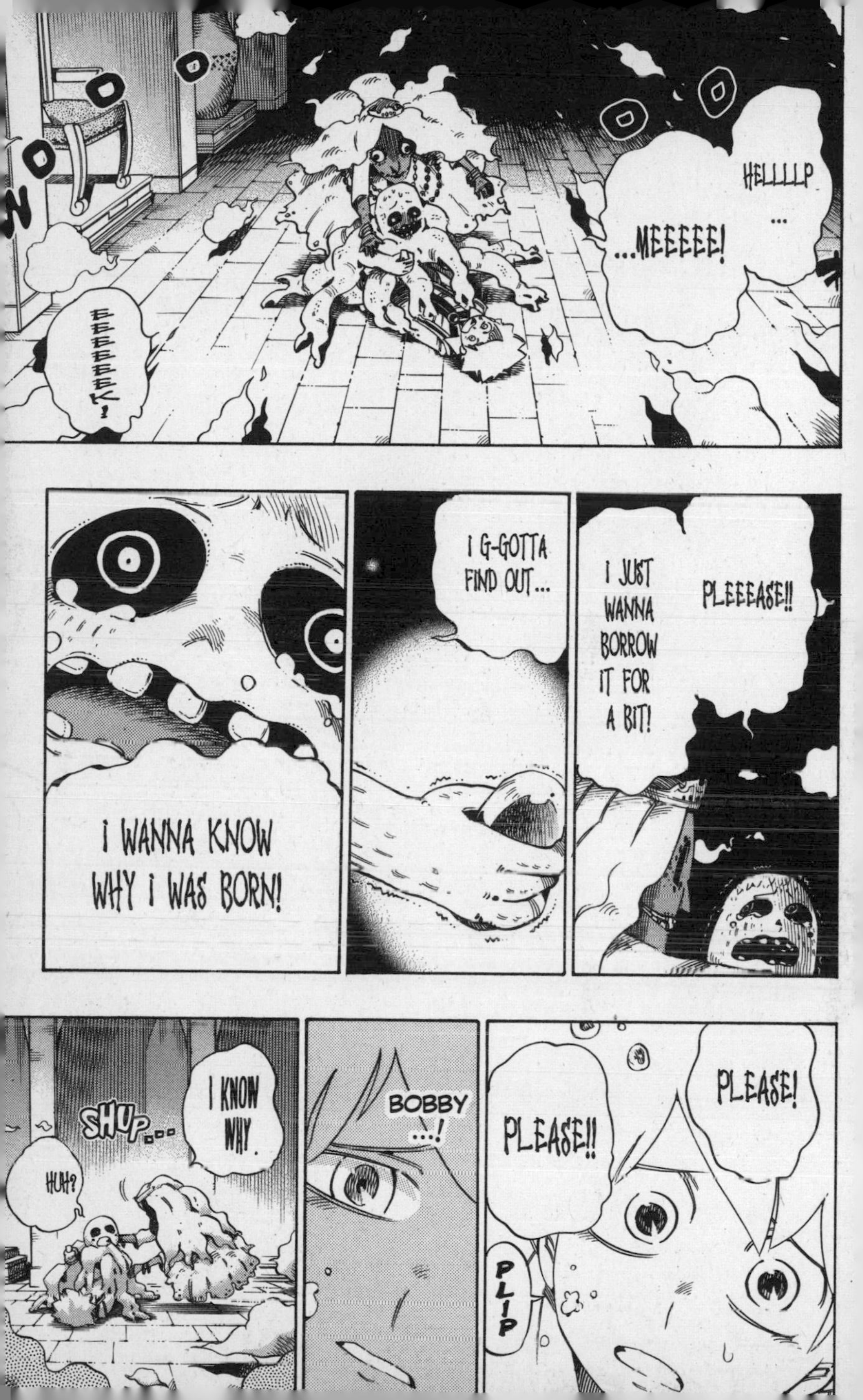
HELLLLP...
...MEEEEE!
EEEEEEK!
I JUST WANNA BORROW IT FOR A BIT!
PLEEEASE!!
I G-GOTTA FIND OUT...
I WANNA KNOW WHY I WAS BORN!
PLEASE!
PLEASE!!
PLIP
BOBBY...!
I KNOW WHY.
SHUP...
HUH?

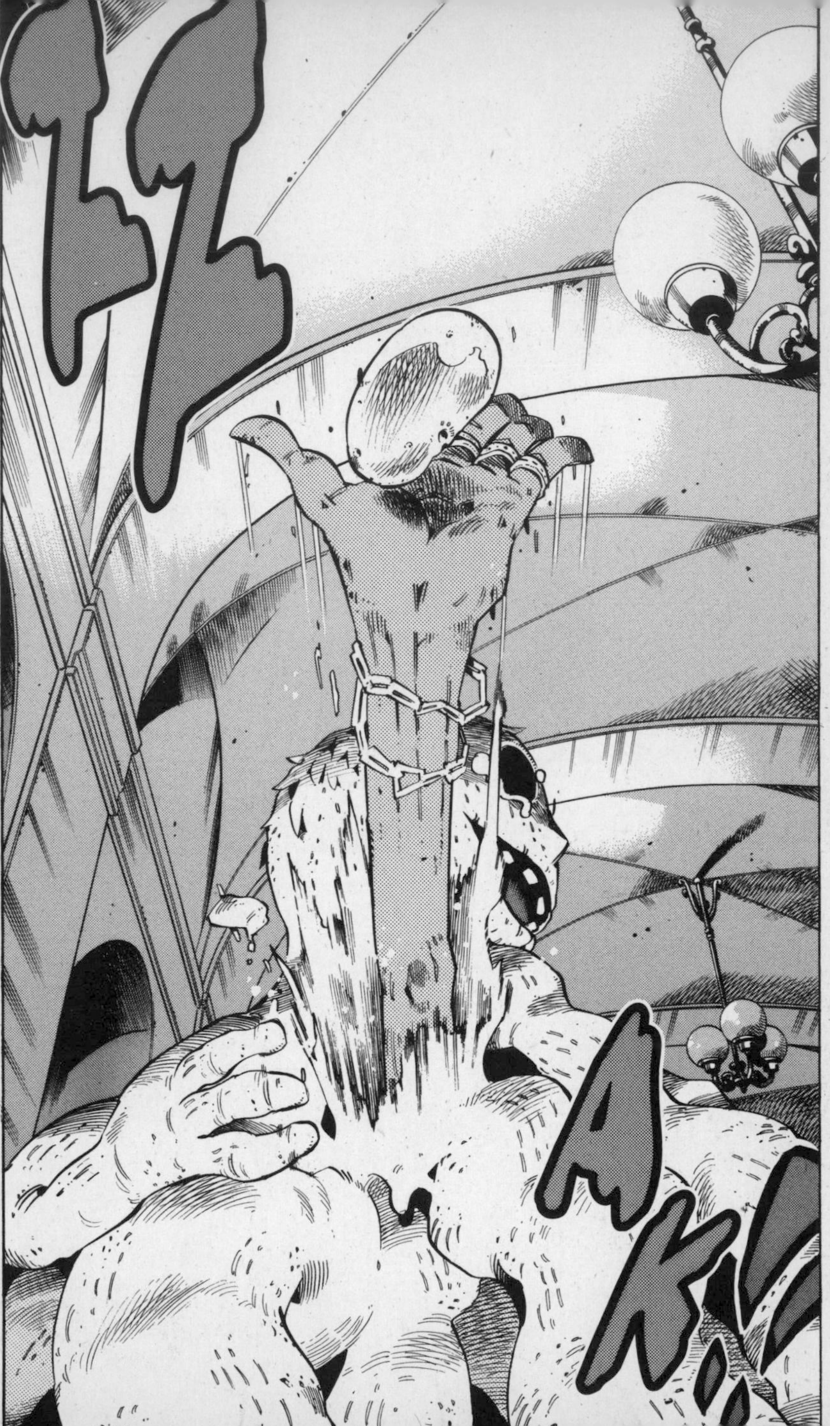
AK!!

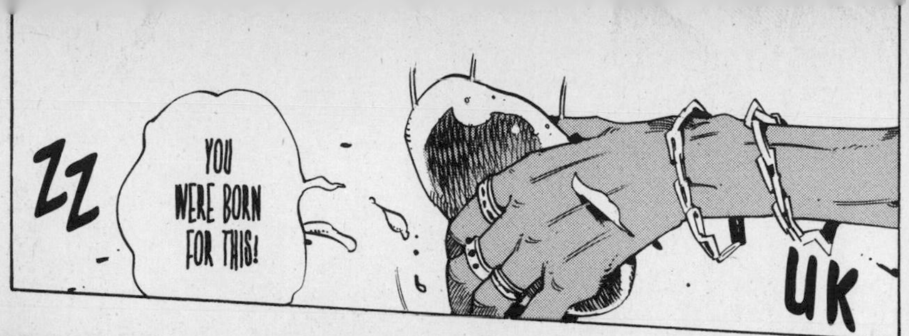
YOU WERE BORN FOR THIS!
ZZ
UK

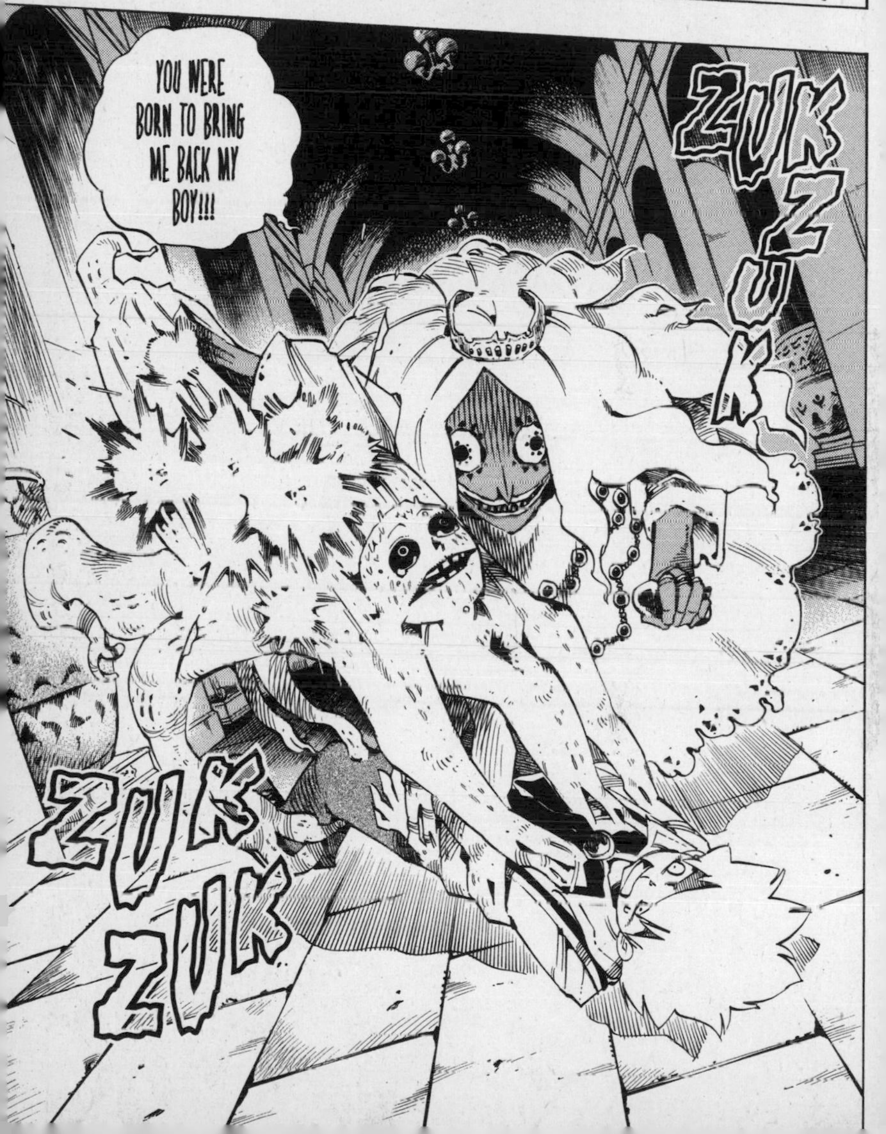
ZUK ZUK
YOU WERE BORN TO BRING ME BACK MY BOY!!!
ZUK ZUK

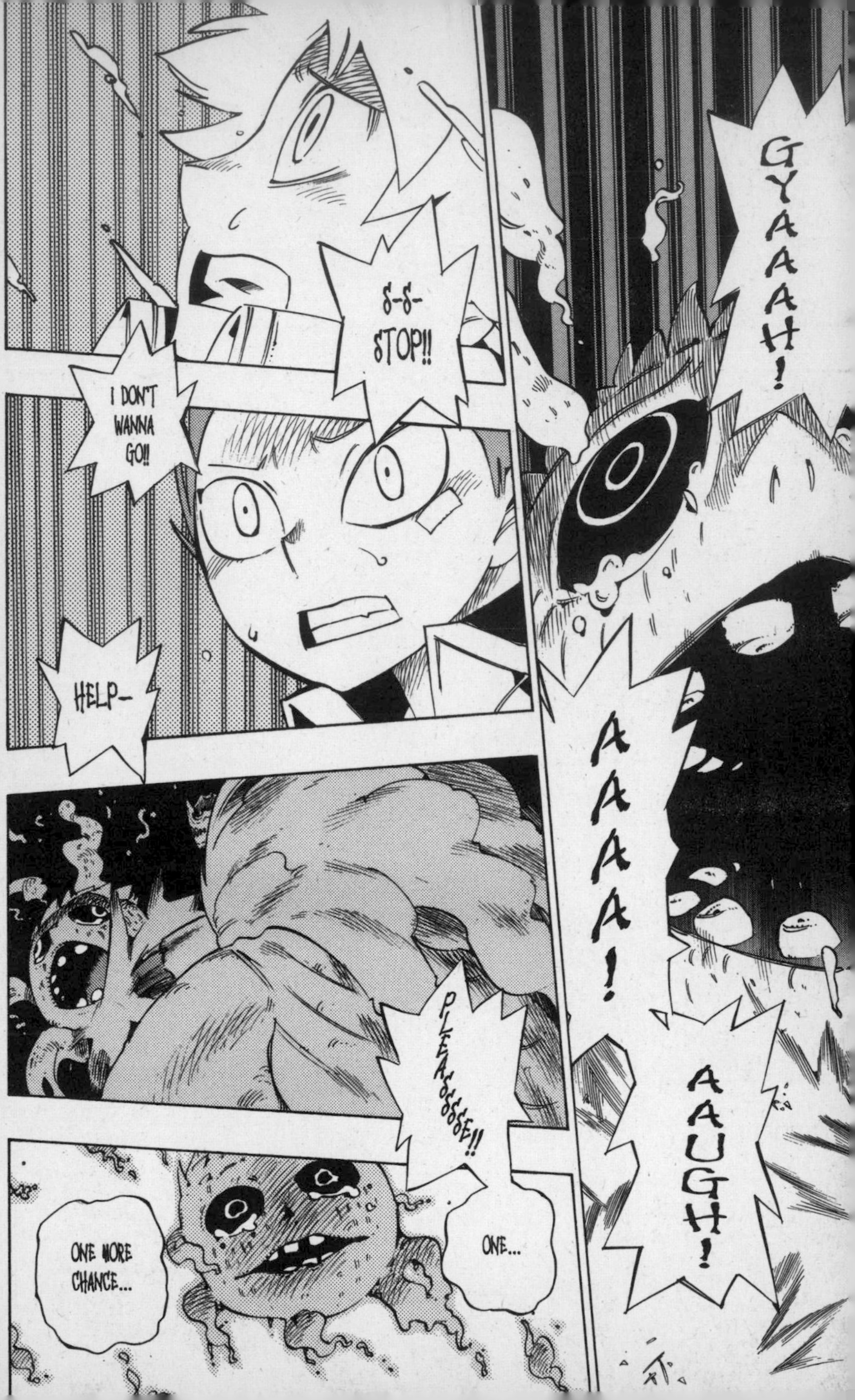
GYAAAAH!
AAAAA!
AAUGH!
S-S-STOP!!
I DON'T WANNA GO!!
HELP-
PLEASSSSE!!
ONE...
ONE MORE CHANCE...

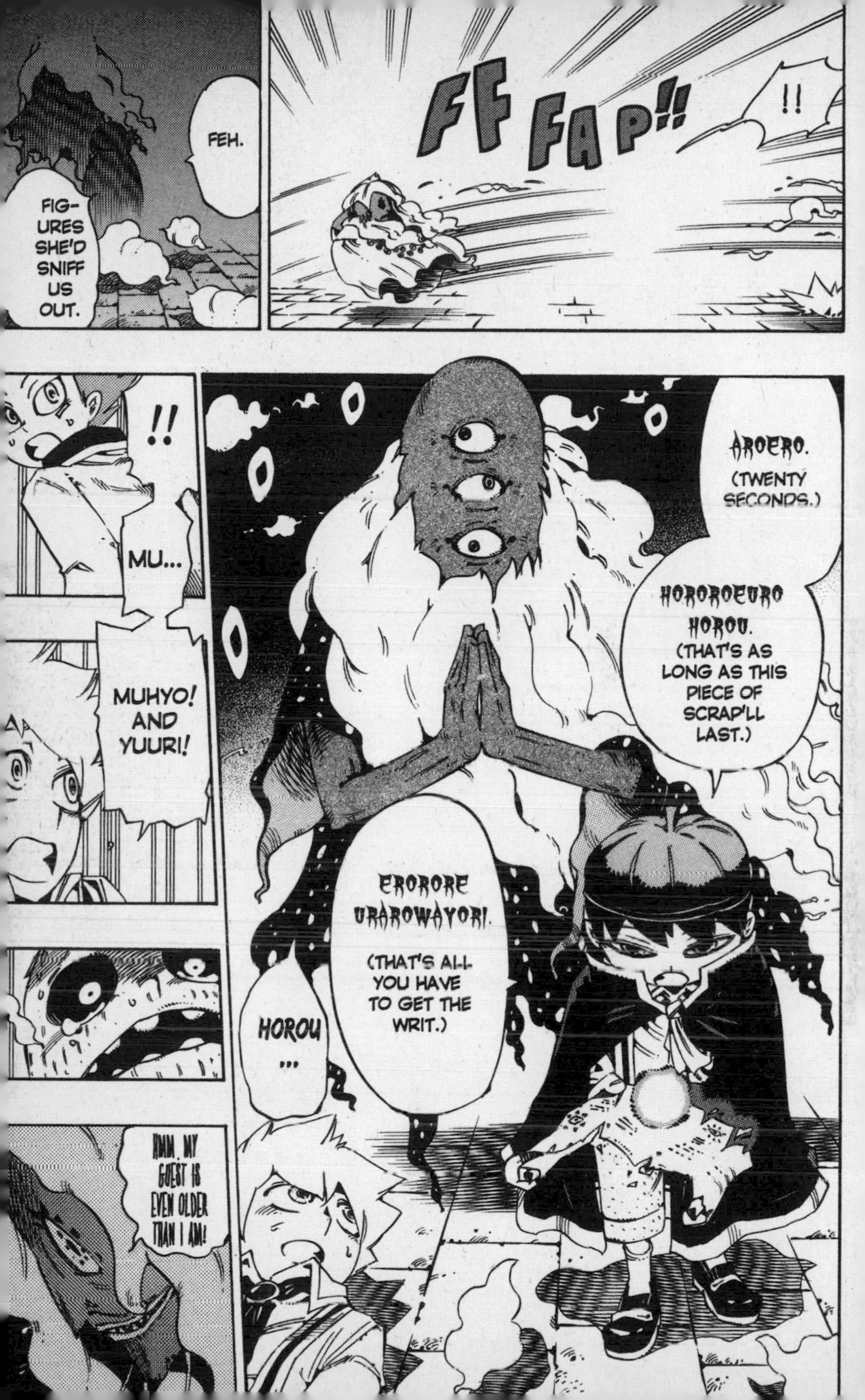
FF FAP!!
!!
FEH.
FIG-URES SHE'D SNIFF US OUT.
AROERO.
(TWENTY SECONDS.)
HOROROEURO HOROU.
(THAT'S AS LONG AS THIS PIECE OF SCRAP'LL LAST.)
ERORORE URAROWAYORI.
(THAT'S ALL YOU HAVE TO GET THE WRIT.)
HOROU ...
!!
MU...
MUHYO! AND YUURI!
HMM. MY GUEST IS EVEN OLDER THAN I AM!

Q1: OKAY, SO THE SIX KINGS OF THE UNDERWORLD ARE HADES, THE FLY LORD, THE KINGCRUSHER, PLUTO, AND WHO ELSE?
Q2: DOES GORYO ALWAYS WEAR TRADITIONAL JAPANESE CLOTHES? DOES HE ONLY EAT JAPANESE FOOD?
Q3: IF YOU NEED A CERTAIN ENVOY TO ADMINISTER A CERTAIN SENTENCE, WHAT HAPPENS IF THE ENVOY IS DEFEATED? CAN A DIFFERENT ENVOY TAKE HIS PLACE?
Q4: WHY DO THE LETTERS LOOK DIFFERENT WHEN GORYO IS PRONOUNCING A SENTENCE [IN THE ORIGINAL JAPANESE VERSION]?
Q5: HOW OLD ARE ENVOYS? LIKE, 2,000 YEARS OLD? 10,000?
Q6: WHAT WOULD HAPPEN IF YOU WERE USING REMOTE MAGIC LAW AND DELIVERED THE WRONG SENTENCE?

-S.A, SHIZUOKA PREFECTURE

A1: YOU GOT HADES, THE KING OF THE MAGIC REALM, THE KING-CRUSHER AND PLUTO RIGHT. AS FOR THE LAST TWO... WELL, YOU'LL JUST HAVE TO WAIT TILL THEY SHOW UP! OH, AND ACTUALLY, THE FLY LORD ISN'T ONE OF THE SIX KINGS. NOT EVERYONE WHO CALLS HIMSELF A KING REALLY IS, YOU KNOW.

A2:

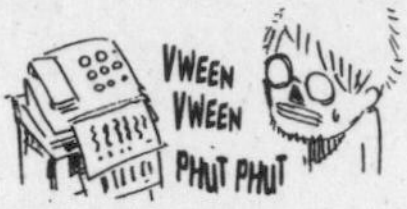
VWEEN
VWEEN
PHUT PHUT

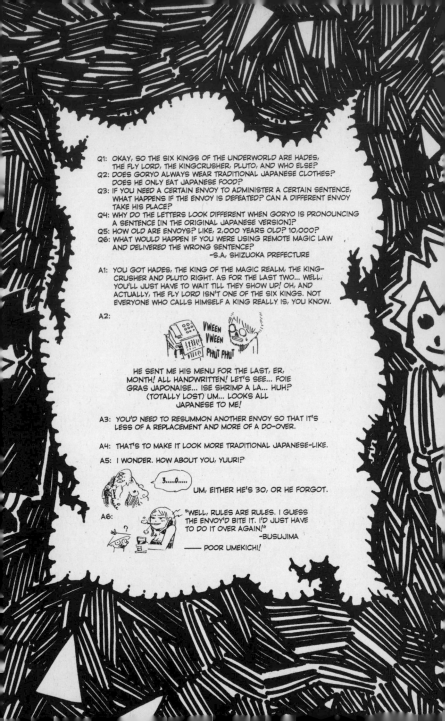

HE SENT ME HIS MENU FOR THE LAST, ER, MONTH! ALL HANDWRITTEN! LET'S SEE... FOIE GRAS JAPONAISE... ISE SHRIMP A LA... HUH? (TOTALLY LOST) UM... LOOKS ALL JAPANESE TO ME!

A3: YOU'D NEED TO RESUMMON ANOTHER ENVOY SO THAT IT'S LESS OF A REPLACEMENT AND MORE OF A DO-OVER.

A4: THAT'S TO MAKE IT LOOK MORE TRADITIONAL JAPANESE-LIKE.

A5: I WONDER. HOW ABOUT YOU, YUURI?

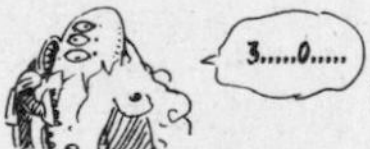
3.....0.....

UM, EITHER HE'S 30, OR HE FORGOT.

A6:

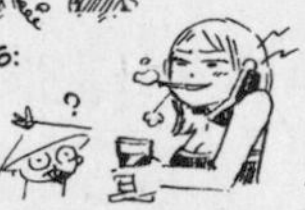
?

"WELL, RULES ARE RULES. I GUESS THE ENVOY'D BITE IT. I'D JUST HAVE TO DO IT OVER AGAIN!"

-BUSUJIMA

—— POOR UMEKICHI!

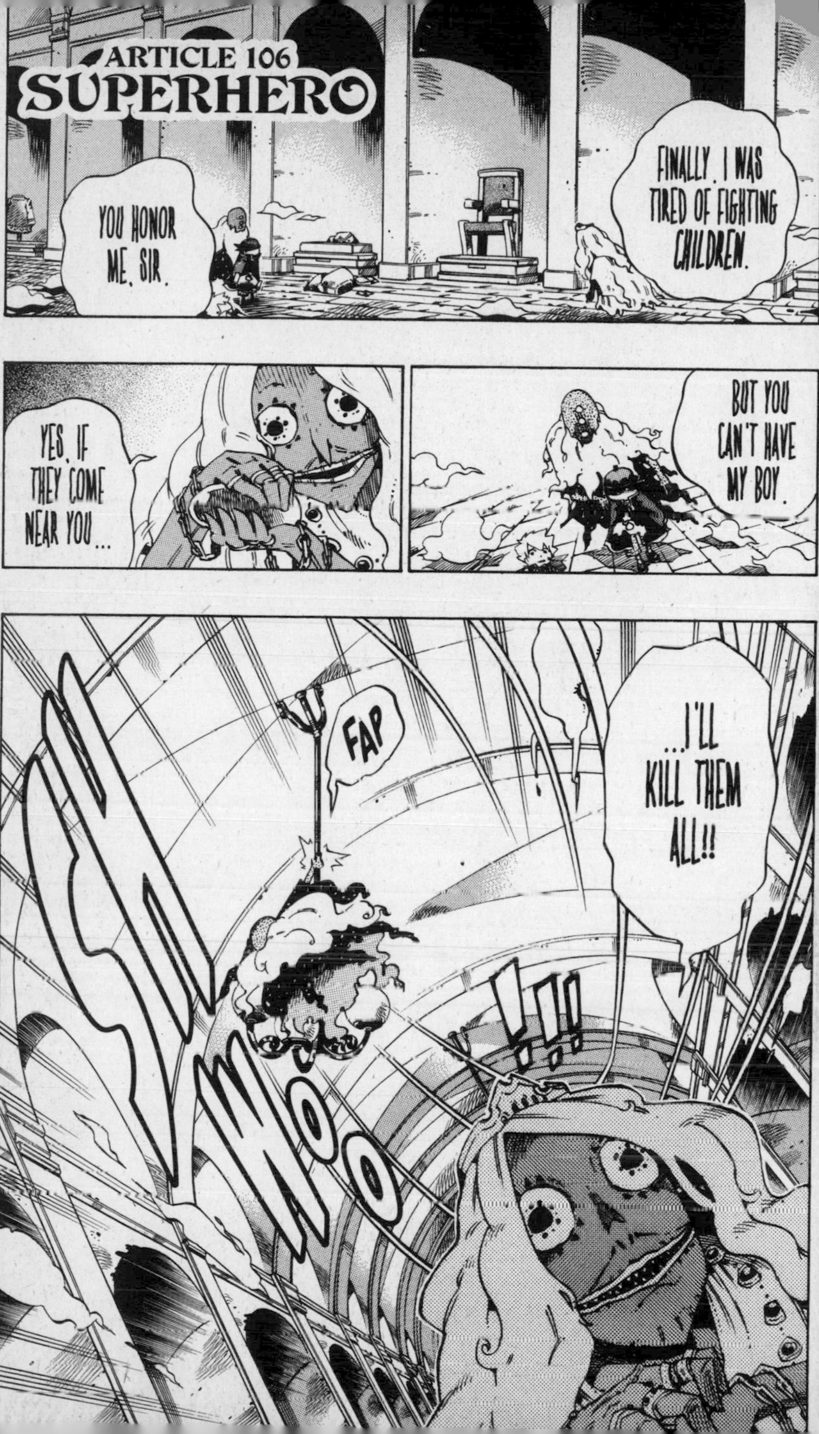
ARTICLE 106
SUPERHERO
FINALLY. I WAS TIRED OF FIGHTING CHILDREN.
YOU HONOR ME, SIR.
BUT YOU CAN'T HAVE MY BOY.
YES. IF THEY COME NEAR YOU...
...I'LL KILL THEM ALL!!
FAP

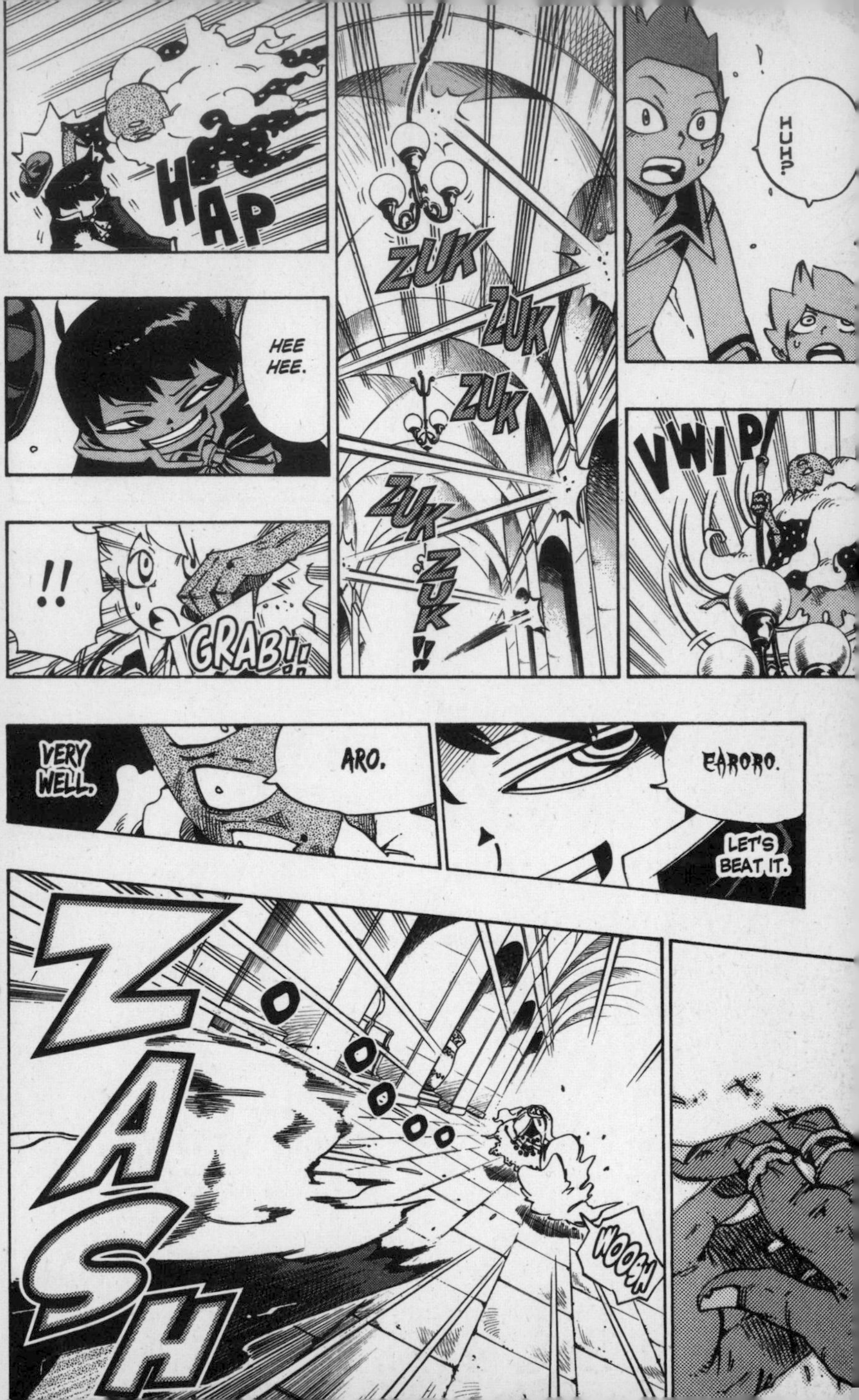
HUH?
VWIP
ZUK
ZUK
ZUK
ZUK
ZUK!!
HAP HAP
HEE HEE.
!!
GRAB!!
EARORO.
LET'S BEAT IT.
ARO.
VERY WELL.
ZASH
WOOSH

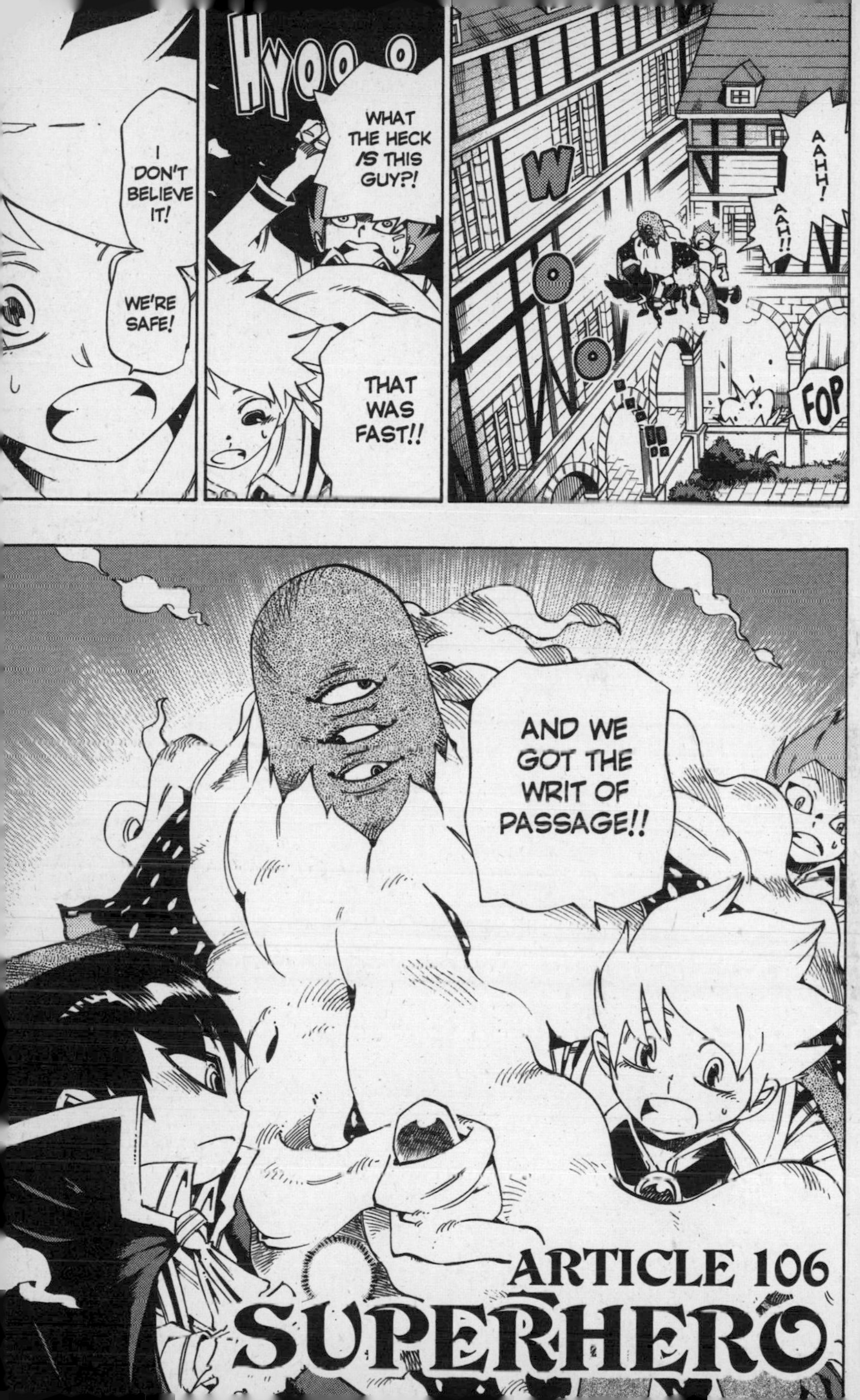
AAHH!
AAH!!
WOO
FOP
HYOO O
WHAT THE HECK IS THIS GUY?!
THAT WAS FAST!!
I DON'T BELIEVE IT!
WE'RE SAFE!
AND WE GOT THE WRIT OF PASSAGE!!
ARTICLE 106
SUPERHERO

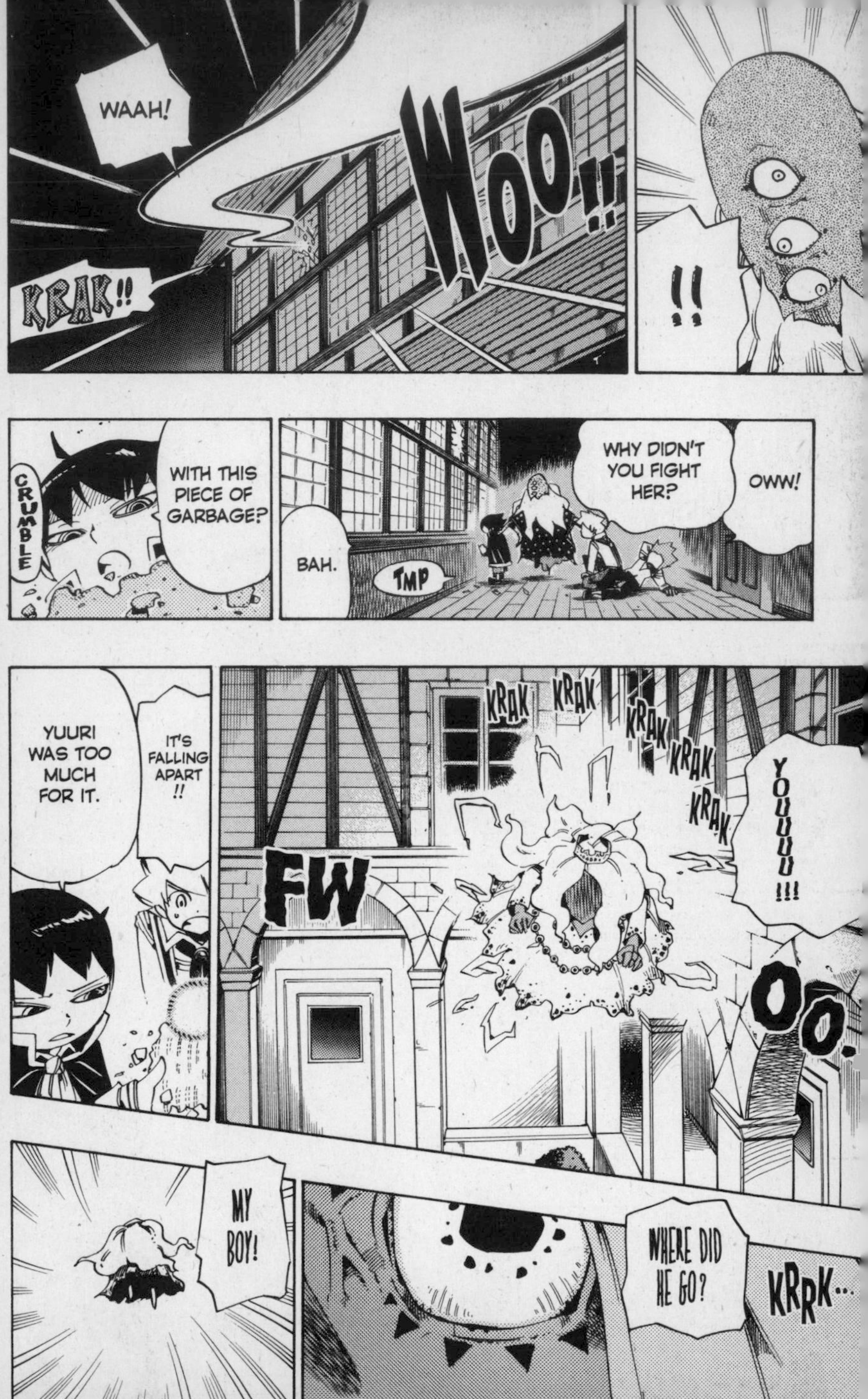
!!
WOO!!
WAAH!
KRAK!!
OWW!
WHY DIDN'T YOU FIGHT HER?
BAH.
TMP
WITH THIS PIECE OF GARBAGE?
CRUMBLE
KRAK
KRAK
KRAK
KRAK
KRAK
YOUUUU!!!
FW
OO
IT'S FALLING APART!!
YUURI WAS TOO MUCH FOR IT.
KRRK...
WHERE DID HE GO?
MY BOY!

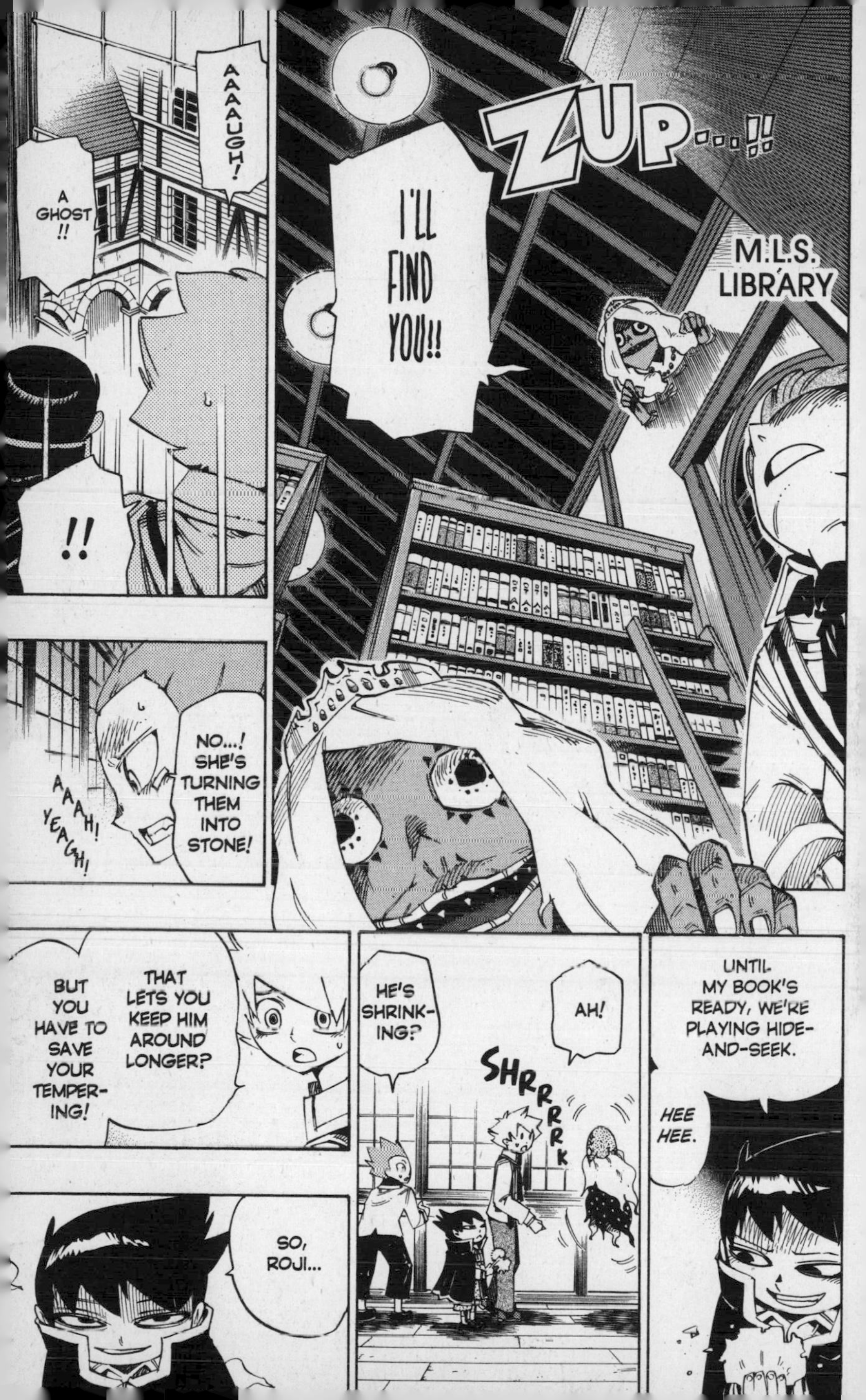
ZUP...!!
M.L.S. LIBRARY
I'LL FIND YOU!!
AAAAUGH!
A GHOST!!
!!
NO...! SHE'S TURNING THEM INTO STONE!
AAAAH! YEAGH!
UNTIL MY BOOK'S READY, WE'RE PLAYING HIDE-AND-SEEK.
HEE HEE.
AH!
SHRRRRK
HE'S SHRINK-ING?
THAT LETS YOU KEEP HIM AROUND LONGER?
BUT YOU HAVE TO SAVE YOUR TEMPER-ING!
SO, ROJI...

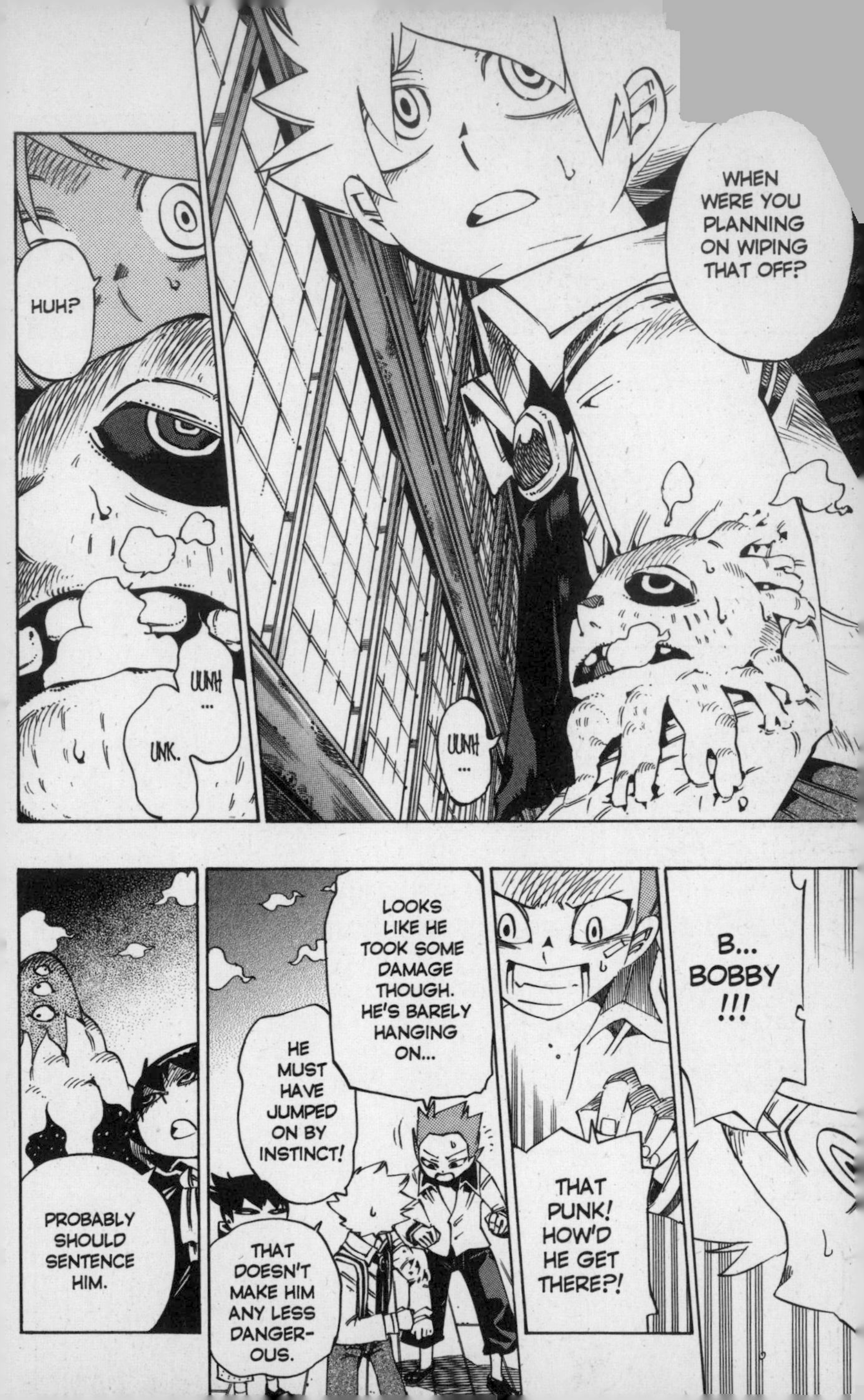
WHEN WERE YOU PLANNING ON WIPING THAT OFF?
UUNH ...
HUH?
UUNH ...
UNK.
B... BOBBY !!!
THAT PUNK! HOW'D HE GET THERE?!
LOOKS LIKE HE TOOK SOME DAMAGE THOUGH. HE'S BARELY HANGING ON...
HE MUST HAVE JUMPED ON BY INSTINCT!
THAT DOESN'T MAKE HIM ANY LESS DANGER-OUS.
PROBABLY SHOULD SENTENCE HIM.

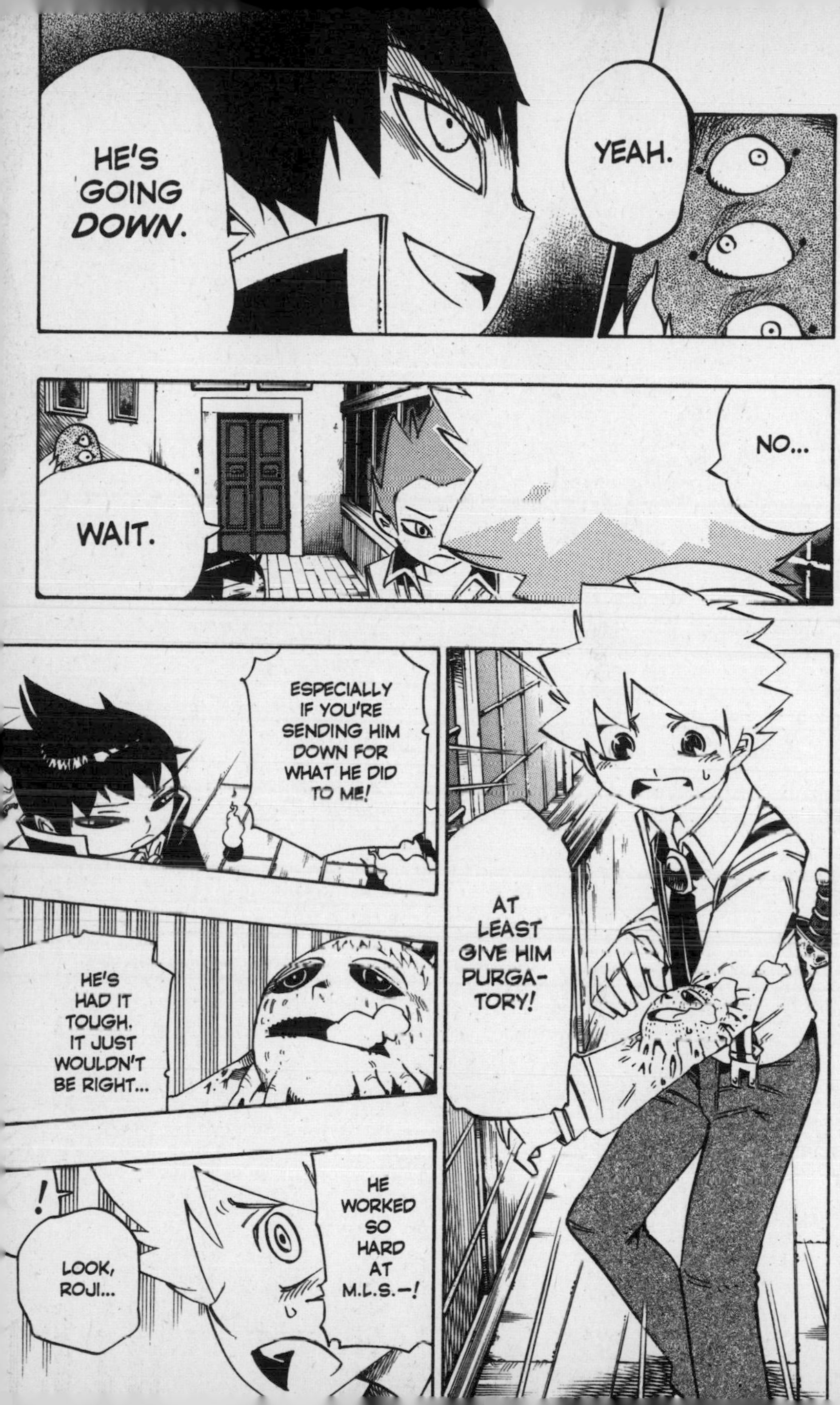
YEAH.
HE'S GOING *DOWN*.
NO...
WAIT.
AT LEAST GIVE HIM PURGATORY!
ESPECIALLY IF YOU'RE SENDING HIM DOWN FOR WHAT HE DID TO ME!
HE'S HAD IT TOUGH. IT JUST WOULDN'T BE RIGHT...
HE WORKED SO HARD AT M.L.S.—!
!
LOOK, ROJI...

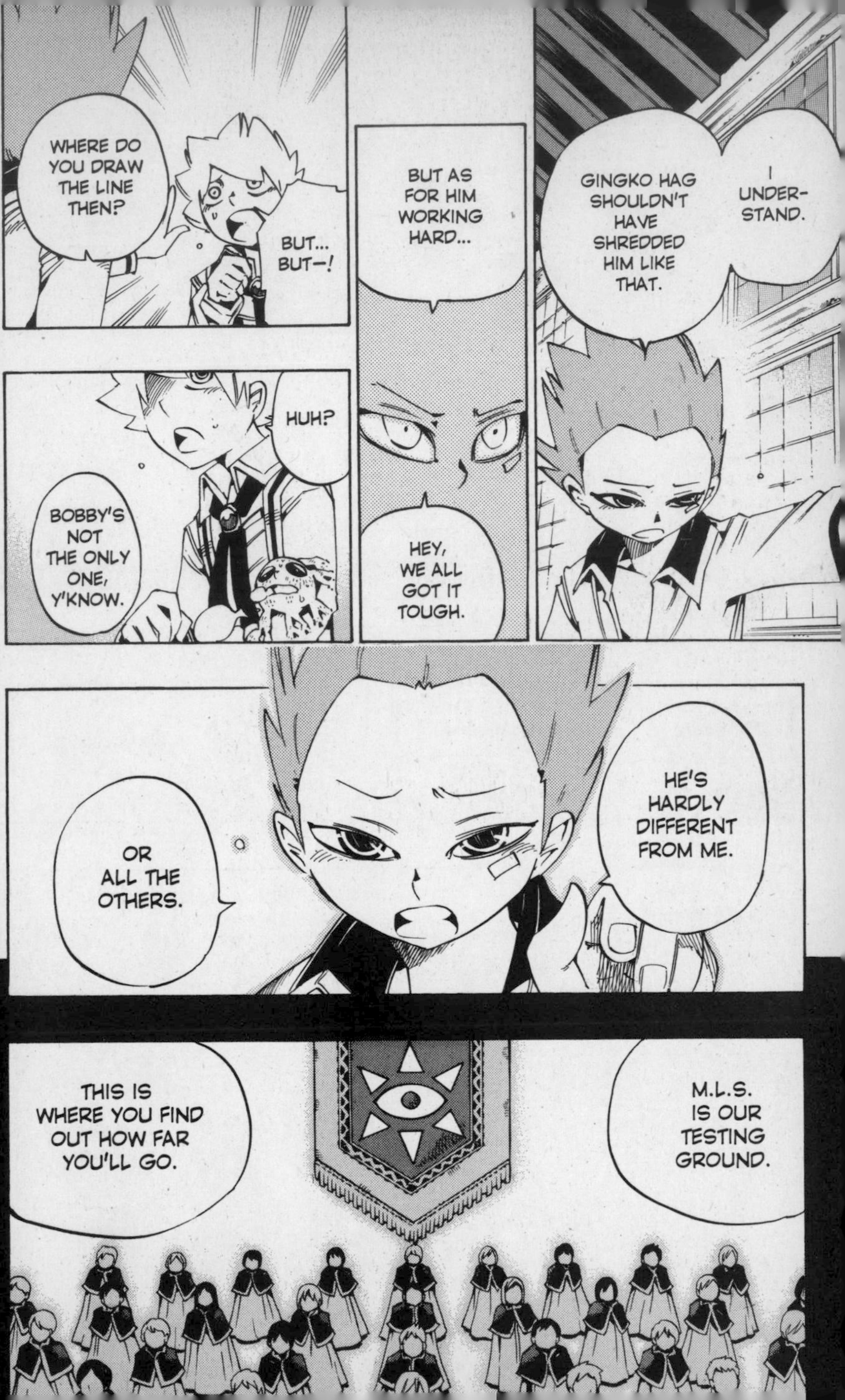
I UNDERSTAND.
GINGKO HAG SHOULDN'T HAVE SHREDDED HIM LIKE THAT.
BUT AS FOR HIM WORKING HARD...
HEY, WE ALL GOT IT TOUGH.
BUT... BUT—!
WHERE DO YOU DRAW THE LINE THEN?
HUH?
BOBBY'S NOT THE ONLY ONE, Y'KNOW.
HE'S HARDLY DIFFERENT FROM ME.
OR ALL THE OTHERS.
M.L.S. IS OUR TESTING GROUND.
THIS IS WHERE YOU FIND OUT HOW FAR YOU'LL GO.

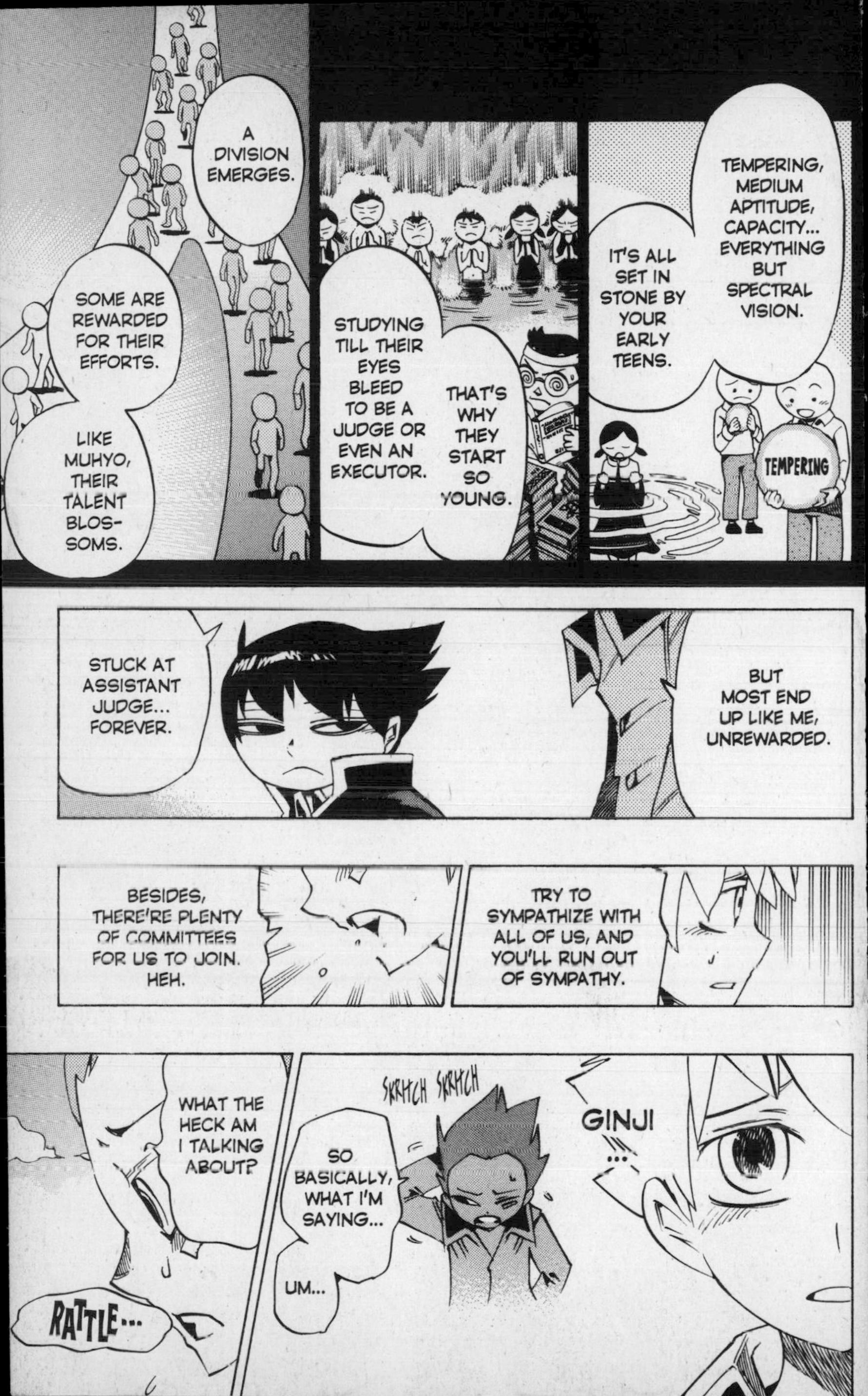
TEMPERING, MEDIUM APTITUDE, CAPACITY... EVERYTHING BUT SPECTRAL VISION.
IT'S ALL SET IN STONE BY YOUR EARLY TEENS.
TEMPERING
STUDYING TILL THEIR EYES BLEED TO BE A JUDGE OR EVEN AN EXECUTOR.
THAT'S WHY THEY START SO YOUNG.
A DIVISION EMERGES.
SOME ARE REWARDED FOR THEIR EFFORTS.
LIKE MUHYO, THEIR TALENT BLOS-SOMS.
BUT MOST END UP LIKE ME, UNREWARDED.
STUCK AT ASSISTANT JUDGE... FOREVER.
TRY TO SYMPATHIZE WITH ALL OF US, AND YOU'LL RUN OUT OF SYMPATHY.
BESIDES, THERE'RE PLENTY OF COMMITTEES FOR US TO JOIN. HEH.
GINJI ...
SKRITCH SKRITCH
SO BASICALLY, WHAT I'M SAYING...
UM...
WHAT THE HECK AM I TALKING ABOUT?
RATTLE...

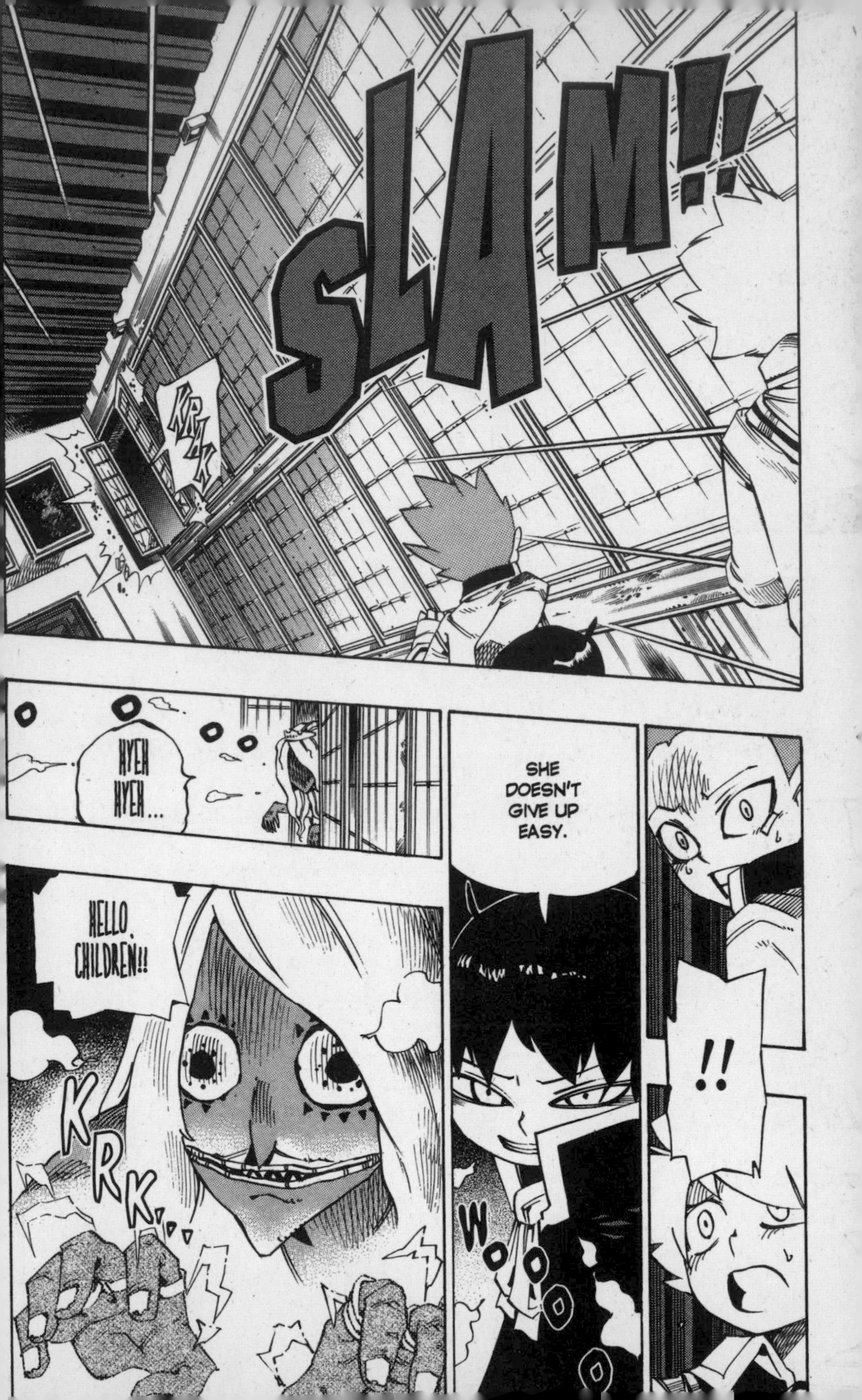
SLAM!!
KRAK
!!
SHE DOESN'T GIVE UP EASY.
WOOO
HYEH HYEH...
HELLO, CHILDREN!!
KRK...

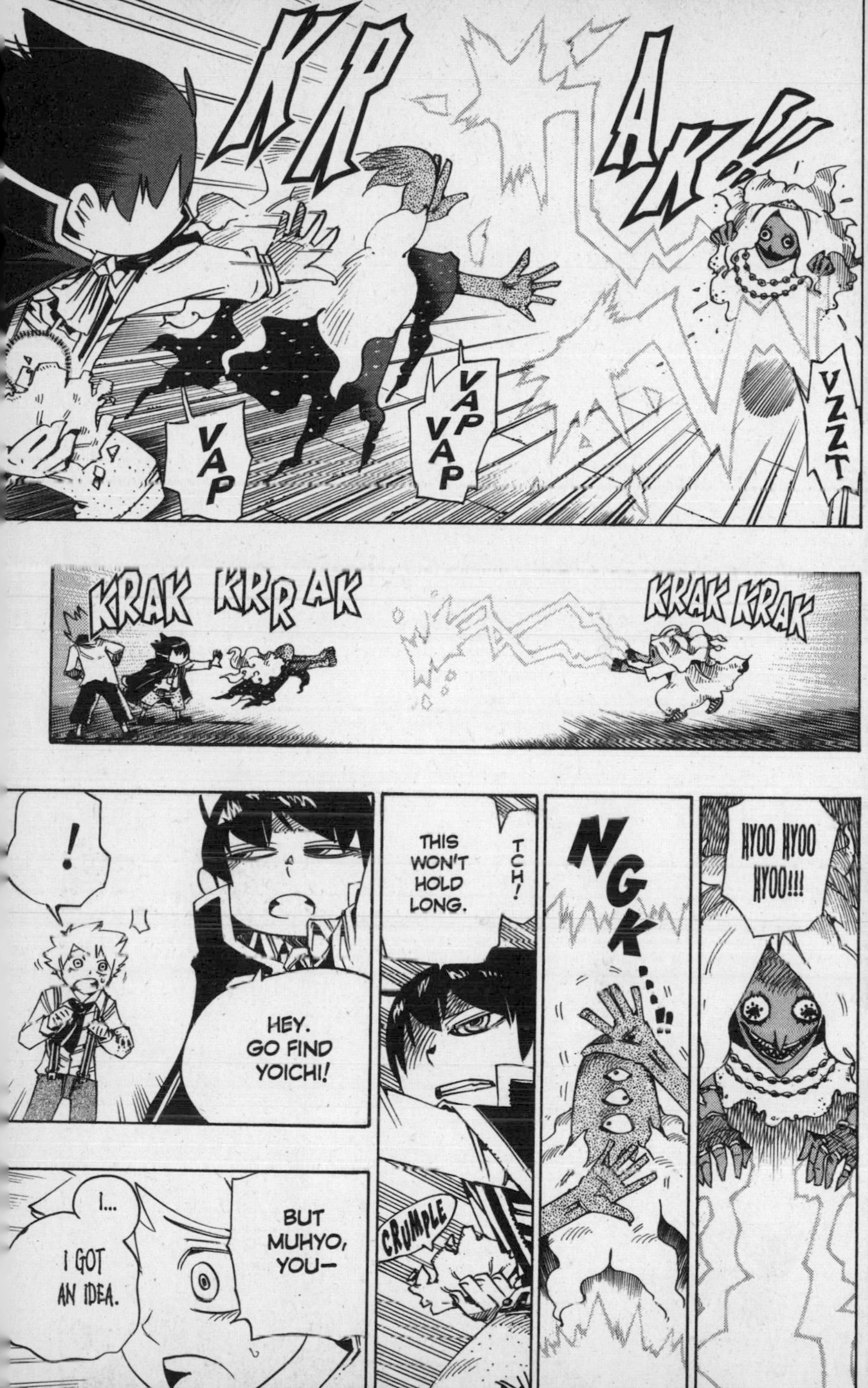
KRAK!!
VZZT
VAP VAP
VAP
KRAK KRAK
KRRAK
KRAK
HYOO HYOO HYOO!!!
NGK...!!
TCH!
THIS WON'T HOLD LONG.
CRUMPLE
!
HEY. GO FIND YOICHI!
BUT MUHYO, YOU—
I...
I GOT AN IDEA.

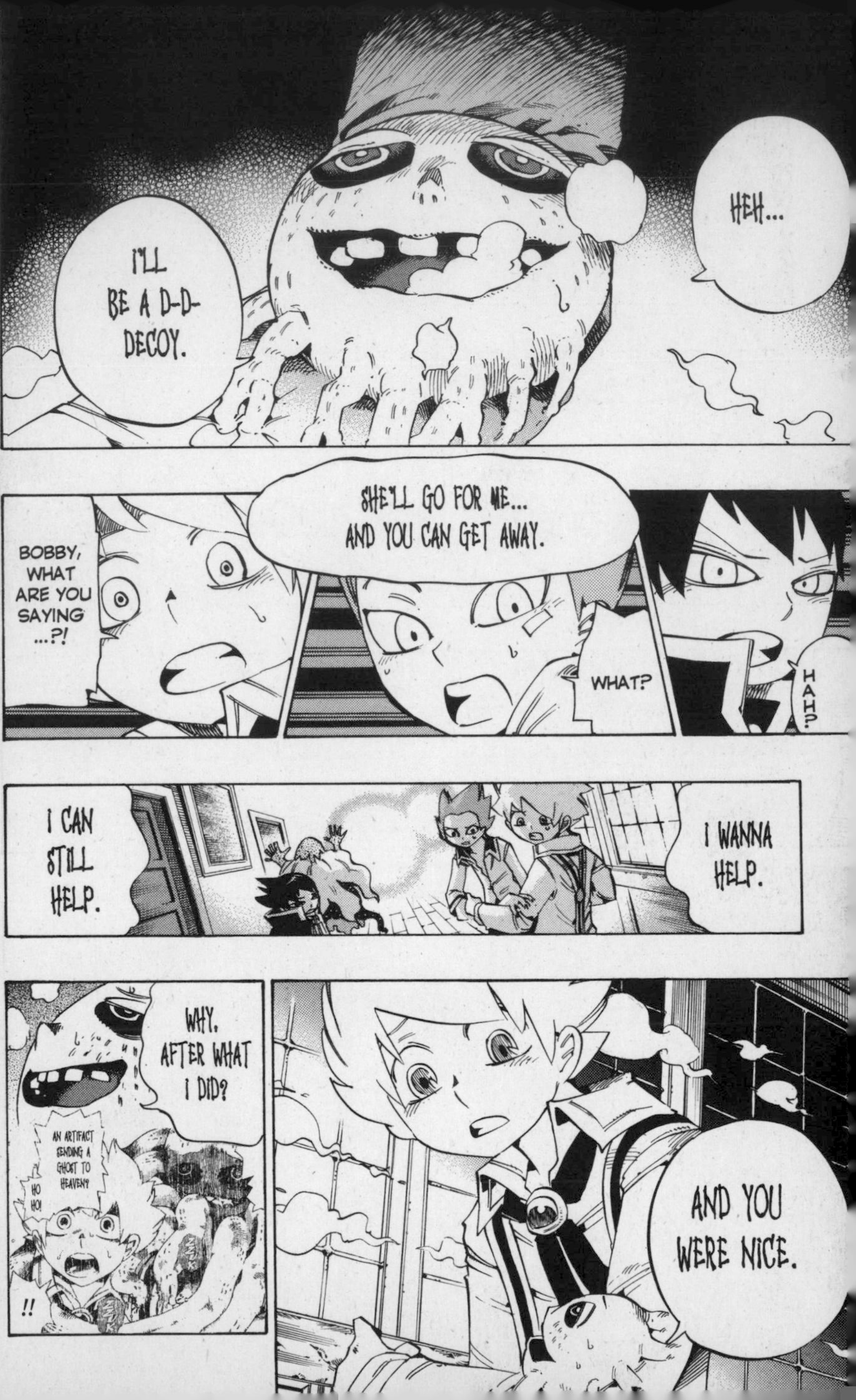
HEH...
I'LL BE A D-D-DECOY.
SHE'LL GO FOR ME... AND YOU CAN GET AWAY.
HAH?
WHAT?
BOBBY, WHAT ARE YOU SAYING ...?!
I WANNA HELP.
I CAN STILL HELP.
AND YOU WERE NICE.
WHY. AFTER WHAT I DID?
AN ARTIFACT SENDING A GHOST TO HEAVEN?
HO HO!
!!

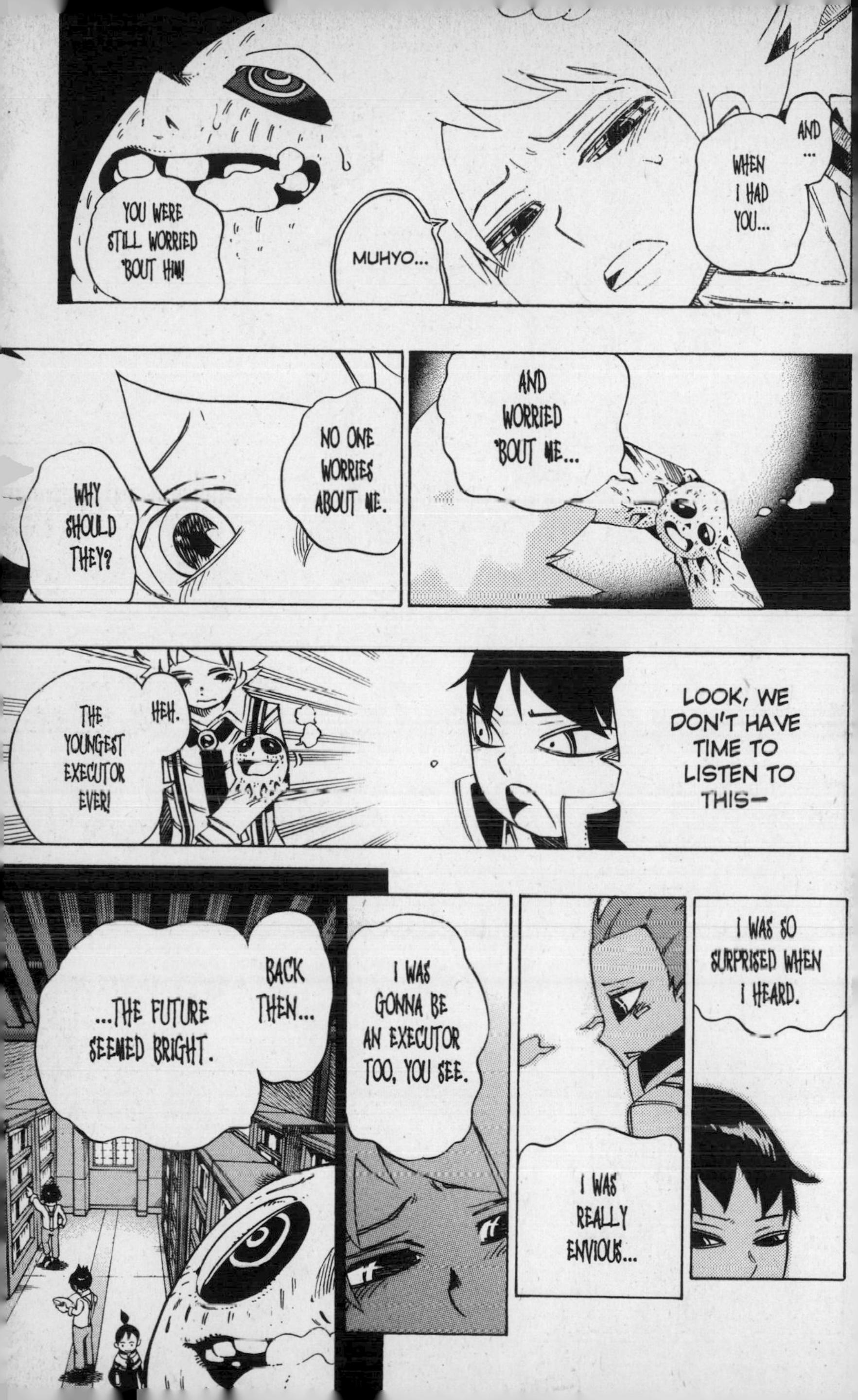
AND... WHEN I HAD YOU...
MUHYO...
YOU WERE STILL WORRIED 'BOUT HIM!
AND WORRIED 'BOUT ME...
NO ONE WORRIES ABOUT ME.
WHY SHOULD THEY?
LOOK, WE DON'T HAVE TIME TO LISTEN TO THIS—
HEH.
THE YOUNGEST EXECUTOR EVER!
I WAS SO SURPRISED WHEN I HEARD.
I WAS REALLY ENVIOUS...
I WAS GONNA BE AN EXECUTOR TOO, YOU SEE.
BACK THEN...
...THE FUTURE SEEMED BRIGHT.

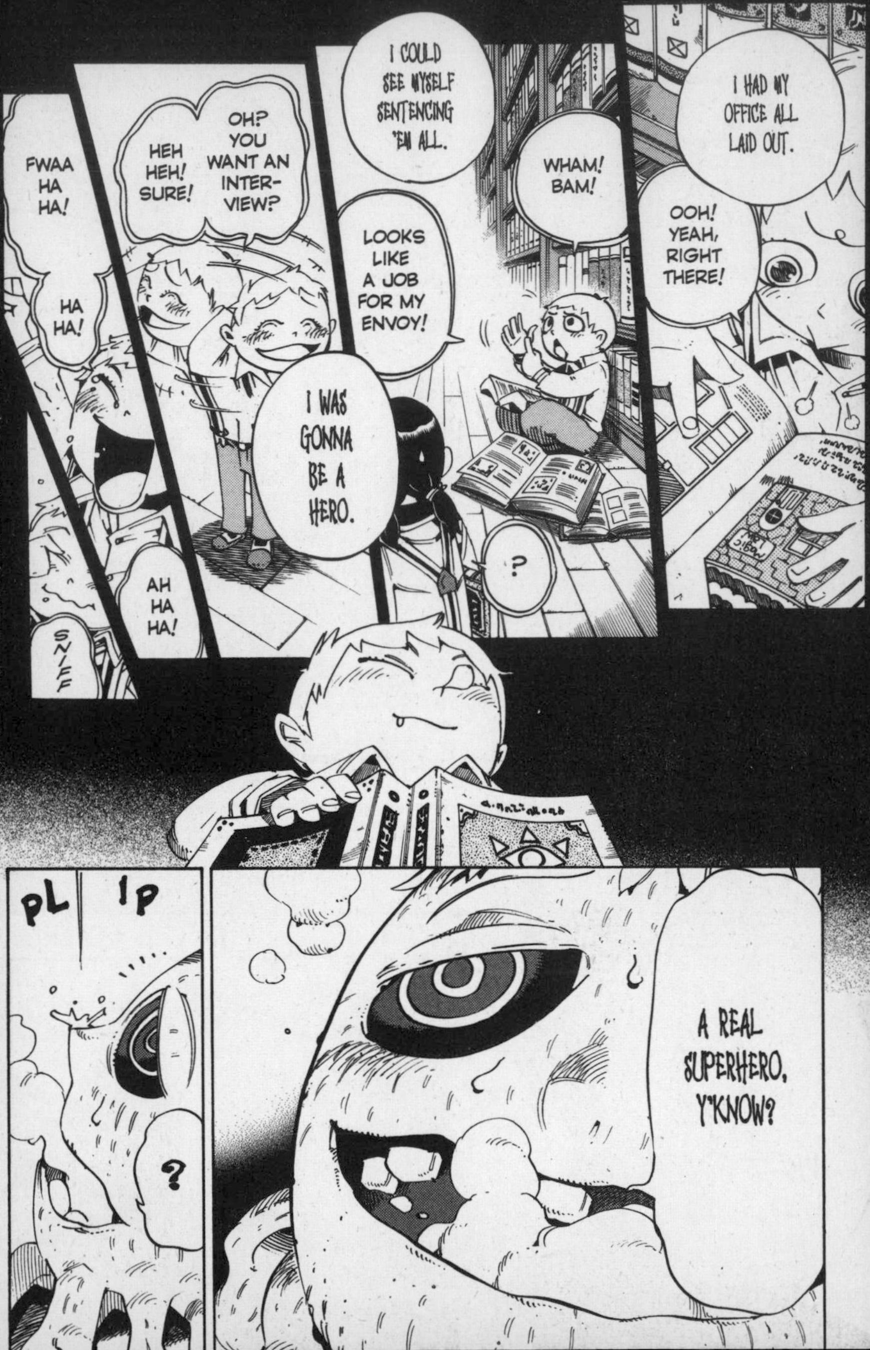
I HAD MY OFFICE ALL LAID OUT.
OOH! YEAH, RIGHT THERE!
I COULD SEE MYSELF SENTENCING 'EM ALL.
WHAM! BAM!
LOOKS LIKE A JOB FOR MY ENVOY!
?
I WAS GONNA BE A HERO.
OH? YOU WANT AN INTER-VIEW?
HEH HEH! SURE!
AH HA HA!
FWAA HA HA!
HA HA!
SNIFF
A REAL SUPERHERO, Y'KNOW?
PLIP
?

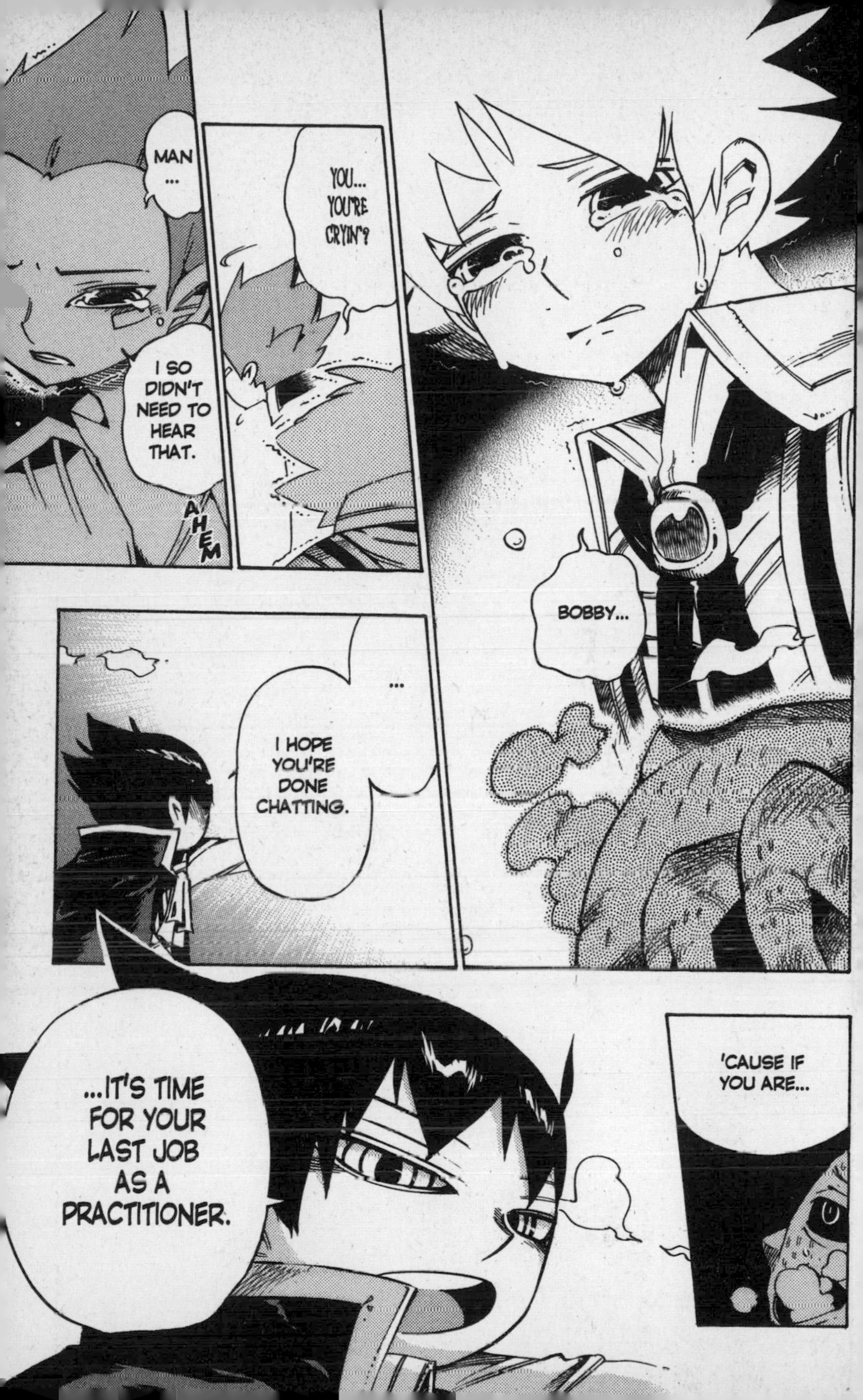
BOBBY...
YOU... YOU'RE CRYIN'?
MAN...
I SO DIDN'T NEED TO HEAR THAT.
AHEM
...
I HOPE YOU'RE DONE CHATTING.
'CAUSE IF YOU ARE...
...IT'S TIME FOR YOUR LAST JOB AS A PRACTITIONER.

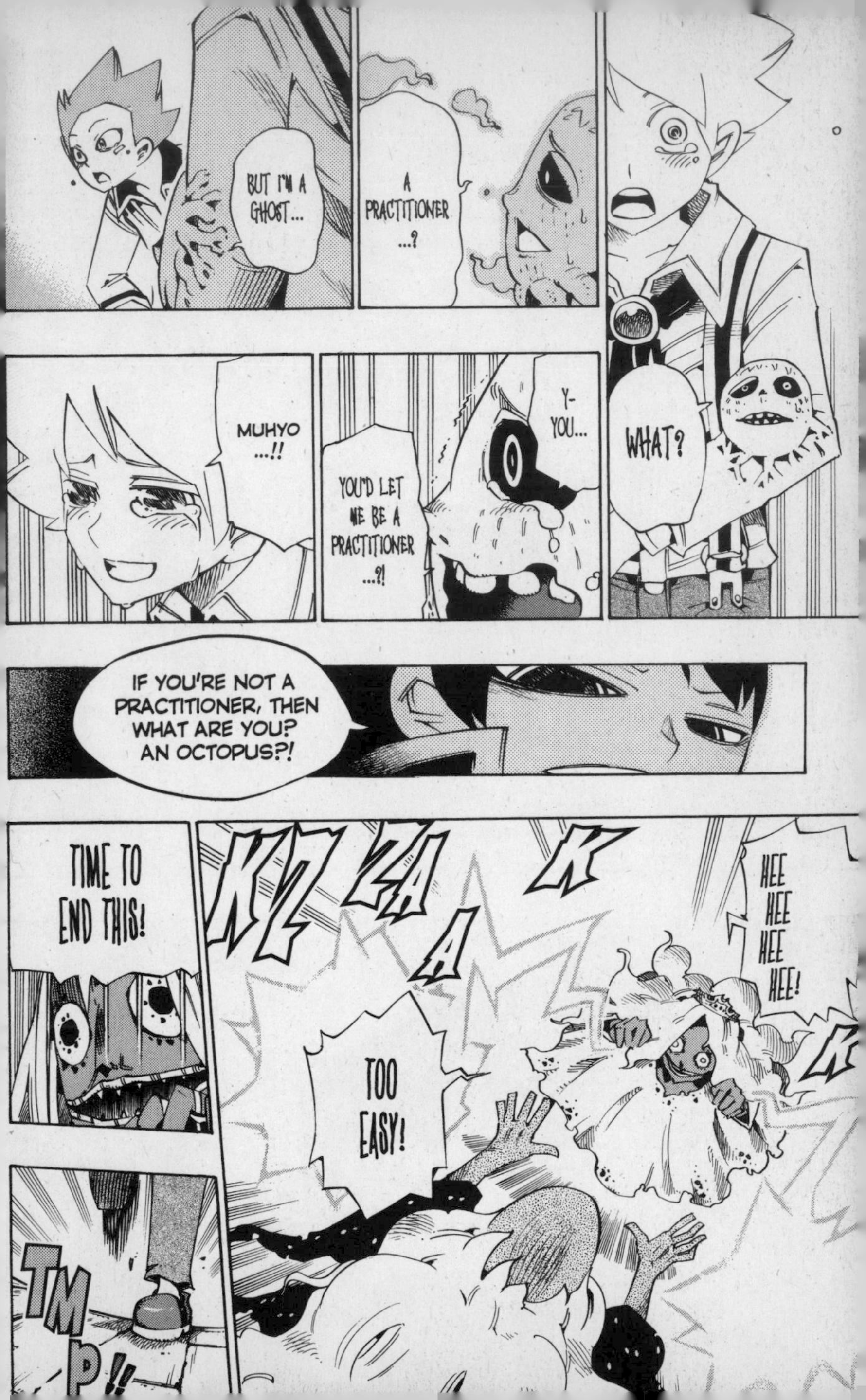
A PRACTITIONER ...?
BUT I'M A GHOST...
WHAT?
Y-YOU...
YOU'D LET ME BE A PRACTITIONER ...?!
MUHYO ...!!
IF YOU'RE NOT A PRACTITIONER, THEN WHAT ARE YOU? AN OCTOPUS?!
HEE HEE HEE HEE HEE!
KZZLAAAK
TOO EASY!
TIME TO END THIS!
TMP!!

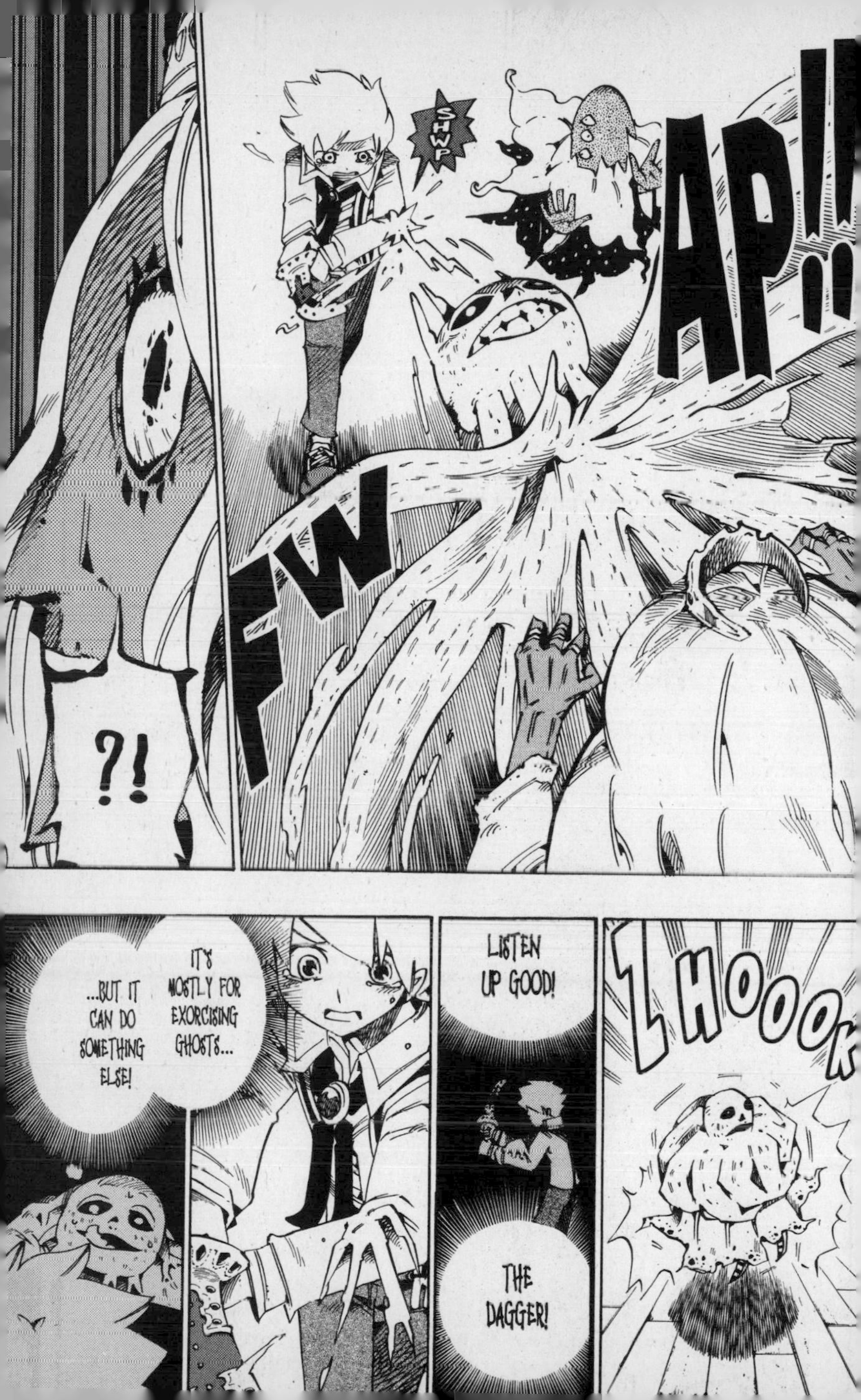
SHWP
FW
AP!!
?!
ZHOOOK
LISTEN UP GOOD!
THE DAGGER!
IT'S MOSTLY FOR EXORCISING GHOSTS...
...BUT IT CAN DO SOMETHING ELSE!

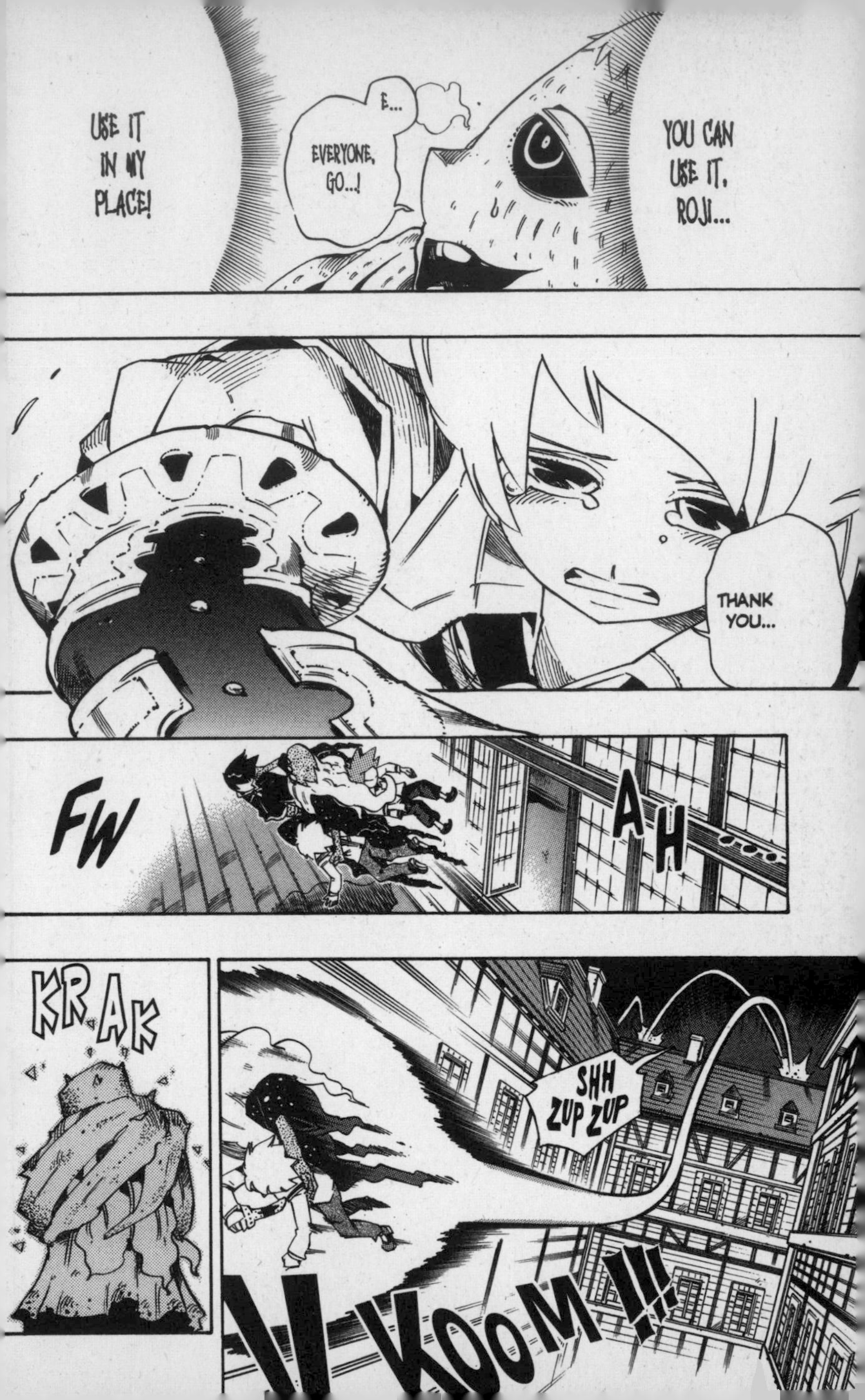
YOU CAN USE IT, ROJI...
E...
EVERYONE, GO...!
USE IT IN MY PLACE!
THANK YOU...
AH
FW
SHH ZUP ZUP
KOOM!!!
KRAK

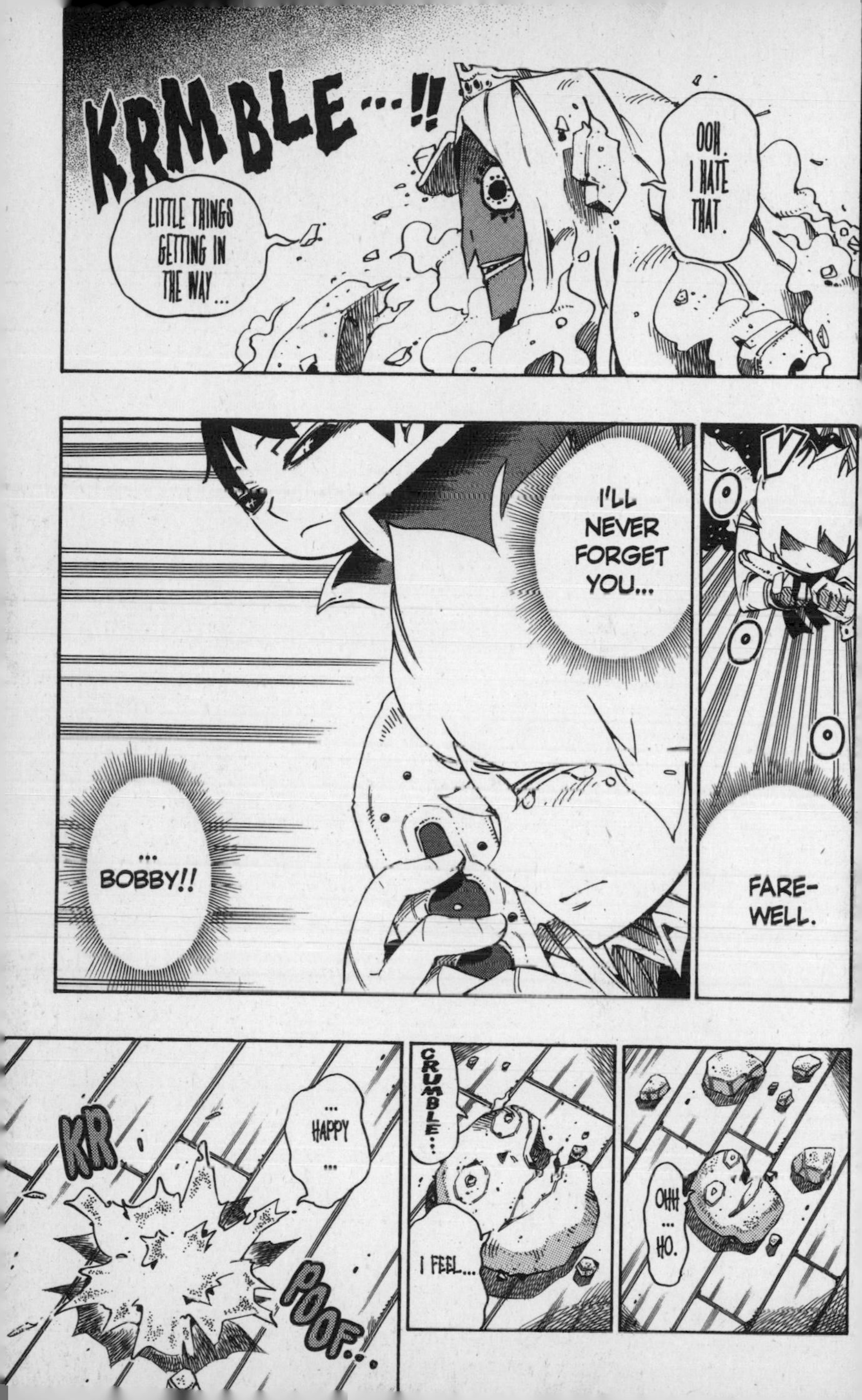
OOH. I HATE THAT.
KRMBLE...!!
LITTLE THINGS GETTING IN THE WAY...
V
FARE-WELL.
I'LL NEVER FORGET YOU...
...BOBBY!!
OHH... HO.
CRUMBLE...
I FEEL...
...HAPPY...
KR
POOF...

ARTICLE 107
THE RING

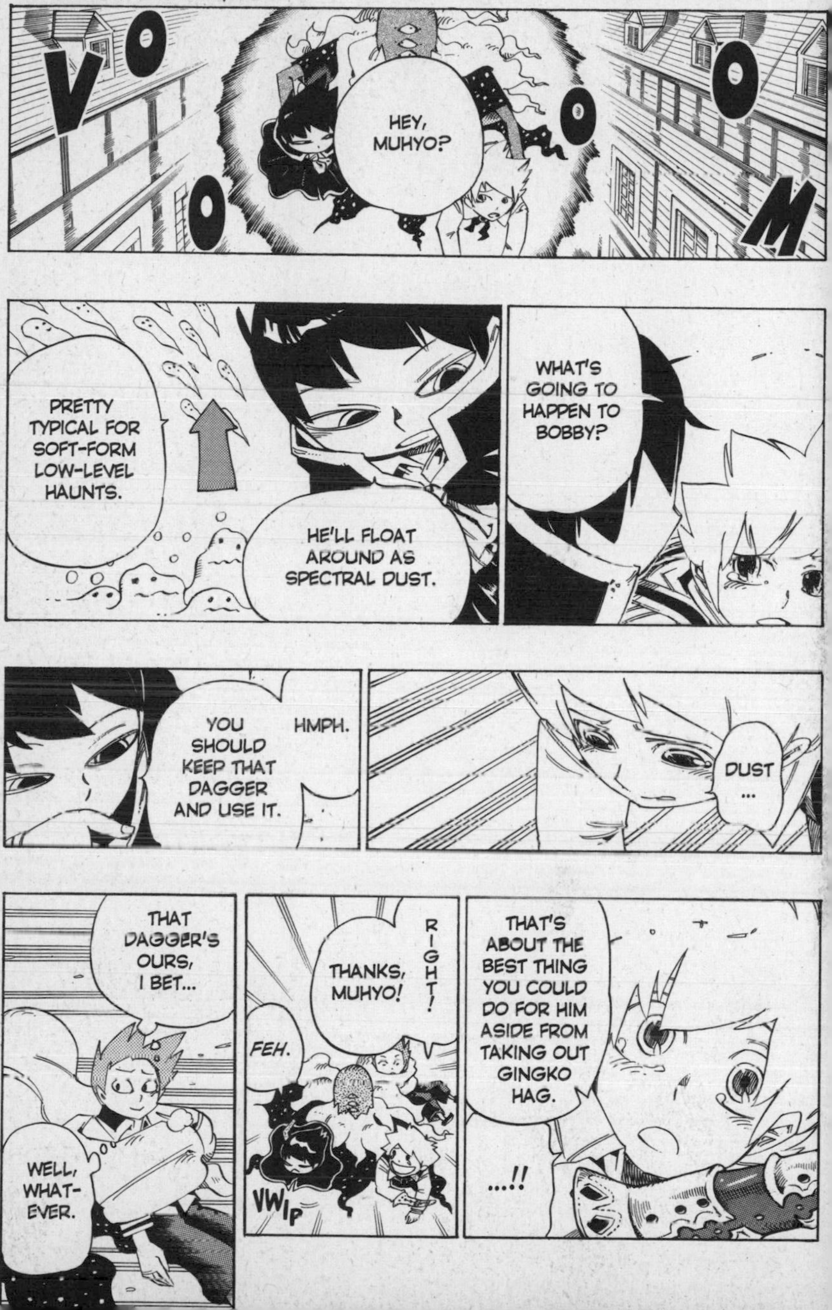
VOOOOM
HEY, MUHYO?
WHAT'S GOING TO HAPPEN TO BOBBY?
HE'LL FLOAT AROUND AS SPECTRAL DUST.
PRETTY TYPICAL FOR SOFT-FORM LOW-LEVEL HAUNTS.
DUST ...
HMPH.
YOU SHOULD KEEP THAT DAGGER AND USE IT.
THAT'S ABOUT THE BEST THING YOU COULD DO FOR HIM ASIDE FROM TAKING OUT GINGKO HAG.
...!!
RIGHT!
THANKS, MUHYO!
FEH.
VWIP
THAT DAGGER'S OURS, I BET...
WELL, WHAT-EVER.

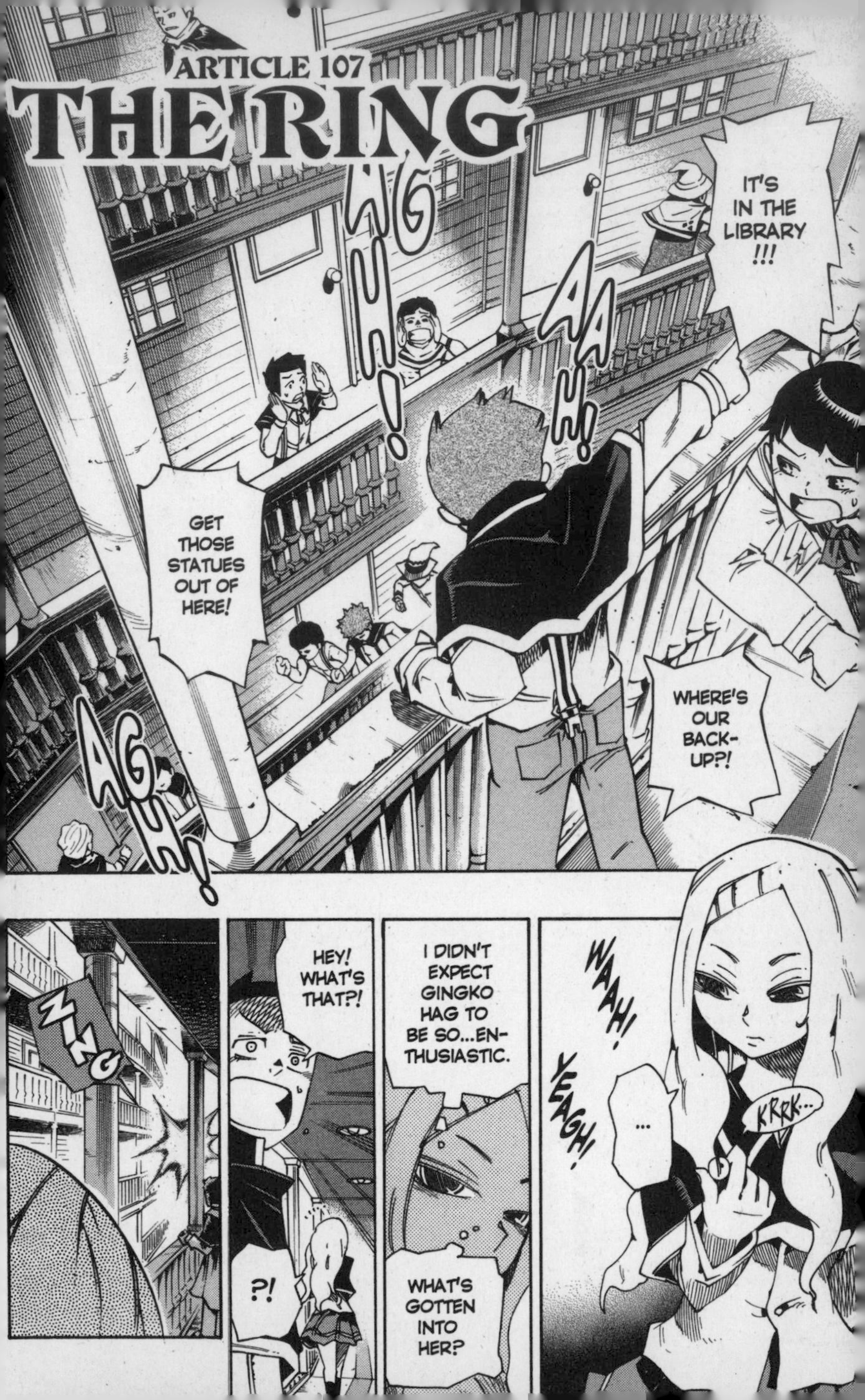
ARTICLE 107
THE RING
IT'S IN THE LIBRARY!!!
AAAH!
NGH!
GET THOSE STATUES OUT OF HERE!
WHERE'S OUR BACK-UP?!
AGUH!
WAAAH!
YEAGH!
...
KRRK...
I DIDN'T EXPECT GINGKO HAG TO BE SO...EN-THUSIASTIC.
WHAT'S GOTTEN INTO HER?
HEY! WHAT'S THAT?!
?!
NNG

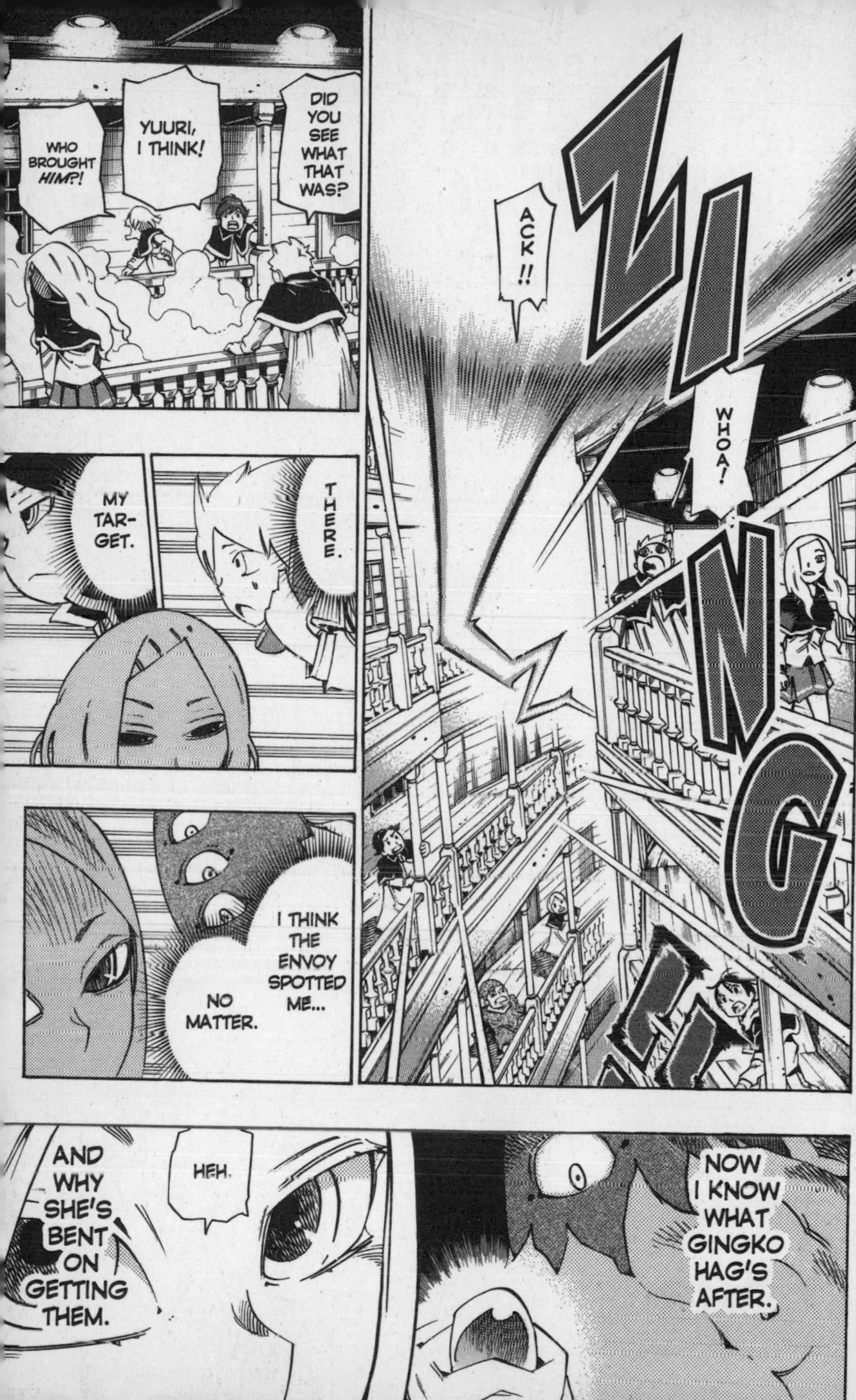
ZING
ACK!!
WHOA!
DID YOU SEE WHAT THAT WAS?
YUURI, I THINK!
WHO BROUGHT *HIM*?!
THERE.
MY TAR-GET.
I THINK THE ENVOY SPOTTED ME...
NO MATTER.
NOW I KNOW WHAT GINGKO HAG'S AFTER.
HEH.
AND WHY SHE'S BENT ON GETTING THEM.

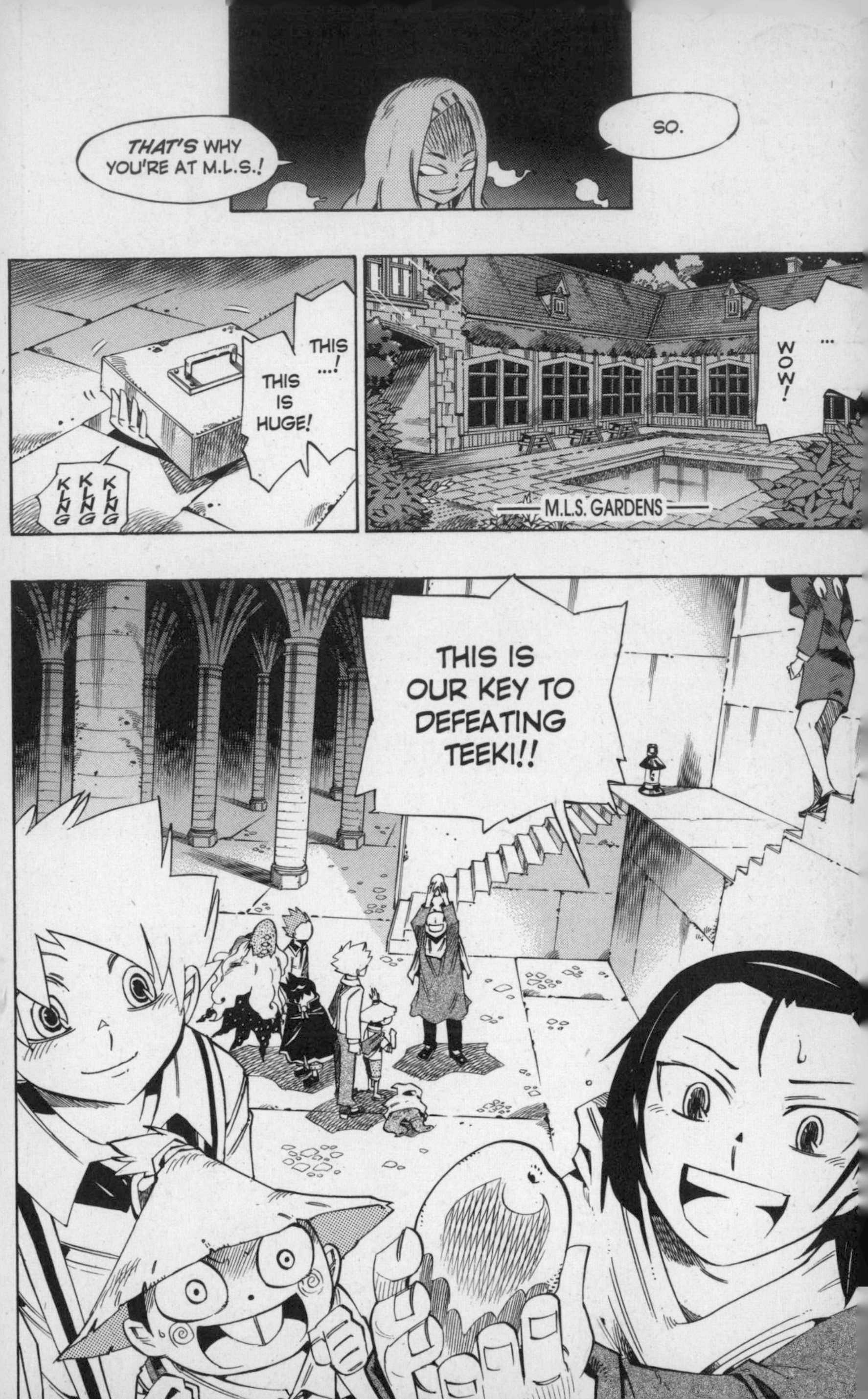
SO.
THAT'S WHY YOU'RE AT M.L.S.!
...WOW!
M.L.S. GARDENS
THIS ...!
THIS IS HUGE!
KLING KLING KLING
THIS IS OUR KEY TO DEFEATING TEEKI!!

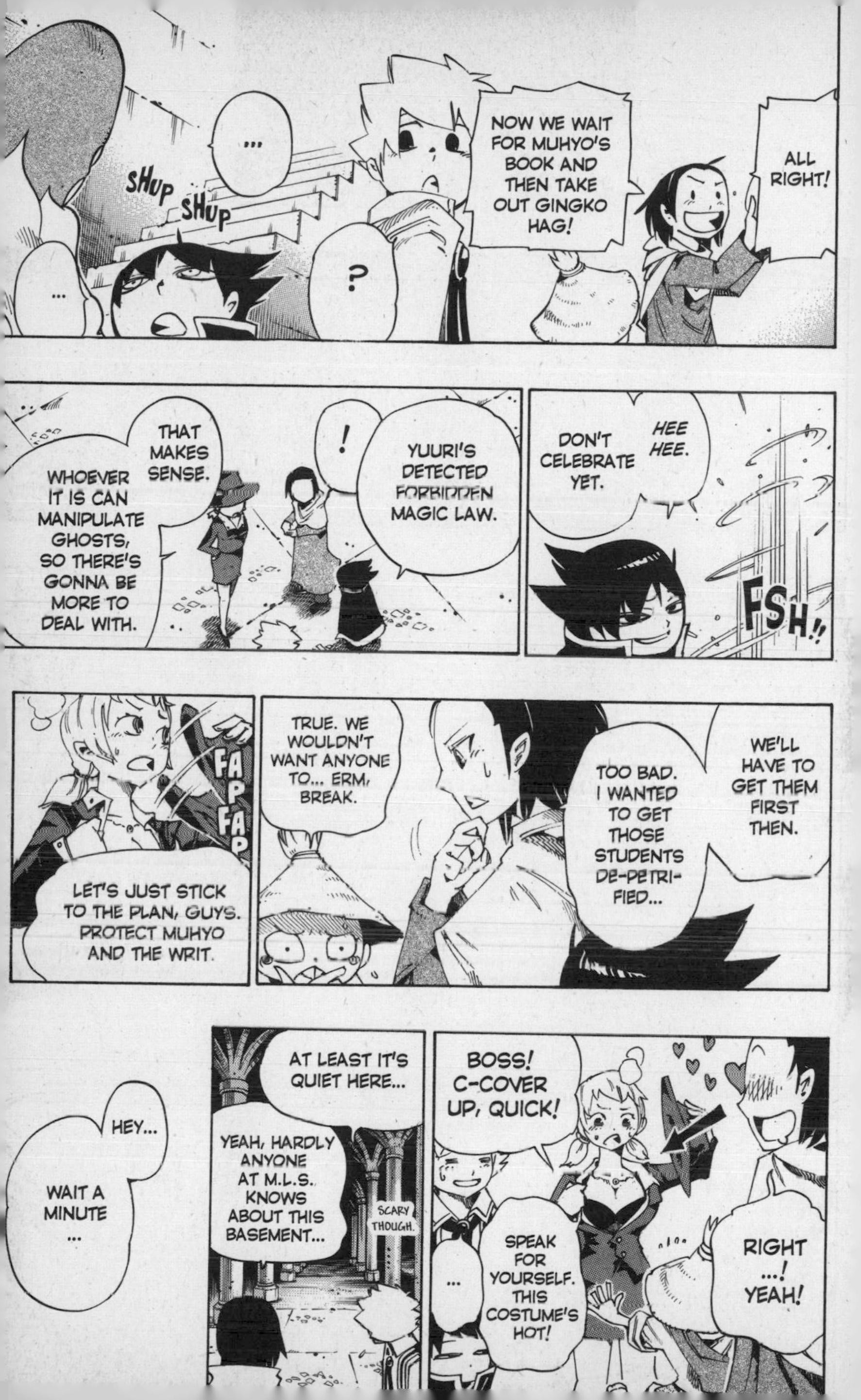
ALL RIGHT!
NOW WE WAIT FOR MUHYO'S BOOK AND THEN TAKE OUT GINGKO HAG!
...
SHUP SHUP
?
...
HEE HEE.
DON'T CELEBRATE YET.
FSH!!
YUURI'S DETECTED FORBIDDEN MAGIC LAW.
!
THAT MAKES SENSE.
WHOEVER IT IS CAN MANIPULATE GHOSTS, SO THERE'S GONNA BE MORE TO DEAL WITH.
WE'LL HAVE TO GET THEM FIRST THEN.
TOO BAD. I WANTED TO GET THOSE STUDENTS DE-PETRI-FIED...
TRUE. WE WOULDN'T WANT ANYONE TO... ERM, BREAK.
FAP FAP
LET'S JUST STICK TO THE PLAN, GUYS. PROTECT MUHYO AND THE WRIT.
BOSS! C-COVER UP, QUICK!
RIGHT ...! YEAH!
SPEAK FOR YOURSELF. THIS COSTUME'S HOT!
...
AT LEAST IT'S QUIET HERE...
YEAH, HARDLY ANYONE AT M.L.S. KNOWS ABOUT THIS BASEMENT...
SCARY THOUGH.
HEY...
WAIT A MINUTE ...

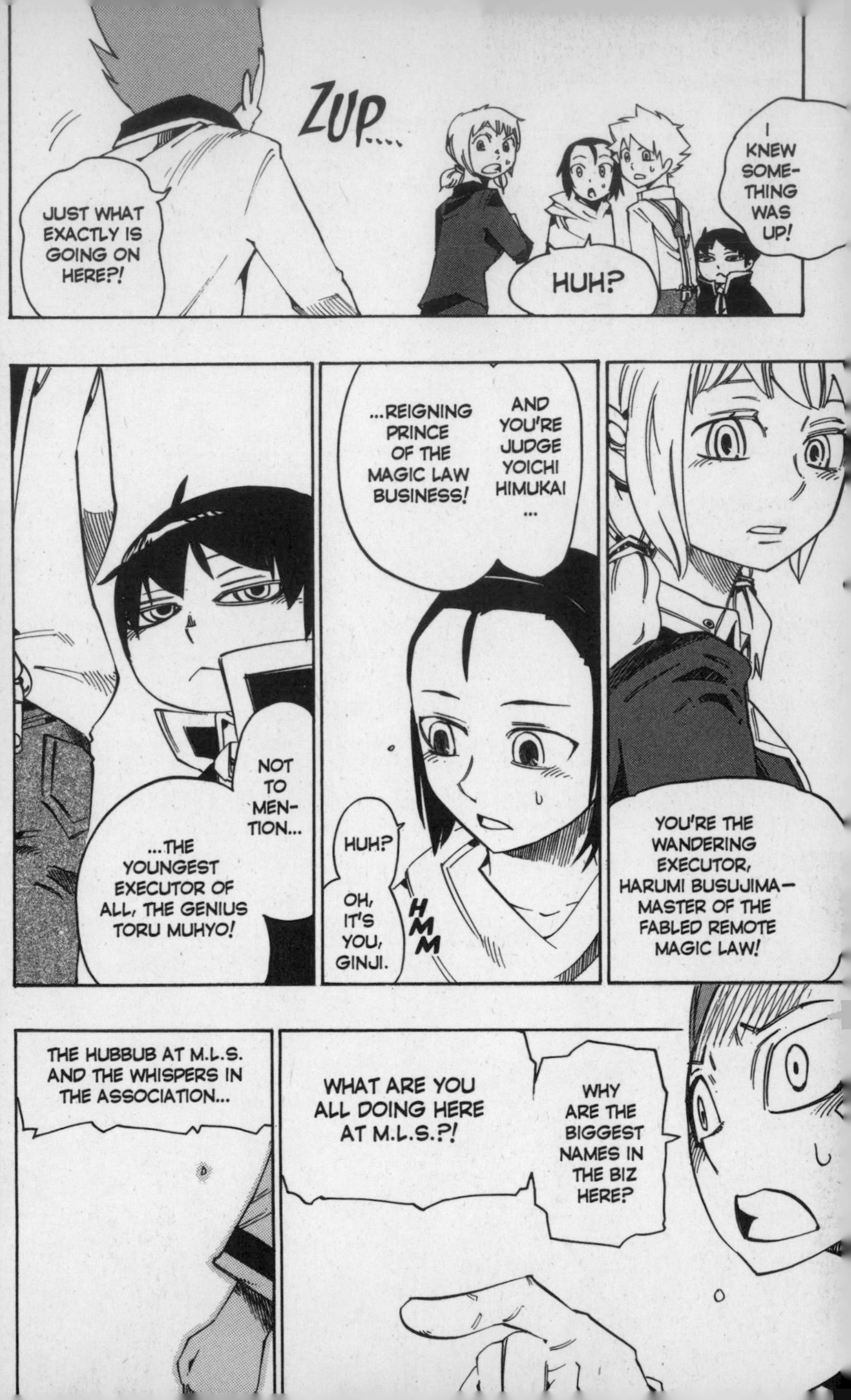
I KNEW SOMETHING WAS UP!
ZUP....
HUH?
JUST WHAT EXACTLY IS GOING ON HERE?!
YOU'RE THE WANDERING EXECUTOR, HARUMI BUSUJIMA—MASTER OF THE FABLED REMOTE MAGIC LAW!
AND YOU'RE JUDGE YOICHI HIMUKAI...
...REIGNING PRINCE OF THE MAGIC LAW BUSINESS!
HMM
HUH?
OH, IT'S YOU, GINJI.
NOT TO MENTION...
...THE YOUNGEST EXECUTOR OF ALL, THE GENIUS TORU MUHYO!
WHY ARE THE BIGGEST NAMES IN THE BIZ HERE?
WHAT ARE YOU ALL DOING HERE AT M.L.S.?!
THE HUBBUB AT M.L.S. AND THE WHISPERS IN THE ASSOCIATION...

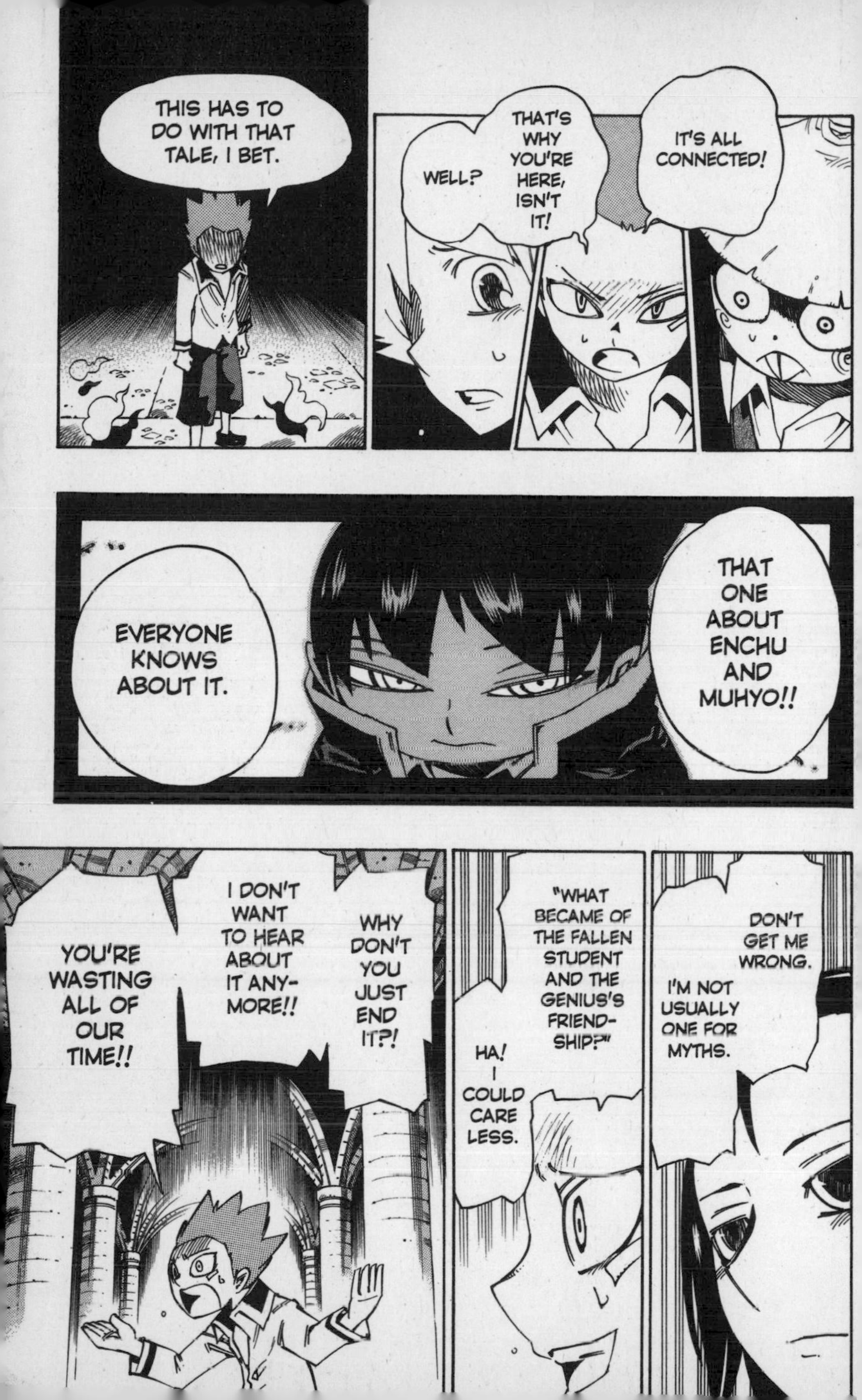
IT'S ALL CONNECTED!
THAT'S WHY YOU'RE HERE, ISN'T IT!
WELL?
THIS HAS TO DO WITH THAT TALE, I BET.
THAT ONE ABOUT ENCHU AND MUHYO!!
EVERYONE KNOWS ABOUT IT.
DON'T GET ME WRONG.
I'M NOT USUALLY ONE FOR MYTHS.
"WHAT BECAME OF THE FALLEN STUDENT AND THE GENIUS'S FRIENDSHIP?"
HA! I COULD CARE LESS.
WHY DON'T YOU JUST END IT?!
I DON'T WANT TO HEAR ABOUT IT ANY-MORE!!
YOU'RE WASTING ALL OF OUR TIME!!

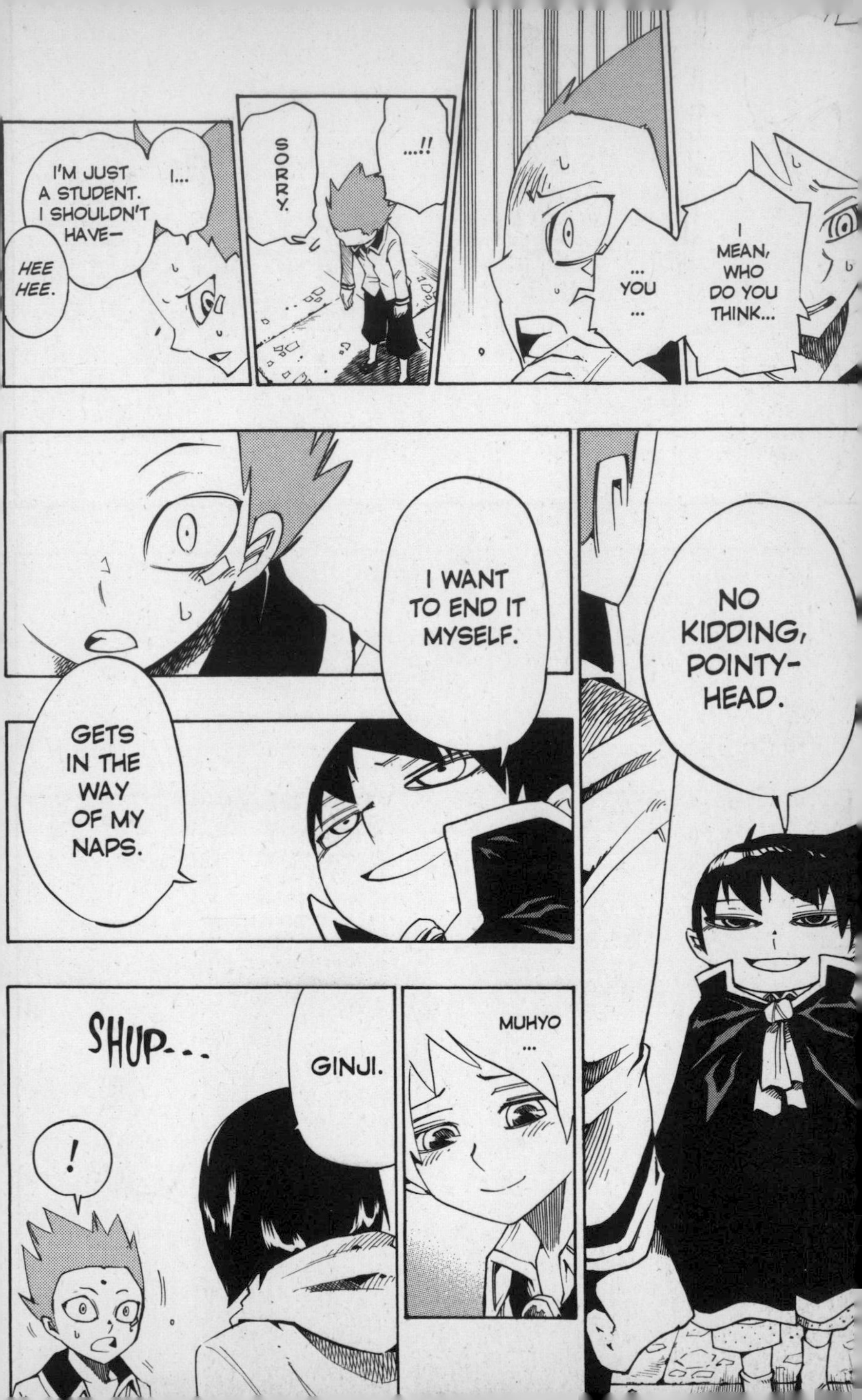
I MEAN, WHO DO YOU THINK...
... YOU ...
...!!
SORRY.
I...
I'M JUST A STUDENT. I SHOULDN'T HAVE—
HEE HEE.
NO KIDDING, POINTY-HEAD.
I WANT TO END IT MYSELF.
GETS IN THE WAY OF MY NAPS.
MUHYO ...
GINJI.
SHUP...
!

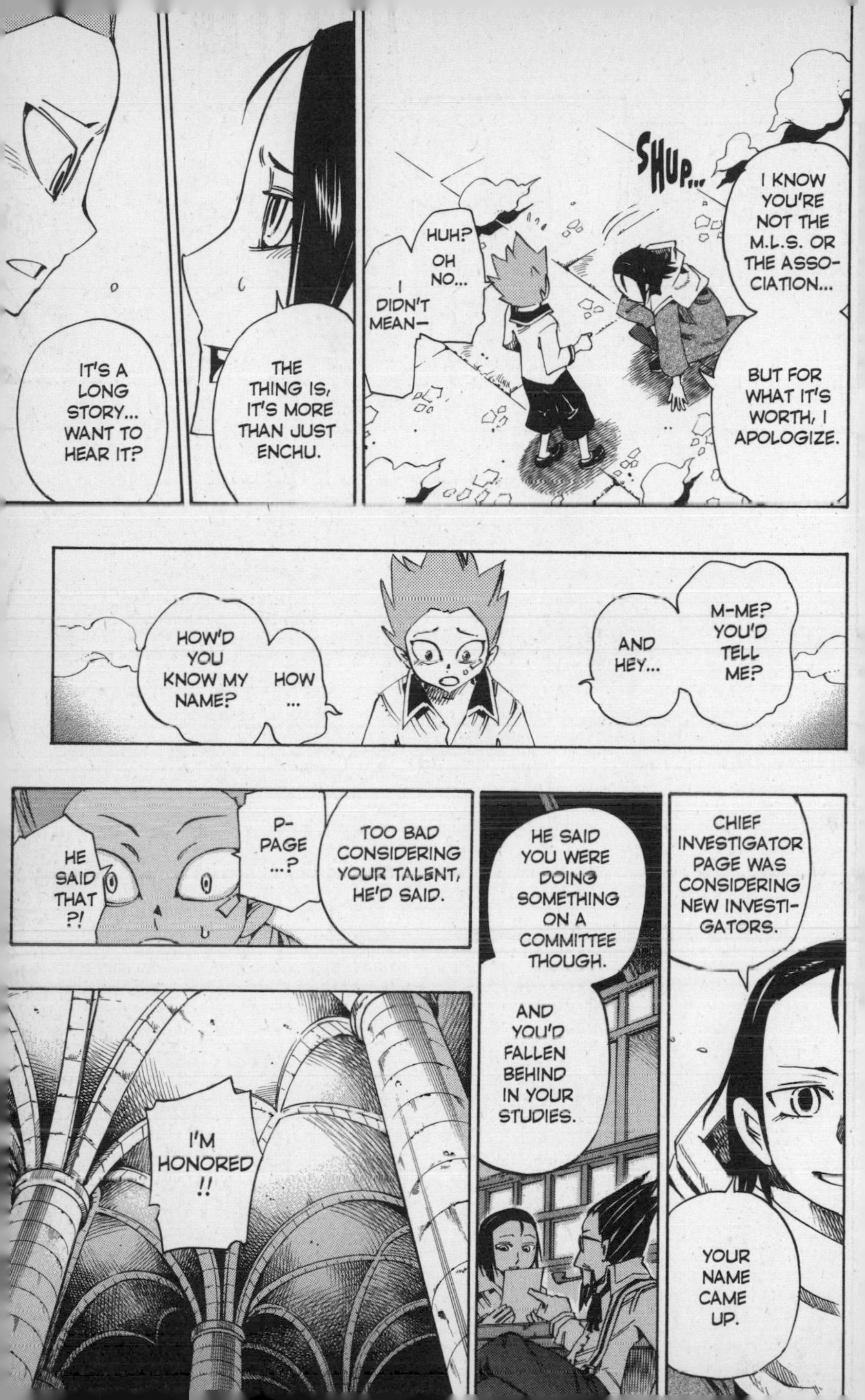
SHUP...
I KNOW YOU'RE NOT THE M.L.S. OR THE ASSOCIATION...
BUT FOR WHAT IT'S WORTH, I APOLOGIZE.
HUH? OH NO... I DIDN'T MEAN—
THE THING IS, IT'S MORE THAN JUST ENCHU.
IT'S A LONG STORY... WANT TO HEAR IT?
M-ME? YOU'D TELL ME?
AND HEY...
HOW ...
HOW'D YOU KNOW MY NAME?
CHIEF INVESTIGATOR PAGE WAS CONSIDERING NEW INVESTIGATORS.
YOUR NAME CAME UP.
HE SAID YOU WERE DOING SOMETHING ON A COMMITTEE THOUGH.
AND YOU'D FALLEN BEHIND IN YOUR STUDIES.
TOO BAD CONSIDERING YOUR TALENT, HE'D SAID.
P-PAGE ...?
HE SAID THAT ?!
I'M HONORED !!

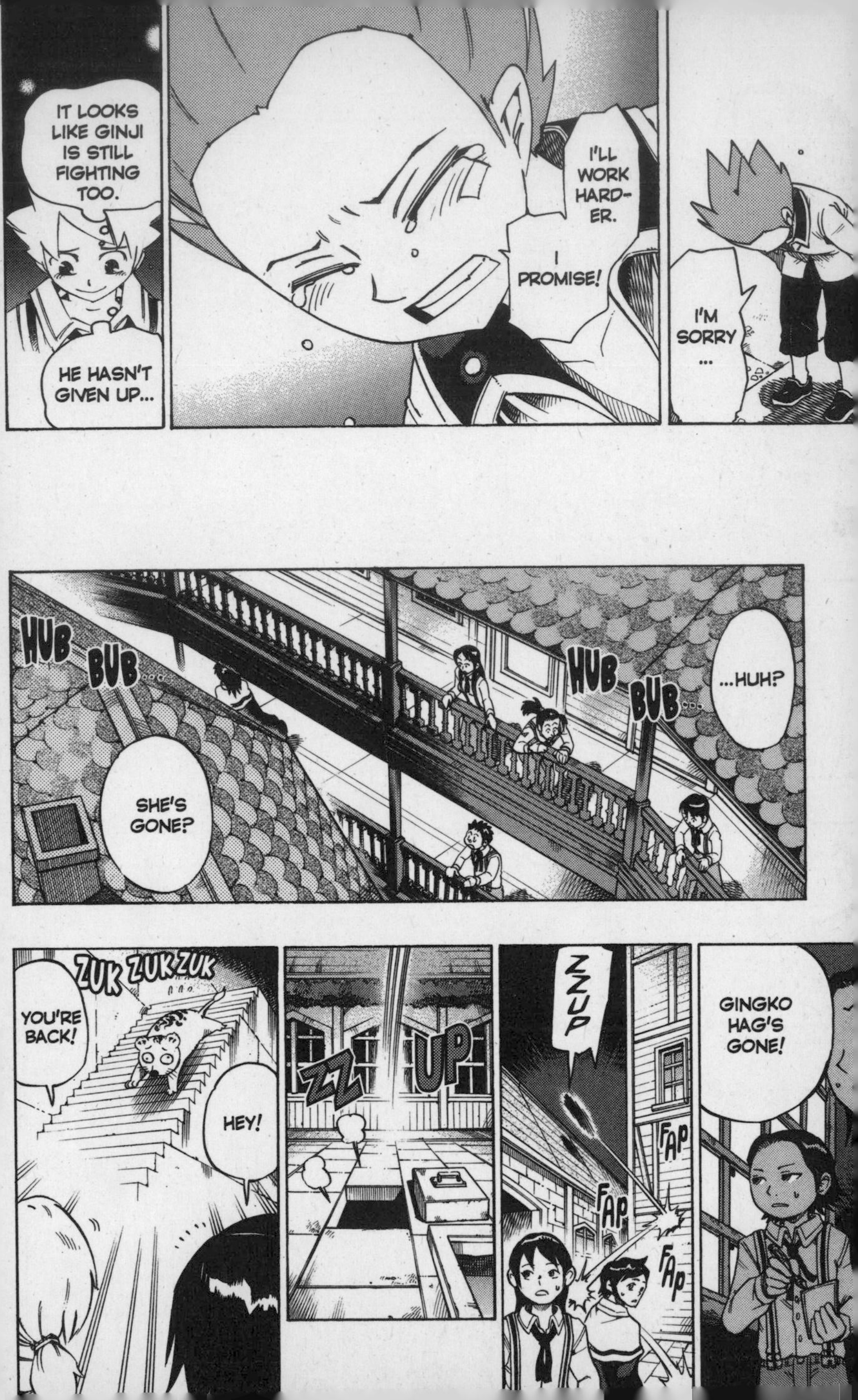
I'M SORRY...
I'LL WORK HARDER.
I PROMISE!
IT LOOKS LIKE GINJI IS STILL FIGHTING TOO.
HE HASN'T GIVEN UP...
...HUH?
HUB BUB...
HUB BUB...
SHE'S GONE?
GINGKO HAG'S GONE!
ZZUP
FAP
FAP
FAP
ZZ UP
ZUK ZUK ZUK
HEY!
YOU'RE BACK!

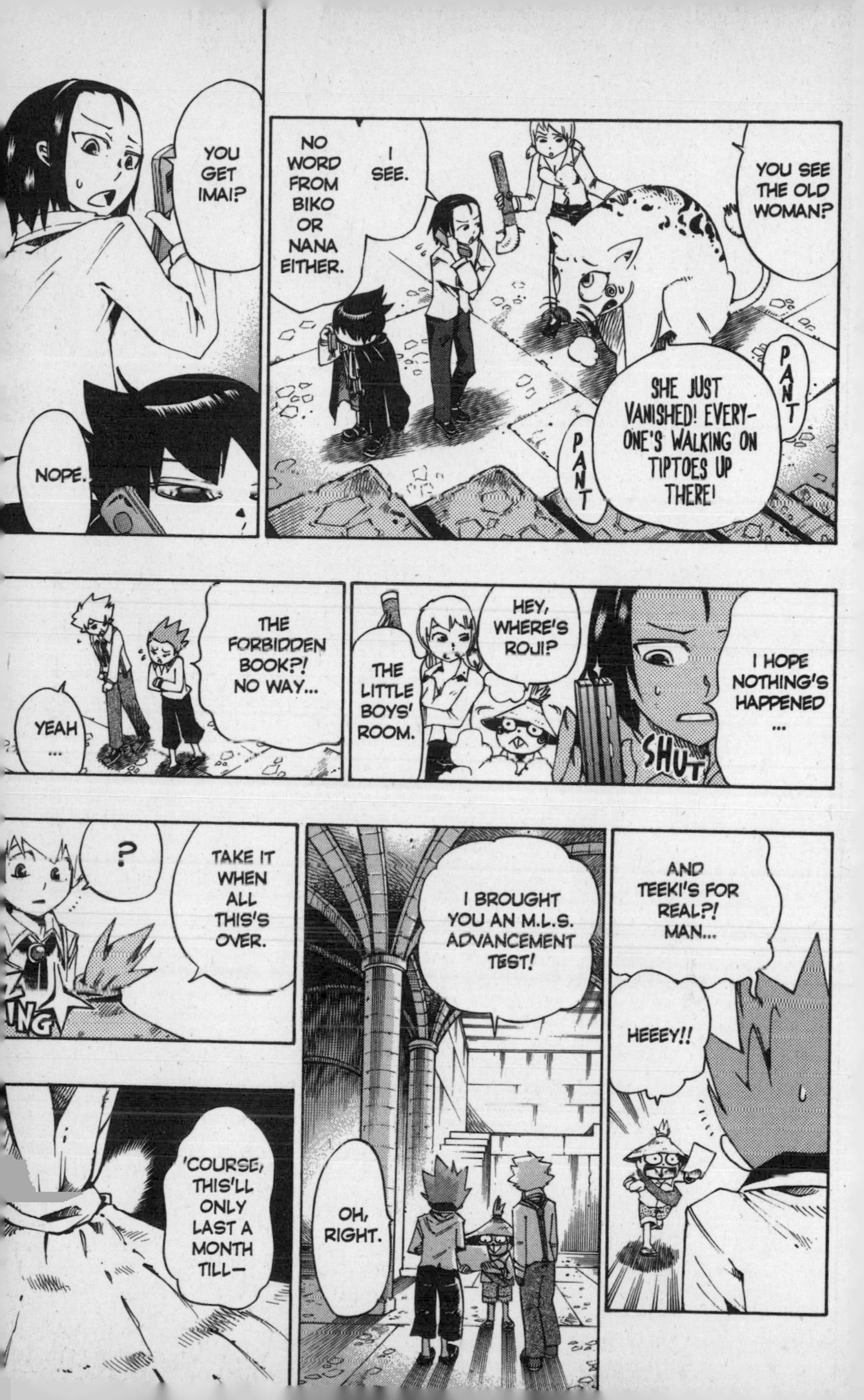
YOU SEE THE OLD WOMAN?
I SEE.
NO WORD FROM BIKO OR NANA EITHER.
PANT
SHE JUST VANISHED! EVERY-ONE'S WALKING ON TIPTOES UP THERE!
PANT
YOU GET IMAI?
NOPE.
I HOPE NOTHING'S HAPPENED...
SHUT
HEY, WHERE'S ROJI?
THE LITTLE BOYS' ROOM.
THE FORBIDDEN BOOK?! NO WAY...
YEAH...
AND TEEKI'S FOR REAL?! MAN...
HEEEY!!
I BROUGHT YOU AN M.L.S. ADVANCEMENT TEST!
OH, RIGHT.
?
TAKE IT WHEN ALL THIS'S OVER.
'COURSE, THIS'LL ONLY LAST A MONTH TILL—

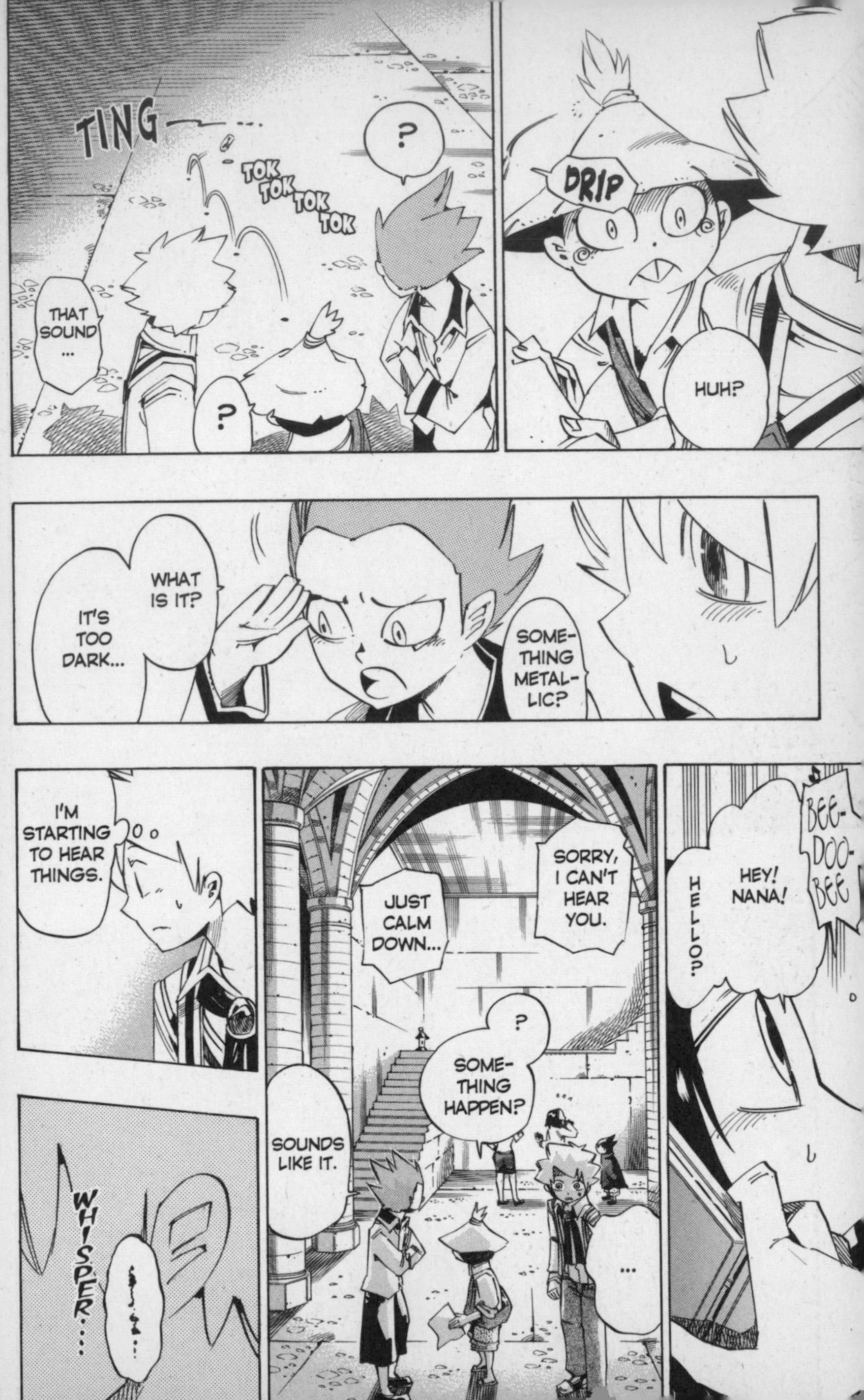
DRIP
HUH?
?
TING
TOK TOK TOK TOK
THAT SOUND ...
?
SOME-THING METAL-LIC?
WHAT IS IT?
IT'S TOO DARK...
BEE-DOO-BEE
HEY! NANA!
HELLO?
SORRY, I CAN'T HEAR YOU.
JUST CALM DOWN...
?
SOME-THING HAPPEN?
SOUNDS LIKE IT.
...
I'M STARTING TO HEAR THINGS.
WHISPER...

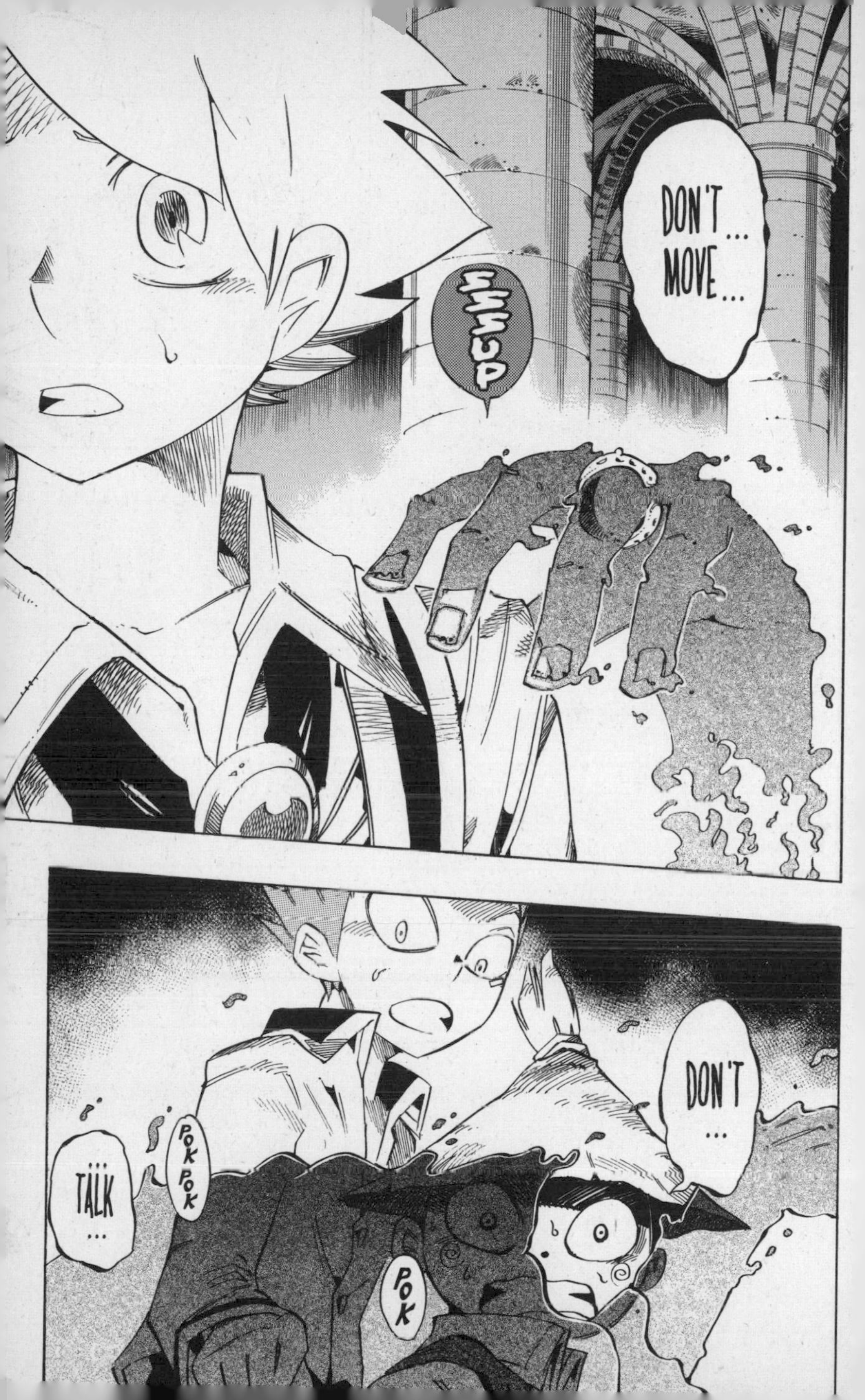
DON'T ... MOVE ...
SSSUP
DON'T ...
POK POK
POK
... TALK ...

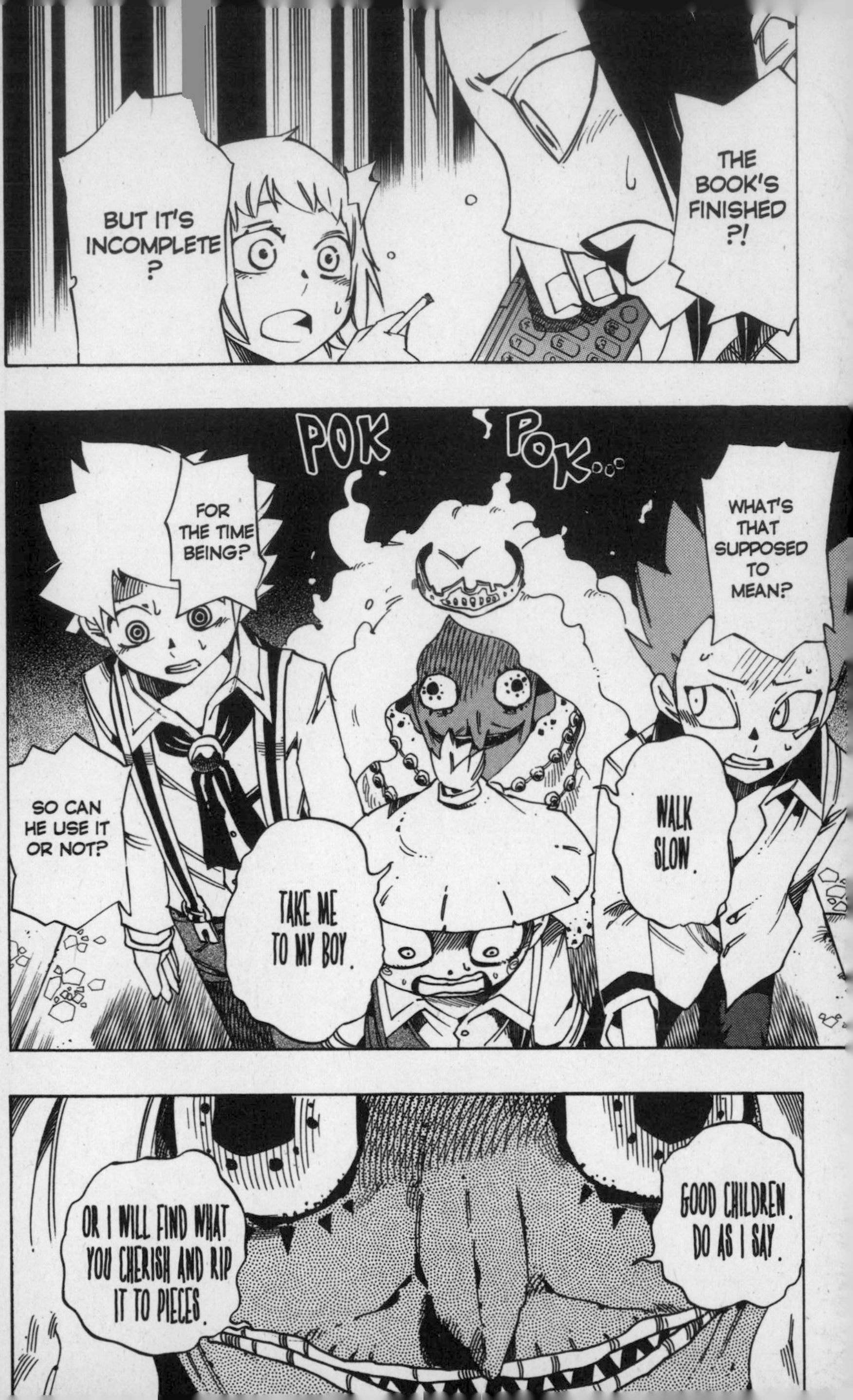
THE BOOK'S FINISHED ?!
BUT IT'S INCOMPLETE ?
WHAT'S THAT SUPPOSED TO MEAN?
POK POK...
FOR THE TIME BEING?
WALK SLOW.
TAKE ME TO MY BOY.
SO CAN HE USE IT OR NOT?
GOOD CHILDREN DO AS I SAY.
OR I WILL FIND WHAT YOU CHERISH AND RIP IT TO PIECES.

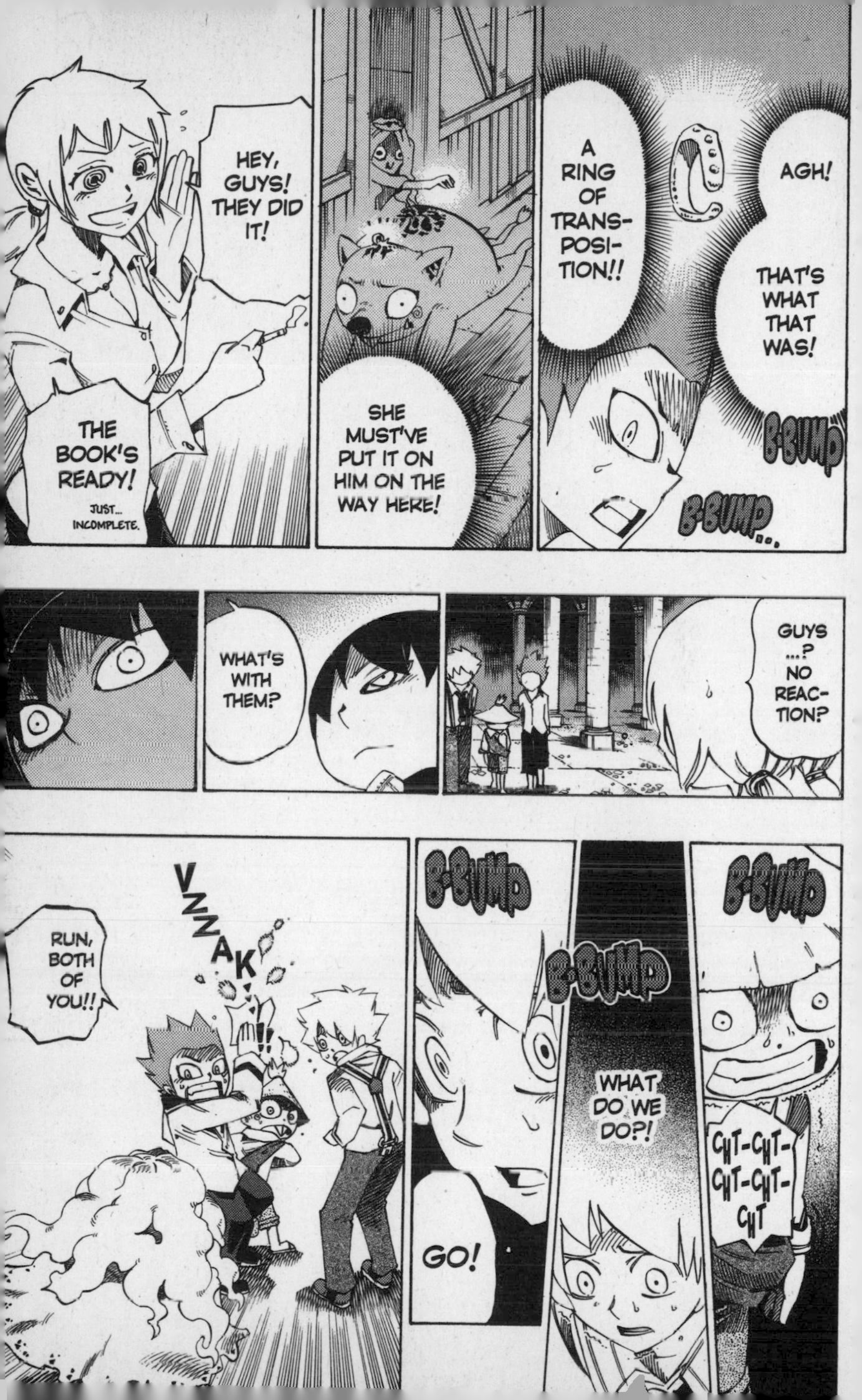
AGH!
A RING OF TRANSPOSITION!!
THAT'S WHAT THAT WAS!
B-BUMP
B-BUMP...
SHE MUST'VE PUT IT ON HIM ON THE WAY HERE!
HEY, GUYS! THEY DID IT!
THE BOOK'S READY!
JUST... INCOMPLETE.
GUYS ...? NO REACTION?
WHAT'S WITH THEM?
B-BUMP
CHT-CHT-CHT-CHT-CHT
B-BUMP
WHAT DO WE DO?!
B-BUMP
GO!
RUN, BOTH OF YOU!!
VZZAK
!!

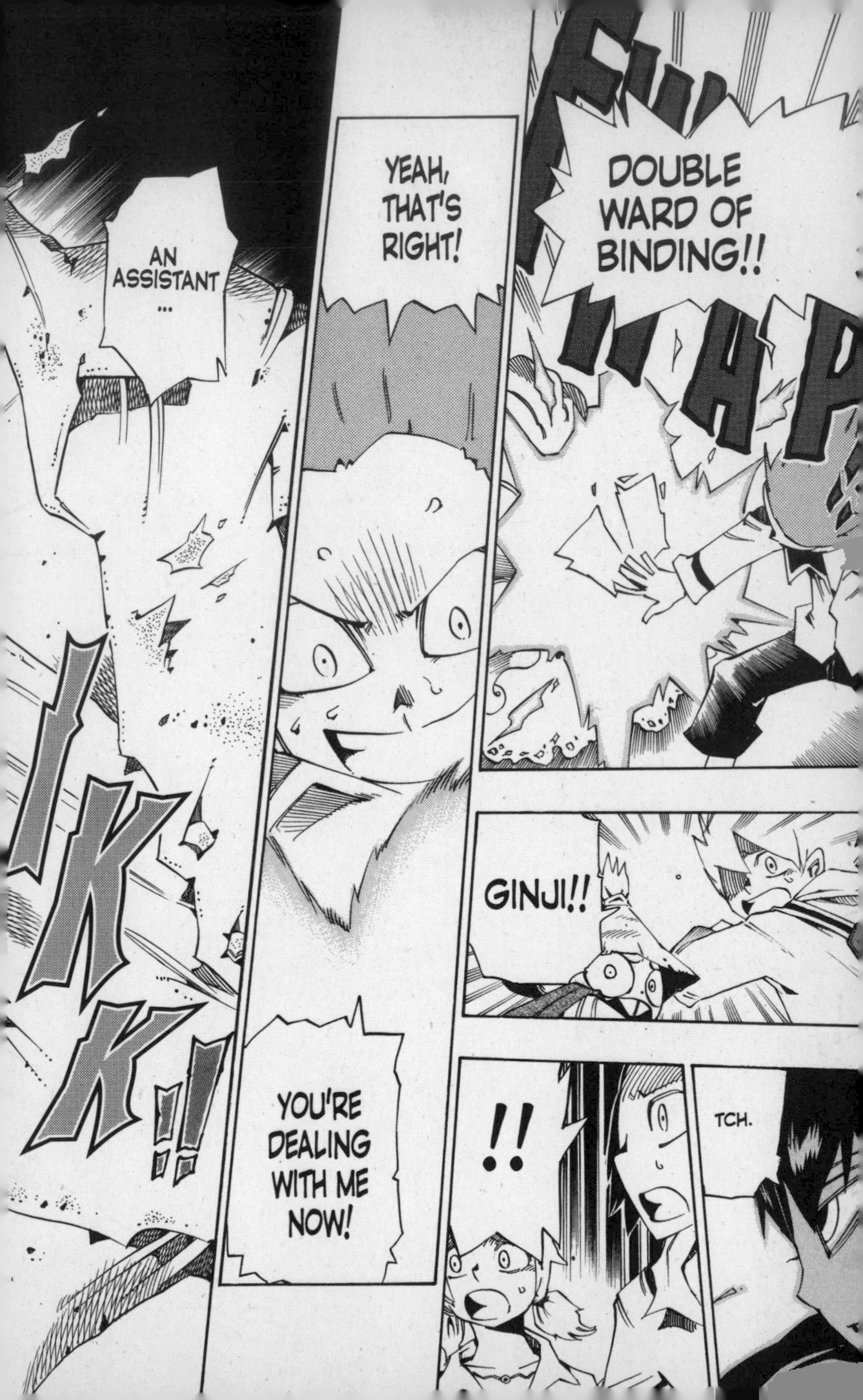
DOUBLE WARD OF BINDING!!
GINJI!!
TCH.
!!
YEAH, THAT'S RIGHT!
YOU'RE DEALING WITH ME NOW!
AN ASSISTANT ...

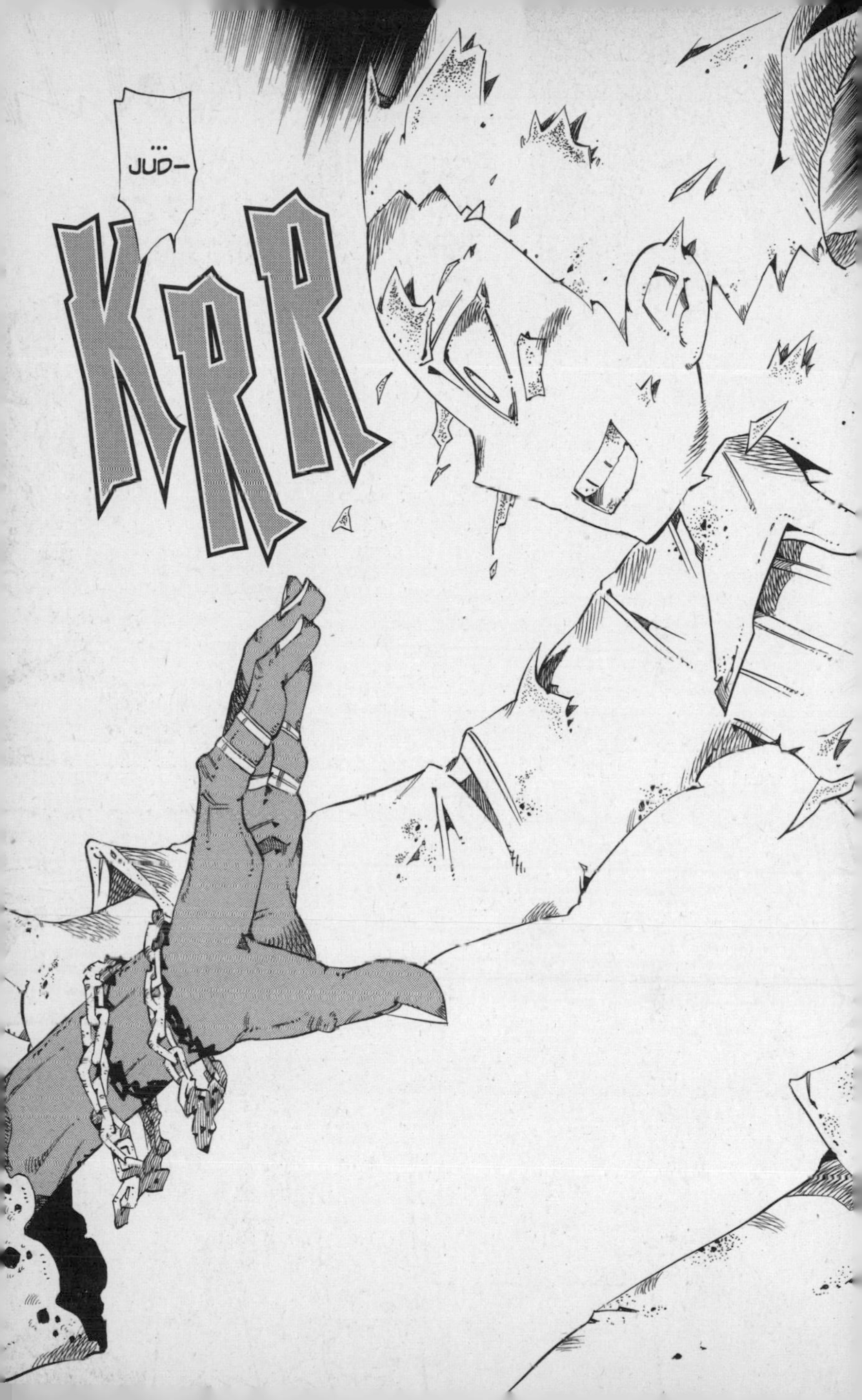
... JUD-
KRR

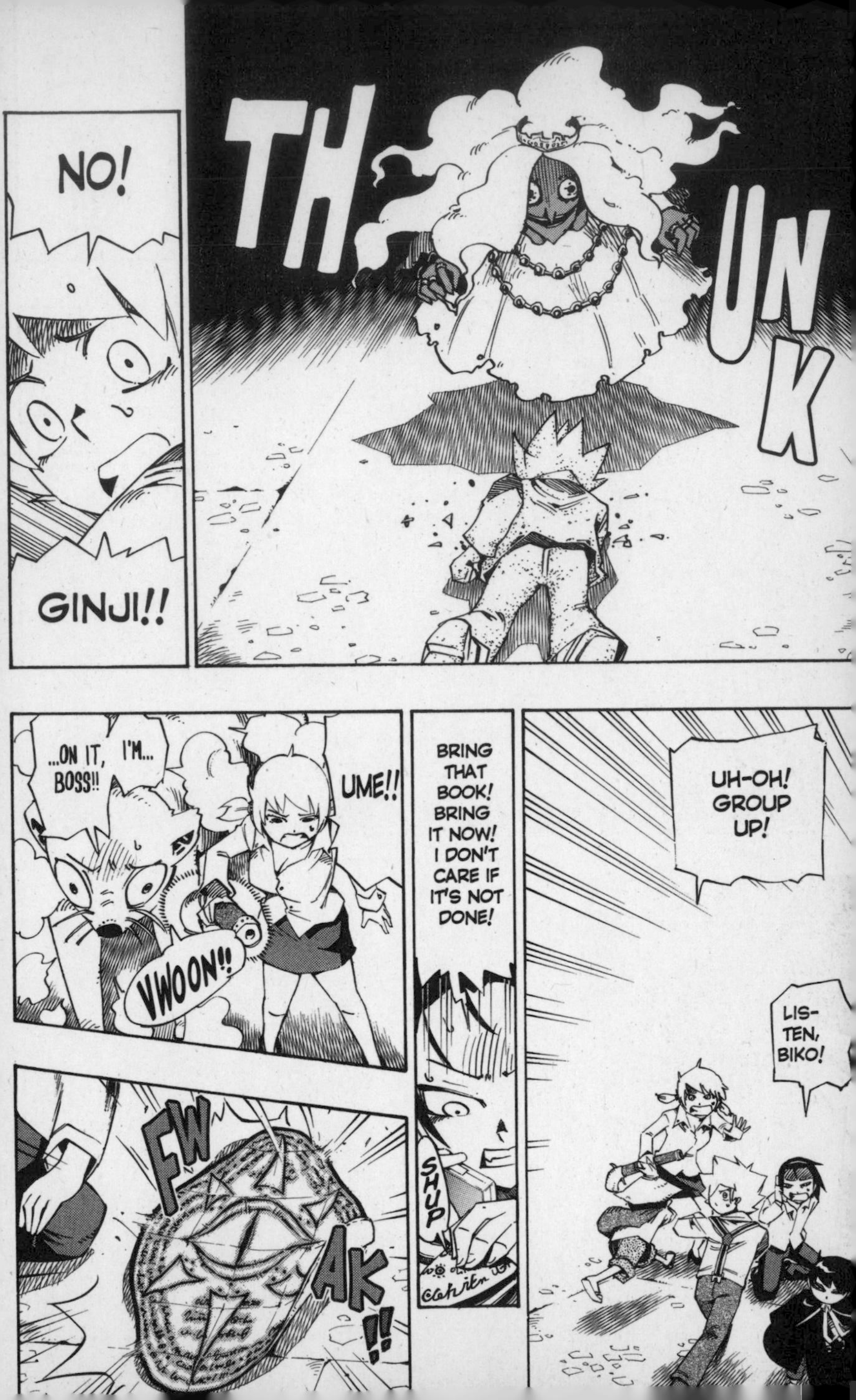
THUNK
NO!
GINJI!!
UH-OH! GROUP UP!
LIS-TEN, BIKO!
BRING THAT BOOK! BRING IT NOW! I DON'T CARE IF IT'S NOT DONE!
SHUP
UME!!
I'M... ...ON IT, BOSS!!
VWOON!!
FWAK!!

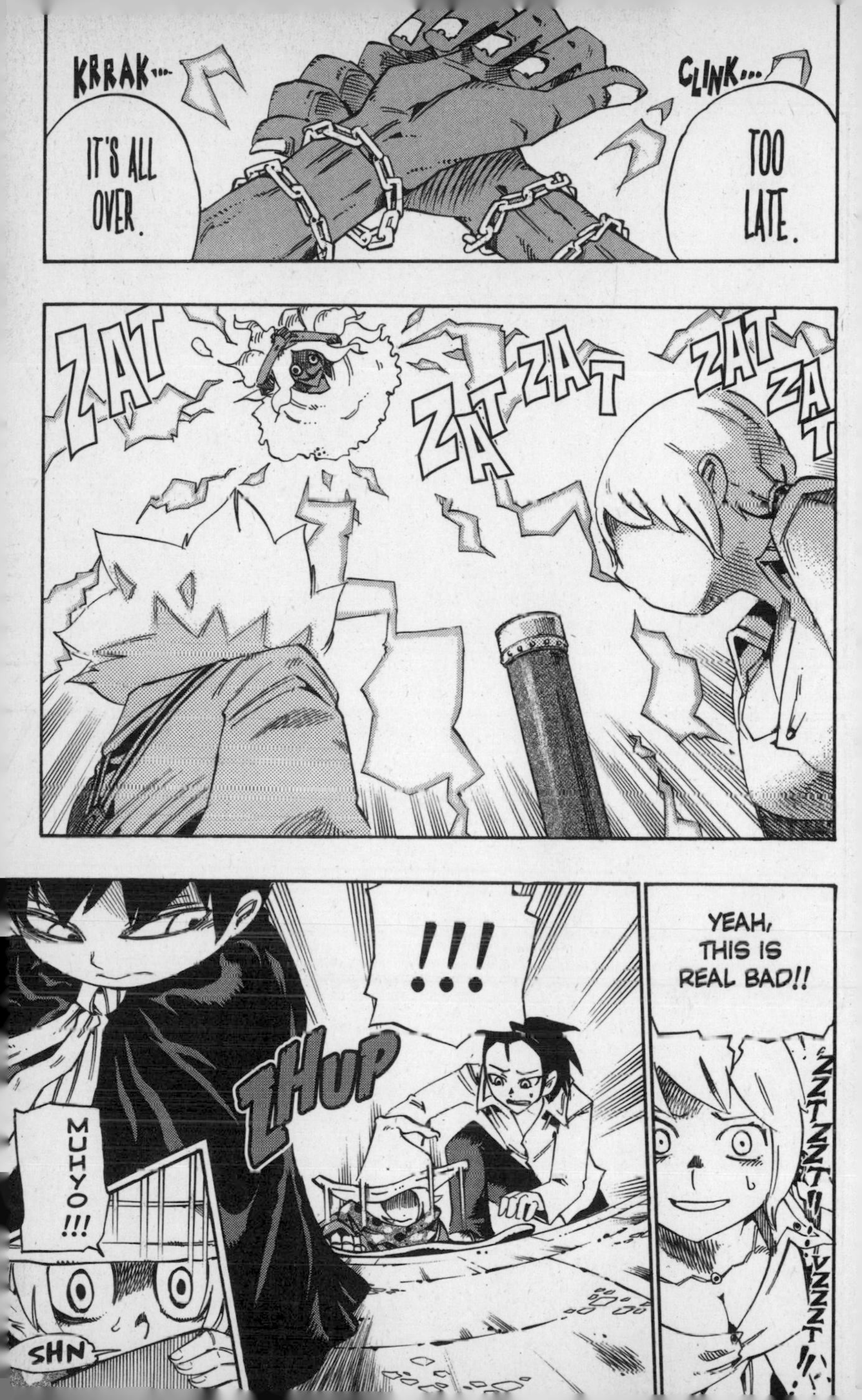
CLINK...
TOO LATE.
KRRAK...
IT'S ALL OVER.
ZAT ZAT
ZAT ZAT
ZAT
YEAH, THIS IS REAL BAD!!
ZZT ZZT!!
VZZZT!!
!!!
ZHUP
MUHYO!!!
SHN

Q1: WAS MUHYO A BAD STUDENT/PRACTITIONER BEFORE HIS TALENT BLOSSOMED?

Q2: AFTER HIS TALENT BLOSSOMED, DID MUHYO GET BETTER AT DOING THINGS LIKE STUDYING?

Q3: HOW WERE YOICHI AND BIKO'S GRADES AT M.L.S.?

-O.R., TOKYO

A1: YES, TERRIBLE. CHECK OUT VOLUME 2 FOR SOME FIRSTHAND EVIDENCE.

A2:

GH...
SEE?
?
?
SI
WHEW

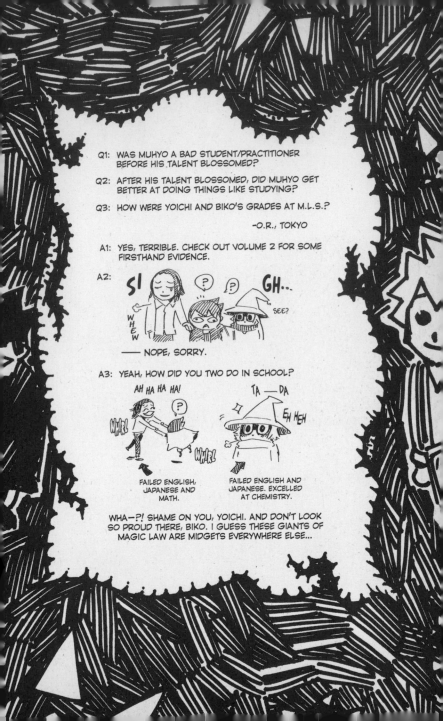

—— NOPE, SORRY.

A3: YEAH, HOW DID YOU TWO DO IN SCHOOL?

TA —DA
EH HEH
AH HA HA HA!
?
WHIRL
WHIRL

FAILED ENGLISH, JAPANESE AND MATH.

FAILED ENGLISH AND JAPANESE. EXCELLED AT CHEMISTRY.

WHA—?! SHAME ON YOU, YOICHI. AND DON'T LOOK SO PROUD THERE, BIKO. I GUESS THESE GIANTS OF MAGIC LAW ARE MIDGETS EVERYWHERE ELSE...

ARTICLE 108

A NEW BOOK OF MAGIC LAW

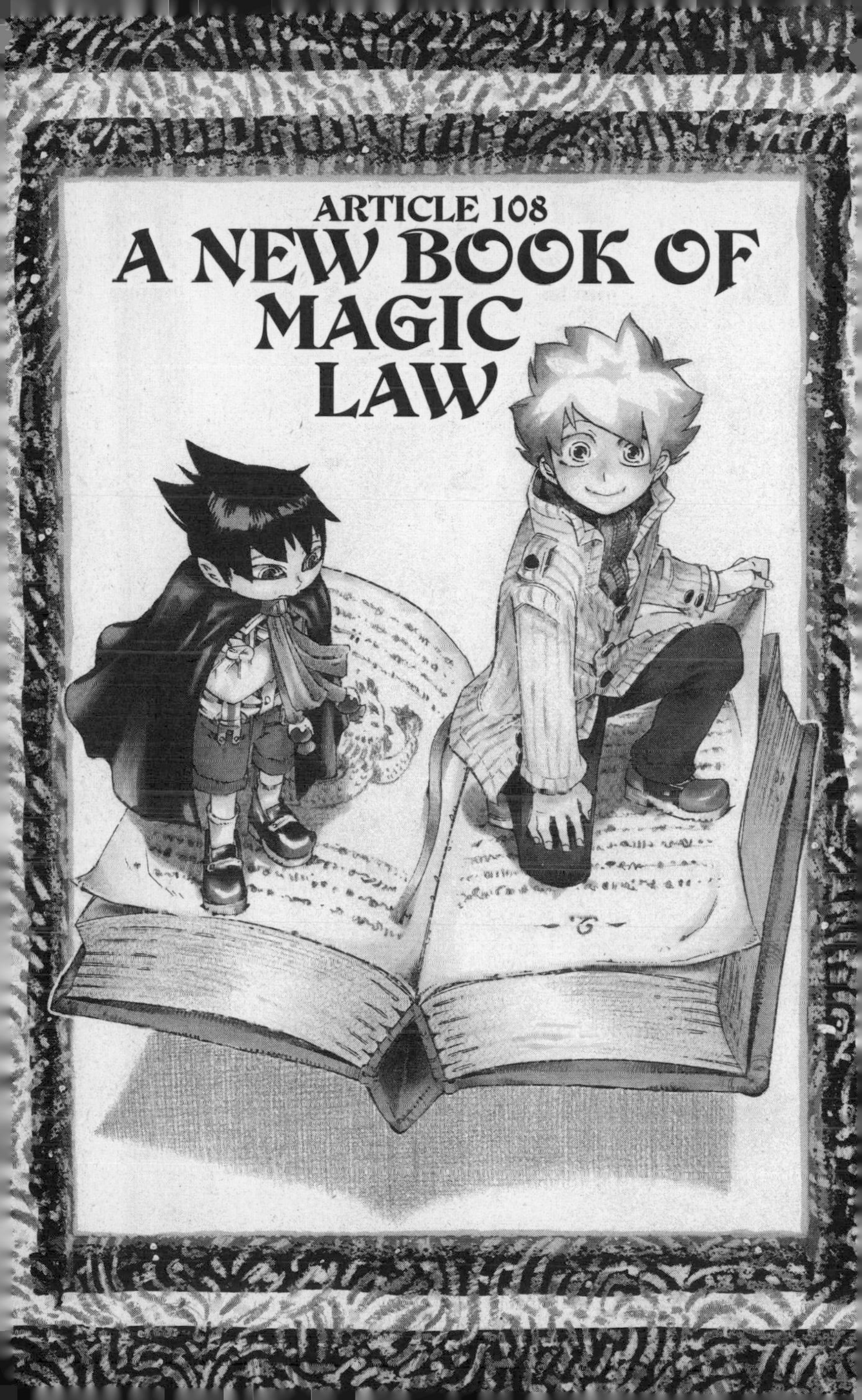

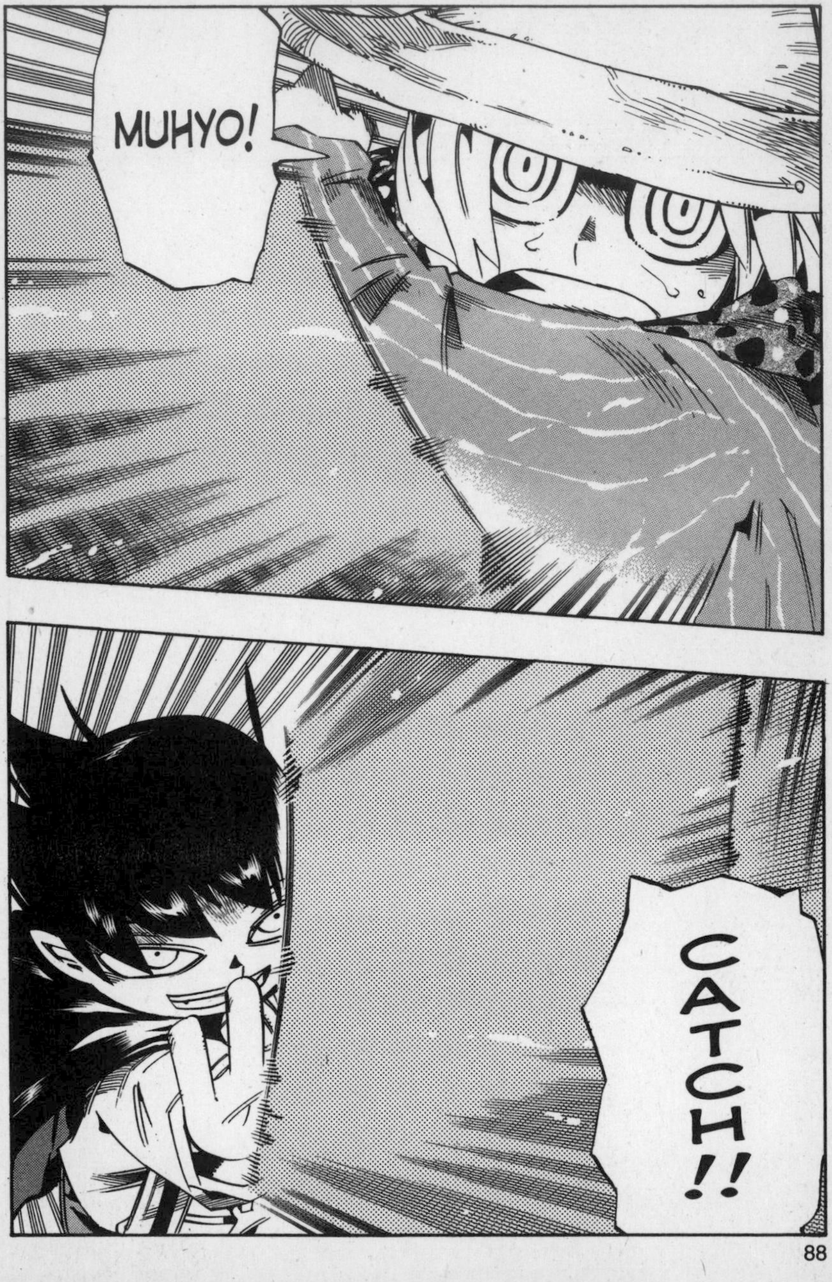
MUHYO!
CATCH!!

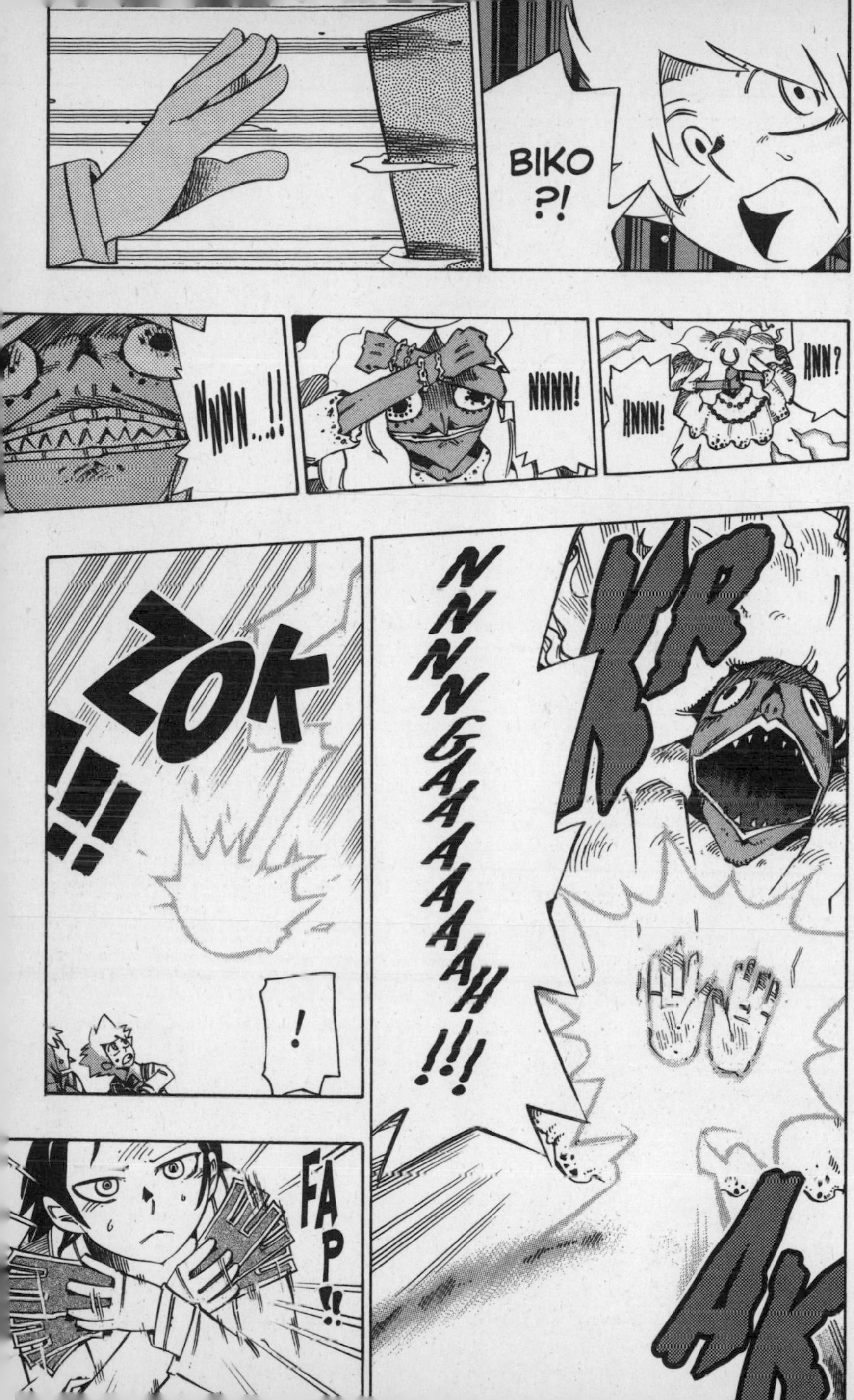
BIKO ?!
HNN?
HNNN!
NNNN!
NNNN...!!
KR
AK
NNNNGAAAAAAH!!!
ZOK!!!
!
FAP!!

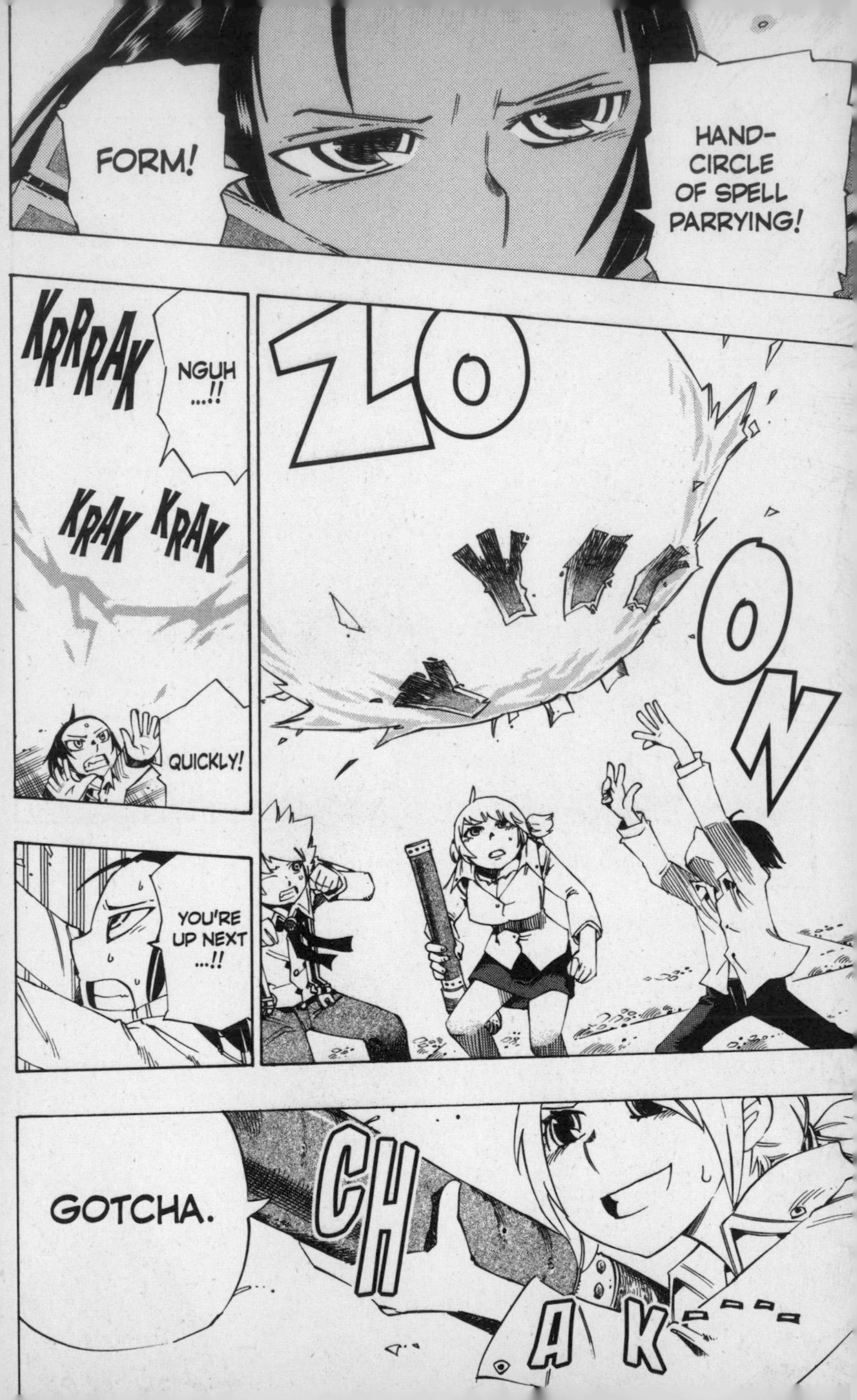
HAND-CIRCLE OF SPELL PARRYING!
FORM!
ZOOON
KRRRAK
NGUH ...!!
KRAK KRAK
QUICKLY!
YOU'RE UP NEXT ...!!
CHAK
GOTCHA.

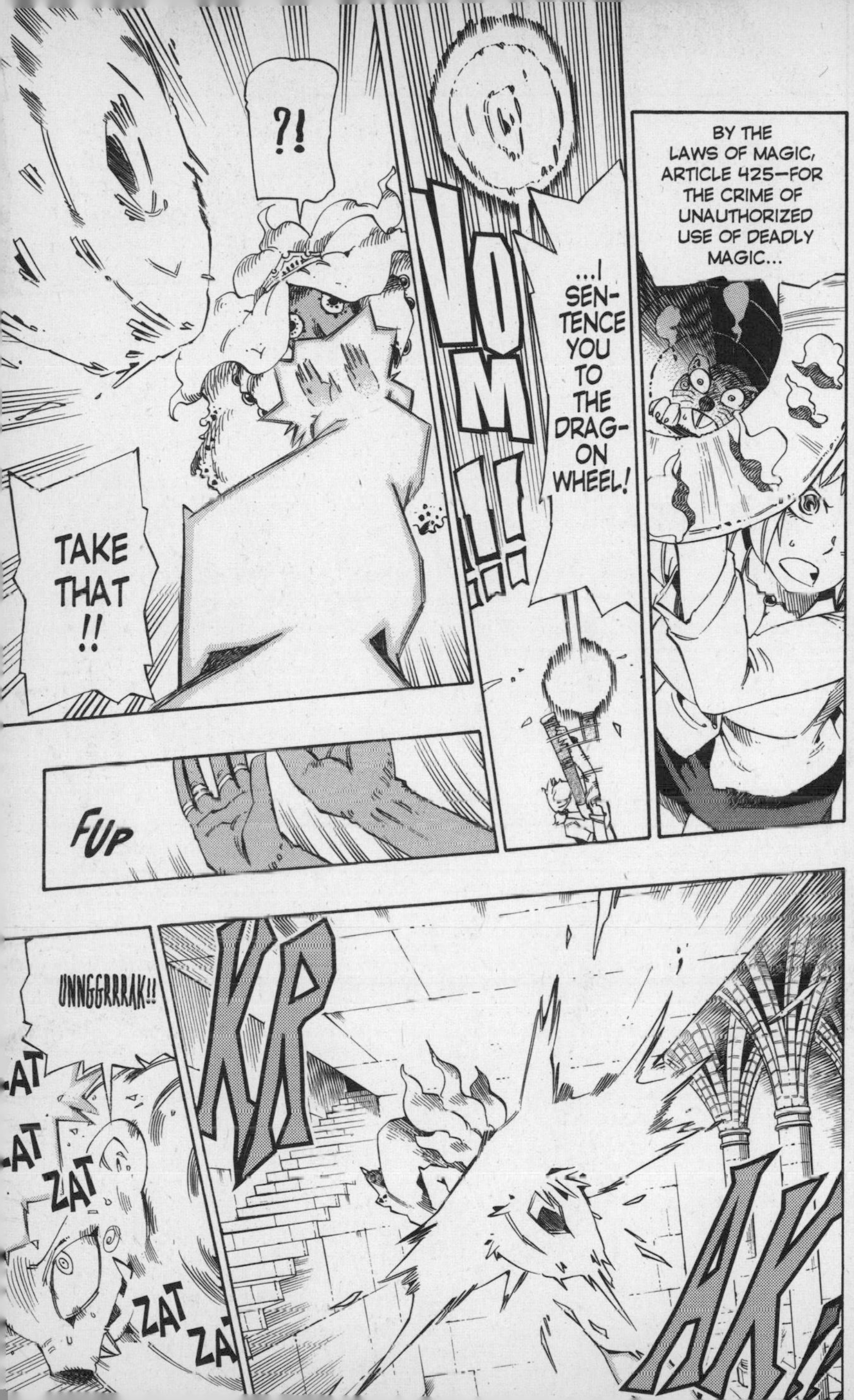
BY THE LAWS OF MAGIC, ARTICLE 425—FOR THE CRIME OF UNAUTHORIZED USE OF DEADLY MAGIC...
...I SEN-TENCE YOU TO THE DRAG-ON WHEEL!
VOM!!
?!
TAKE THAT!!
FUP
AK!
KR
UNNGGRRRAK!!
-AT -AT ZAT ZAT ZAT ZAT

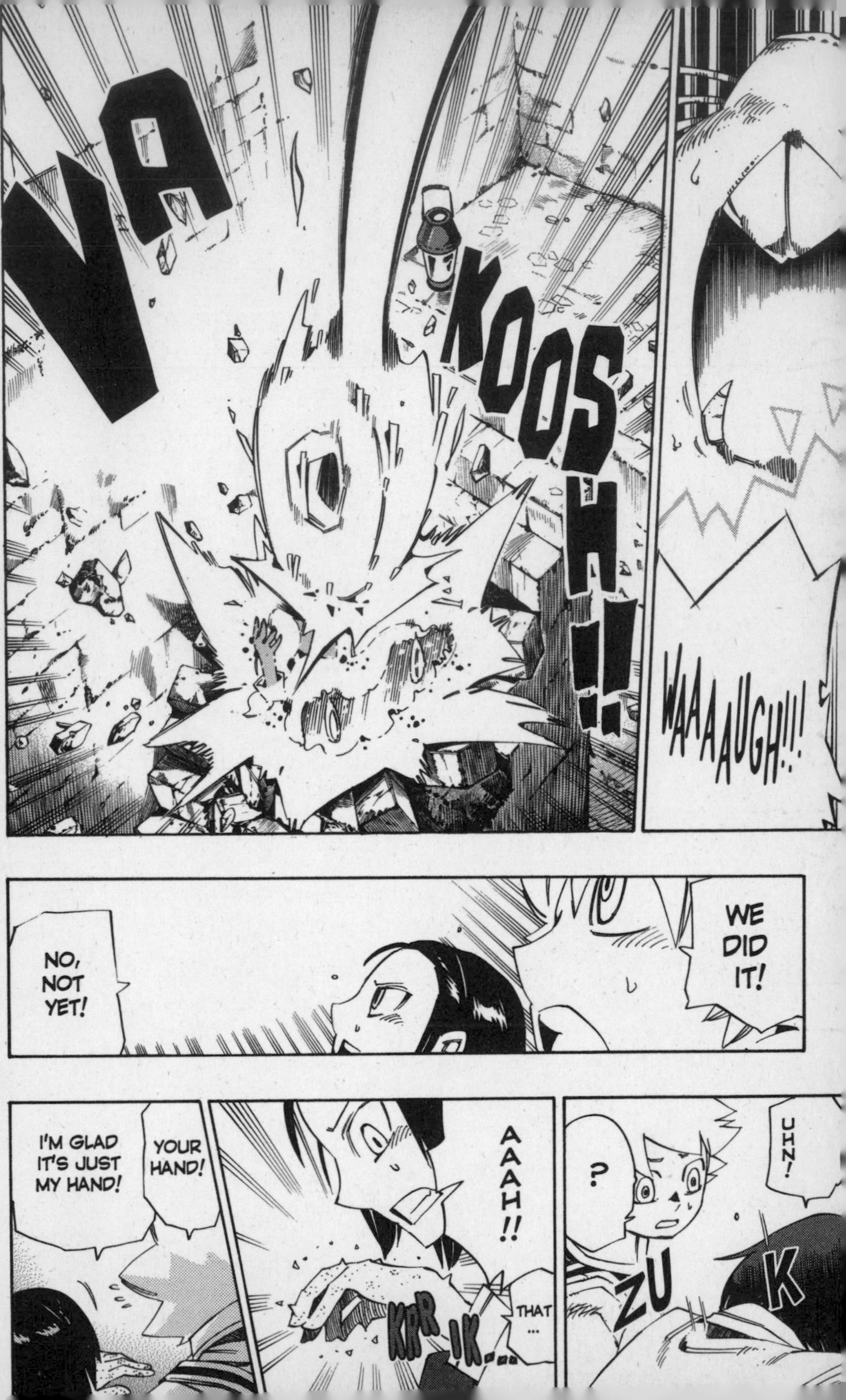
WAAAAUGH!!!
VA
KOOSH!!
WE DID IT!
NO, NOT YET!
UHN!
?
ZU
K
AAAH!!
THAT ...
KRRIK...
YOUR HAND!
I'M GLAD IT'S JUST MY HAND!

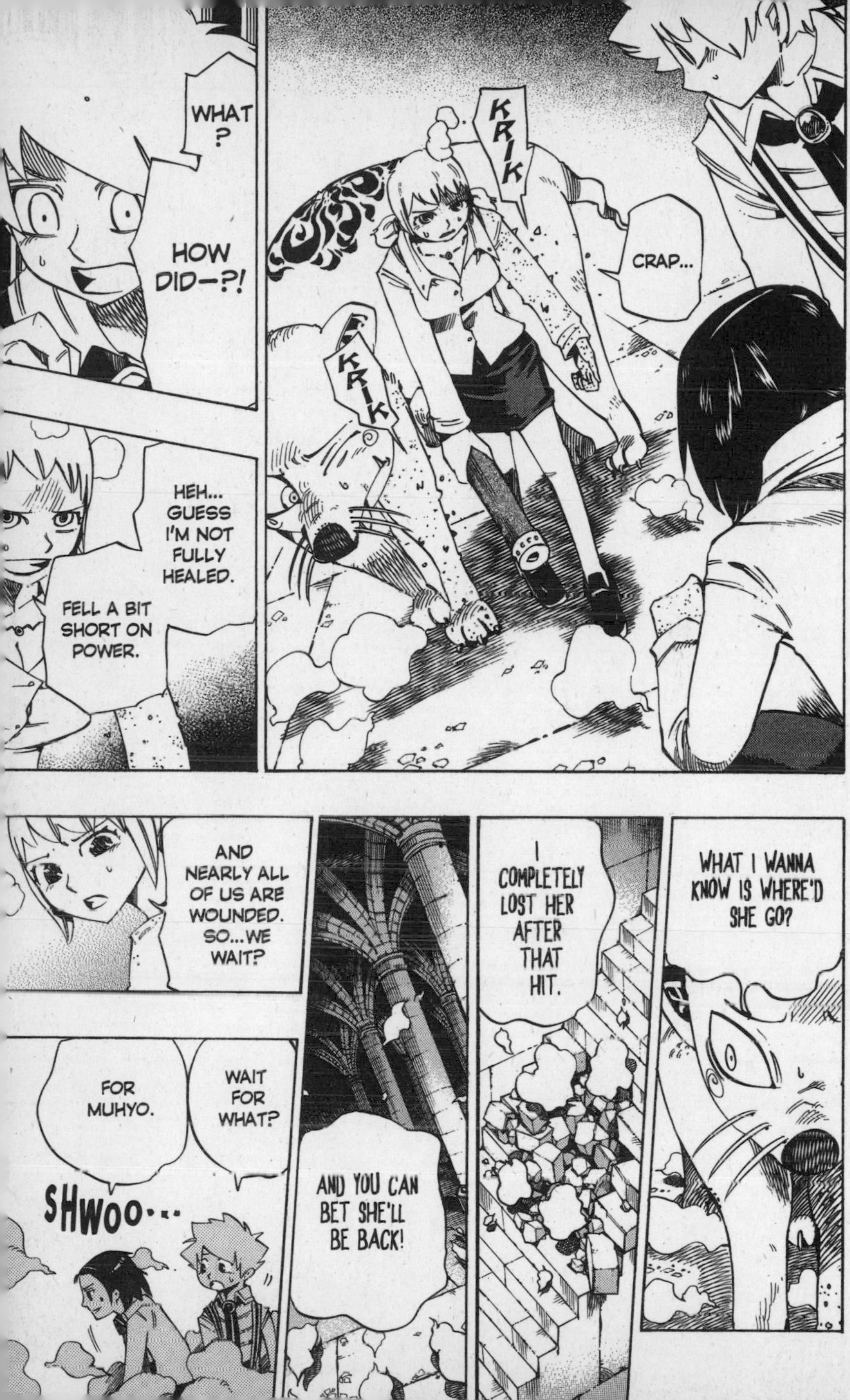
KRIK
CRAP...
KRIK
WHAT ?
HOW DID—?!
HEH... GUESS I'M NOT FULLY HEALED.
FELL A BIT SHORT ON POWER.
WHAT I WANNA KNOW IS WHERE'D SHE GO?
I COMPLETELY LOST HER AFTER THAT HIT.
AND YOU CAN BET SHE'LL BE BACK!
AND NEARLY ALL OF US ARE WOUNDED. SO...WE WAIT?
WAIT FOR WHAT?
FOR MUHYO.
SHWOO...

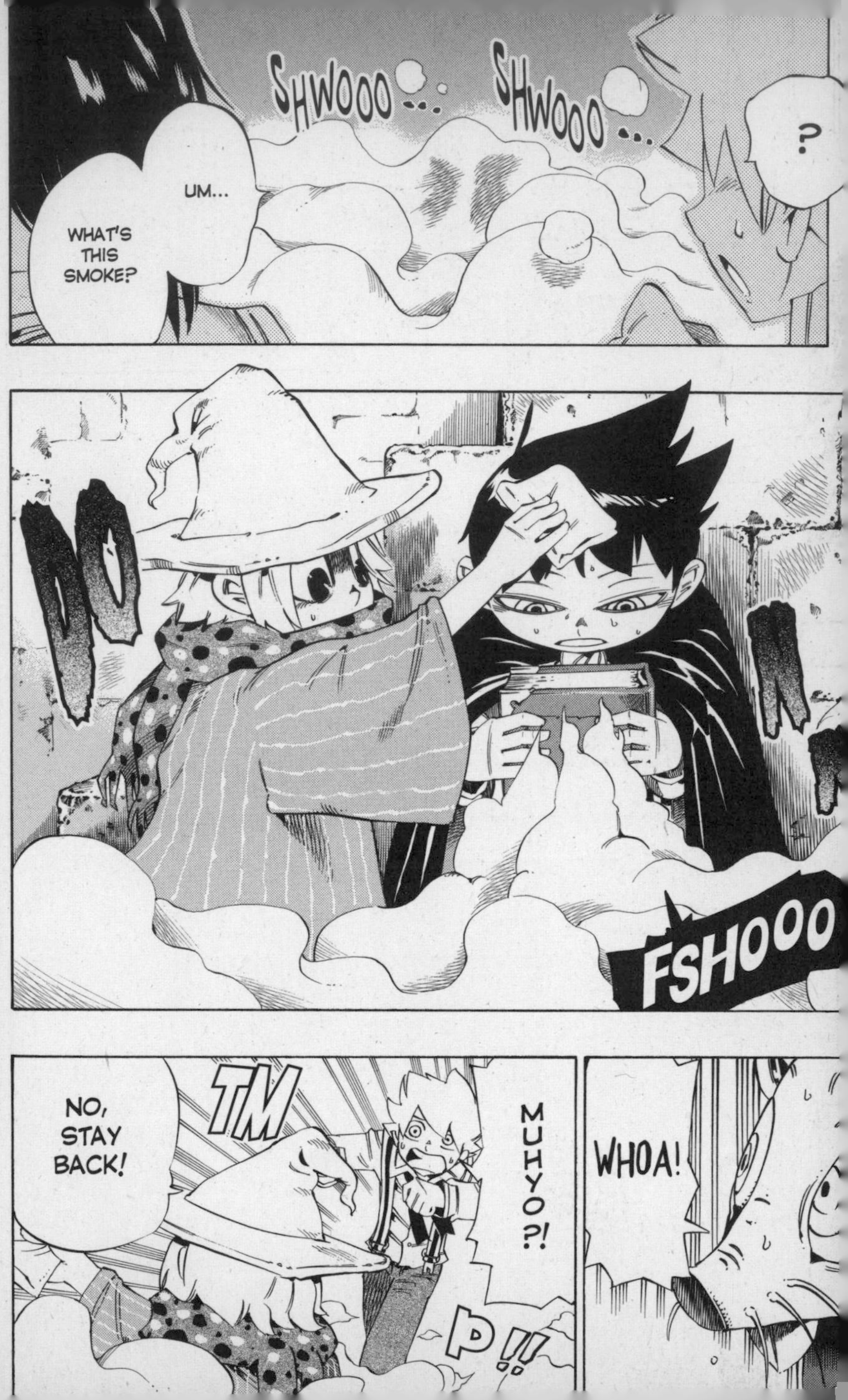
?
SHWOOO...
SHWOOO...
UM...
WHAT'S THIS SMOKE?
FSHOOO
WHOA!
MUHYO?!
TM
NO, STAY BACK!
P!!

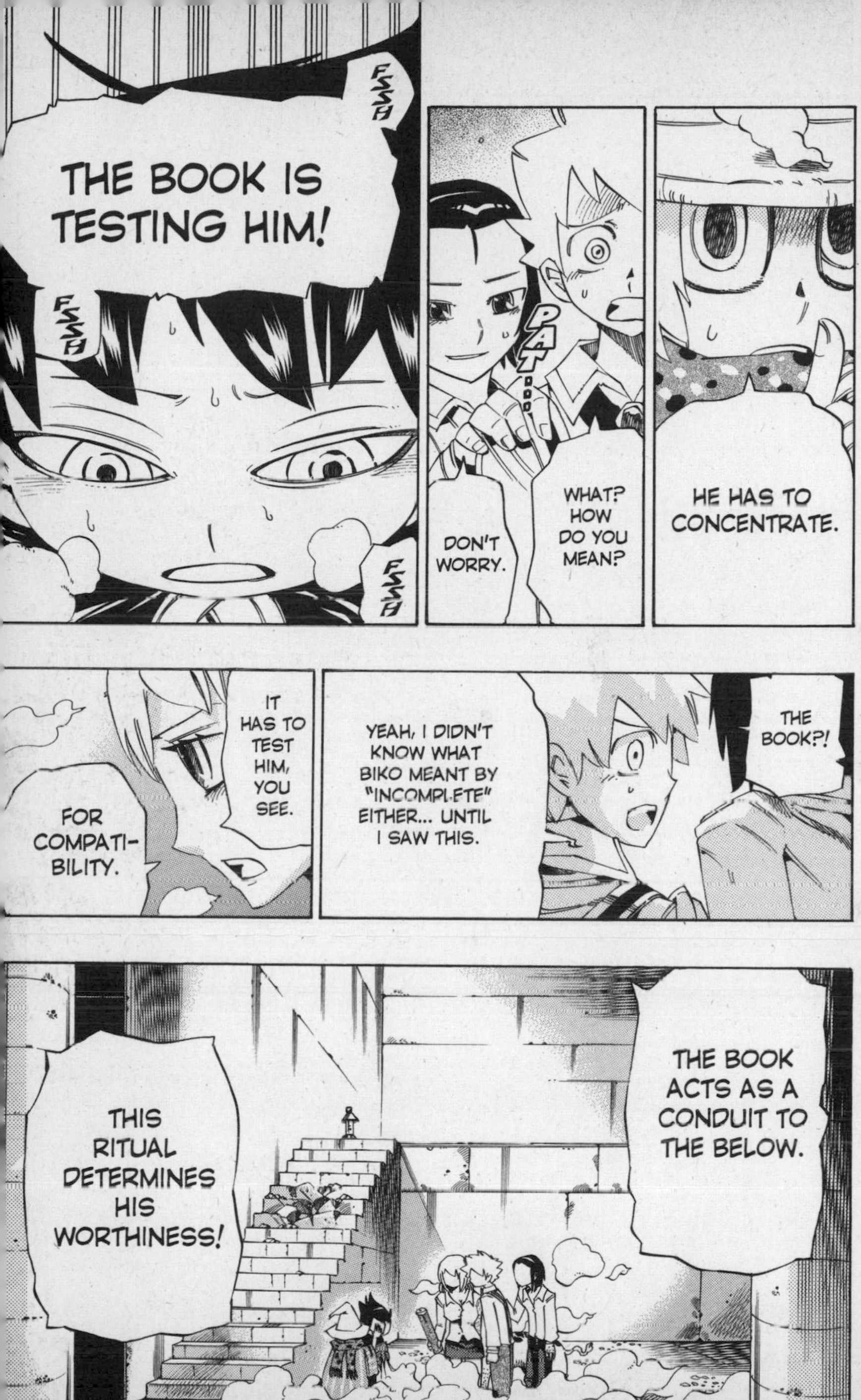
HE HAS TO CONCENTRATE.
WHAT? HOW DO YOU MEAN?
PAT
DON'T WORRY.
FSSH
THE BOOK IS TESTING HIM!
FSSH
FSSH
THE BOOK?!
YEAH, I DIDN'T KNOW WHAT BIKO MEANT BY "INCOMPLETE" EITHER... UNTIL I SAW THIS.
IT HAS TO TEST HIM, YOU SEE.
FOR COMPATI-BILITY.
THE BOOK ACTS AS A CONDUIT TO THE BELOW.
THIS RITUAL DETERMINES HIS WORTHINESS!

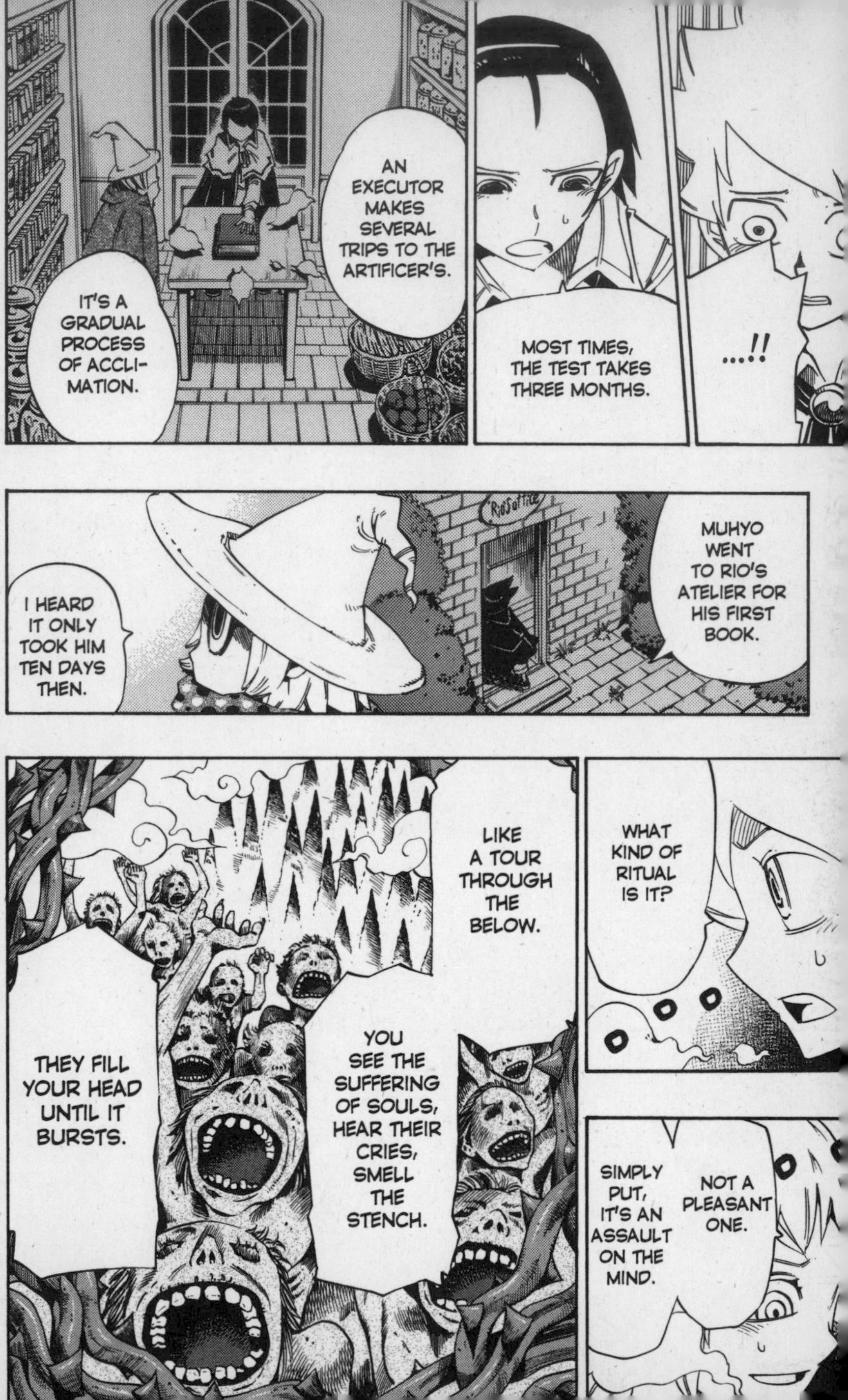
...!!
MOST TIMES, THE TEST TAKES THREE MONTHS.
AN EXECUTOR MAKES SEVERAL TRIPS TO THE ARTIFICER'S.
IT'S A GRADUAL PROCESS OF ACCLI-MATION.
MUHYO WENT TO RIO'S ATELIER FOR HIS FIRST BOOK.
I HEARD IT ONLY TOOK HIM TEN DAYS THEN.
WHAT KIND OF RITUAL IS IT?
NOT A PLEASANT ONE.
SIMPLY PUT, IT'S AN ASSAULT ON THE MIND.
LIKE A TOUR THROUGH THE BELOW.
YOU SEE THE SUFFERING OF SOULS, HEAR THEIR CRIES, SMELL THE STENCH.
THEY FILL YOUR HEAD UNTIL IT BURSTS.

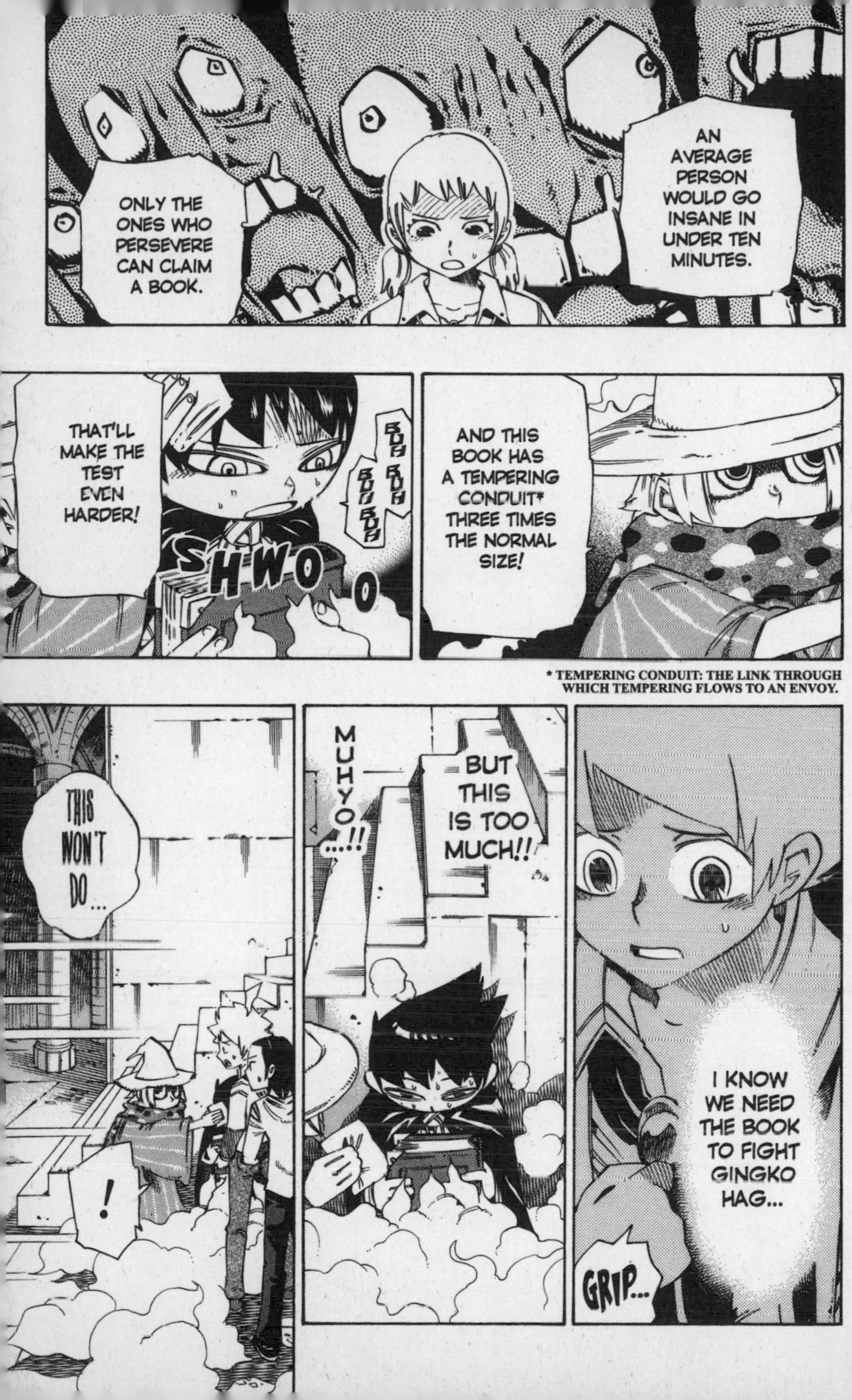
AN AVERAGE PERSON WOULD GO INSANE IN UNDER TEN MINUTES.
ONLY THE ONES WHO PERSEVERE CAN CLAIM A BOOK.
AND THIS BOOK HAS A TEMPERING CONDUIT* THREE TIMES THE NORMAL SIZE!
THAT'LL MAKE THE TEST EVEN HARDER!
SHWOOO
* TEMPERING CONDUIT: THE LINK THROUGH WHICH TEMPERING FLOWS TO AN ENVOY.
I KNOW WE NEED THE BOOK TO FIGHT GINGKO HAG...
GRIP...
BUT THIS IS TOO MUCH!!
MUHYO...!!
THIS WON'T DO...
!

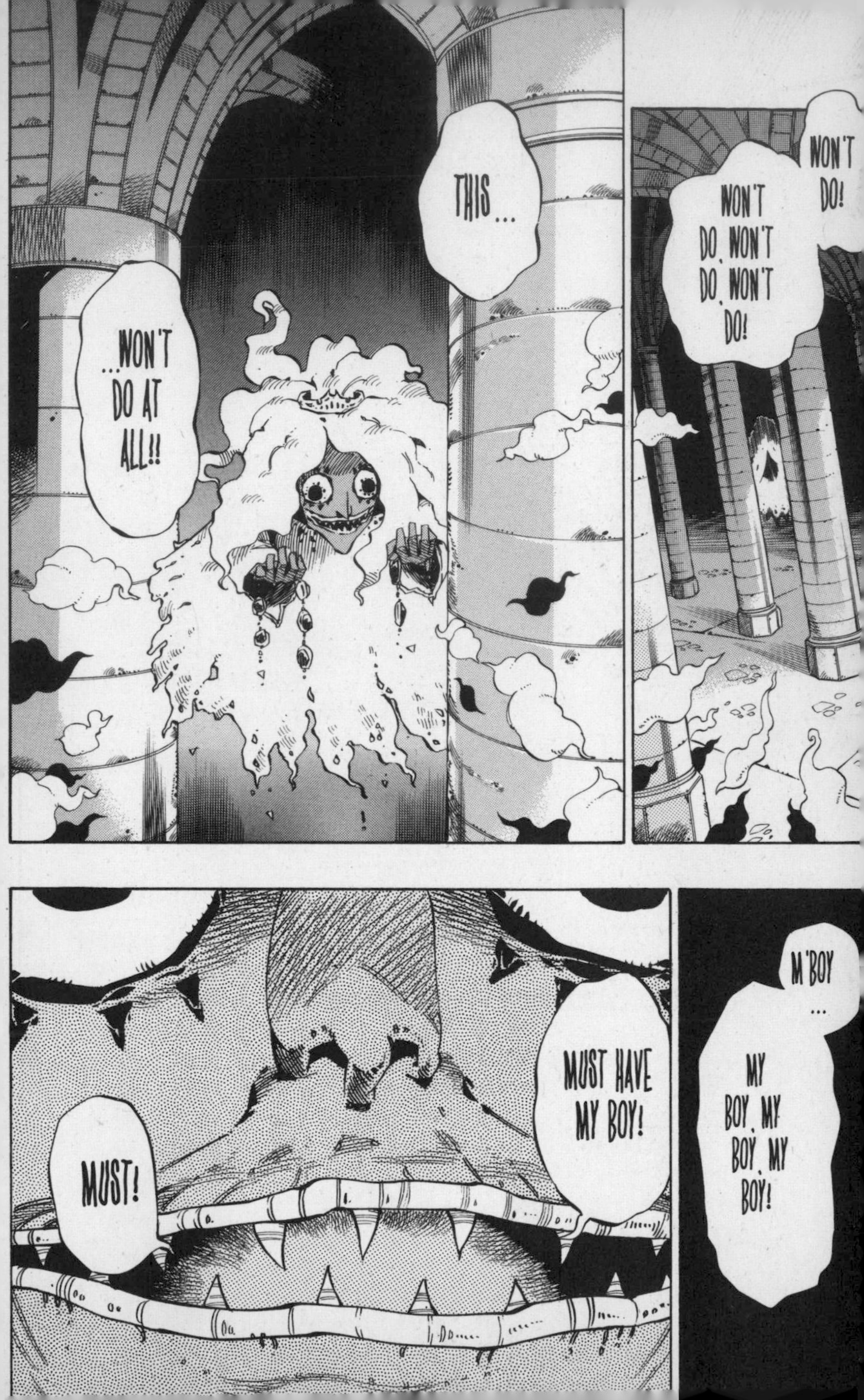
WON'T DO!
WON'T DO, WON'T DO, WON'T DO!
THIS...
...WON'T DO AT ALL!!
M'BOY...
MY BOY, MY BOY, MY BOY!
MUST HAVE MY BOY!
MUST!

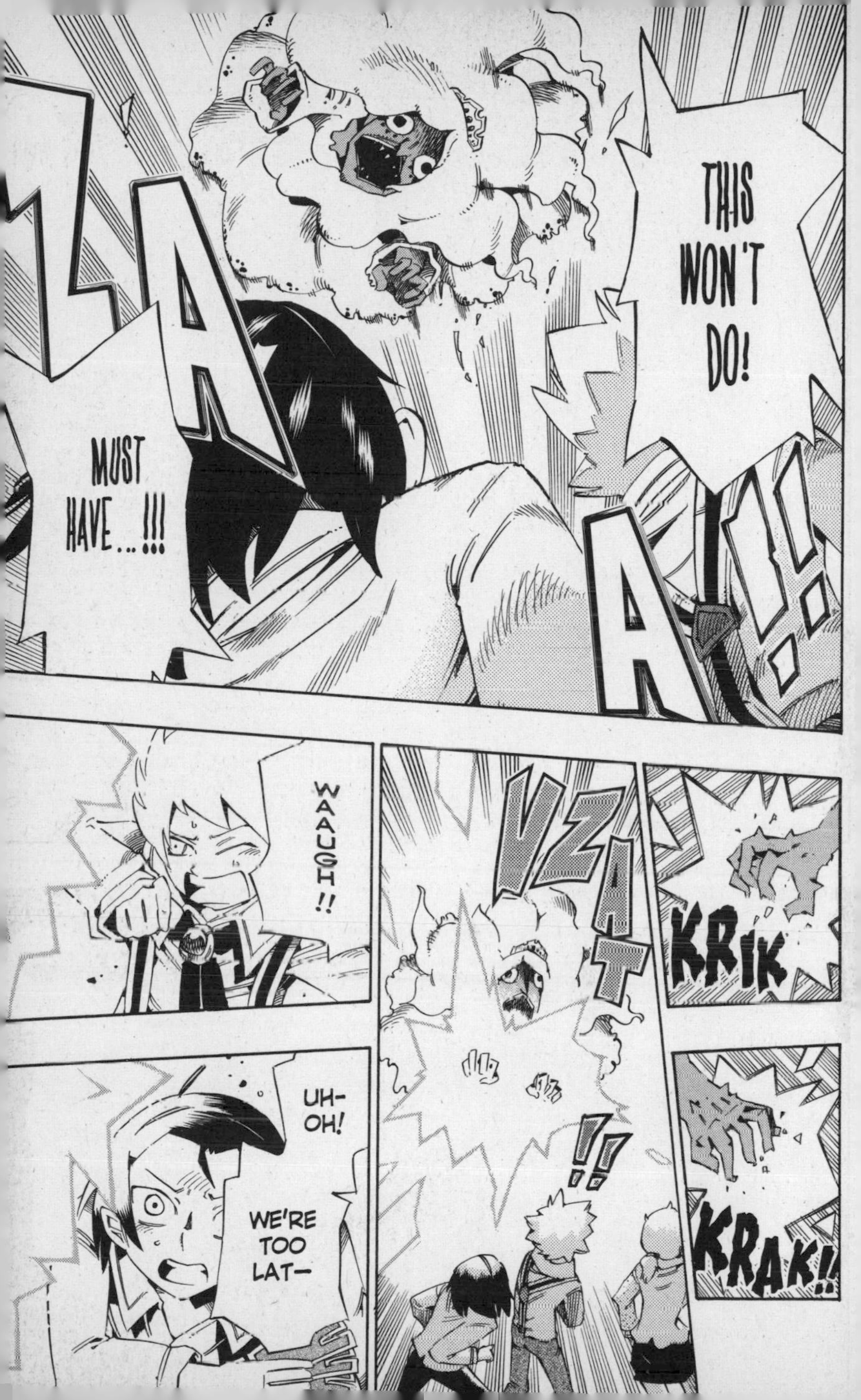
THIS WON'T DO!
MUST HAVE...!!!
ZAA!!
KRIK
KRAK!!
VZAT
!!
WAAUGH!!
UH-OH!
WE'RE TOO LAT—

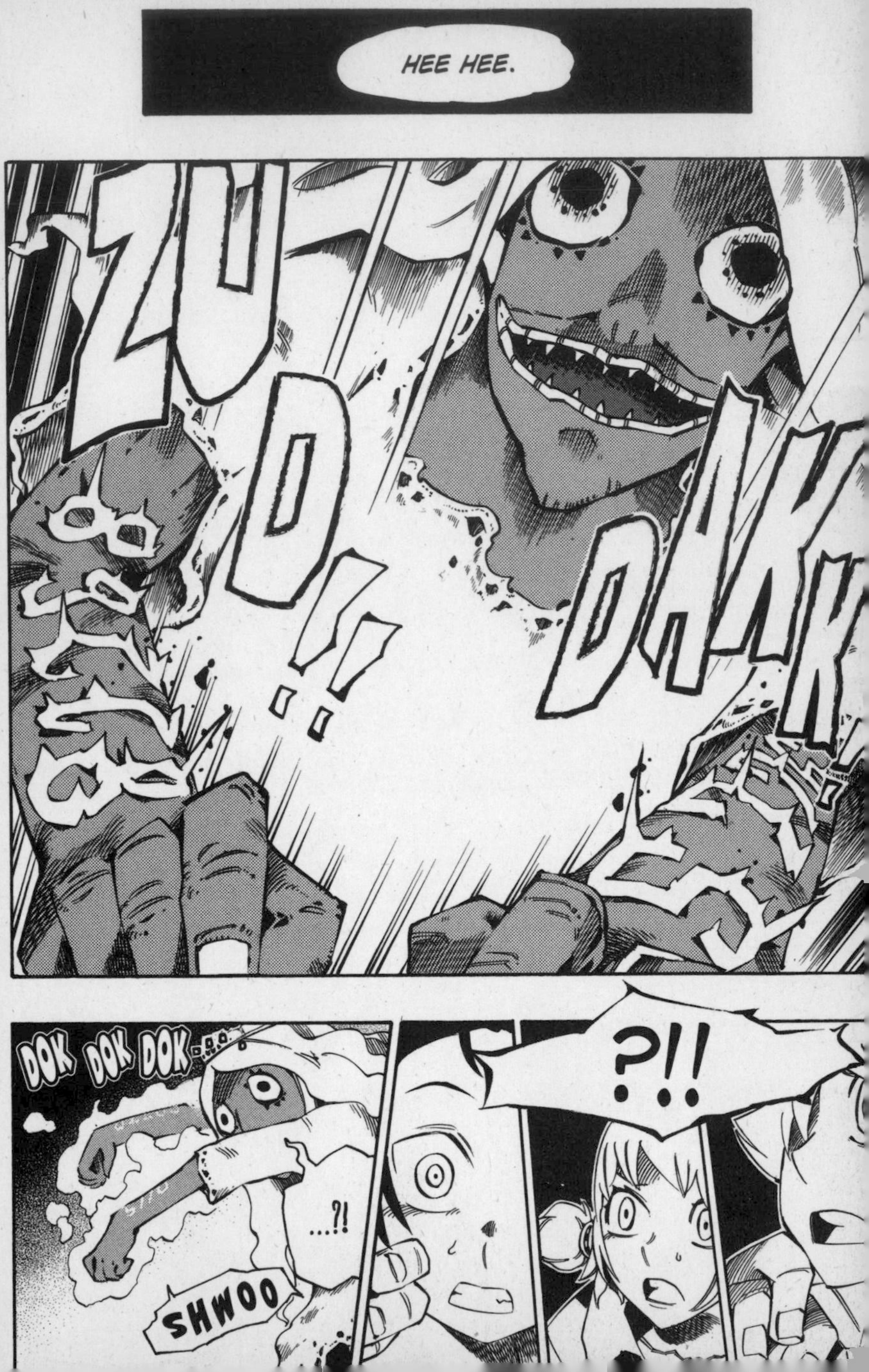
HEE HEE.
ZUD!!
DAK
?!!
DOK DOK DOK...
...?!
SHWOO

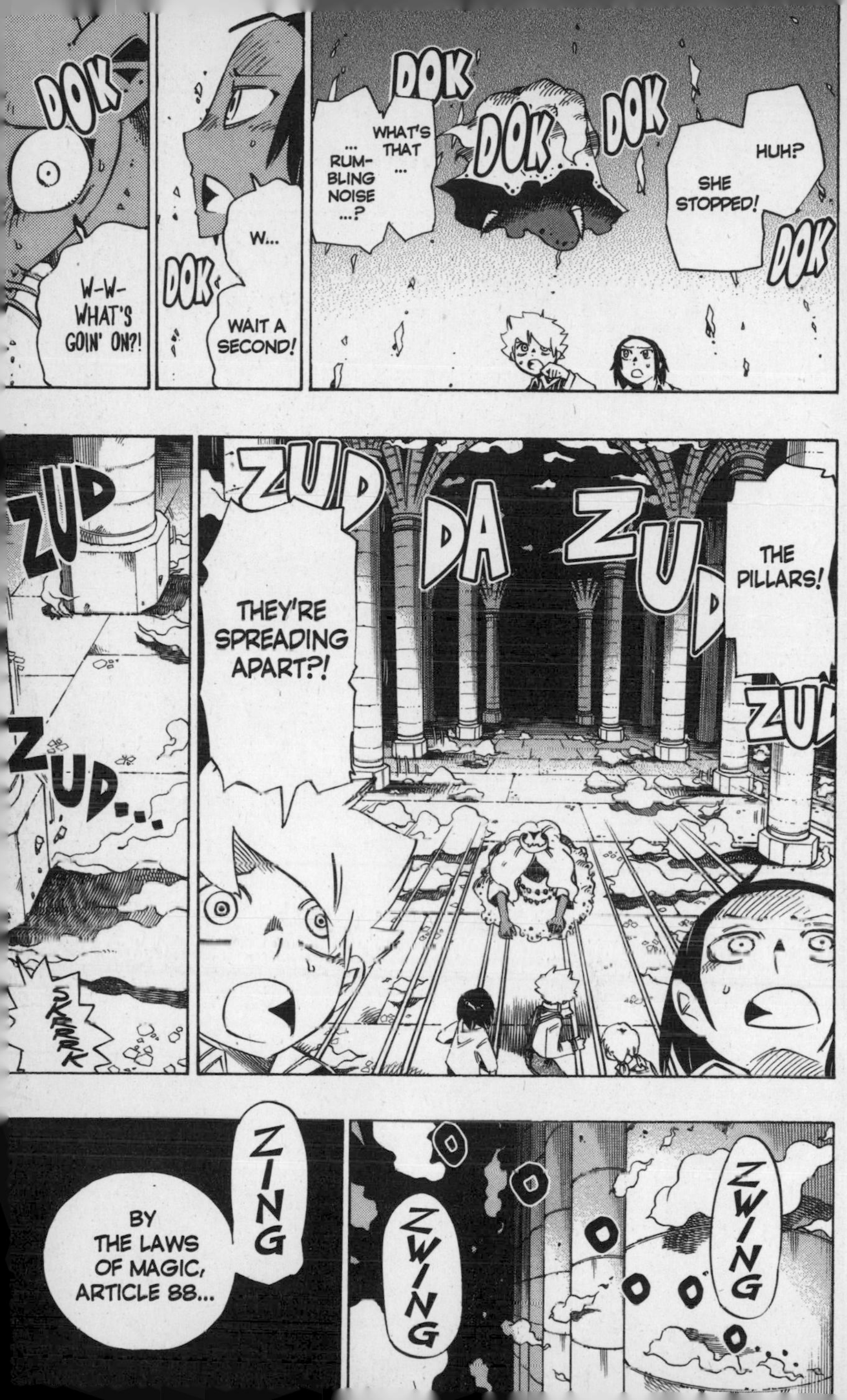
DOK
HUH?
SHE STOPPED!
DOK
WHAT'S THAT ...
... RUMBLING NOISE ...?
DOK
DOK
W...
WAIT A SECOND!
DOK
DOK
W-W-WHAT'S GOIN' ON?!
ZUD
THE PILLARS!
DA
ZUD
ZUD
THEY'RE SPREADING APART?!
ZUD
ZUD...
SKRRRK
ZWING
ZWING
ZING
BY THE LAWS OF MAGIC, ARTICLE 88...

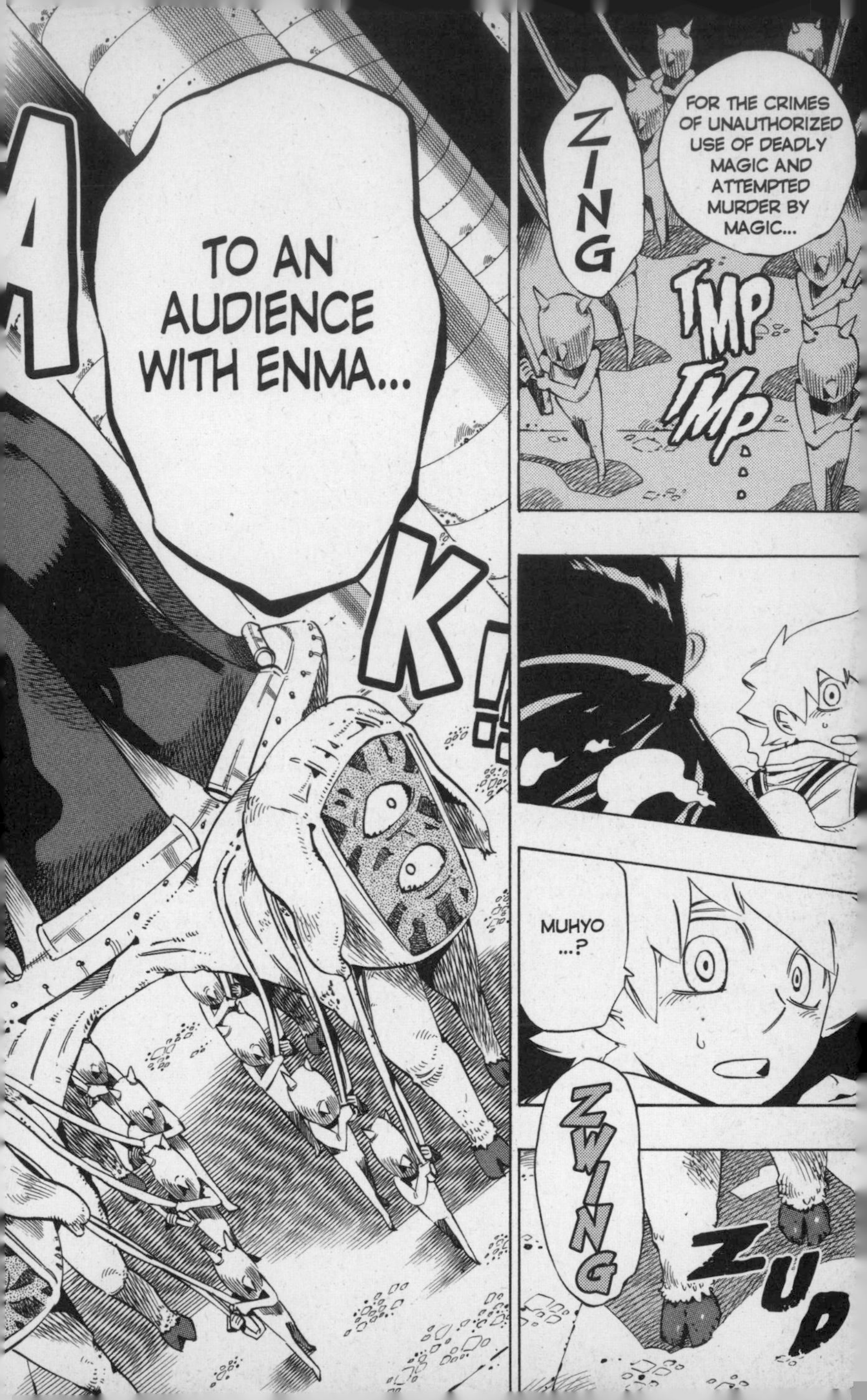
FOR THE CRIMES OF UNAUTHORIZED USE OF DEADLY MAGIC AND ATTEMPTED MURDER BY MAGIC...
ZING
TMP TMP
MUHYO ...?
ZWING
ZUP
TO AN AUDIENCE WITH ENMA...
K!!

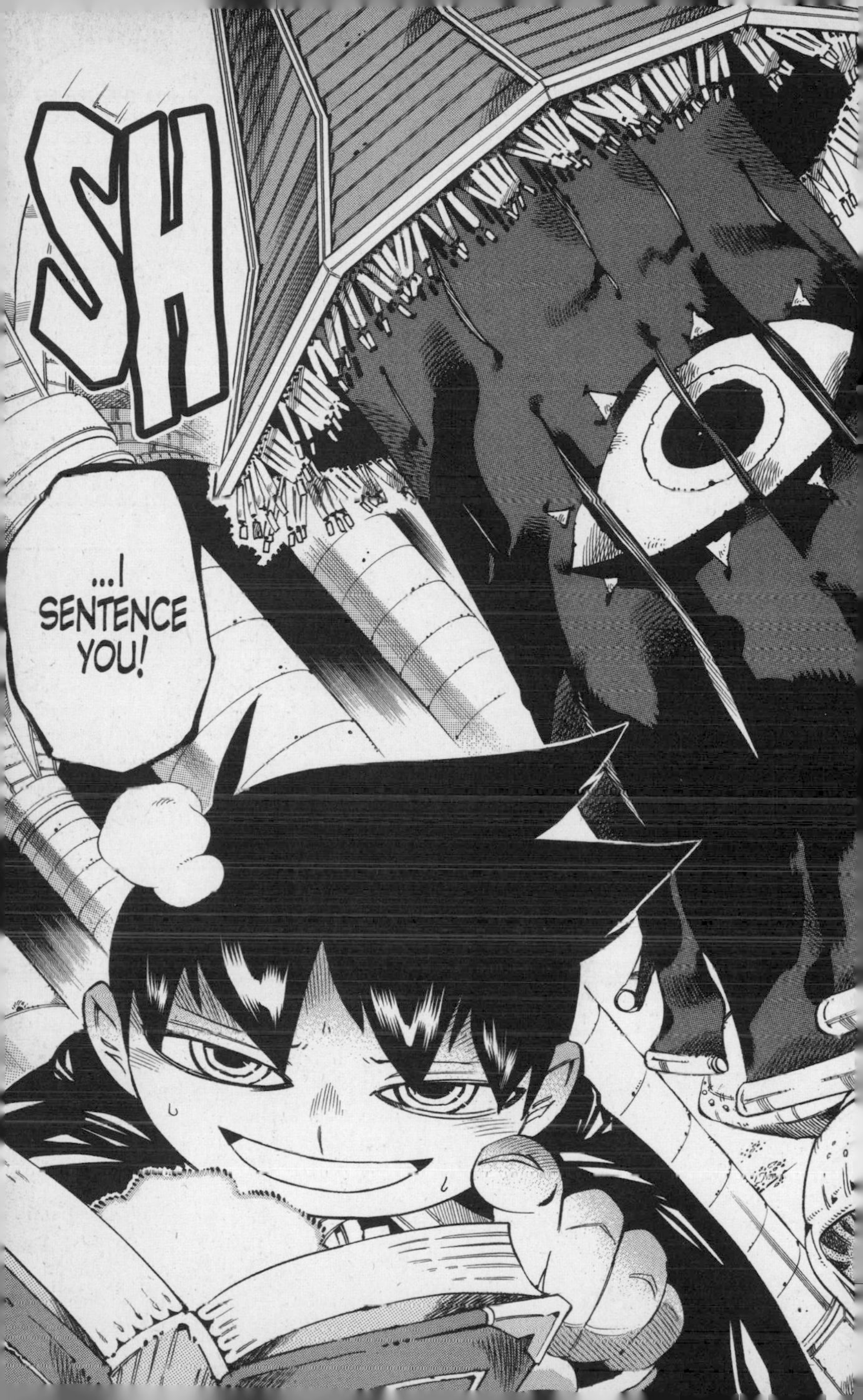
SH
...I SENTENCE YOU!

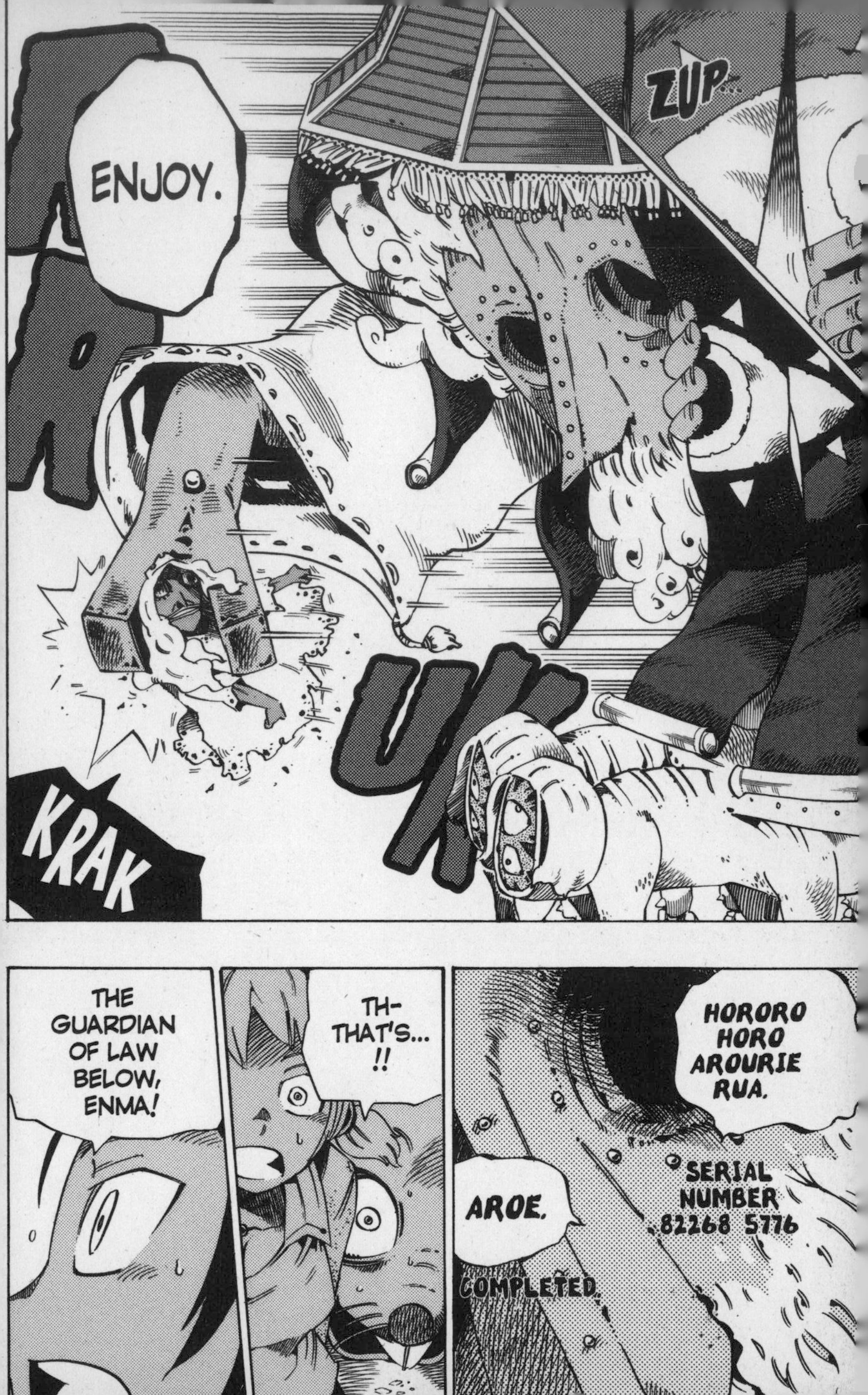
ZUP...
ENJOY.
KRAK
HORORO HORO AROURIE RUA.
SERIAL NUMBER 82268 5776
AROE.
COMPLETED.
TH- THAT'S... !!
THE GUARDIAN OF LAW BELOW, ENMA!

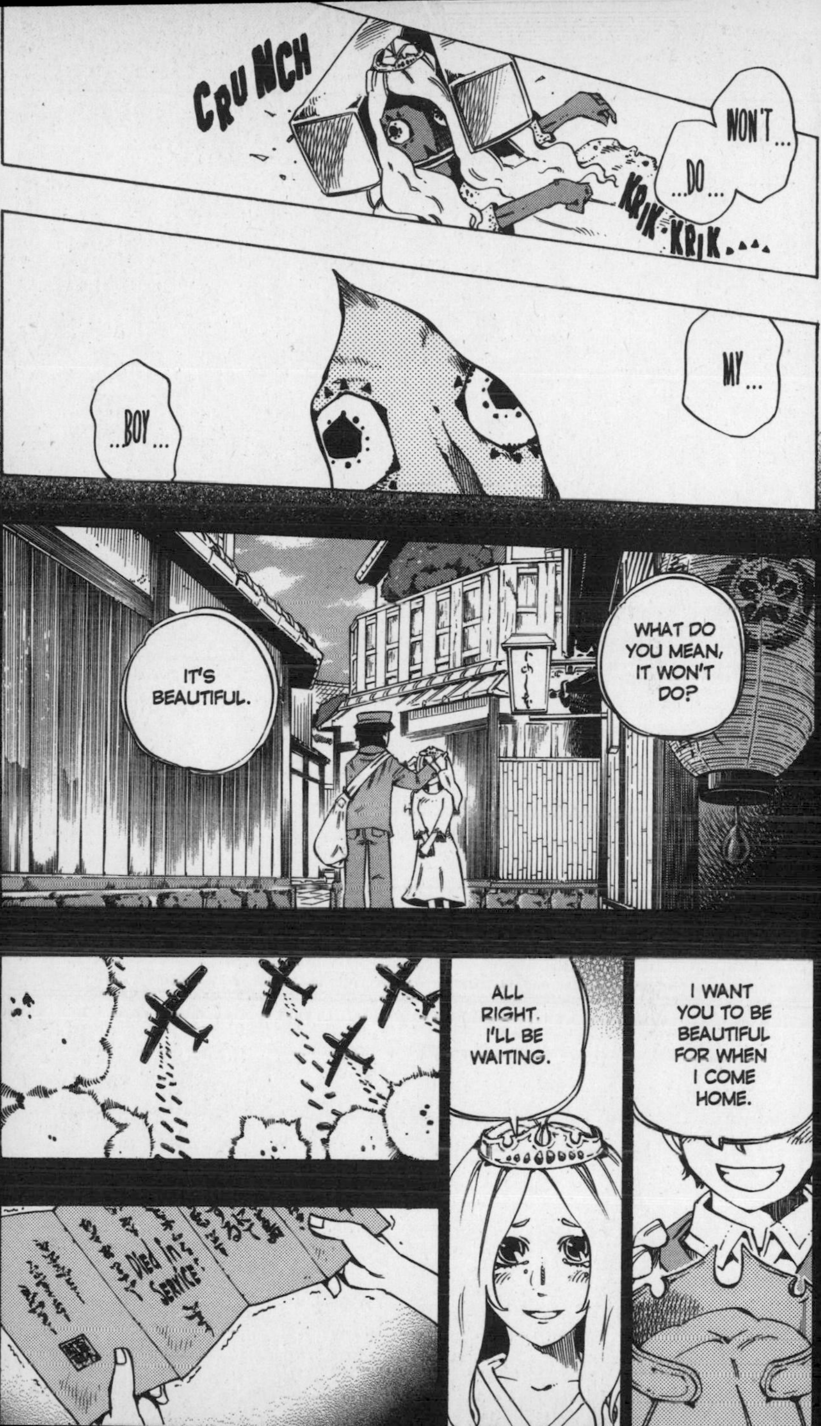
WON'T... ...DO...
CRUNCH
KRIK KRIK...
MY...
...BOY...
WHAT DO YOU MEAN, IT WON'T DO?
IT'S BEAUTIFUL.
I WANT YOU TO BE BEAUTIFUL FOR WHEN I COME HOME.
ALL RIGHT. I'LL BE WAITING.
Died in Service

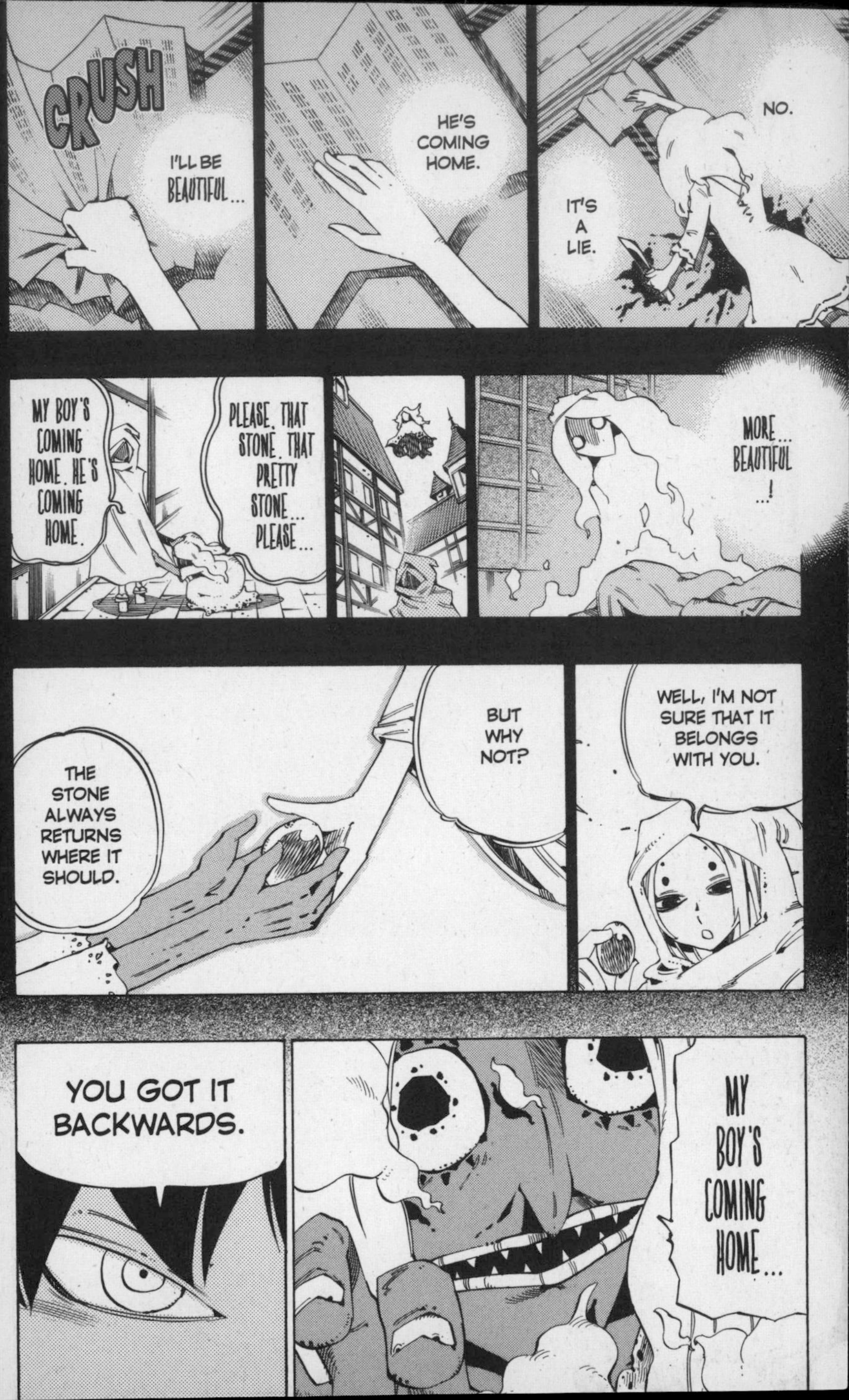
NO.
IT'S A LIE.
HE'S COMING HOME.
CRUSH
I'LL BE BEAUTIFUL...
MORE... BEAUTIFUL...!
PLEASE. THAT STONE. THAT PRETTY STONE... PLEASE...
MY BOY'S COMING HOME. HE'S COMING HOME.
WELL, I'M NOT SURE THAT IT BELONGS WITH YOU.
BUT WHY NOT?
THE STONE ALWAYS RETURNS WHERE IT SHOULD.
MY BOY'S COMING HOME...
YOU GOT IT BACKWARDS.

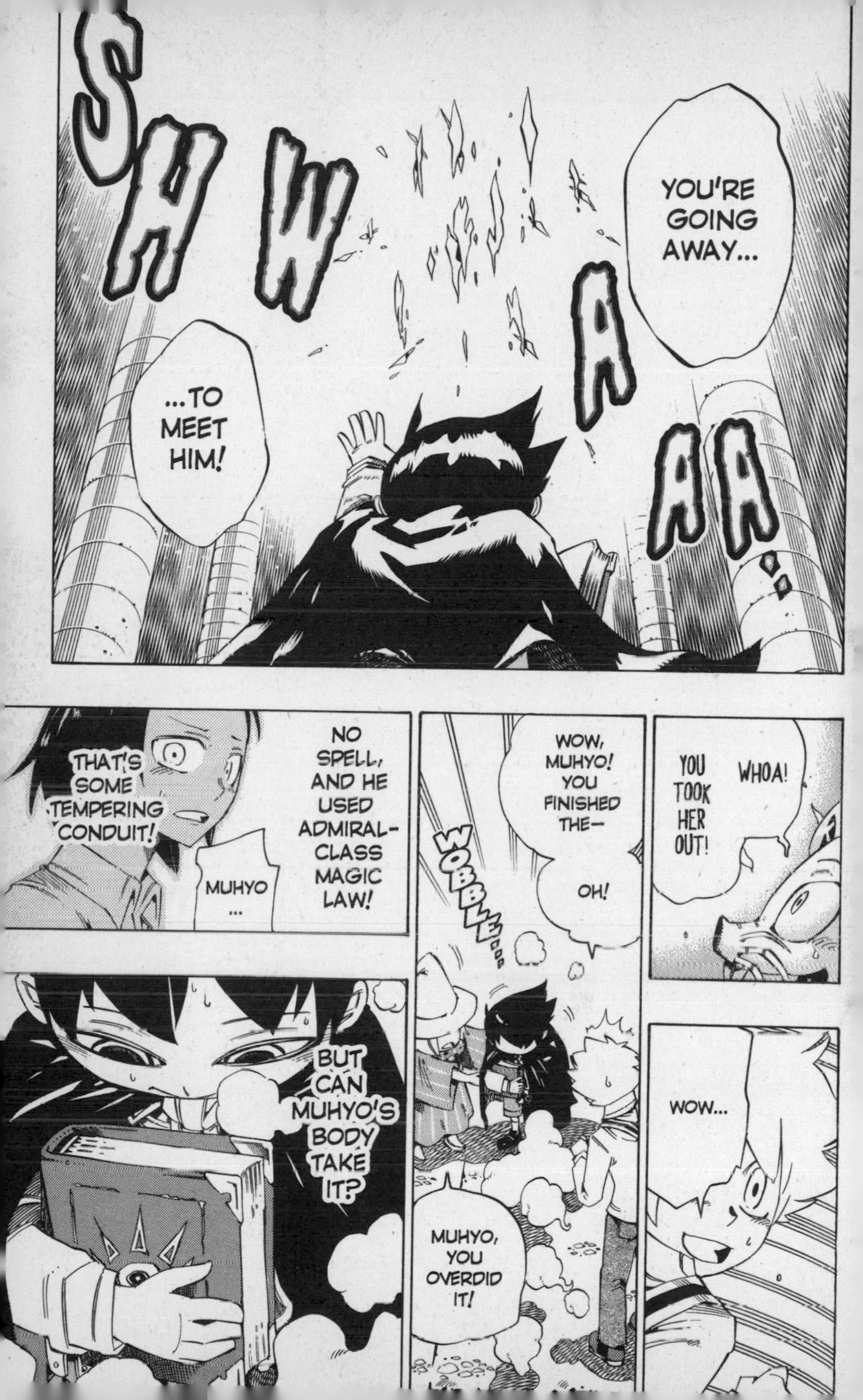
YOU'RE GOING AWAY...
SHWAAAA
...TO MEET HIM!
WHOA!
YOU TOOK HER OUT!
WOW...
WOW, MUHYO! YOU FINISHED THE—
OH!
WOBBLE
MUHYO, YOU OVERDID IT!
NO SPELL, AND HE USED ADMIRAL-CLASS MAGIC LAW!
THAT'S SOME TEMPERING CONDUIT!
MUHYO...
BUT CAN MUHYO'S BODY TAKE IT?

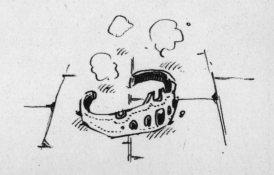

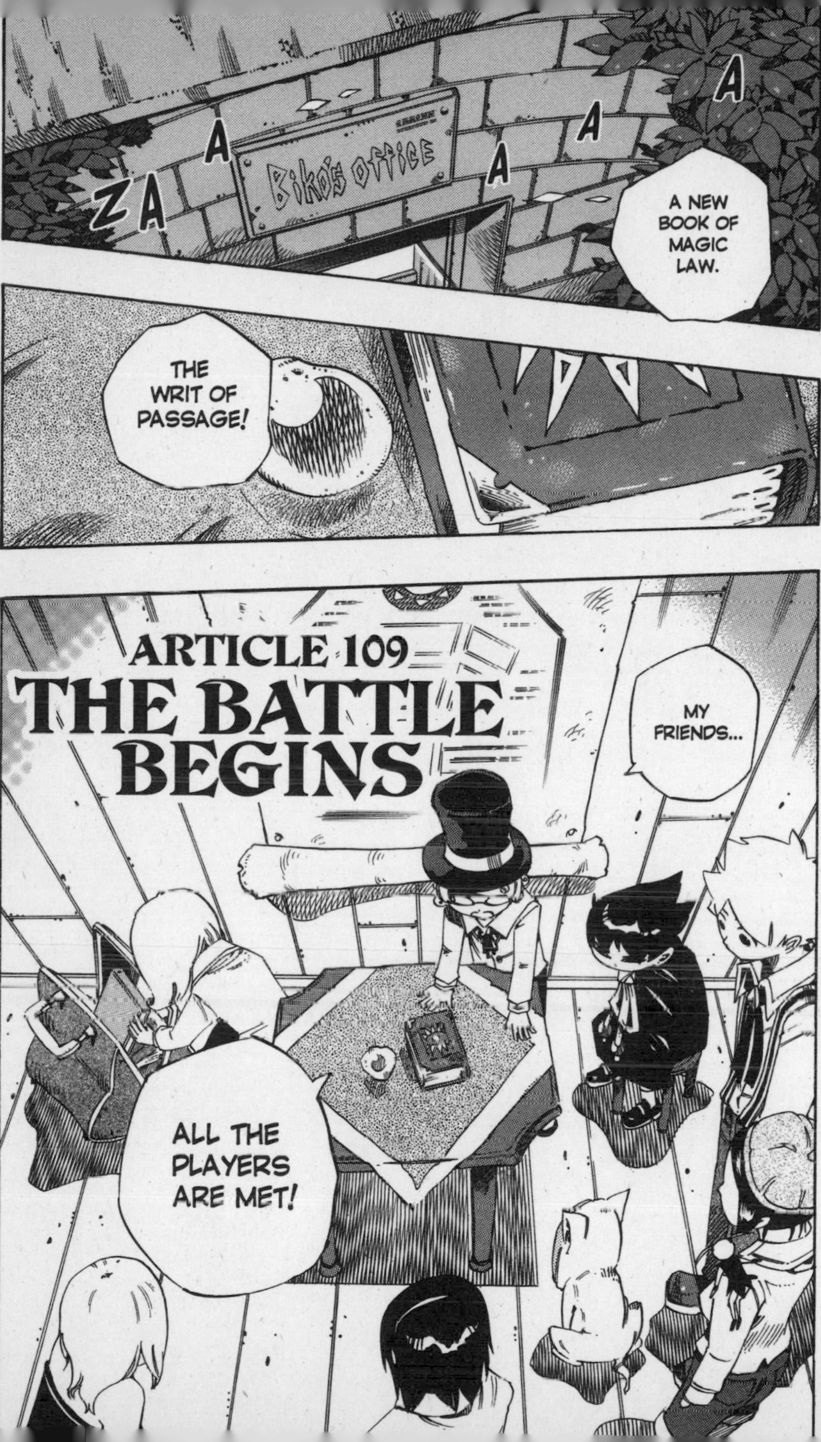
Biko's office
ZA A A A A A
A NEW BOOK OF MAGIC LAW.
THE WRIT OF PASSAGE!
ARTICLE 109
THE BATTLE BEGINS
MY FRIENDS...
ALL THE PLAYERS ARE MET!

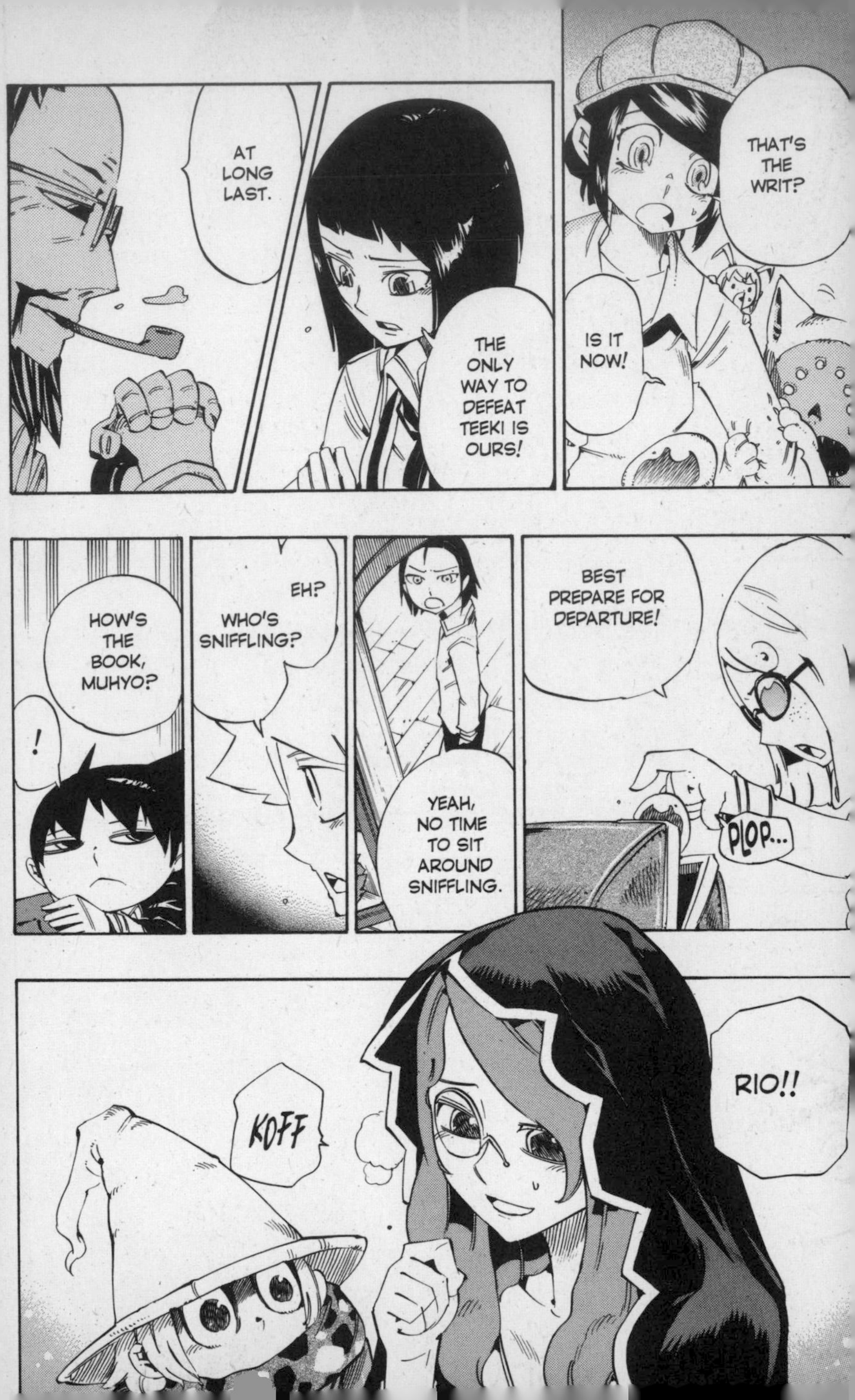
THAT'S THE WRIT?
IS IT NOW!
THE ONLY WAY TO DEFEAT TEEKI IS OURS!
AT LONG LAST.
BEST PREPARE FOR DEPARTURE!
PLOP...
YEAH, NO TIME TO SIT AROUND SNIFFLING.
EH?
WHO'S SNIFFLING?
HOW'S THE BOOK, MUHYO?
!
RIO!!
KOFF

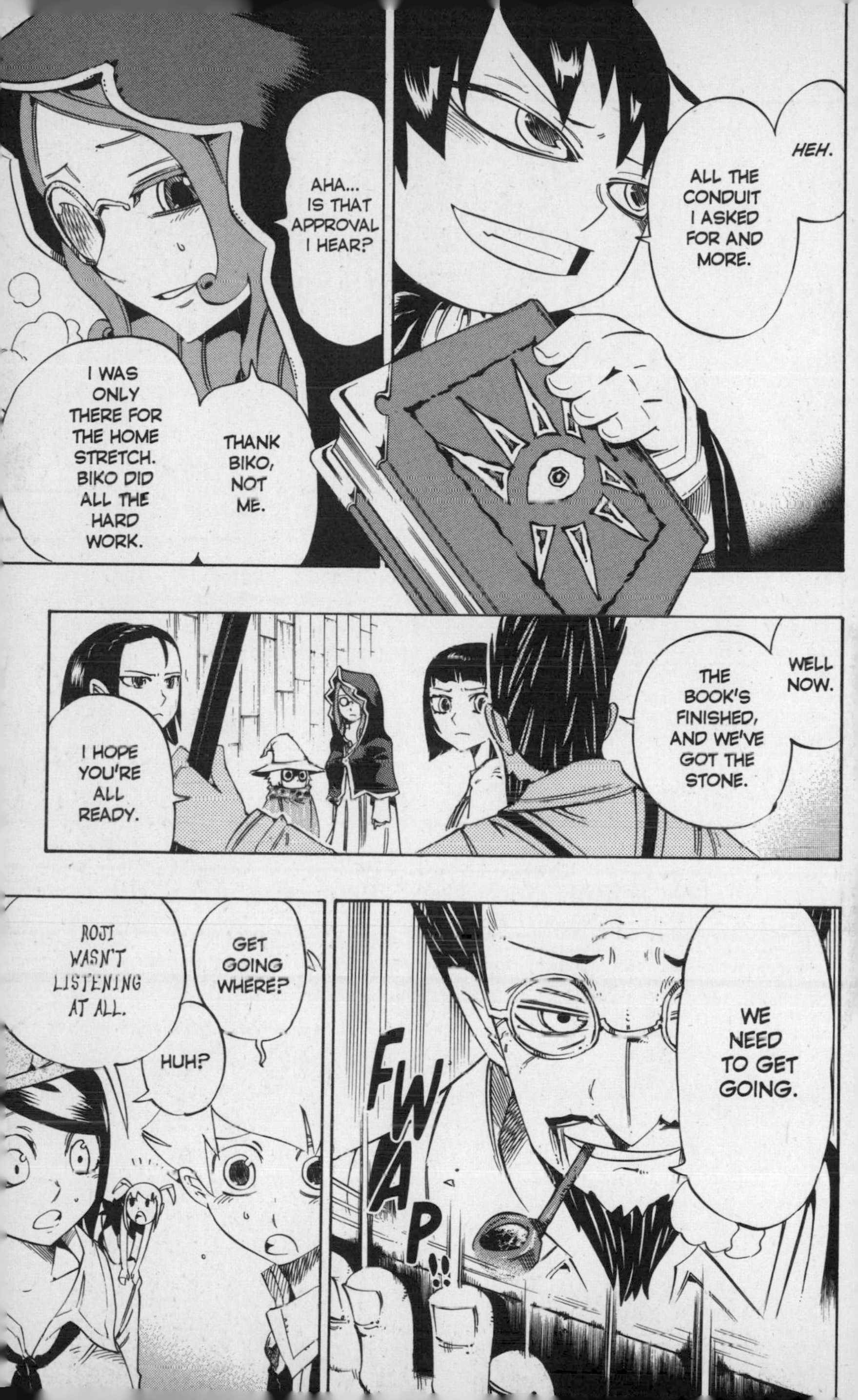
HEH.
ALL THE CONDUIT I ASKED FOR AND MORE.
AHA... IS THAT APPROVAL I HEAR?
I WAS ONLY THERE FOR THE HOME STRETCH. BIKO DID ALL THE HARD WORK.
THANK BIKO, NOT ME.
WELL NOW.
THE BOOK'S FINISHED, AND WE'VE GOT THE STONE.
I HOPE YOU'RE ALL READY.
WE NEED TO GET GOING.
FWAP
GET GOING WHERE?
HUH?
ROJI WASN'T LISTENING AT ALL.

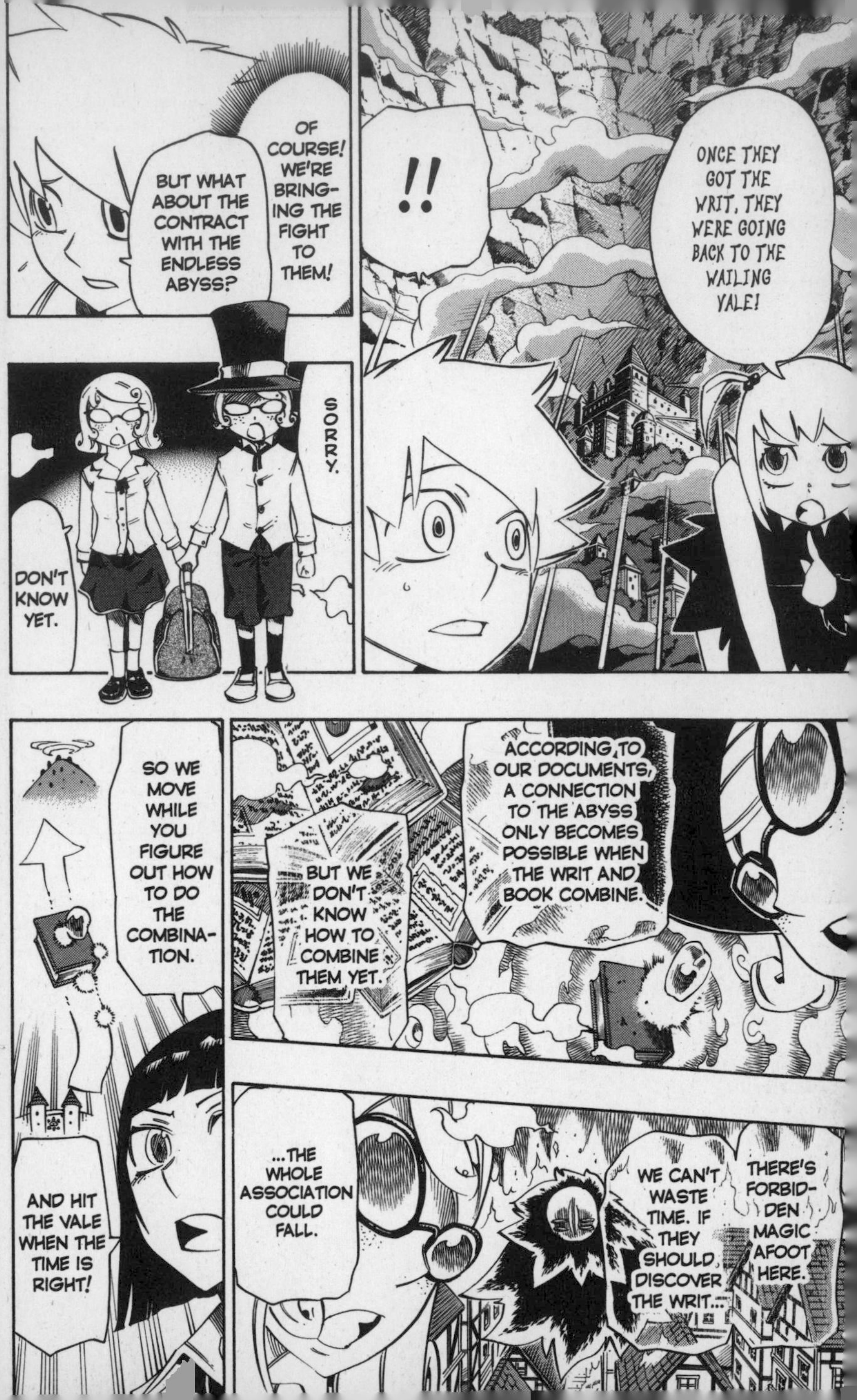
ONCE THEY GOT THE WRIT, THEY WERE GOING BACK TO THE WAILING VALE!
!!
OF COURSE! WE'RE BRINGING THE FIGHT TO THEM!
BUT WHAT ABOUT THE CONTRACT WITH THE ENDLESS ABYSS?
SORRY.
DON'T KNOW YET.
ACCORDING TO OUR DOCUMENTS, A CONNECTION TO THE ABYSS ONLY BECOMES POSSIBLE WHEN THE WRIT AND BOOK COMBINE.
BUT WE DON'T KNOW HOW TO COMBINE THEM YET.
THERE'S FORBIDDEN MAGIC AFOOT HERE.
WE CAN'T WASTE TIME. IF THEY SHOULD DISCOVER THE WRIT...
...THE WHOLE ASSOCIATION COULD FALL.
SO WE MOVE WHILE YOU FIGURE OUT HOW TO DO THE COMBINATION.
AND HIT THE VALE WHEN THE TIME IS RIGHT!

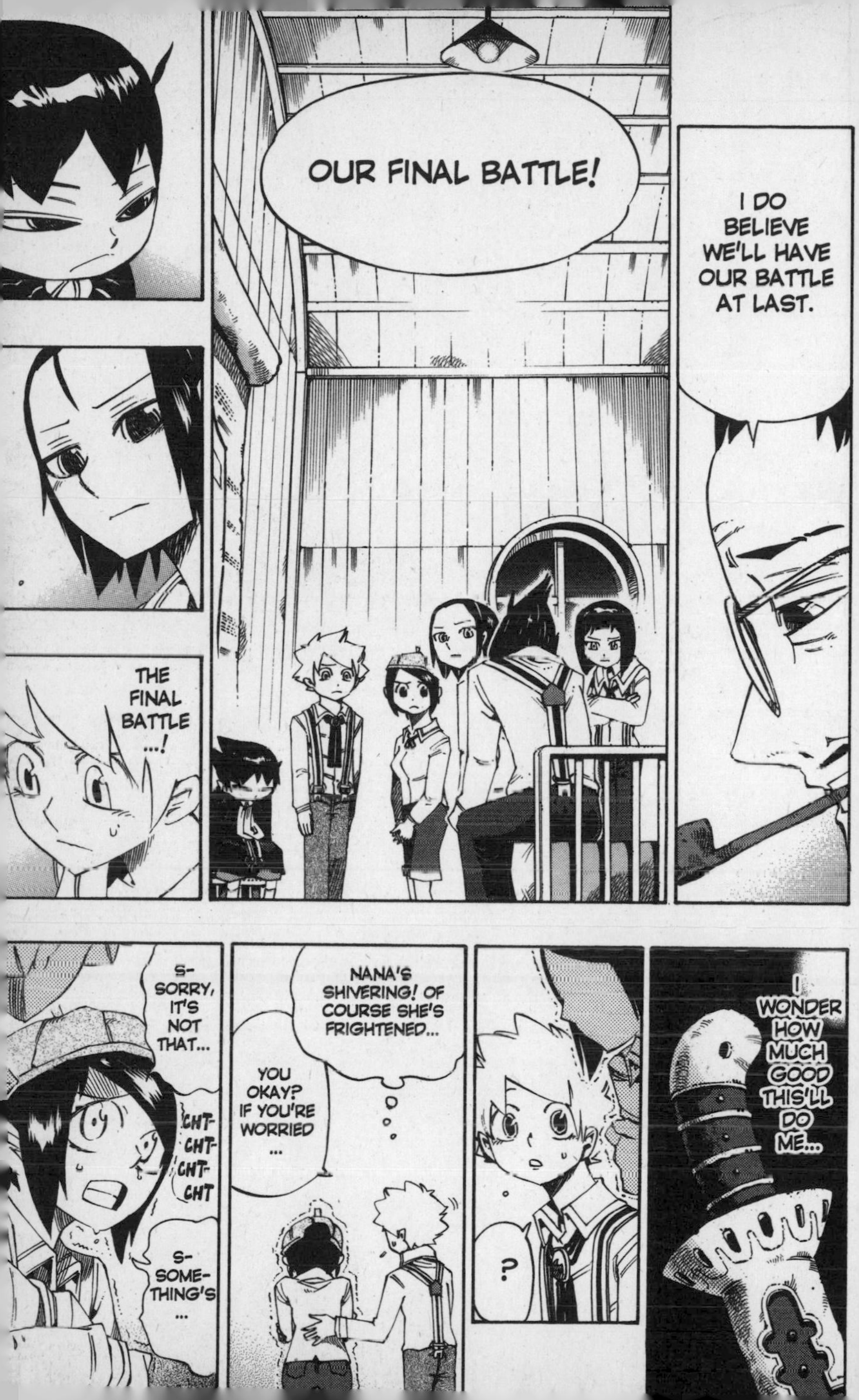
I DO BELIEVE WE'LL HAVE OUR BATTLE AT LAST.
OUR FINAL BATTLE!
THE FINAL BATTLE ...!
I WONDER HOW MUCH GOOD THIS'LL DO ME...
?
NANA'S SHIVERING! OF COURSE SHE'S FRIGHTENED...
YOU OKAY? IF YOU'RE WORRIED ...
S-SORRY, IT'S NOT THAT...
CHT-CHT-CHT-CHT
S-SOMETHING'S ...

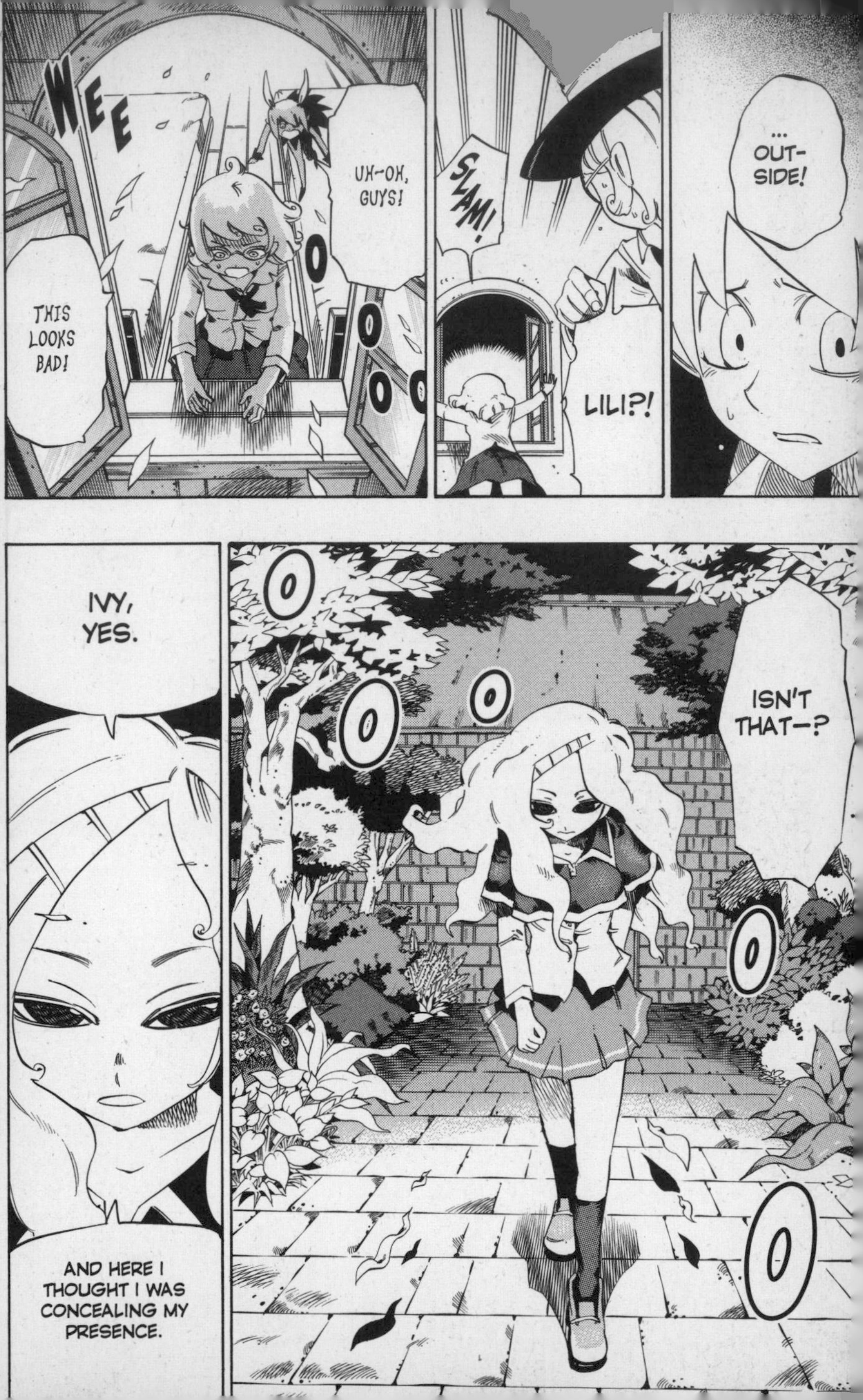
... OUT-SIDE!
SLAM!
LILI?!
WEE
UH-OH, GUYS!
OOOO
THIS LOOKS BAD!
OOOO
ISN'T THAT—?
IVY, YES.
AND HERE I THOUGHT I WAS CONCEALING MY PRESENCE.

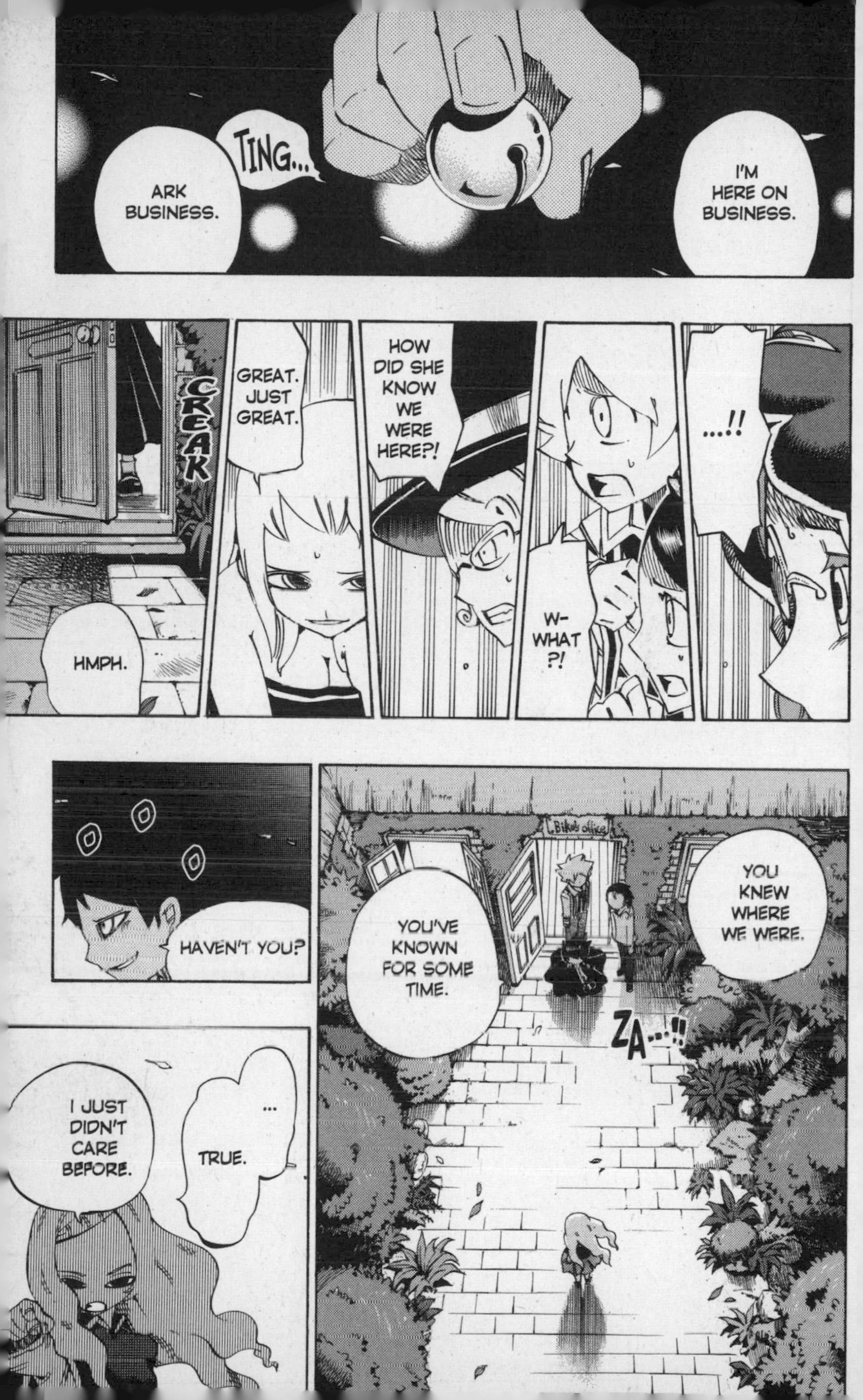
I'M HERE ON BUSINESS.
TING...
ARK BUSINESS.
...!!
W- WHAT?!
HOW DID SHE KNOW WE WERE HERE?!
GREAT. JUST GREAT.
CREAK
HMPH.
YOU KNEW WHERE WE WERE.
YOU'VE KNOWN FOR SOME TIME.
ZA...!!
HAVEN'T YOU?
... TRUE.
I JUST DIDN'T CARE BEFORE.

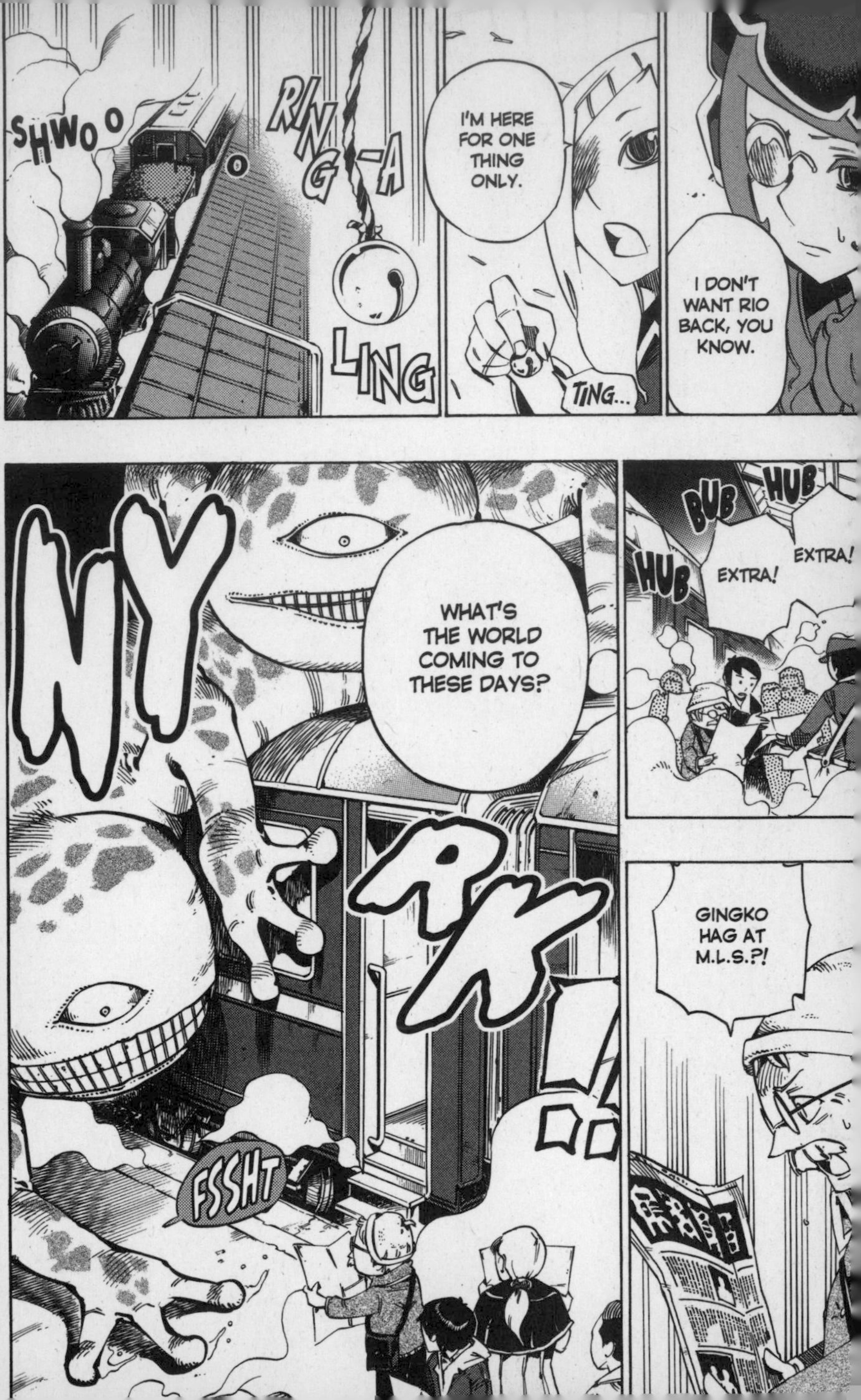

I DON'T WANT RIO BACK, YOU KNOW.
I'M HERE FOR ONE THING ONLY.
TING...
RING-A
LING
SHWOOO
HUB HUB
BUB
EXTRA!
EXTRA!
GINGKO HAG AT M.L.S.?!
WHAT'S THE WORLD COMING TO THESE DAYS?
MY
FSSHT!

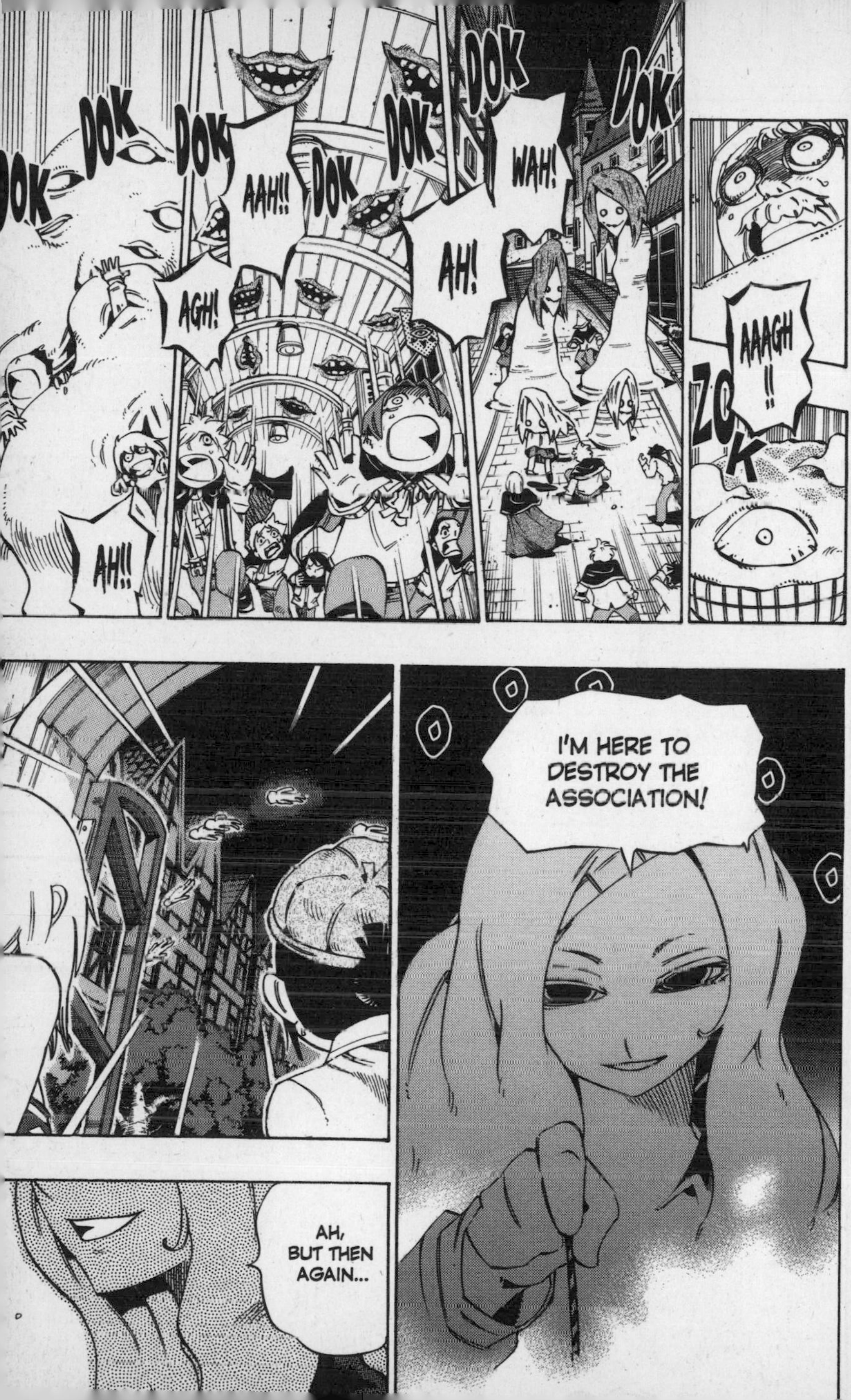
AAAGH!!
ZOK
DOK
DOK
WAH!
AH!
DOK
DOK
AAH!!
AGH!
DOK
DOK
AH!!
I'M HERE TO DESTROY THE ASSOCIATION!
AH, BUT THEN AGAIN...

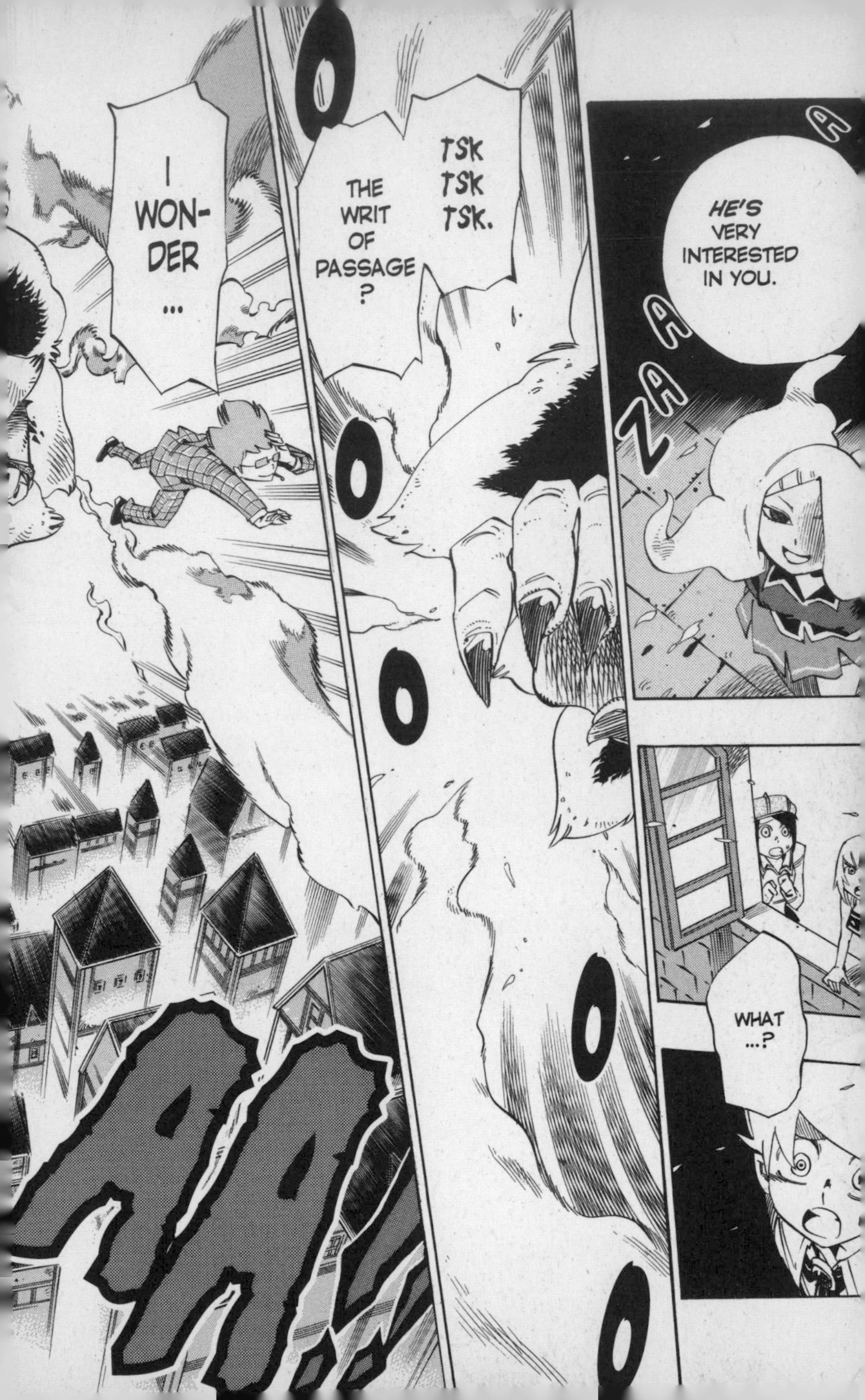
HE'S VERY INTERESTED IN YOU.
ZAAA
WHAT ...?
TSK TSK TSK.
THE WRIT OF PASSAGE ?
I WON-DER ...

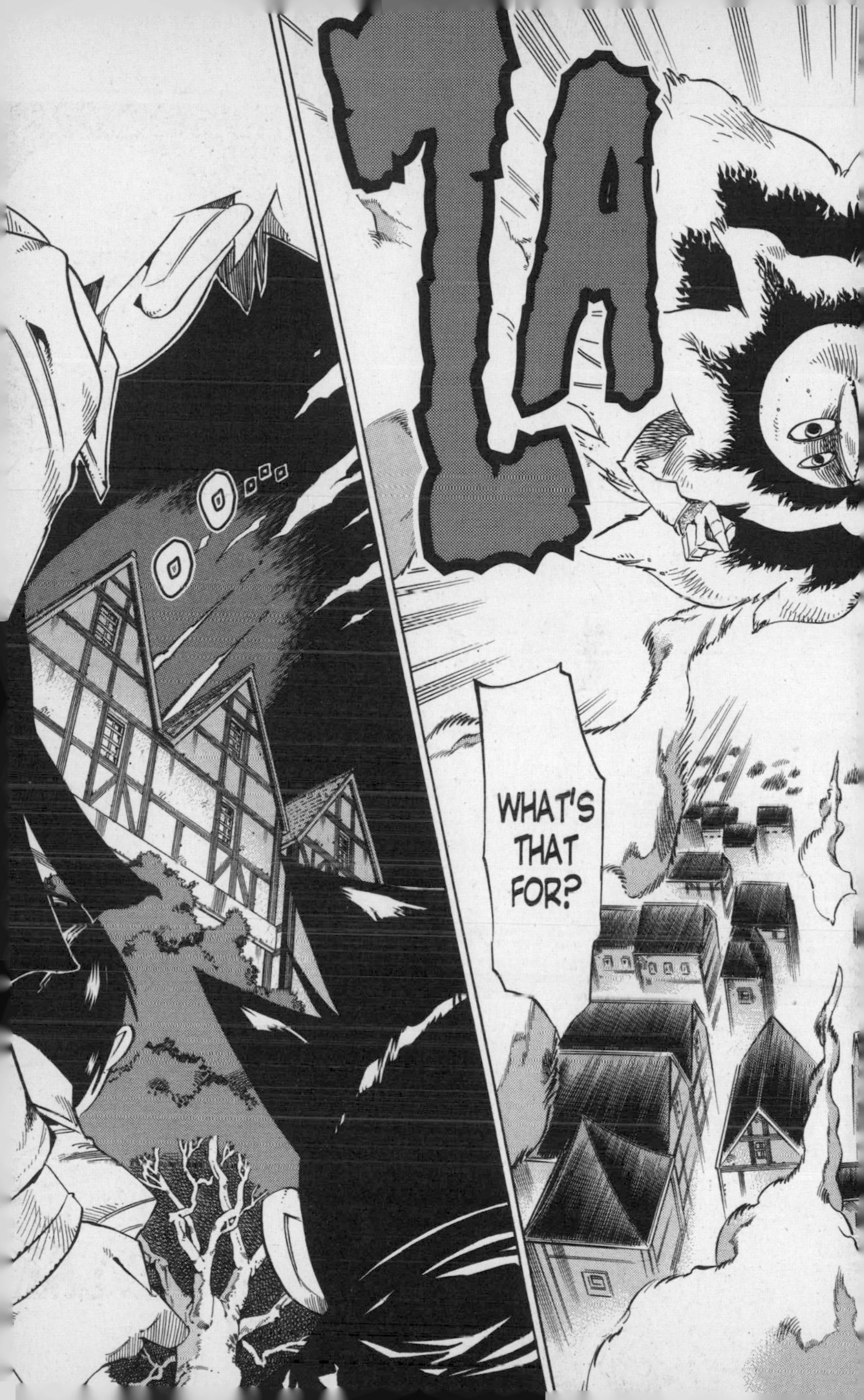
TA
WHAT'S THAT FOR?

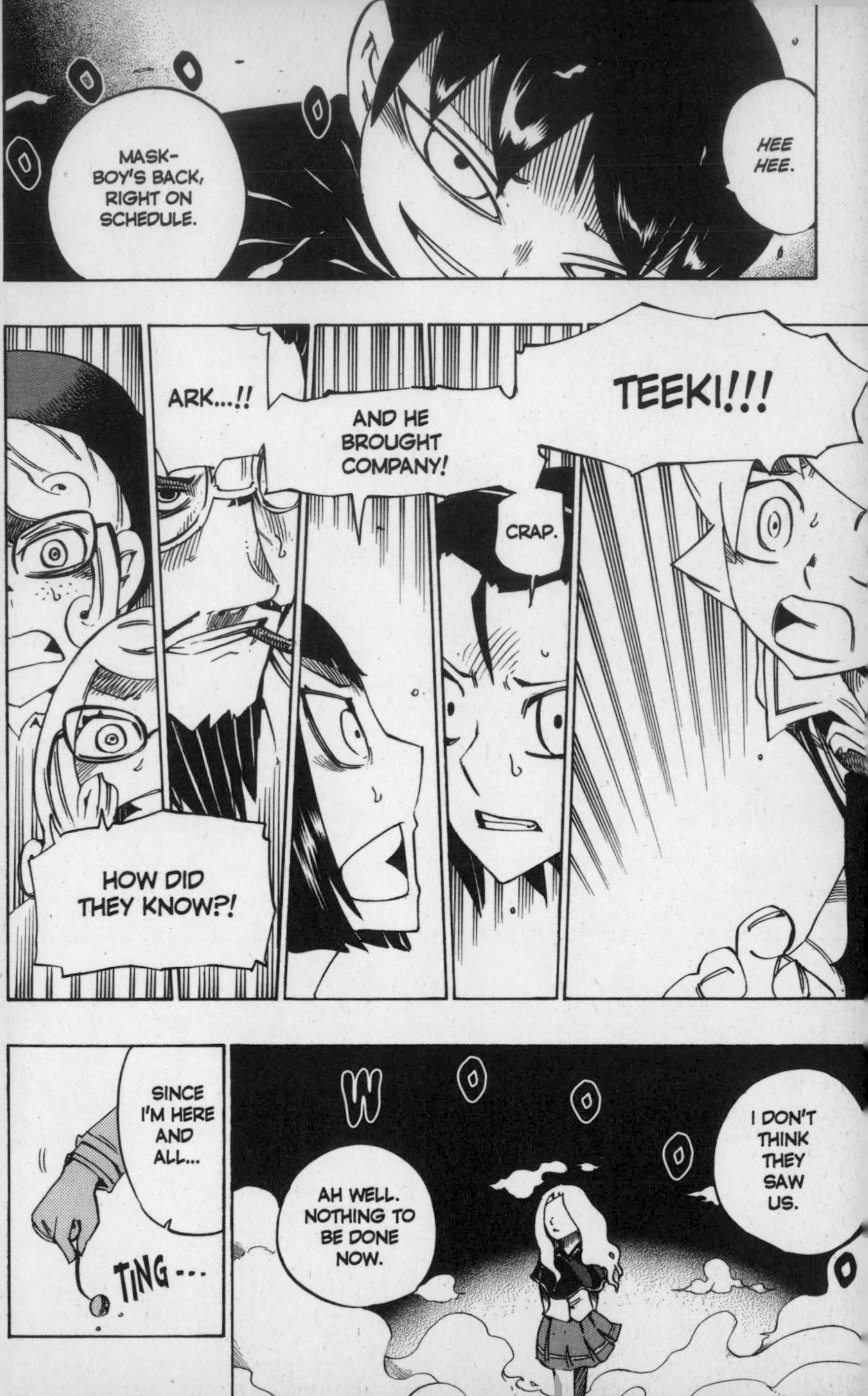
HEE HEE.
MASK-BOY'S BACK, RIGHT ON SCHEDULE.
TEEKI!!!
CRAP.
AND HE BROUGHT COMPANY!
ARK...!!
HOW DID THEY KNOW?!
I DON'T THINK THEY SAW US.
AH WELL. NOTHING TO BE DONE NOW.
SINCE I'M HERE AND ALL...
TING...

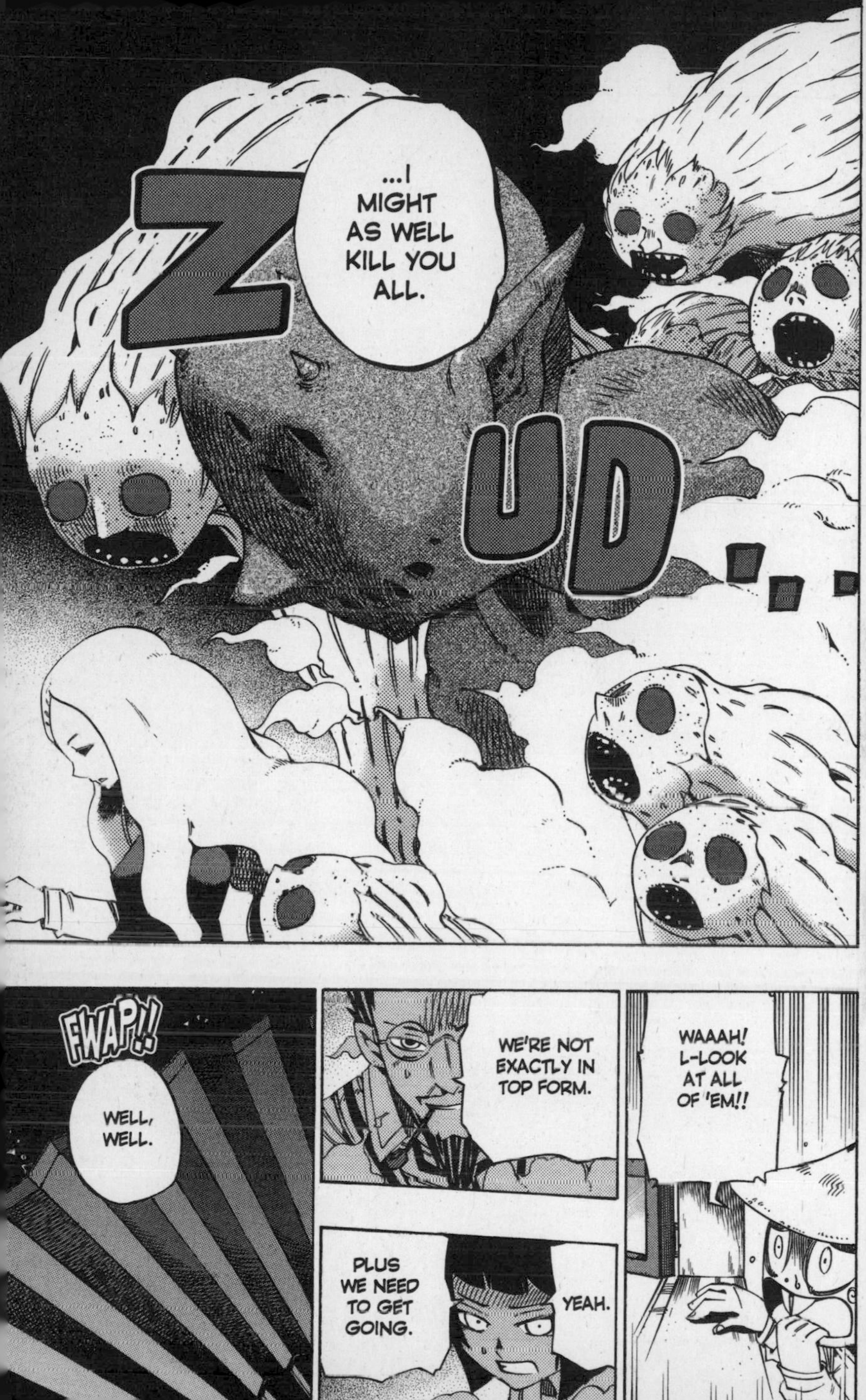
...I MIGHT AS WELL KILL YOU ALL.
ZUD...
WAAAH! L-LOOK AT ALL OF 'EM!!
WE'RE NOT EXACTLY IN TOP FORM.
YEAH.
PLUS WE NEED TO GET GOING.
FWAP!!
WELL, WELL.

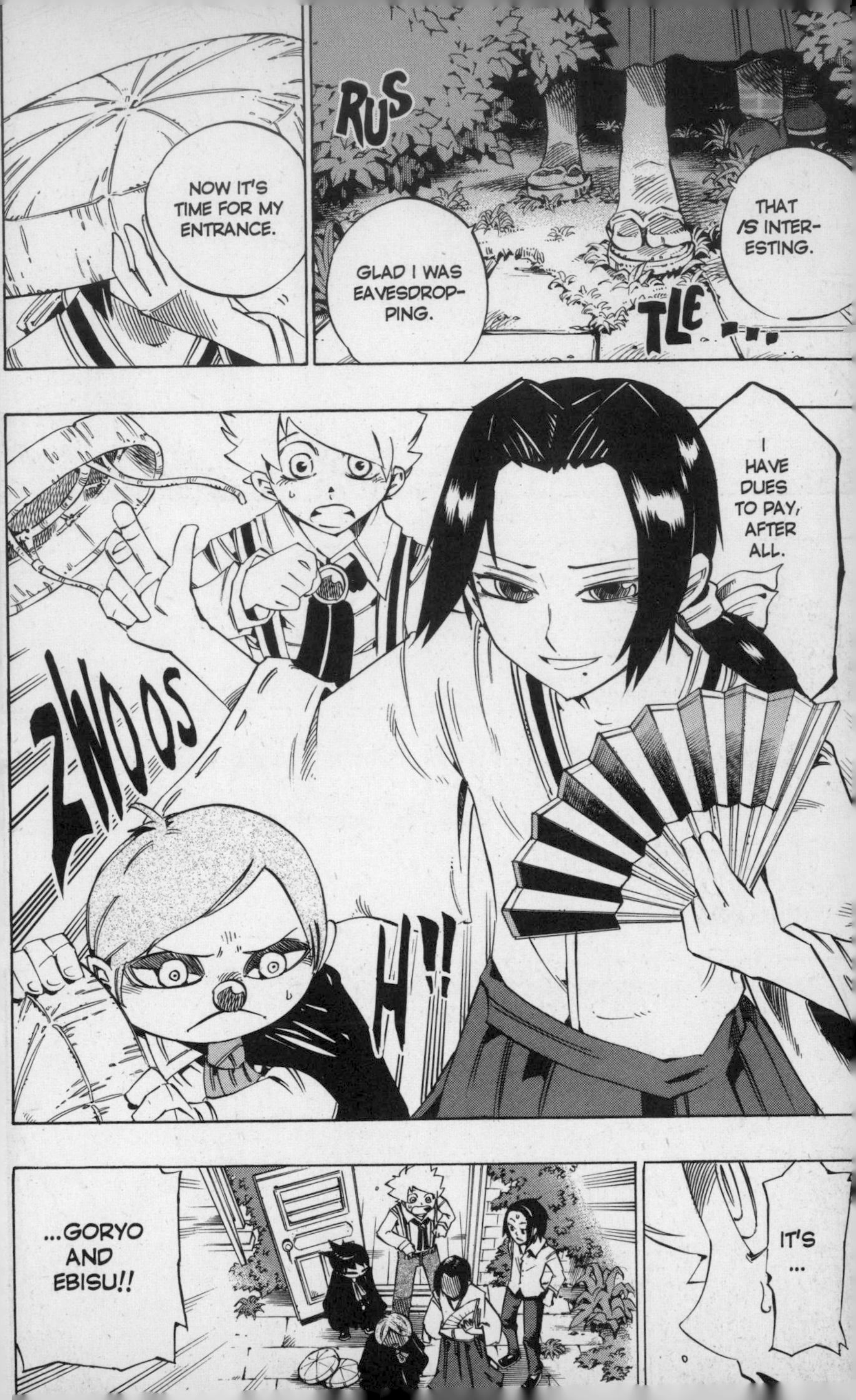
RUS
TLE...
THAT IS INTER-ESTING.
GLAD I WAS EAVESDROP-PING.
NOW IT'S TIME FOR MY ENTRANCE.
I HAVE DUES TO PAY, AFTER ALL.
ZWOOSH!!
IT'S...
...GORYO AND EBISU!!

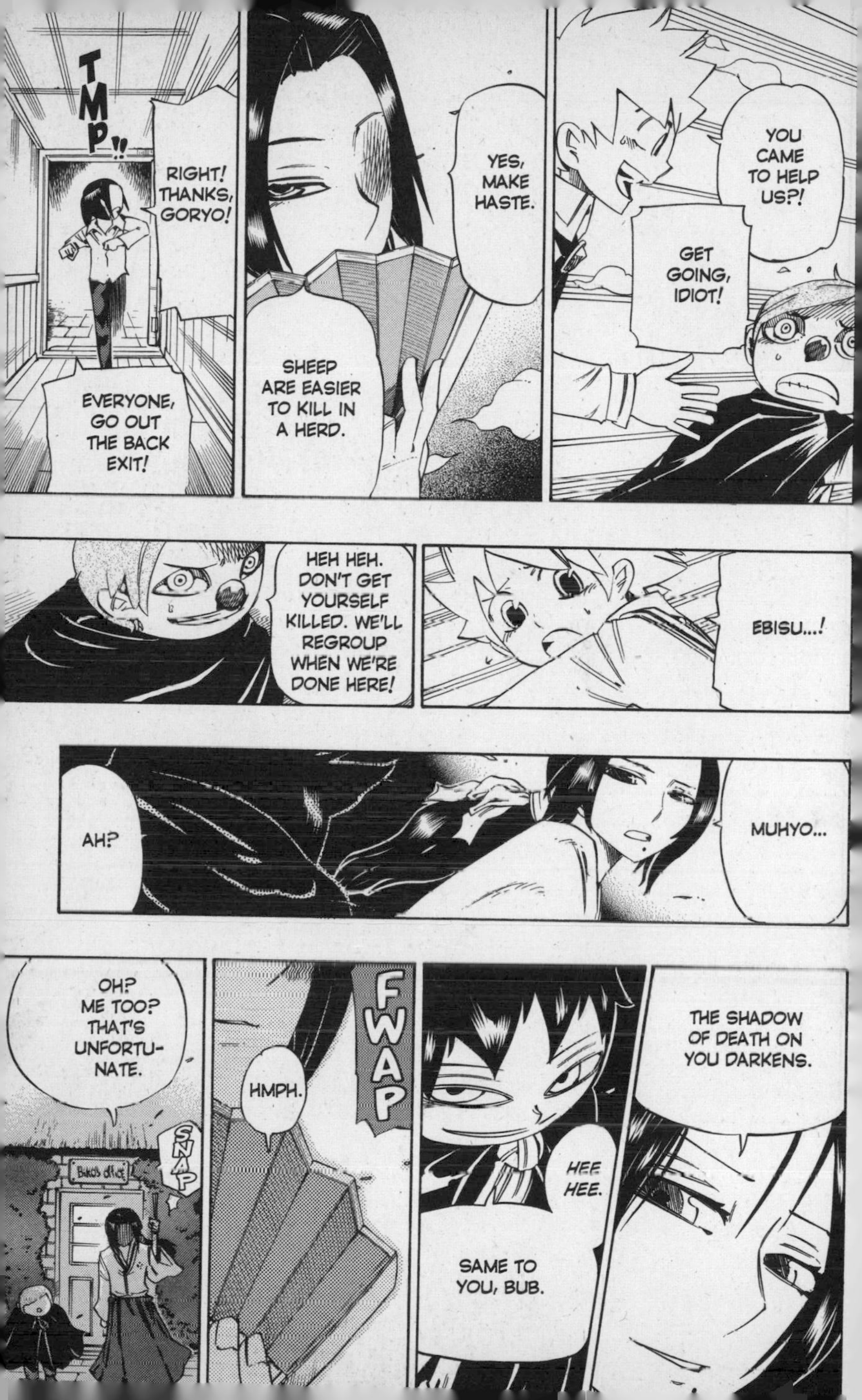
YOU CAME TO HELP US?!
GET GOING, IDIOT!
YES, MAKE HASTE.
SHEEP ARE EASIER TO KILL IN A HERD.
TMP!!
RIGHT! THANKS, GORYO!
EVERYONE, GO OUT THE BACK EXIT!
EBISU...!
HEH HEH. DON'T GET YOURSELF KILLED. WE'LL REGROUP WHEN WE'RE DONE HERE!
MUHYO...
AH?
THE SHADOW OF DEATH ON YOU DARKENS.
HEE HEE.
SAME TO YOU, BUB.
FWAP
HMPH.
OH? ME TOO? THAT'S UNFORTU-NATE.
SNAP
Biko's office

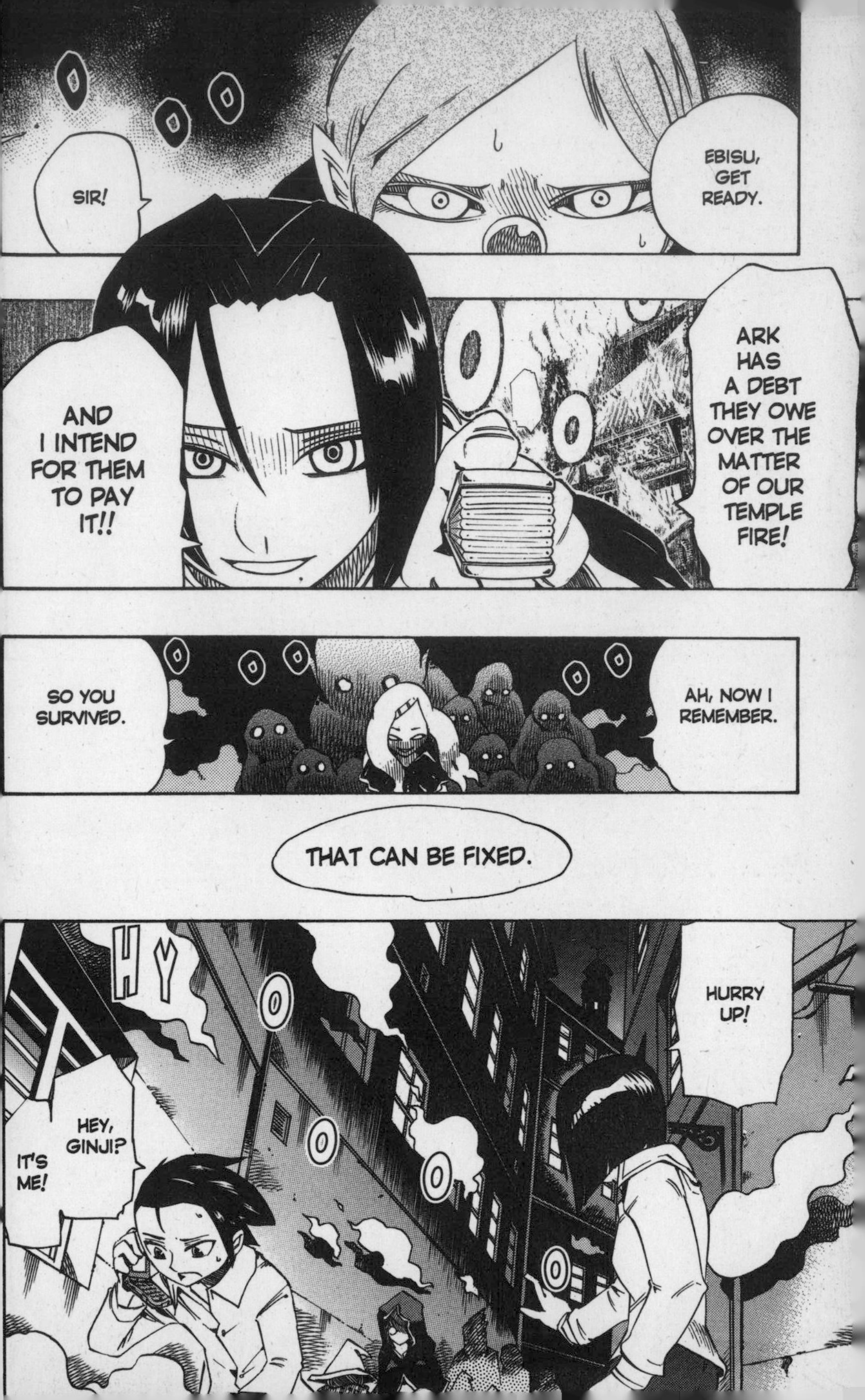
EBISU, GET READY.
SIR!
ARK HAS A DEBT THEY OWE OVER THE MATTER OF OUR TEMPLE FIRE!
AND I INTEND FOR THEM TO PAY IT!!
AH, NOW I REMEMBER.
SO YOU SURVIVED.
THAT CAN BE FIXED.
HURRY UP!
HY
HEY, GINJI?
IT'S ME!

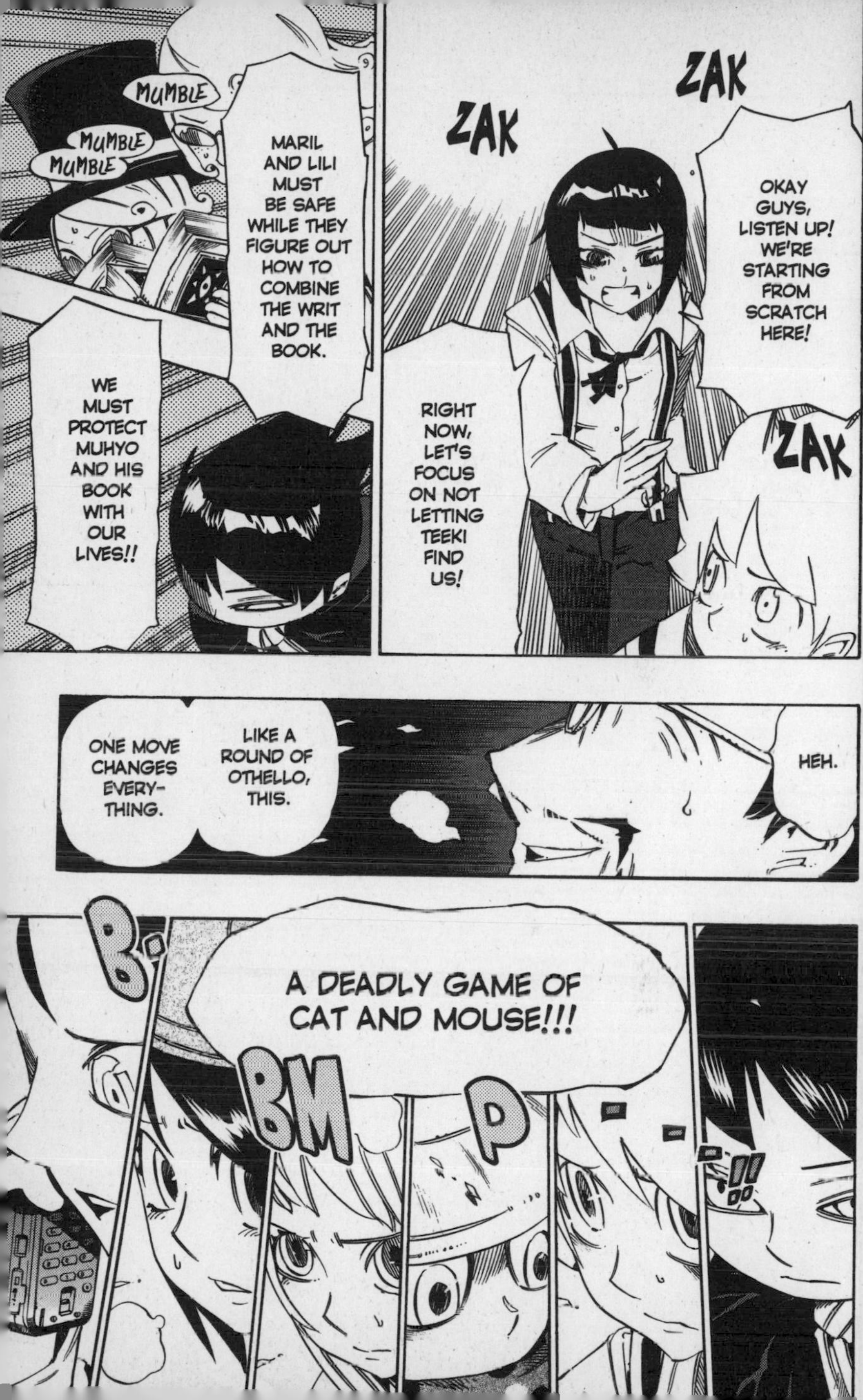
ZAK
OKAY GUYS, LISTEN UP! WE'RE STARTING FROM SCRATCH HERE!
ZAK
ZAK
RIGHT NOW, LET'S FOCUS ON NOT LETTING TEEKI FIND US!
MARIL AND LILI MUST BE SAFE WHILE THEY FIGURE OUT HOW TO COMBINE THE WRIT AND THE BOOK.
MUMBLE
MUMBLE MUMBLE
WE MUST PROTECT MUHYO AND HIS BOOK WITH OUR LIVES!!
HEH.
LIKE A ROUND OF OTHELLO, THIS.
ONE MOVE CHANGES EVERY-THING.
A DEADLY GAME OF CAT AND MOUSE!!!
B-BMP---!!

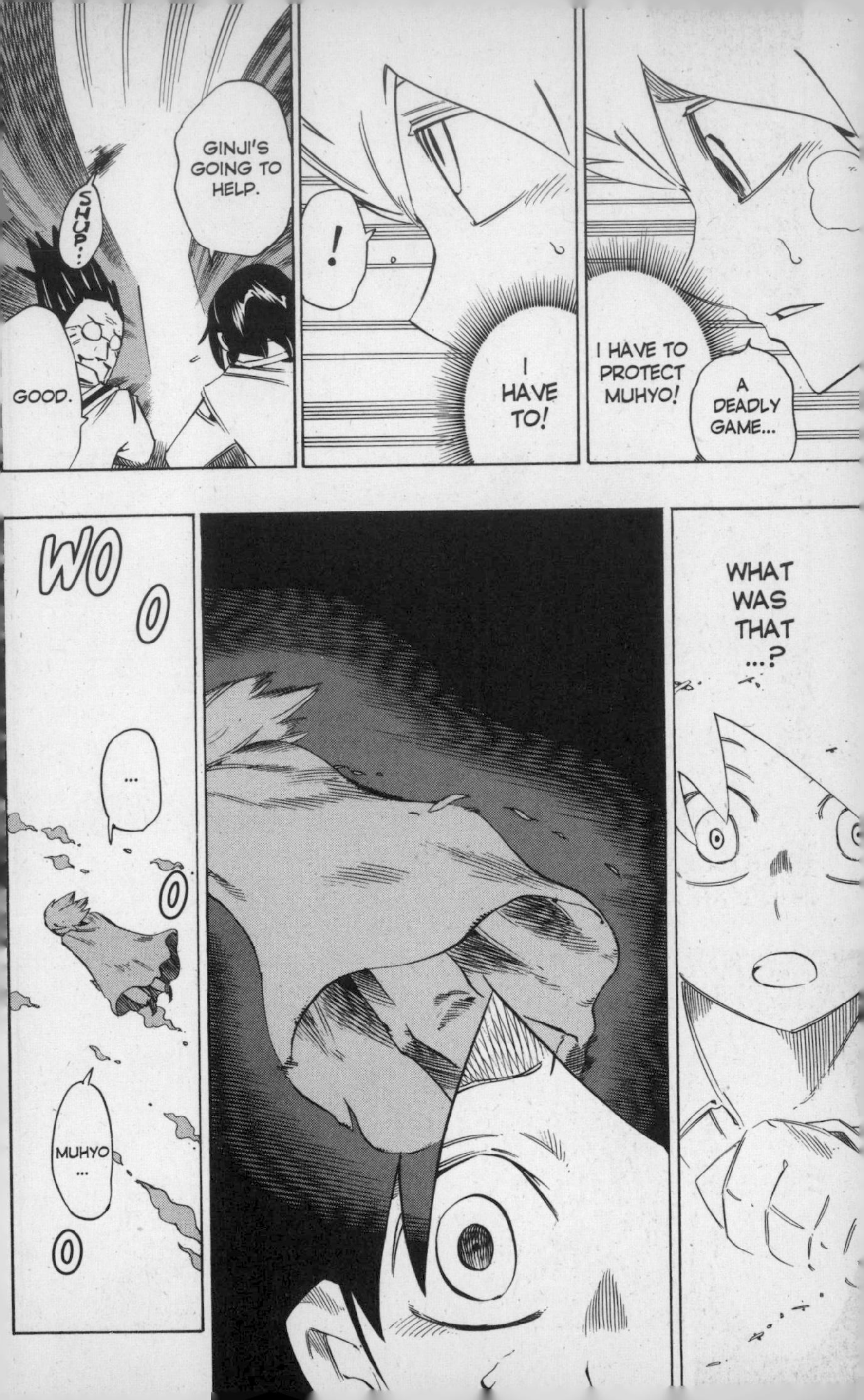
A DEADLY GAME...
I HAVE TO PROTECT MUHYO!
!
I HAVE TO!
GINJI'S GOING TO HELP.
SHUP...
GOOD.
WHAT WAS THAT ...?
WO
O
...
O
MUHYO ...
O

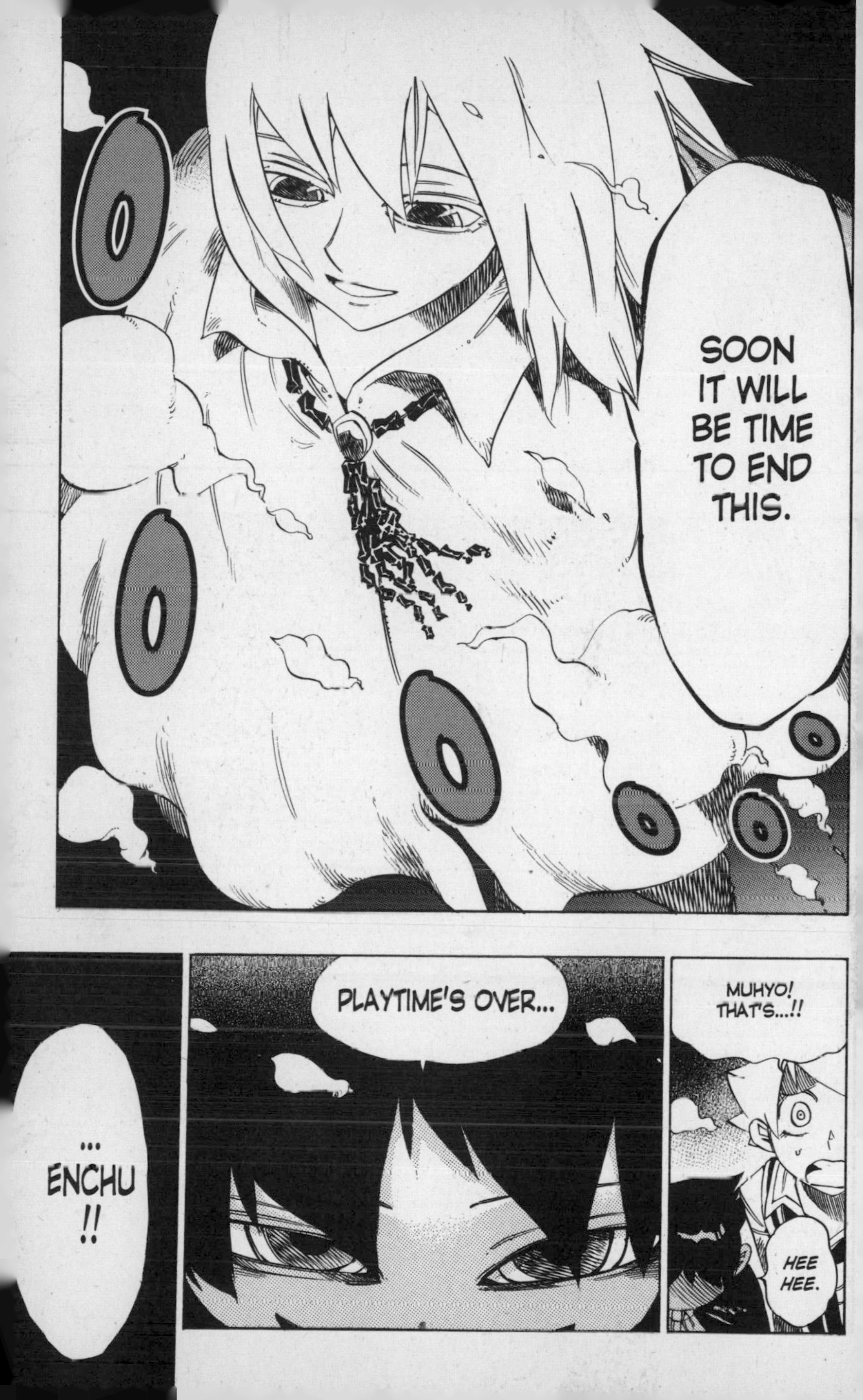
SOON IT WILL BE TIME TO END THIS.
MUHYO! THAT'S...!!
HEE HEE.
PLAYTIME'S OVER...
...ENCHU!!

Q: IN VOLUME 9, MUHYO'S MUNCHING ON THIS BIG RADISH. WHERE'D HE GET IT?!

-A.N., KANAGAWA PREFECTURE

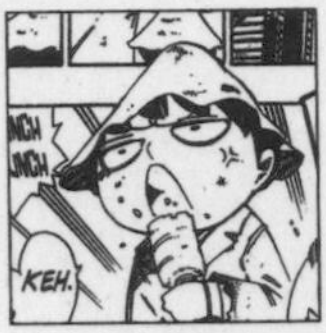
KEH.

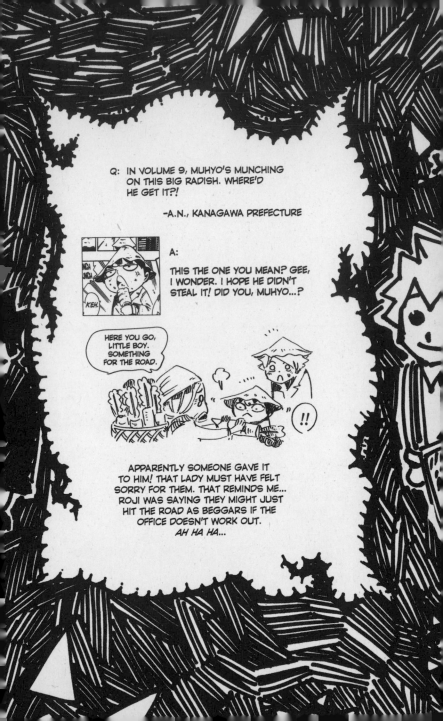

A:

THIS THE ONE YOU MEAN? GEE, I WONDER. I HOPE HE DIDN'T STEAL IT! DID YOU, MUHYO...?

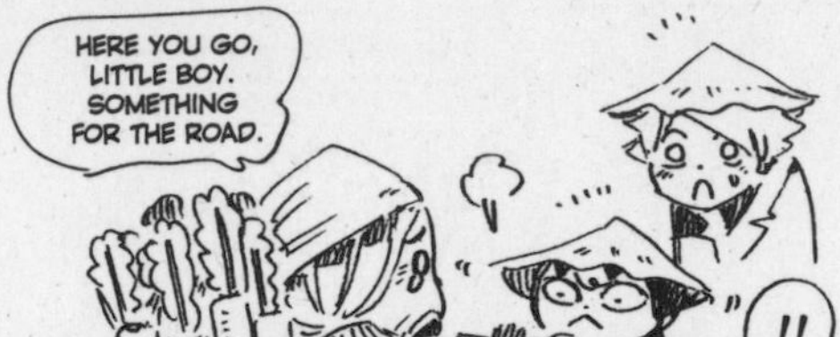
HERE YOU GO, LITTLE BOY. SOMETHING FOR THE ROAD.
!!

APPARENTLY SOMEONE GAVE IT TO HIM! THAT LADY MUST HAVE FELT SORRY FOR THEM. THAT REMINDS ME... ROJI WAS SAYING THEY MIGHT JUST HIT THE ROAD AS BEGGARS IF THE OFFICE DOESN'T WORK OUT. *AH HA HA...*

ARTICLE 110
WHAT GOES AROUND

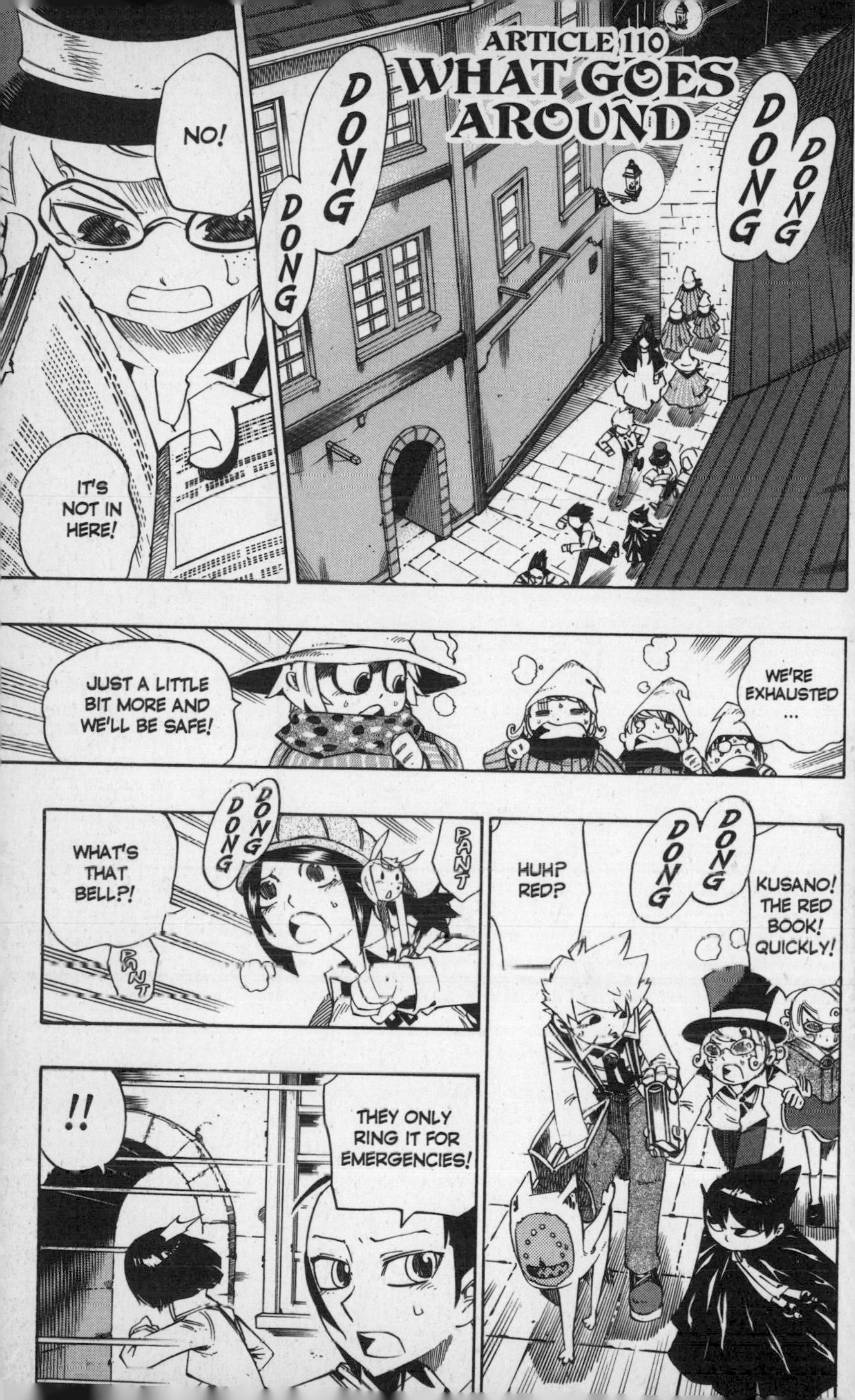

DONG DONG
DONG DONG
NO!
IT'S NOT IN HERE!
WE'RE EXHAUSTED ...
JUST A LITTLE BIT MORE AND WE'LL BE SAFE!
KUSANO! THE RED BOOK! QUICKLY!
DONG DONG
HUH? RED?
PANT
DONG DONG
WHAT'S THAT BELL?!
PANT
THEY ONLY RING IT FOR EMERGENCIES!
!!

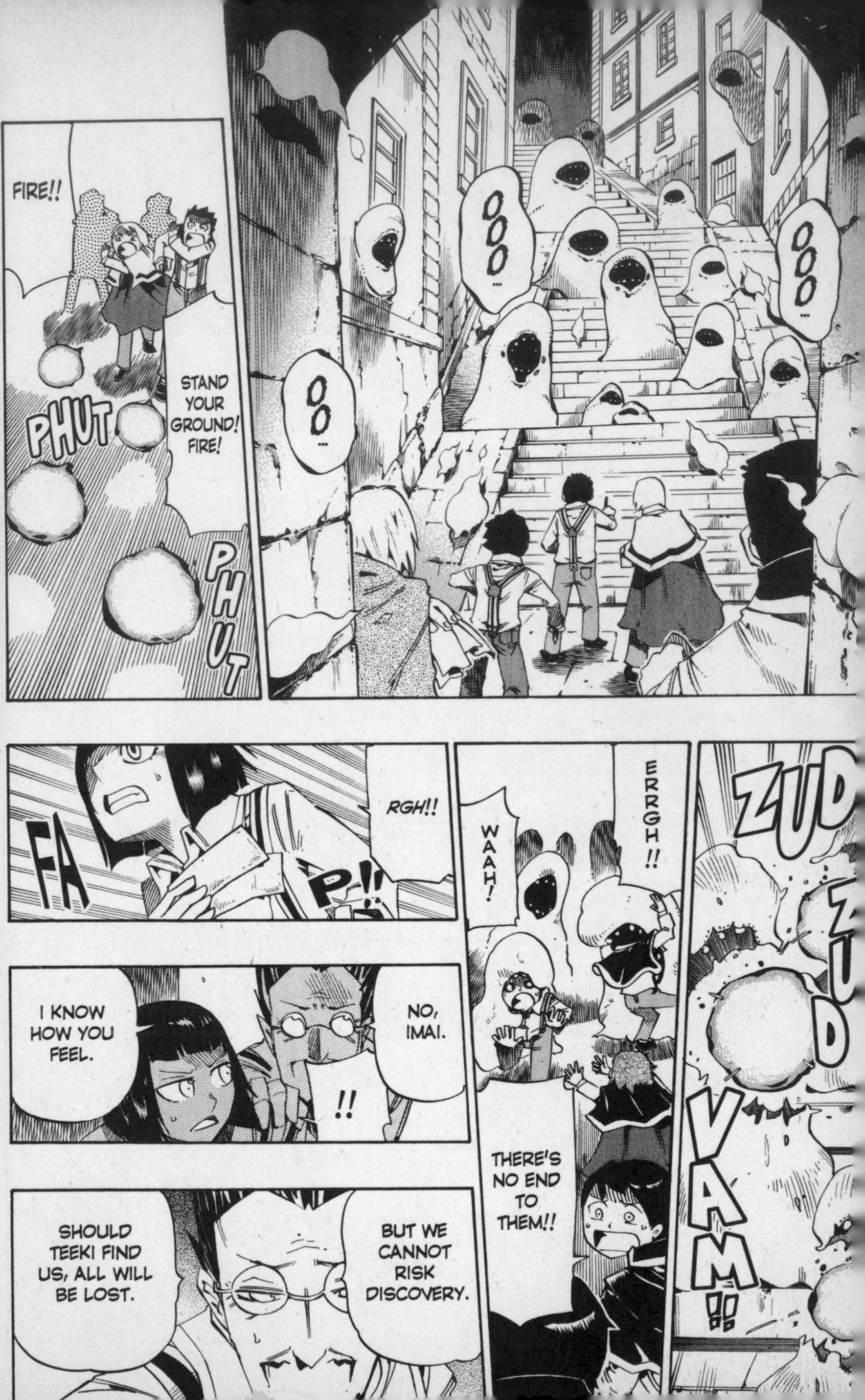
OOO...
OOO...
OO...
FIRE!!
STAND YOUR GROUND! FIRE!
PHUT
PHUT
ZUD
ZUD
ZUD
VAM!!
ERRGH!!
WAAH!
THERE'S NO END TO THEM!!
RGH!!
FA
P!!
NO, IMAI.
I KNOW HOW YOU FEEL.
!!
BUT WE CANNOT RISK DISCOVERY.
SHOULD TEEKI FIND US, ALL WILL BE LOST.

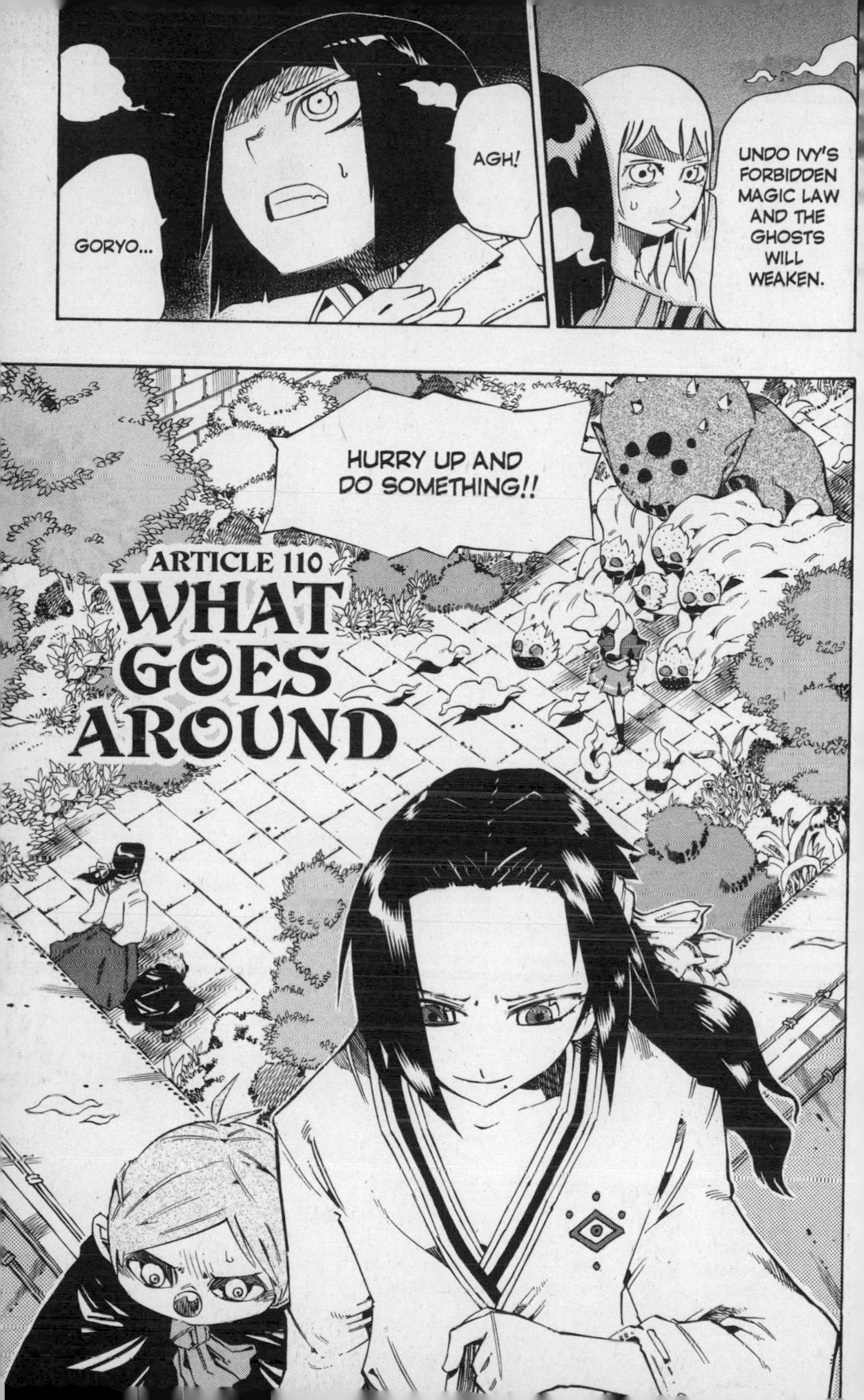
UNDO IVY'S FORBIDDEN MAGIC LAW AND THE GHOSTS WILL WEAKEN.
AGH!
GORYO...
HURRY UP AND DO SOMETHING!!
ARTICLE 110
WHAT GOES AROUND

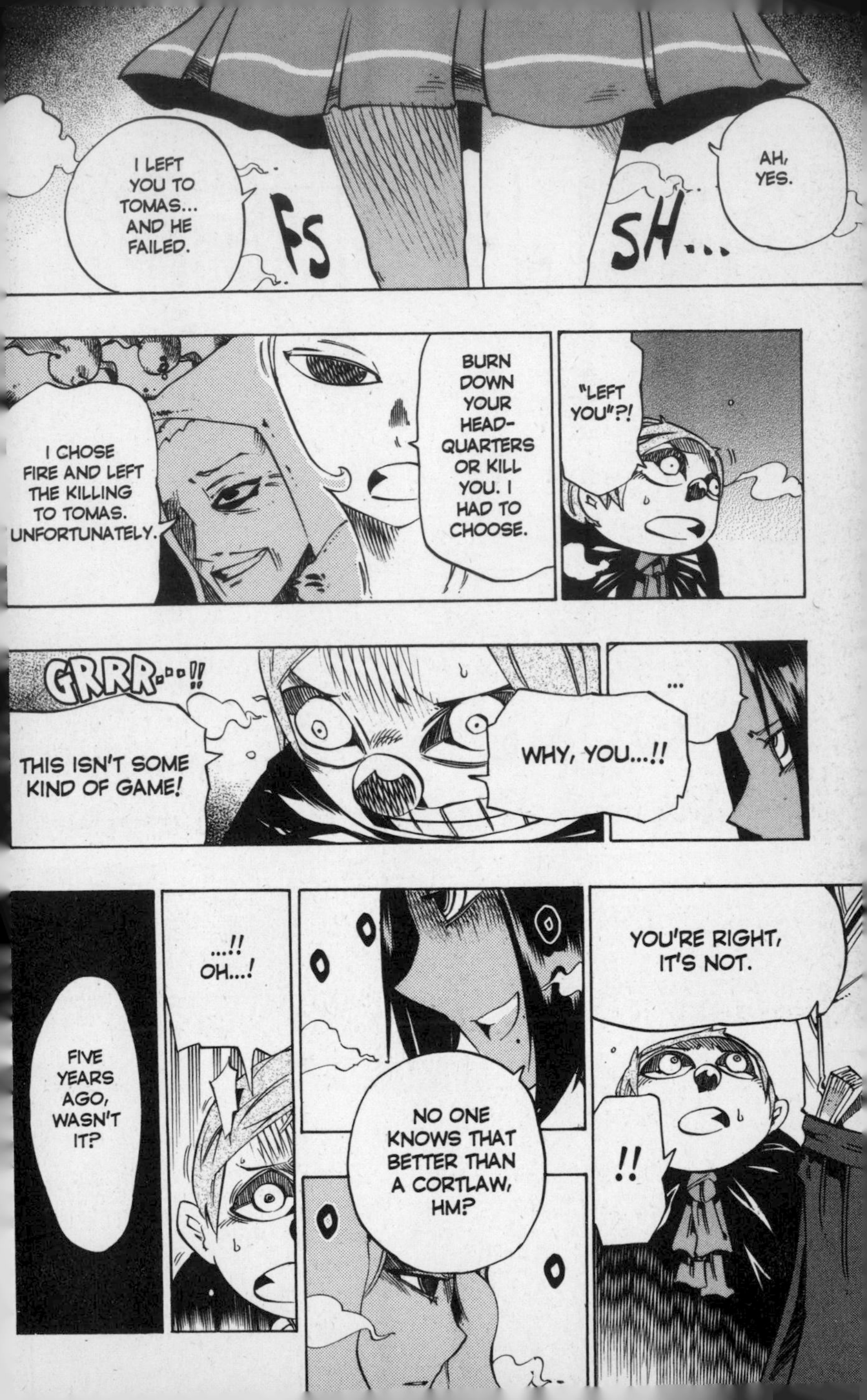
AH, YES.
FS
SH...
I LEFT YOU TO TOMAS... AND HE FAILED.
"LEFT YOU"?!
BURN DOWN YOUR HEAD-QUARTERS OR KILL YOU. I HAD TO CHOOSE.
I CHOSE FIRE AND LEFT THE KILLING TO TOMAS. UNFORTUNATELY.
...
WHY, YOU...!!
GRRR...!!
THIS ISN'T SOME KIND OF GAME!
YOU'RE RIGHT, IT'S NOT.
!!
NO ONE KNOWS THAT BETTER THAN A CORTLAW, HM?
...!! OH...!
FIVE YEARS AGO, WASN'T IT?

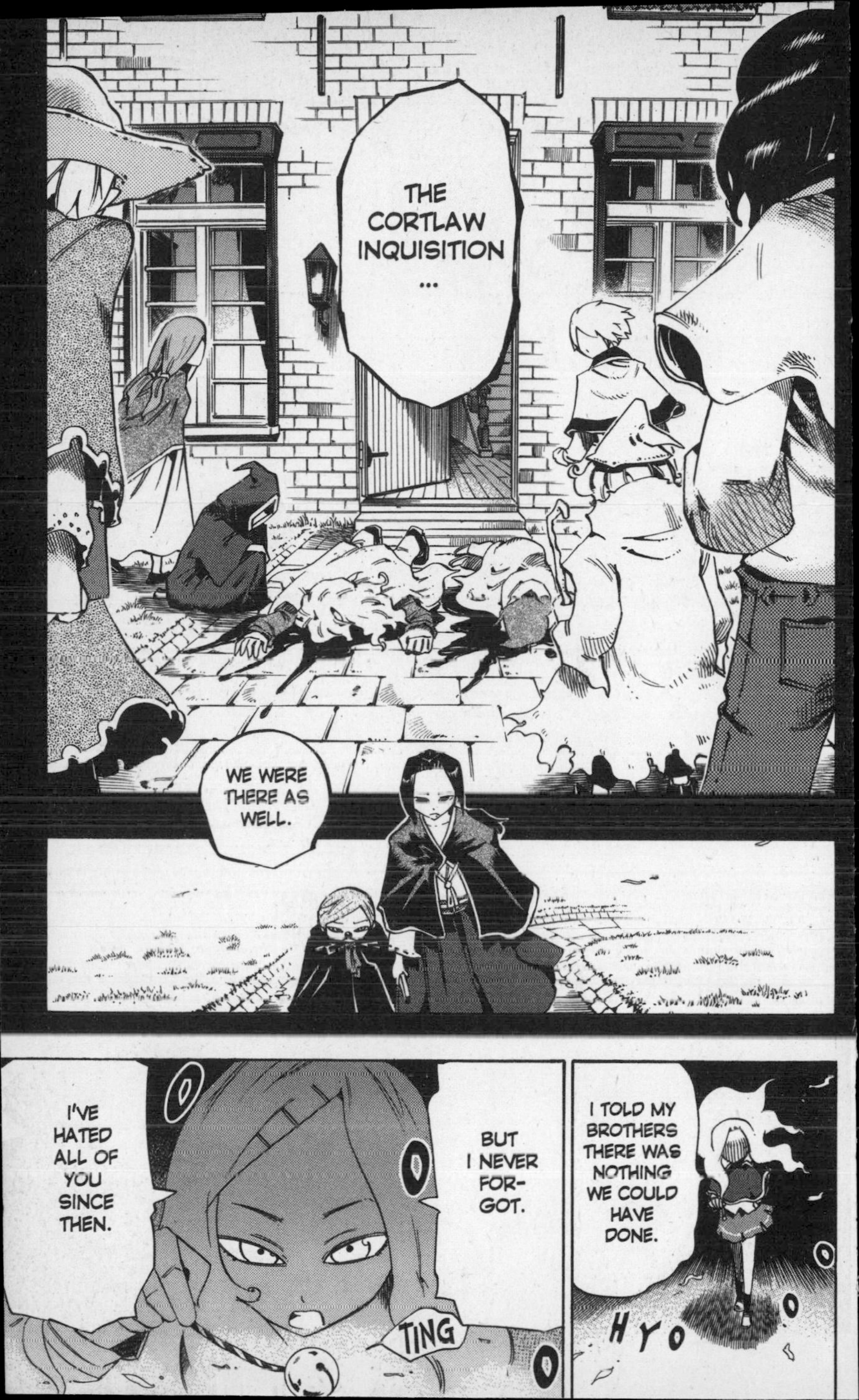
THE CORTLAW INQUISITION ...
WE WERE THERE AS WELL.
I TOLD MY BROTHERS THERE WAS NOTHING WE COULD HAVE DONE.
HYOO
BUT I NEVER FOR-GOT.
I'VE HATED ALL OF YOU SINCE THEN.
TING

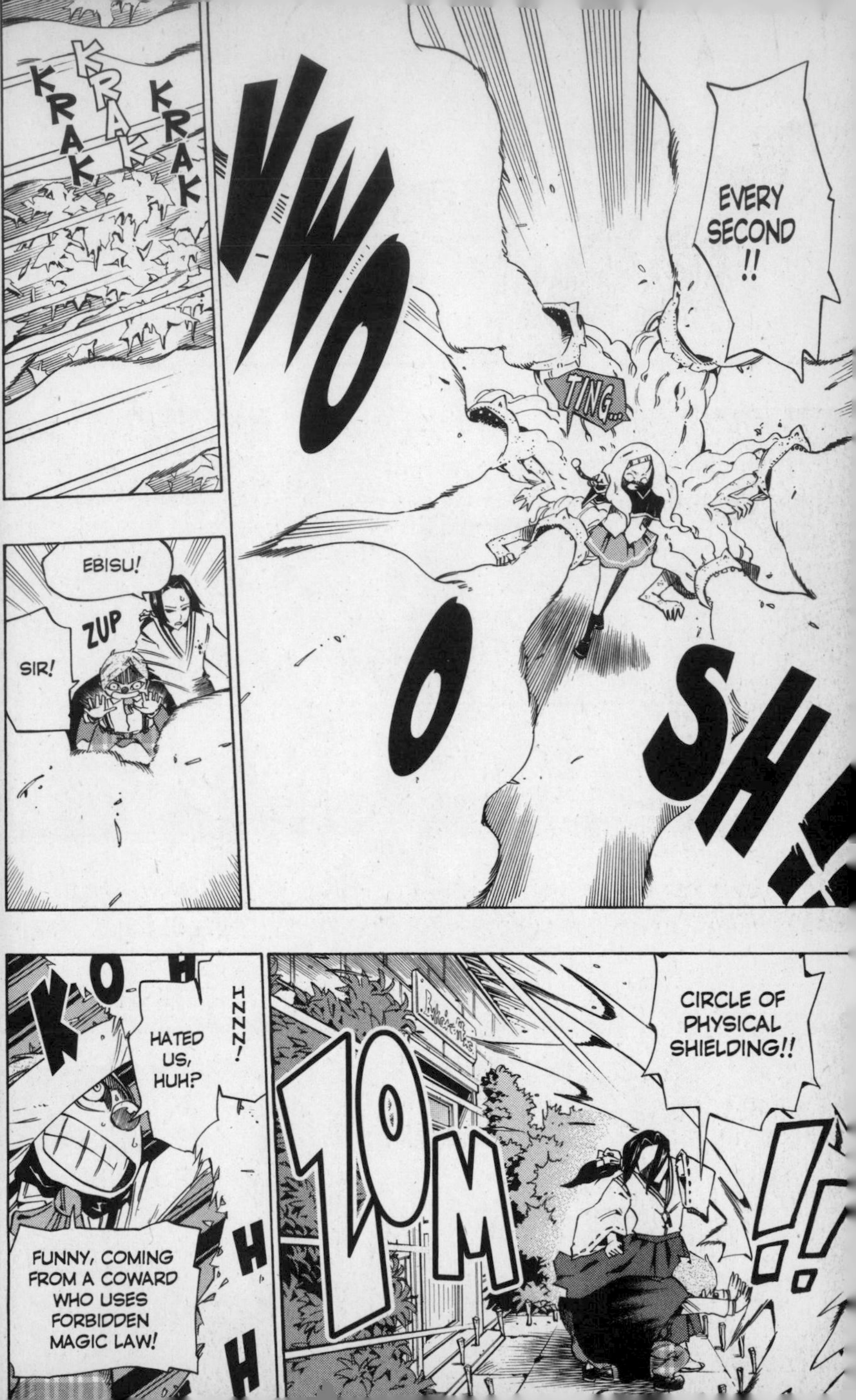
EVERY SECOND!!
VWOOSH!!
TING...
KRAK KRAK KRAK
EBISU!
ZUP
SIR!
CIRCLE OF PHYSICAL SHIELDING!!
ZOM!!
HNNN!
HATED US, HUH?
KOH
FUNNY, COMING FROM A COWARD WHO USES FORBIDDEN MAGIC LAW!
HH

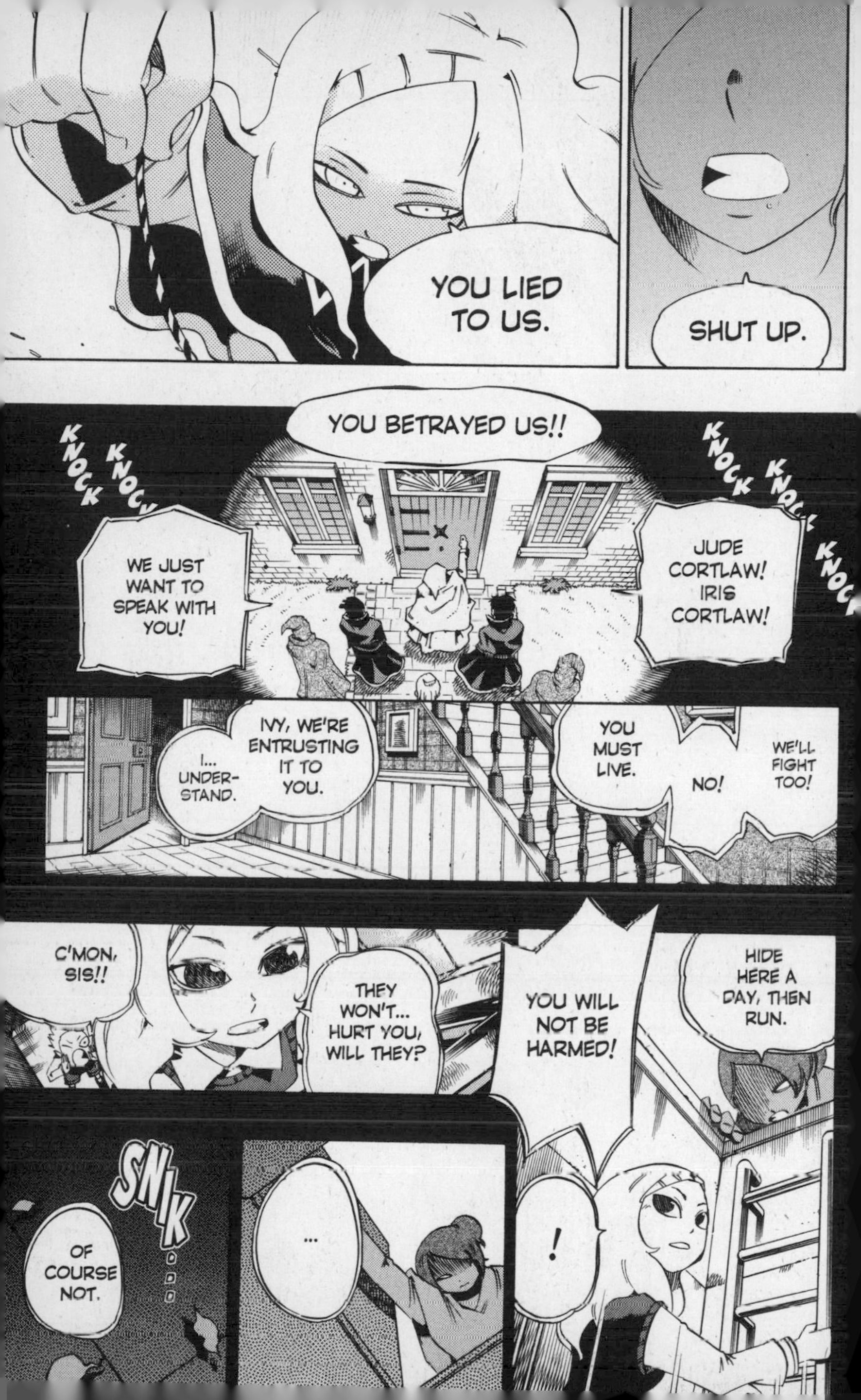
SHUT UP.
YOU LIED TO US.
YOU BETRAYED US!!
KNOCK KNOCK KNOCK
JUDE CORTLAW! IRIS CORTLAW!
KNOCK KNOCK
WE JUST WANT TO SPEAK WITH YOU!
WE'LL FIGHT TOO!
NO!
YOU MUST LIVE.
IVY, WE'RE ENTRUSTING IT TO YOU.
I... UNDERSTAND.
HIDE HERE A DAY, THEN RUN.
YOU WILL NOT BE HARMED!
THEY WON'T... HURT YOU, WILL THEY?
C'MON, SIS!!
!
...
SNIK
OF COURSE NOT.

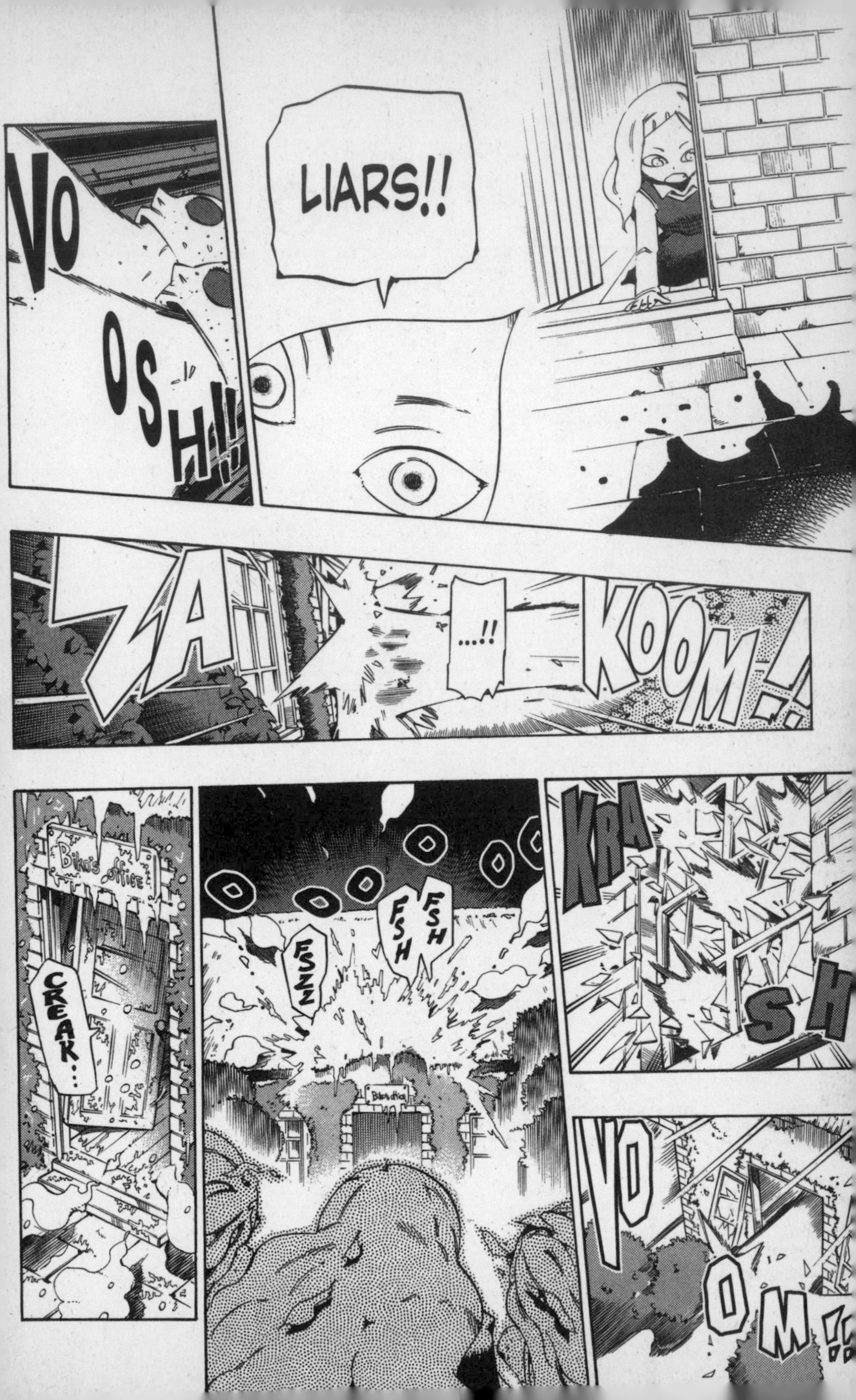
LIARS!!
VOOSH!!
KOOM!!
...!!
ZA
KRASH
VOOM!!
FSH
FSH
FSZZ
Biko's office
CREAK...

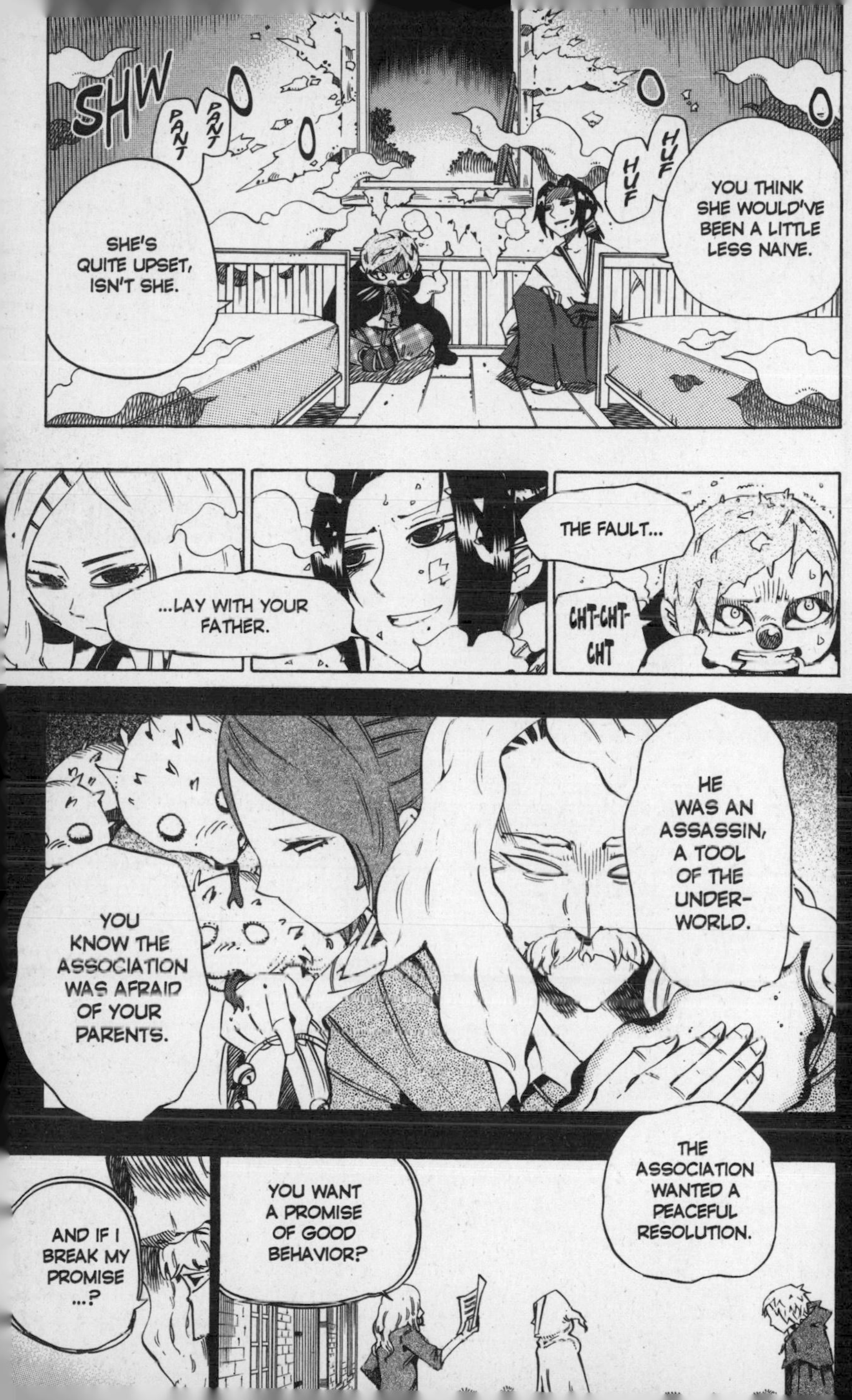
YOU THINK SHE WOULD'VE BEEN A LITTLE LESS NAIVE.
HUF HUF
O O O
SHE'S QUITE UPSET, ISN'T SHE.
PANT PANT
SHW O O
THE FAULT...
CHT-CHT-CHT
...LAY WITH YOUR FATHER.
HE WAS AN ASSASSIN, A TOOL OF THE UNDER-WORLD.
YOU KNOW THE ASSOCIATION WAS AFRAID OF YOUR PARENTS.
THE ASSOCIATION WANTED A PEACEFUL RESOLUTION.
YOU WANT A PROMISE OF GOOD BEHAVIOR?
AND IF I BREAK MY PROMISE ...?

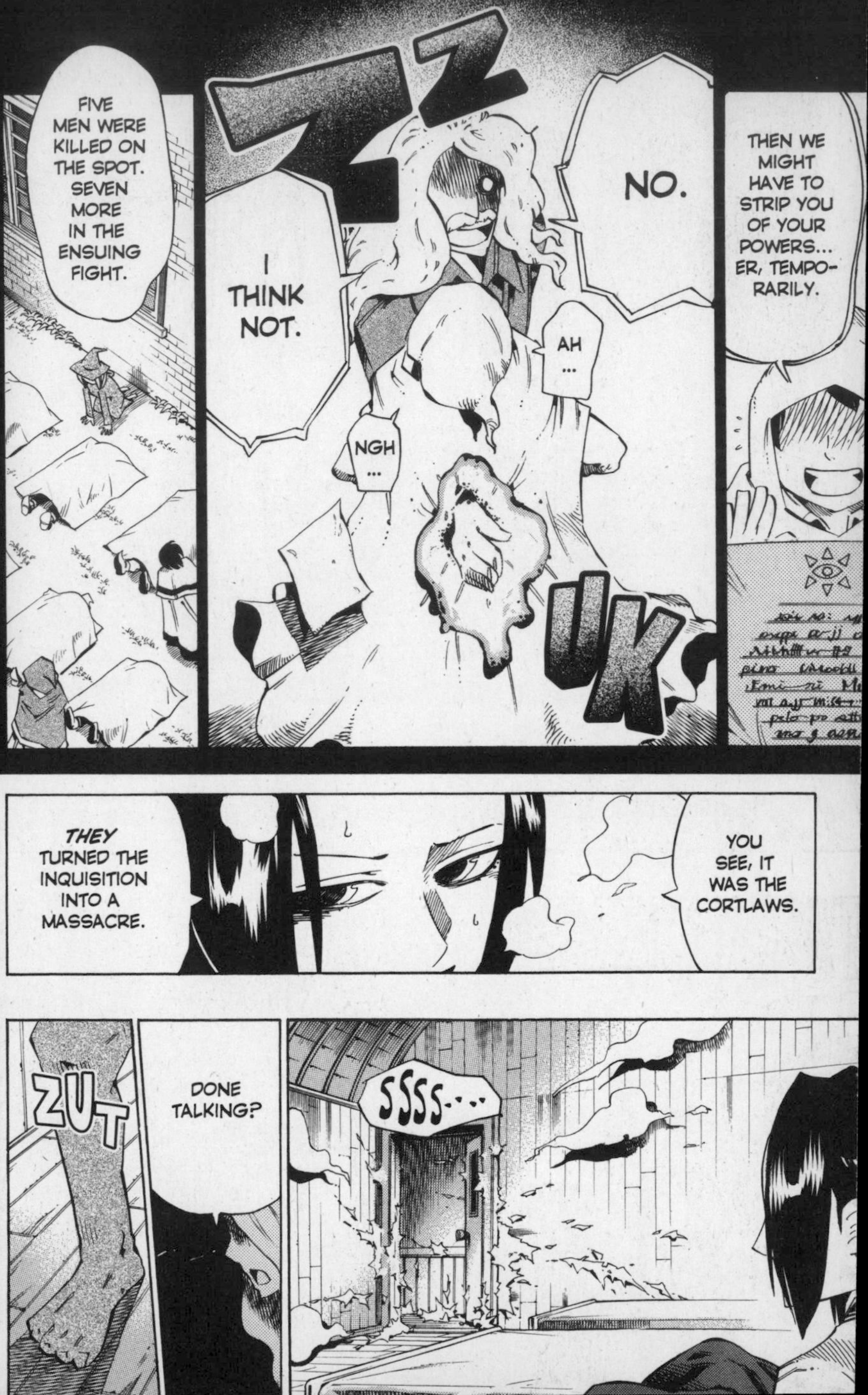
THEN WE MIGHT HAVE TO STRIP YOU OF YOUR POWERS... ER, TEMPO-RARILY.
NO.
ZZ
I THINK NOT.
AH ...
NGH ...
UK
FIVE MEN WERE KILLED ON THE SPOT. SEVEN MORE IN THE ENSUING FIGHT.
YOU SEE, IT WAS THE CORTLAWS.
THEY TURNED THE INQUISITION INTO A MASSACRE.
SSSS....
DONE TALKING?
ZUT

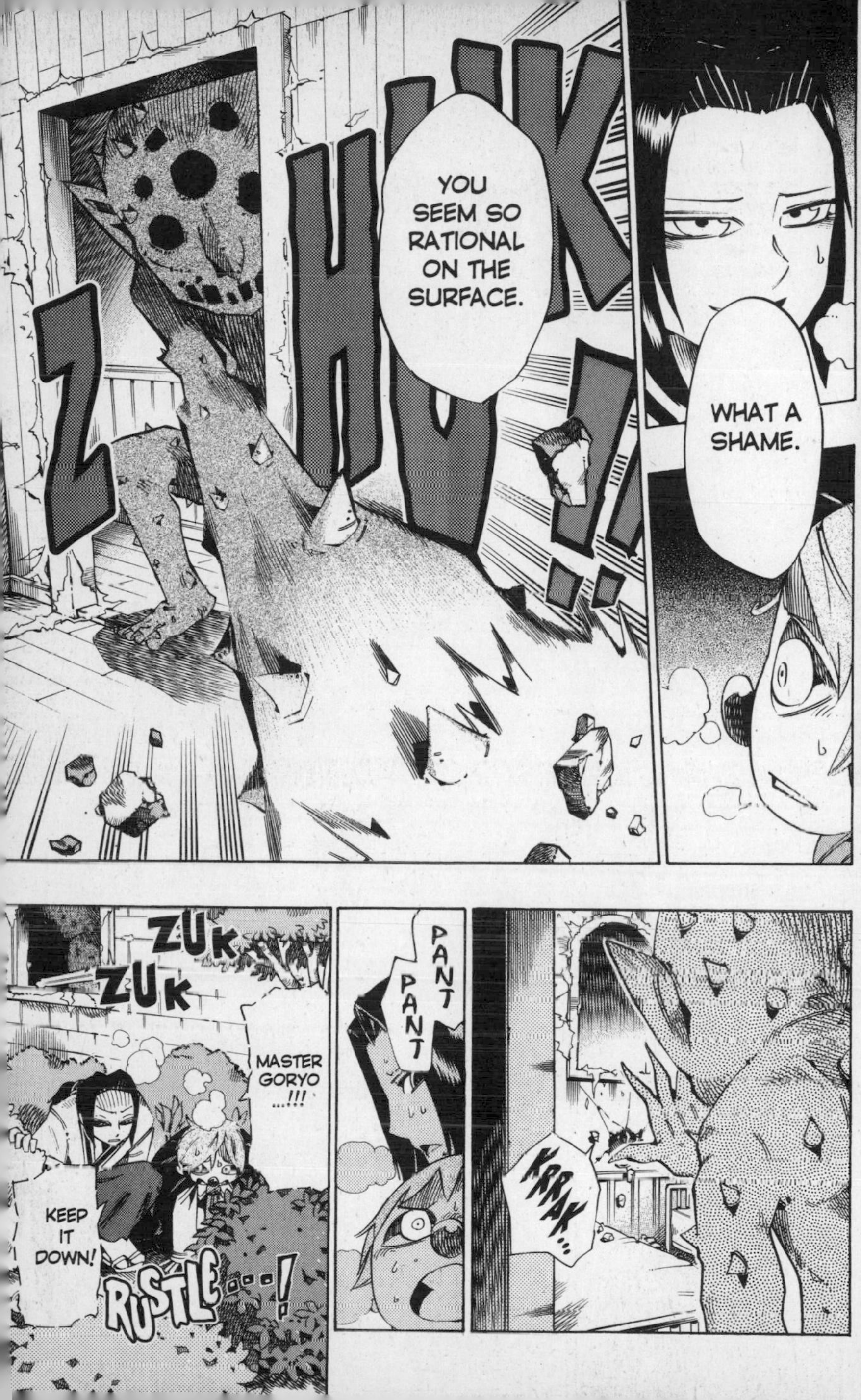
WHAT A SHAME.
ZHUK!!
YOU SEEM SO RATIONAL ON THE SURFACE.
KRRAK...
PANT PANT
ZUK ZUK
MASTER GORYO ...!!!
KEEP IT DOWN!
RUSTLE...!

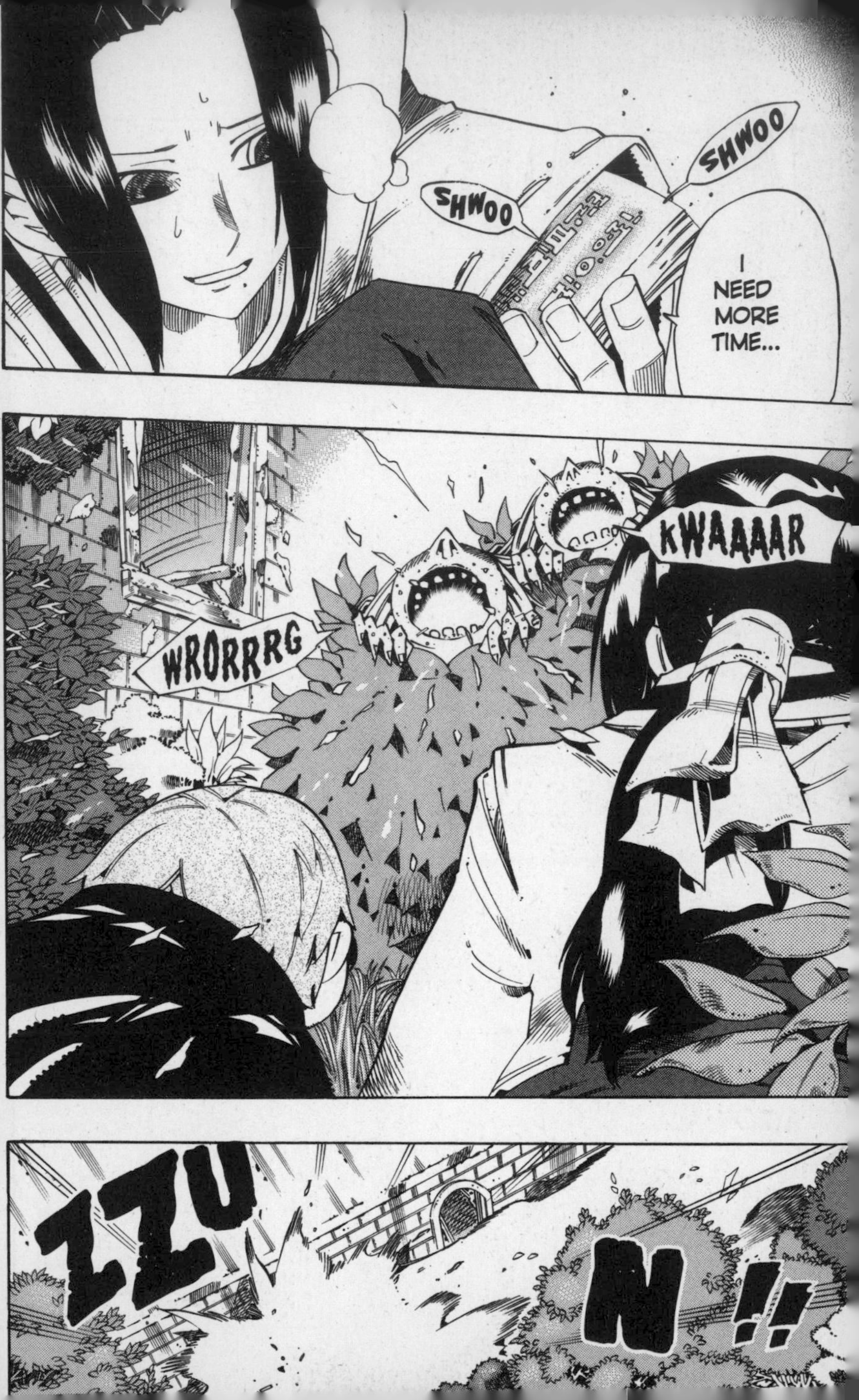
SHWOO
SHWOO
I NEED MORE TIME...
KWAAAAR
WRORRRG
ZZU
N!!

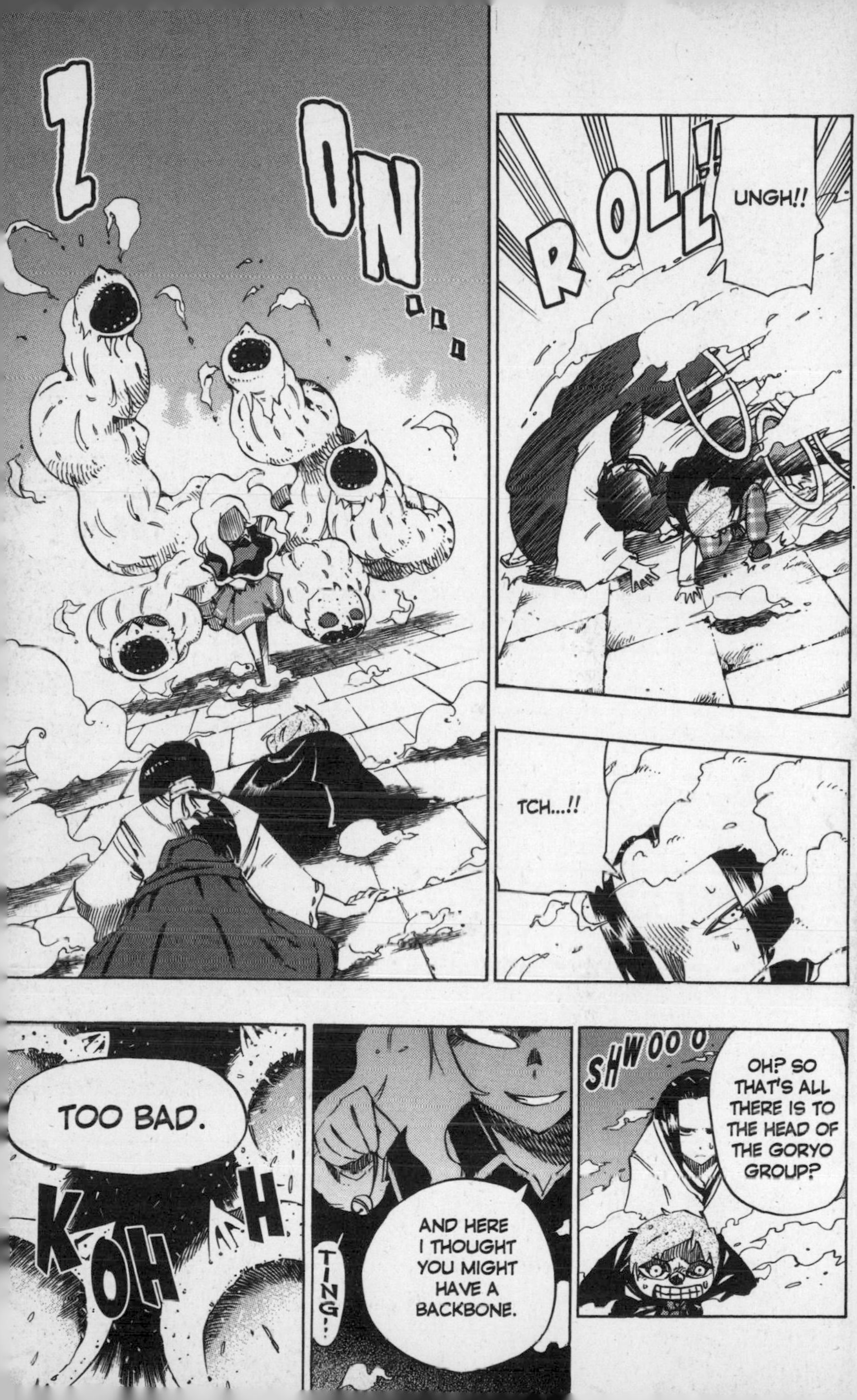
ROLL!!
UNGH!!
TCH...!!
ZOON
SHWOOO
OH? SO THAT'S ALL THERE IS TO THE HEAD OF THE GORYO GROUP?
TING!
AND HERE I THOUGHT YOU MIGHT HAVE A BACKBONE.
TOO BAD.
KOHH

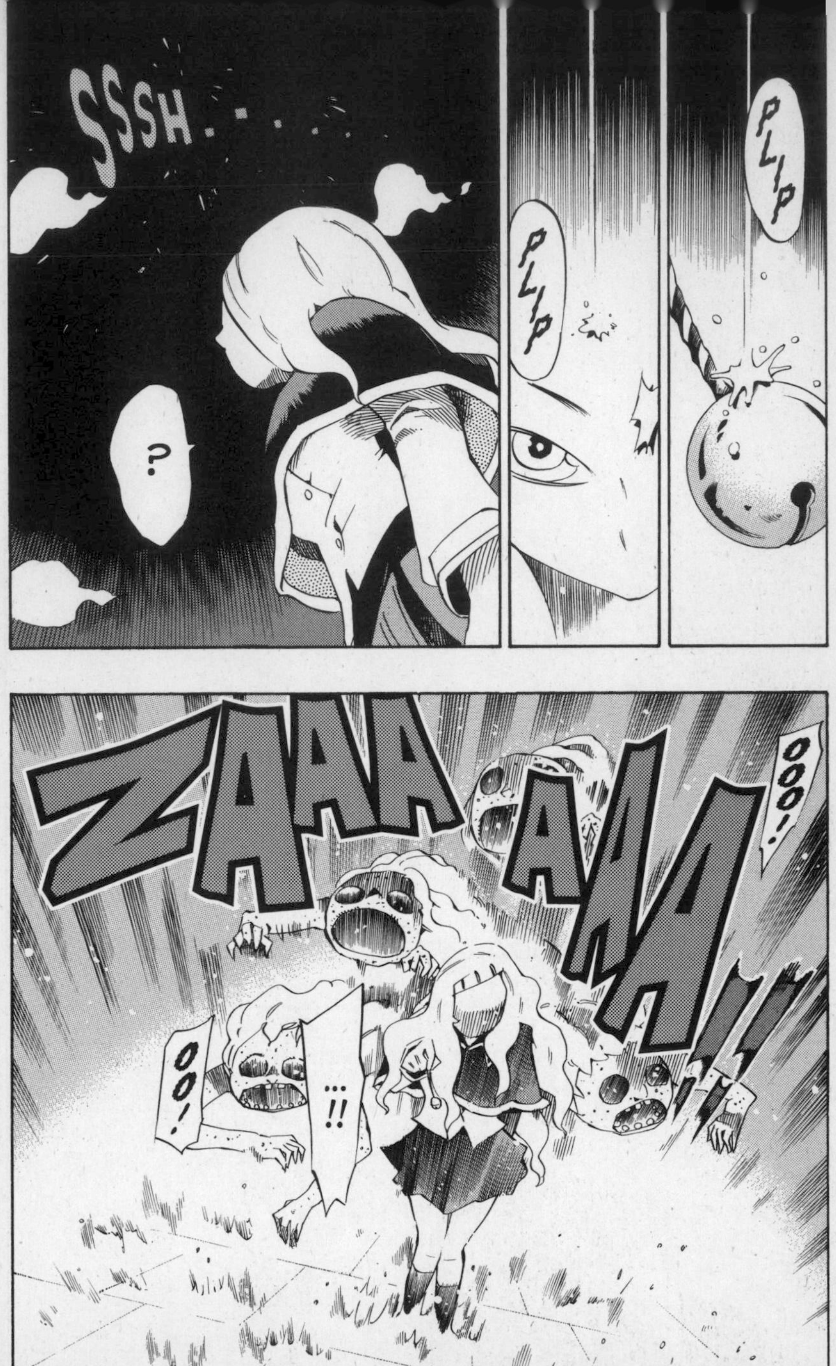
PLIP
PLIP
?
SSSH. . . .
ZAAAAAA!!
OOO!
...!!
OO!

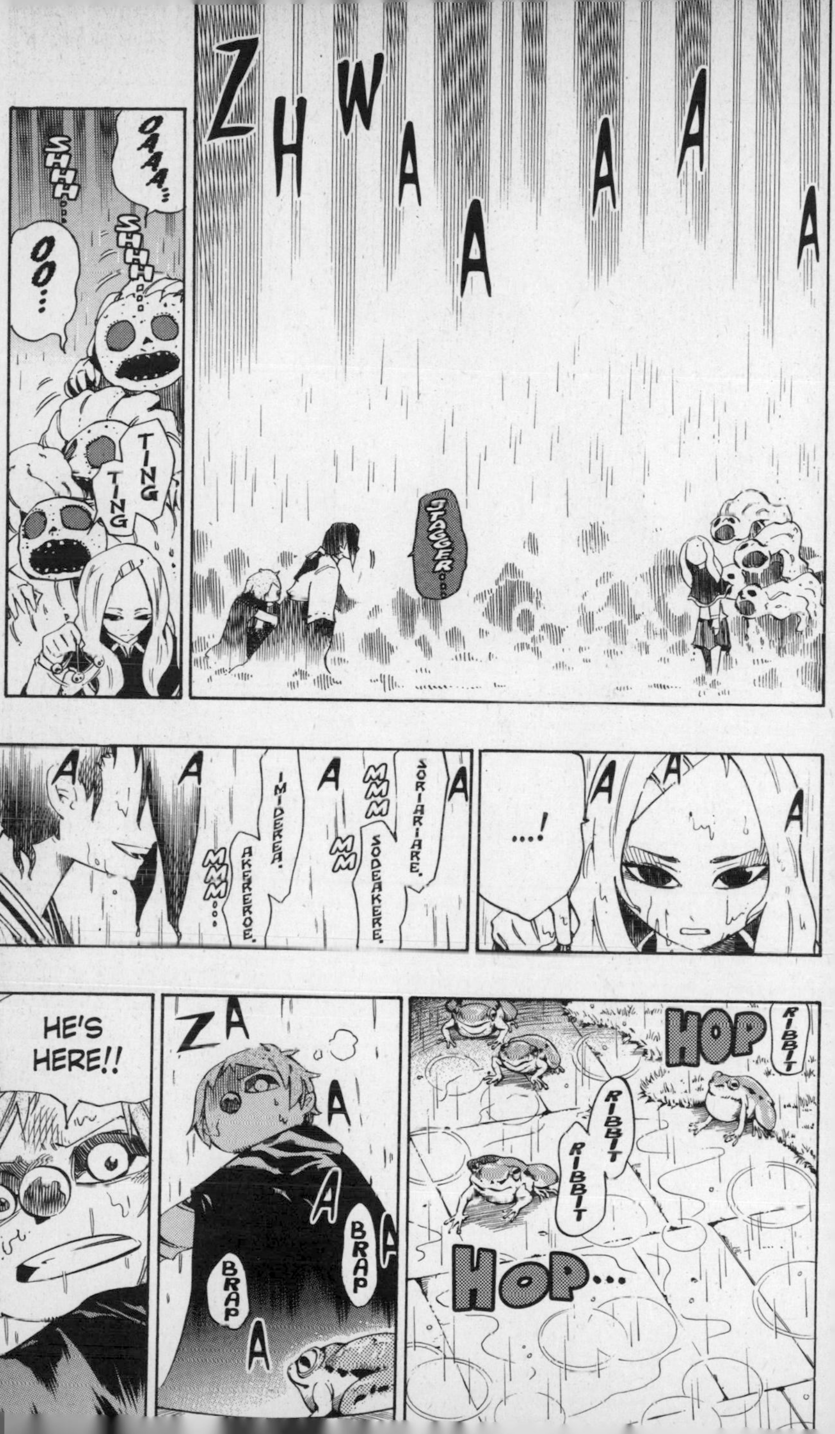

ZHWAAAAAAA
STAGGER...
OAAAA...
SHHH...
SHHHH...
OO...
TING
TING
AAA
...!
AAAA
SORIARIARE.
SODEAKERE.
MMM
MM
IMIDEREA.
AKEREROE.
MMM...
HOP
RIBBIT
RIBBIT
RIBBIT
HOP...
ZA
A
A
BRAP
BRAP
A
A
HE'S HERE!!

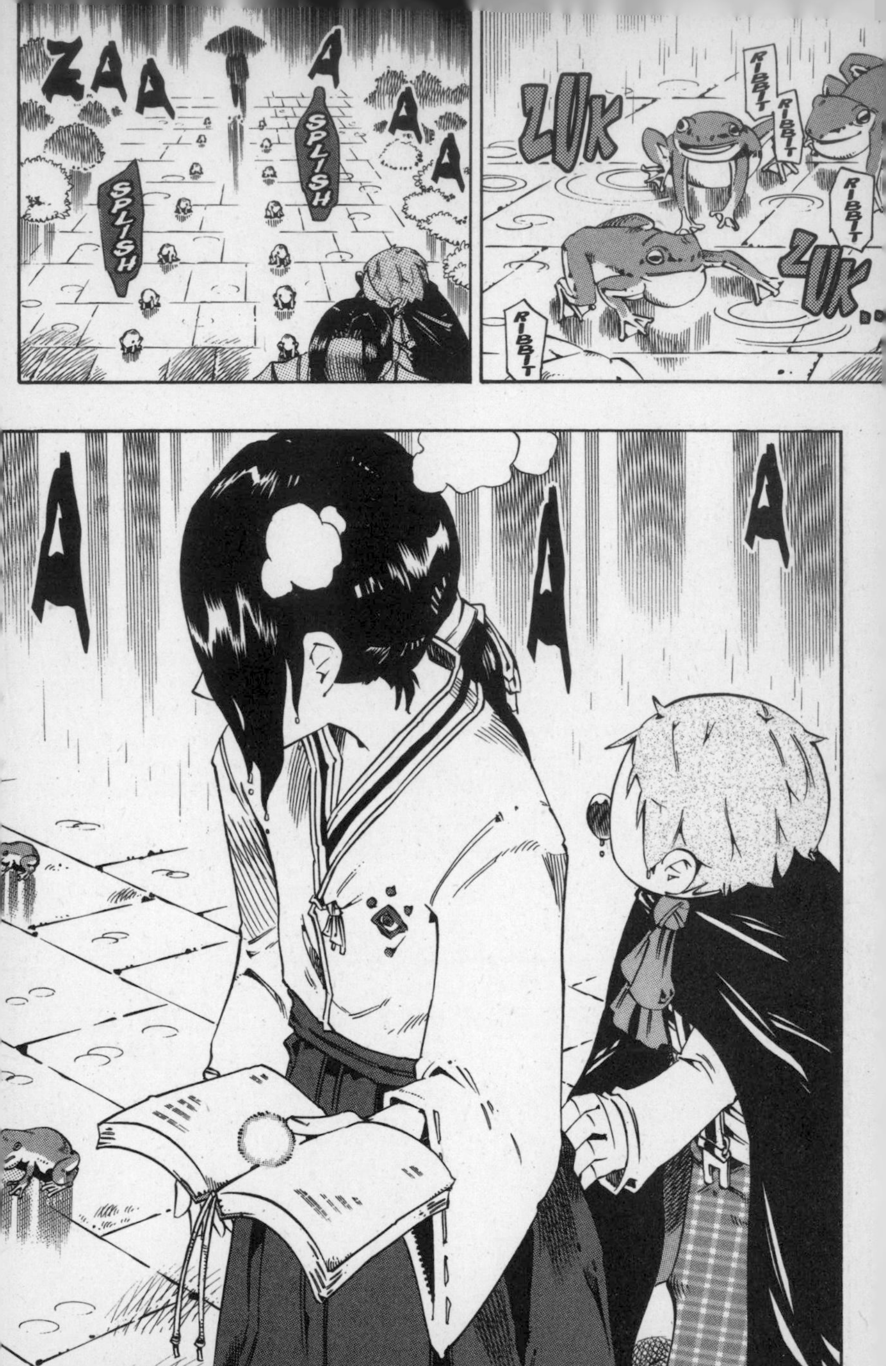
RIBBIT
RIBBIT
ZUK
RIBBIT
ZUK..
RIBBIT
ZAA
A
A
A
SPLISH
SPLISH
A
A
A

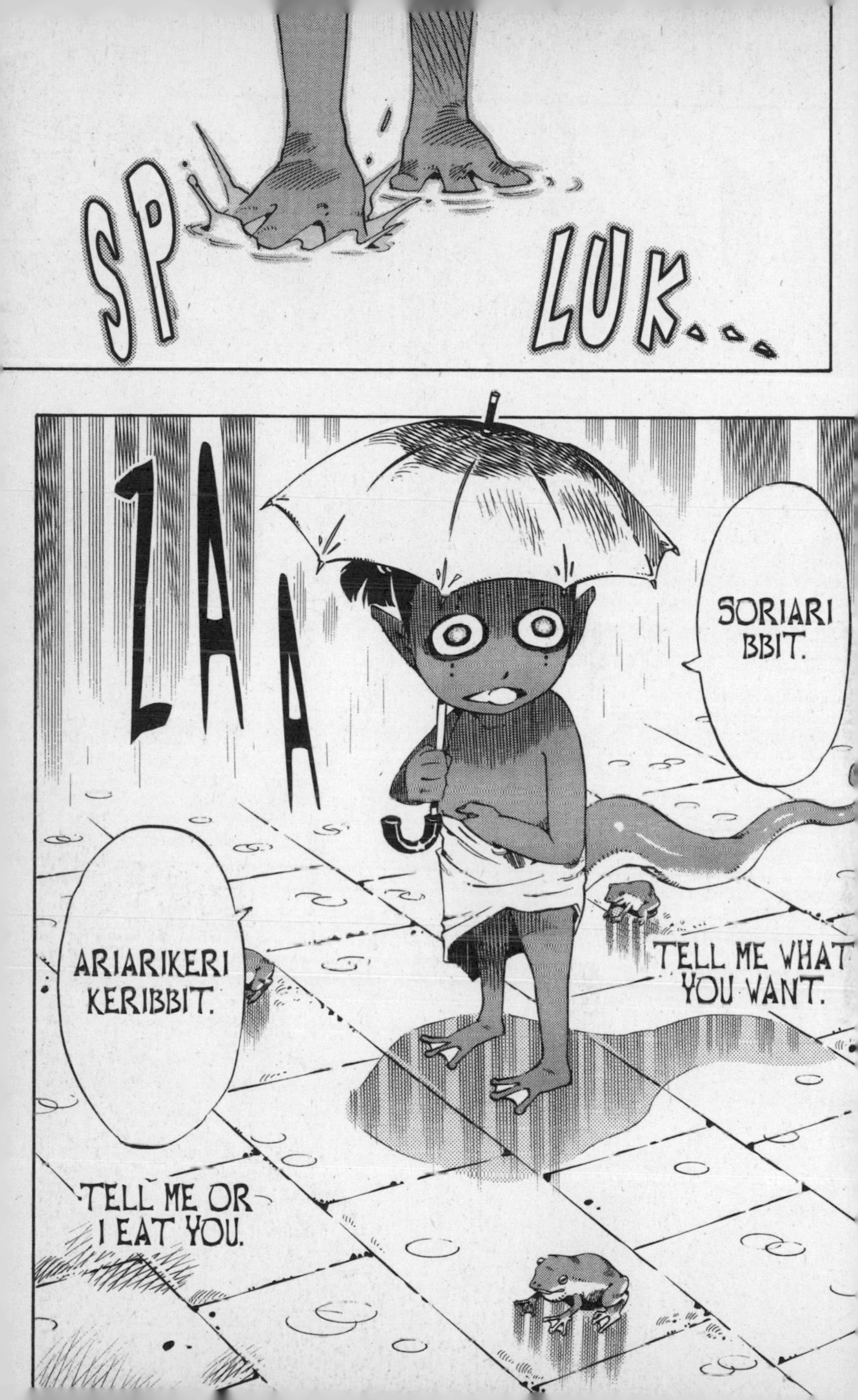
SPLUK...
SORIARI BBIT.
ZAA
TELL ME WHAT YOU WANT.
ARIARIKERI KERIBBIT.
TELL ME OR I EAT YOU.

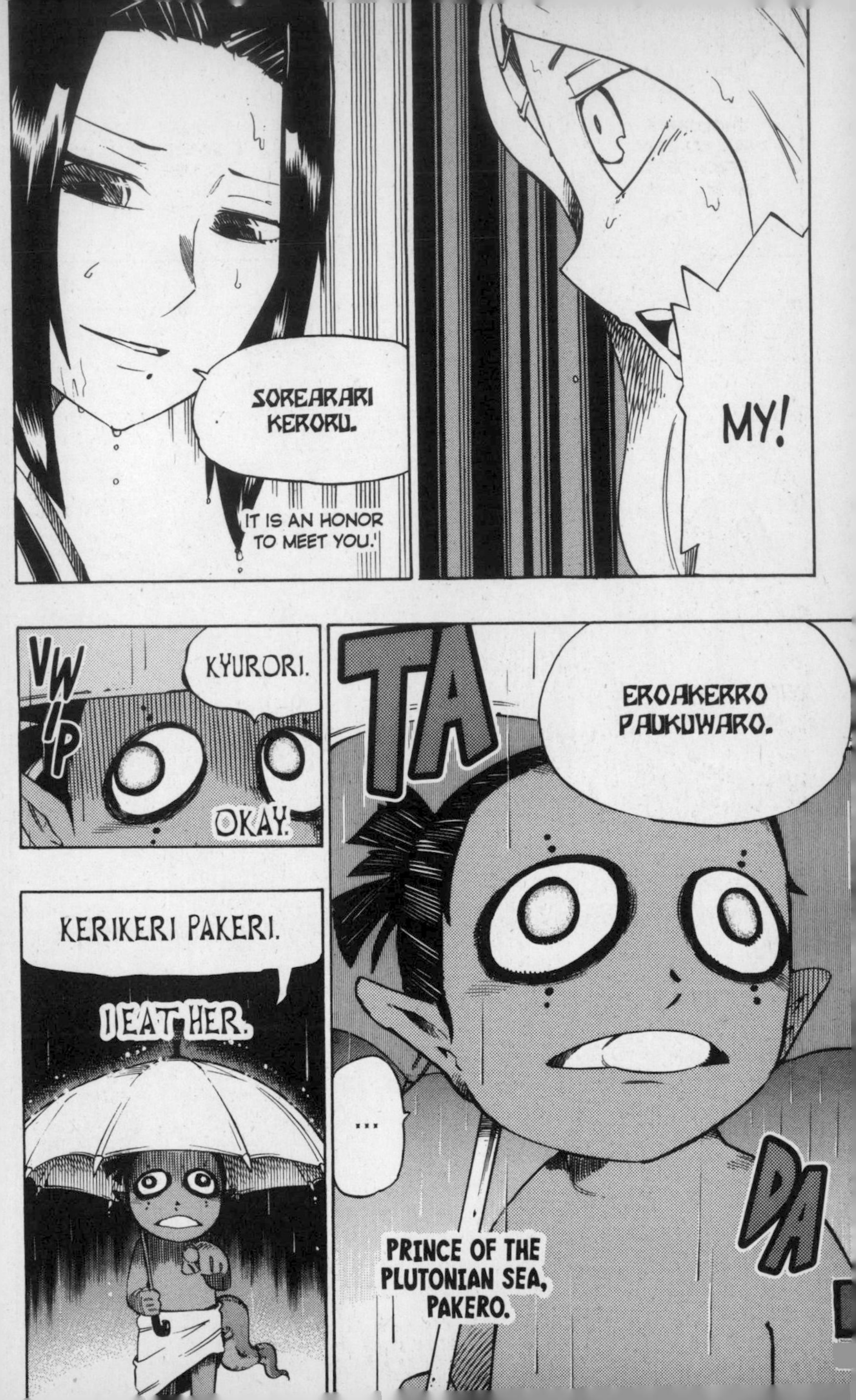
MY!
SOREARARI KERORU.
IT IS AN HONOR TO MEET YOU.
TA
EROAKERRO PAUKUWARO.
...
DA
PRINCE OF THE PLUTONIAN SEA, PAKERO.
VWIP
KYURORI.
OKAY.
KERIKERI PAKERI.
I EAT HER.

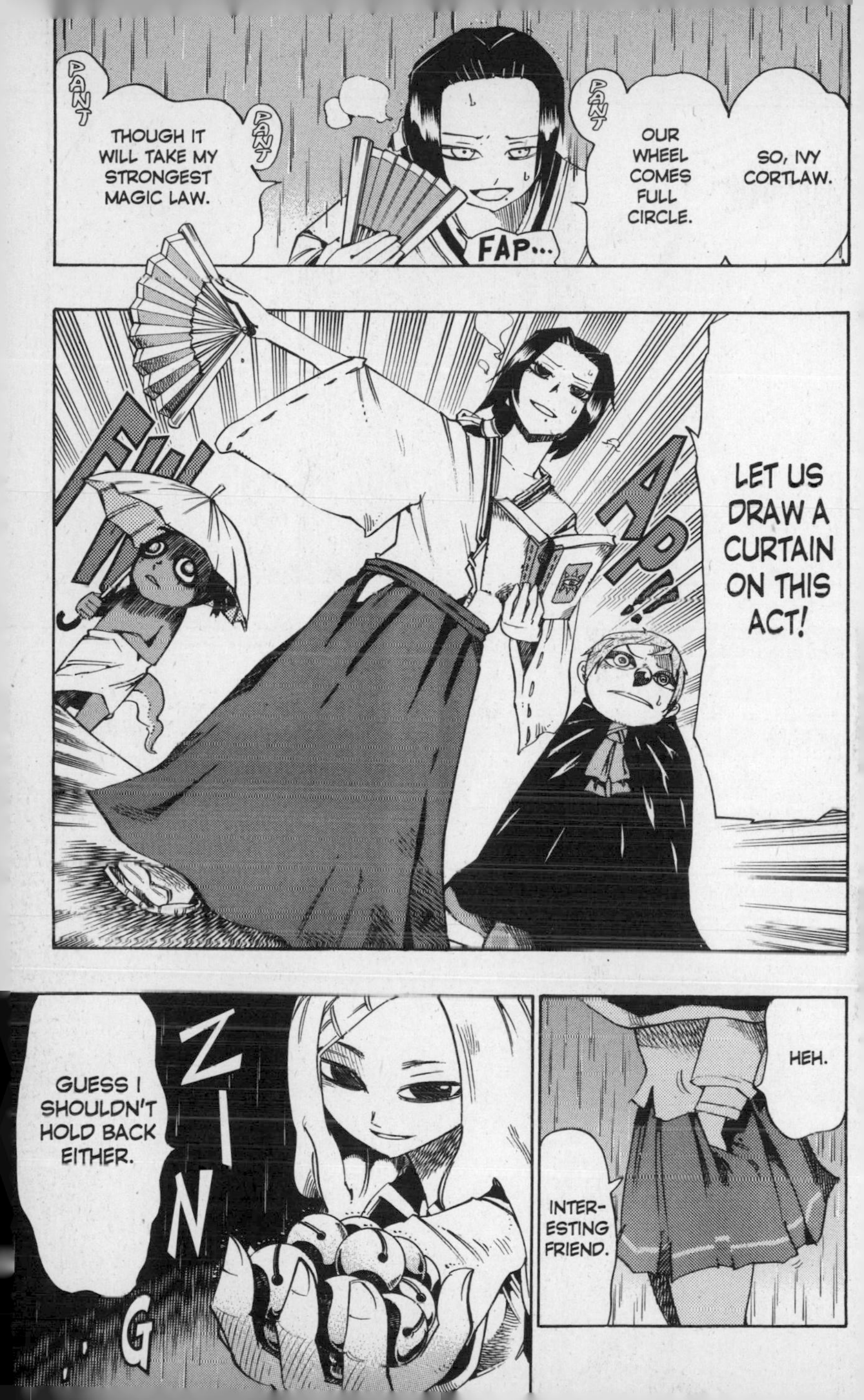
SO, IVY CORTLAW.
PANT
OUR WHEEL COMES FULL CIRCLE.
PANT
PANT
THOUGH IT WILL TAKE MY STRONGEST MAGIC LAW.
FAP...
LET US DRAW A CURTAIN ON THIS ACT!
FWAP!!
HEH.
INTER-ESTING FRIEND.
GUESS I SHOULDN'T HOLD BACK EITHER.
ZING

Muhyo & Roji's
Bureau of Supernatural Investigation
BSI

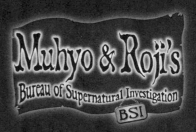

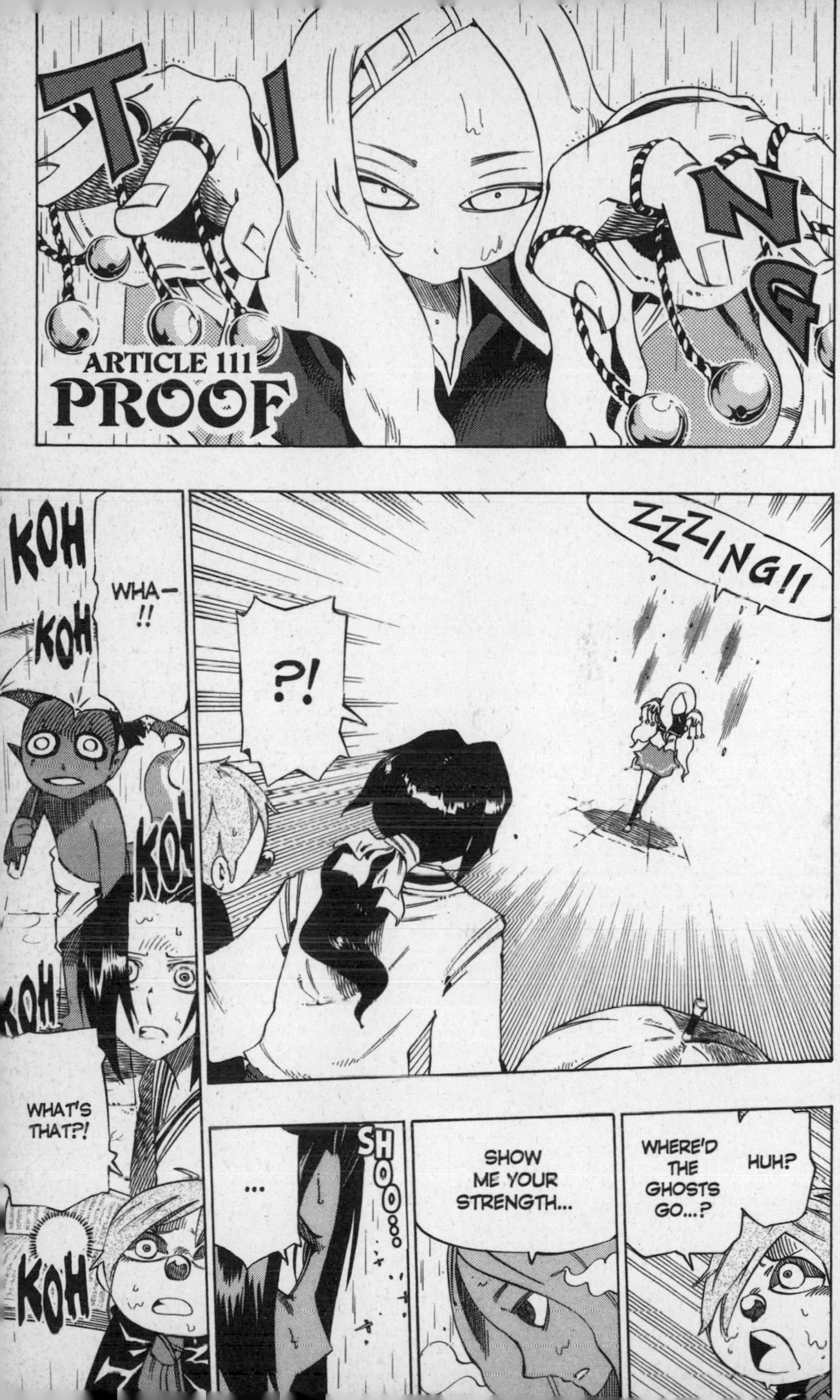
TING
ARTICLE 111
PROOF
ZZZING!!
?!
HUH?
WHERE'D THE GHOSTS GO...?
SHOW ME YOUR STRENGTH...
SHOOOO...
...
WHA— !!
KOH KOH KOH KOH
WHAT'S THAT?!
KOH

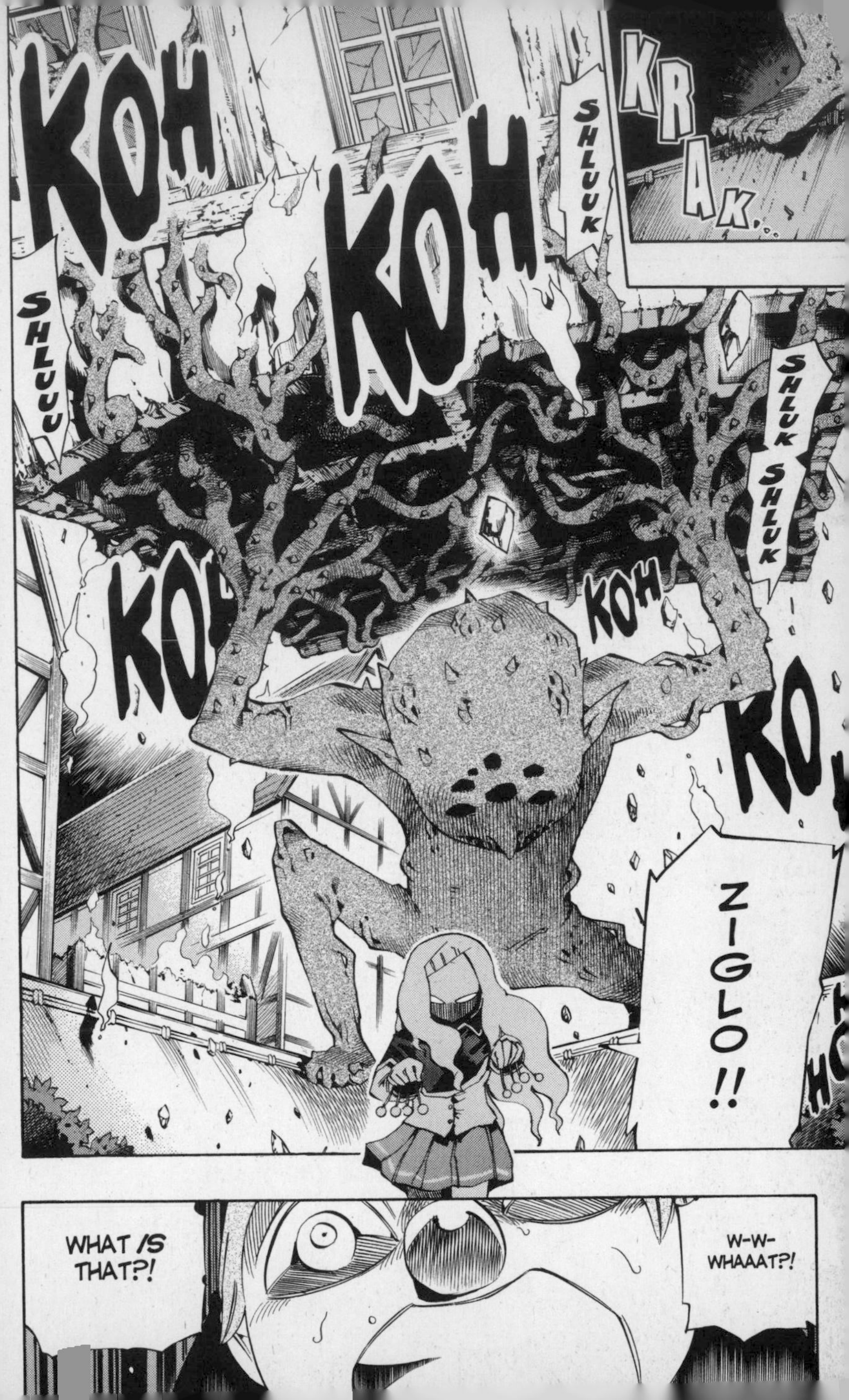
KRAK...
SHLUUK
KOH
KOH
SHLUK SHLUK
SHLUUU
KOH
KO
KO
ZIGLO!!
W-W-WHAAAT?!
WHAT IS THAT?!

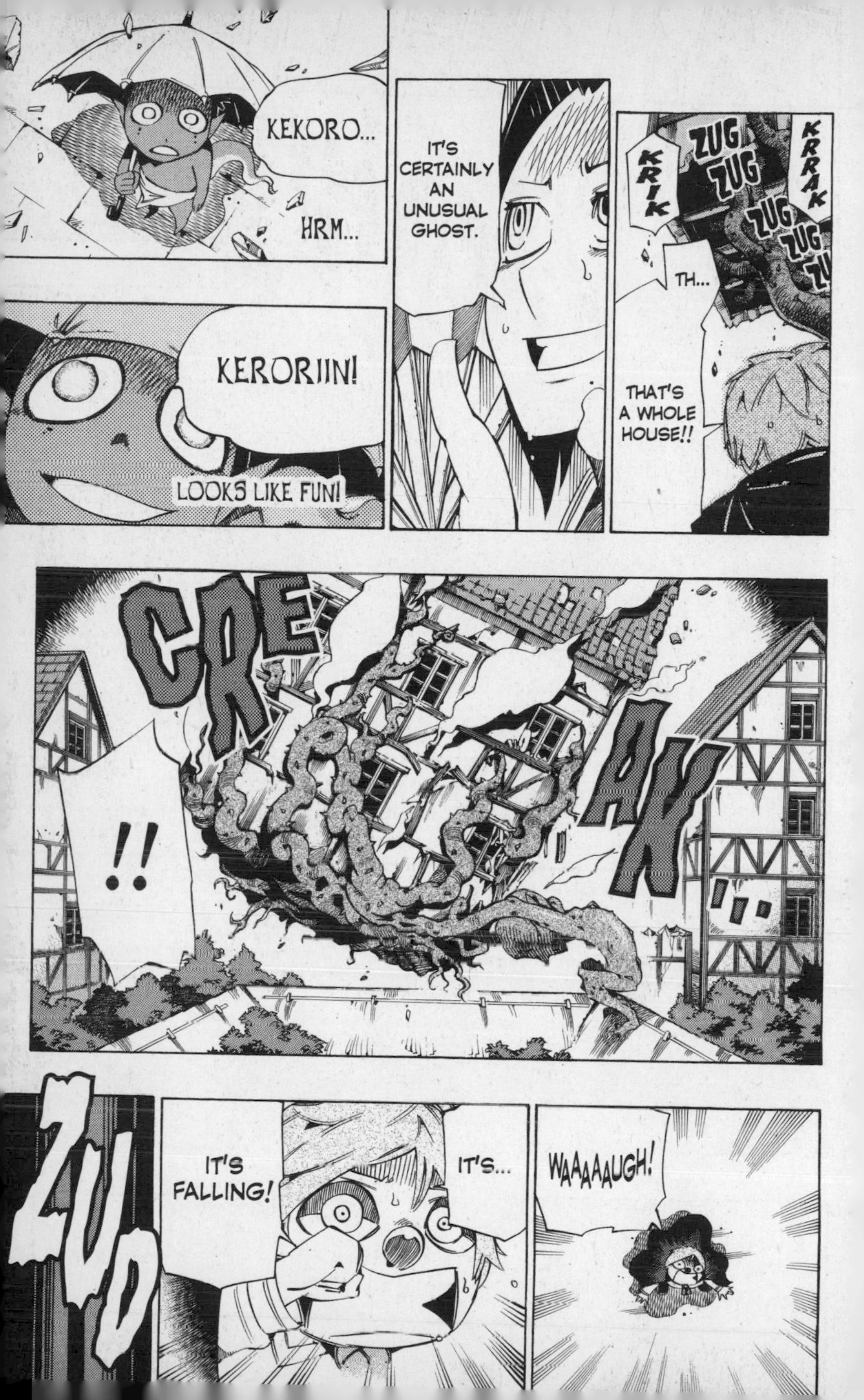
KRRAK
ZUG ZUG
KRIK
ZUG ZUG ZU
TH...
THAT'S A WHOLE HOUSE!!
IT'S CERTAINLY AN UNUSUAL GHOST.
KEKORO...
HRM...
KERORIIN!
LOOKS LIKE FUN!
CREAK...
!!
WAAAAAUGH!
IT'S...
IT'S FALLING!
ZUD

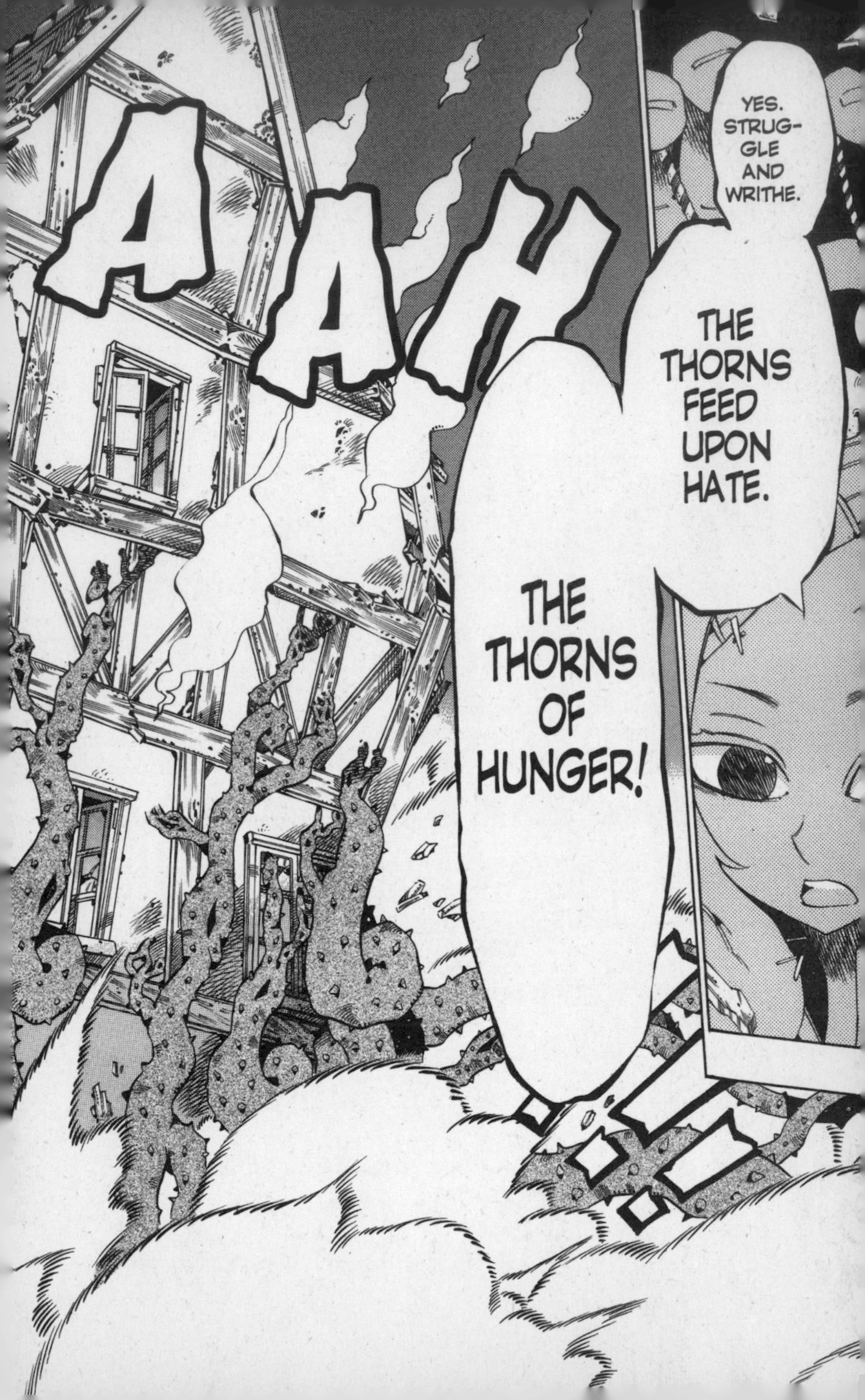
YES. STRUG-GLE AND WRITHE.
THE THORNS FEED UPON HATE.
AAH
THE THORNS OF HUNGER!

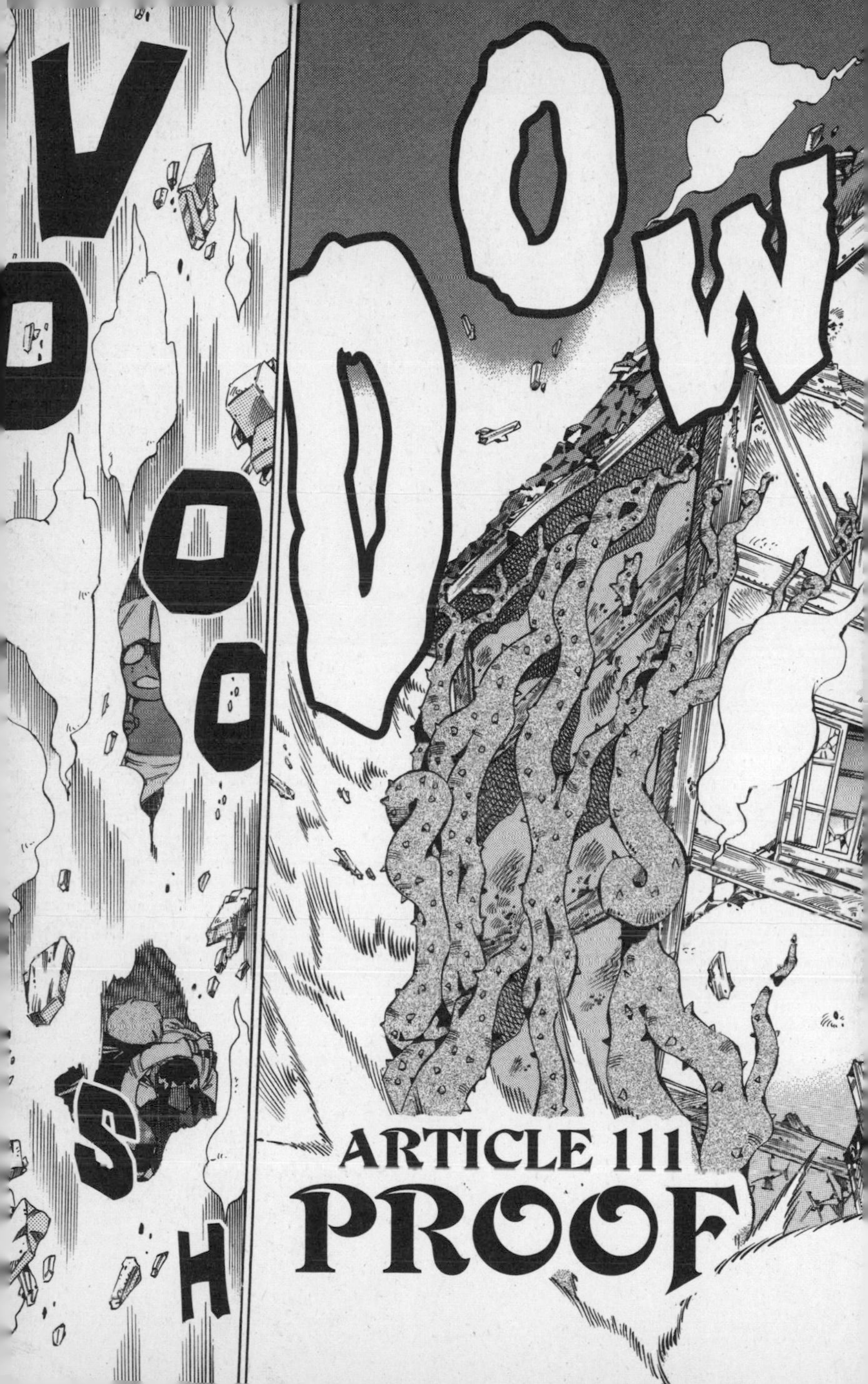
DOW
ARTICLE 111
PROOF
VOOOSH

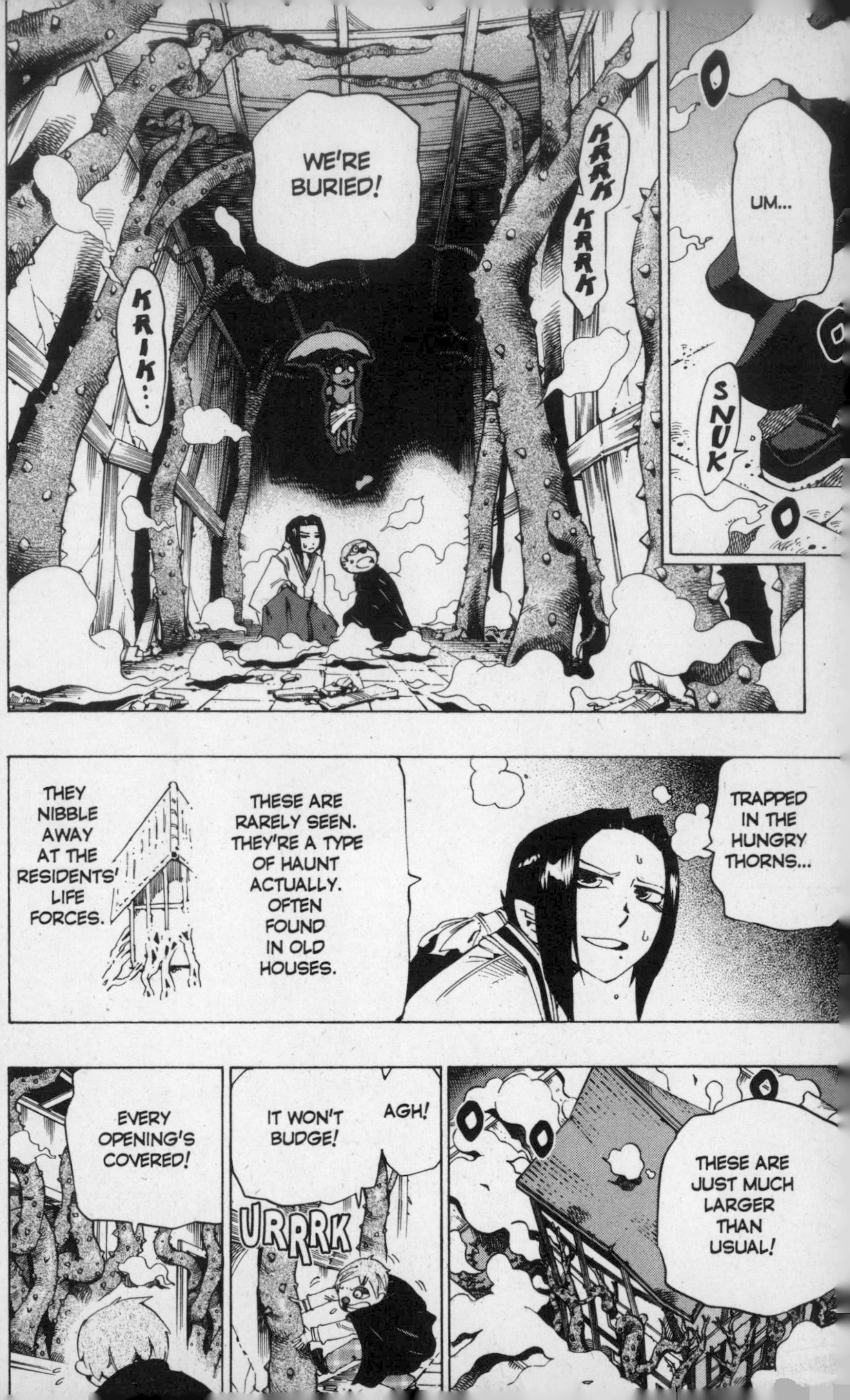
UM...
SNUK
KRRK KRRK
WE'RE BURIED!
KRIK...
TRAPPED IN THE HUNGRY THORNS...
THESE ARE RARELY SEEN. THEY'RE A TYPE OF HAUNT ACTUALLY. OFTEN FOUND IN OLD HOUSES.
THEY NIBBLE AWAY AT THE RESIDENTS' LIFE FORCES.
THESE ARE JUST MUCH LARGER THAN USUAL!
AGH!
IT WON'T BUDGE!
URRRK
EVERY OPENING'S COVERED!

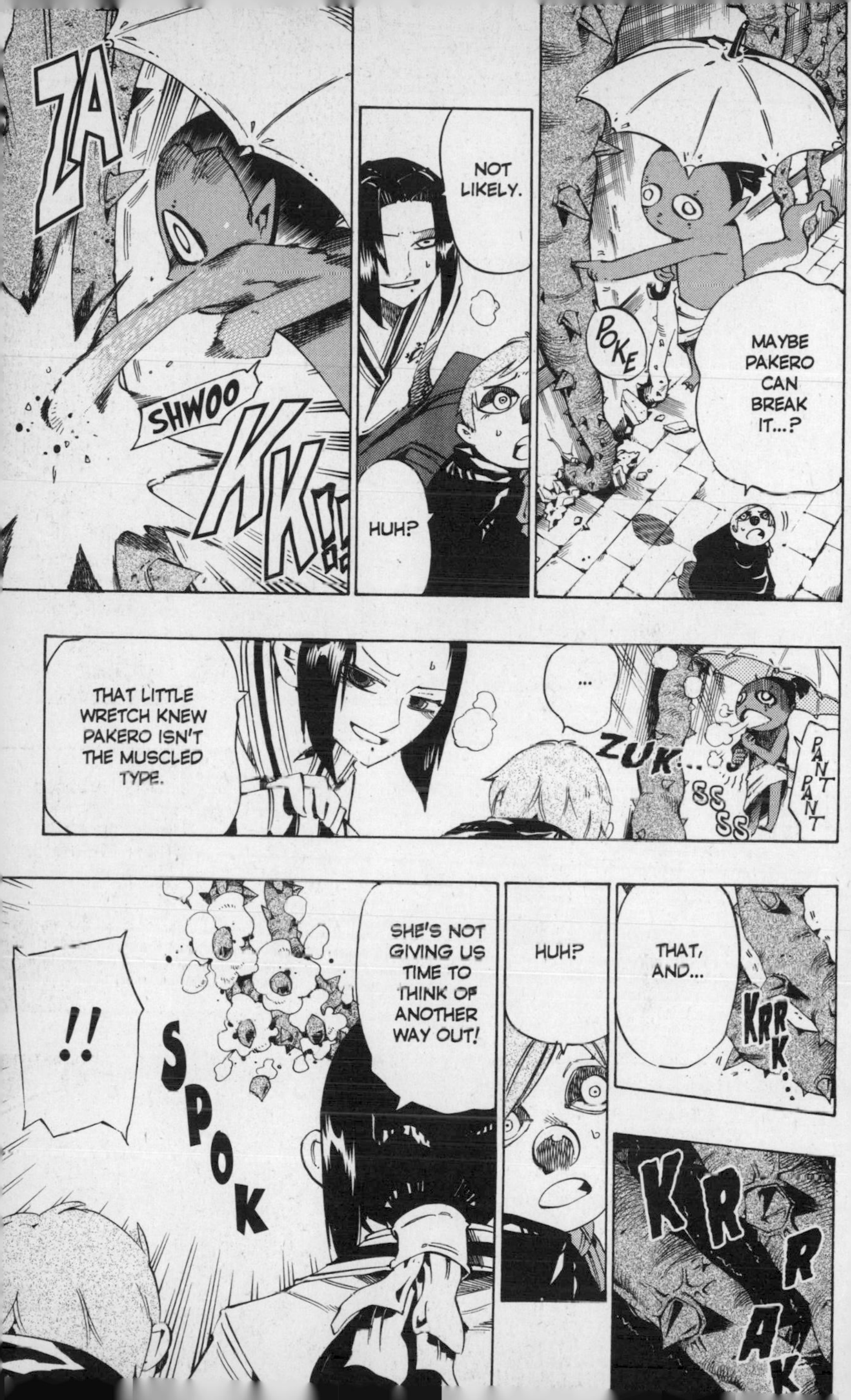

POKE
MAYBE PAKERO CAN BREAK IT...?
NOT LIKELY.
HUH?
ZA
SHWOOKK!!
...
ZUK...
SSSS
PANT PANT
THAT LITTLE WRETCH KNEW PAKERO ISN'T THE MUSCLED TYPE.
THAT, AND...
KRRRK
KRRRAK
HUH?
SHE'S NOT GIVING US TIME TO THINK OF ANOTHER WAY OUT!
!!
SPOK

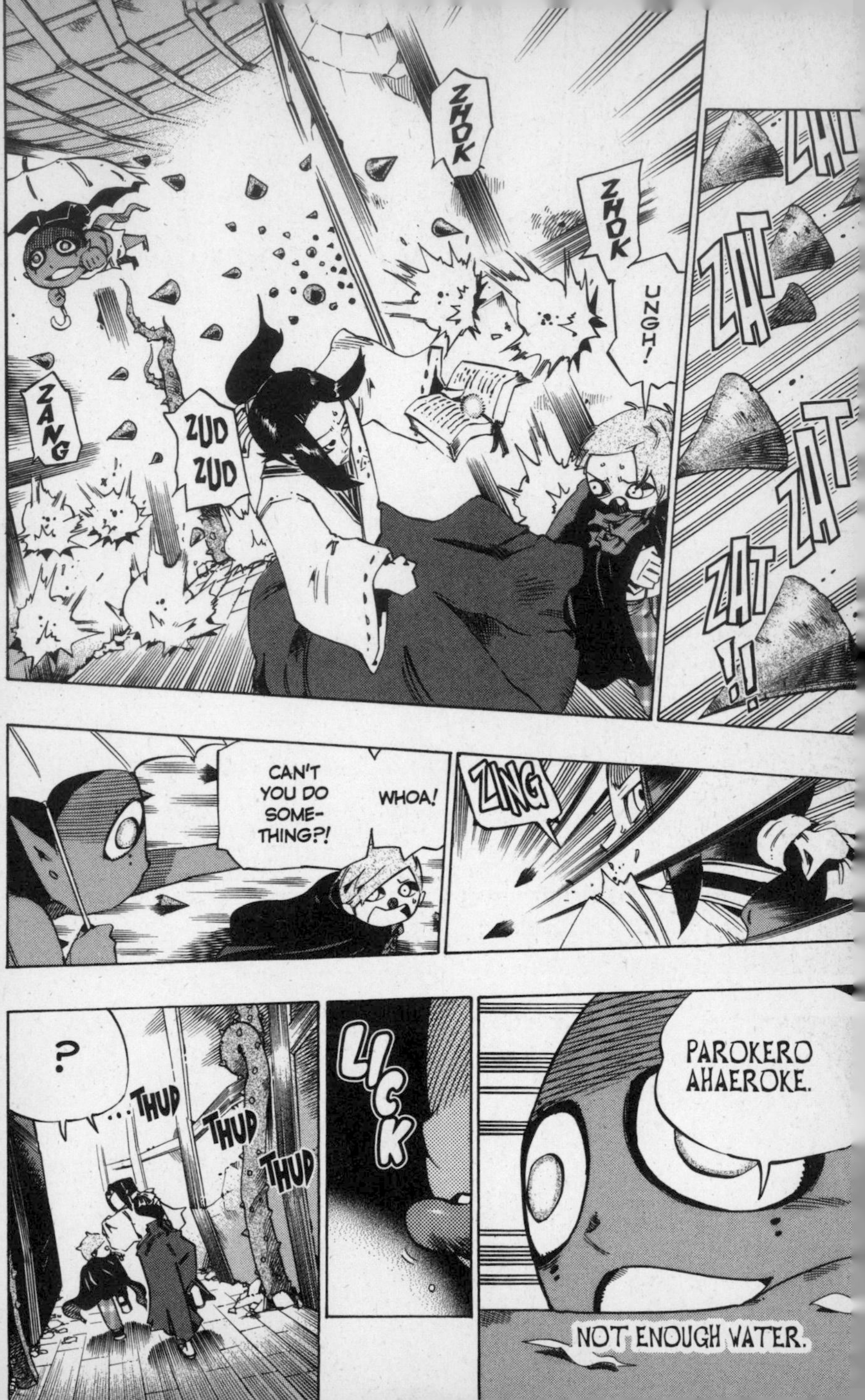
LHU
ZAT
ZAT
ZAT
ZAT!!
ZHOK
ZHOK
UNGH!
ZUD ZUD
ZANG
ZING
WHOA!
CAN'T YOU DO SOME-THING?!
PAROKERO AHAEROKE.
NOT ENOUGH WATER.
LICK
?
...THUD
THUD
THUD

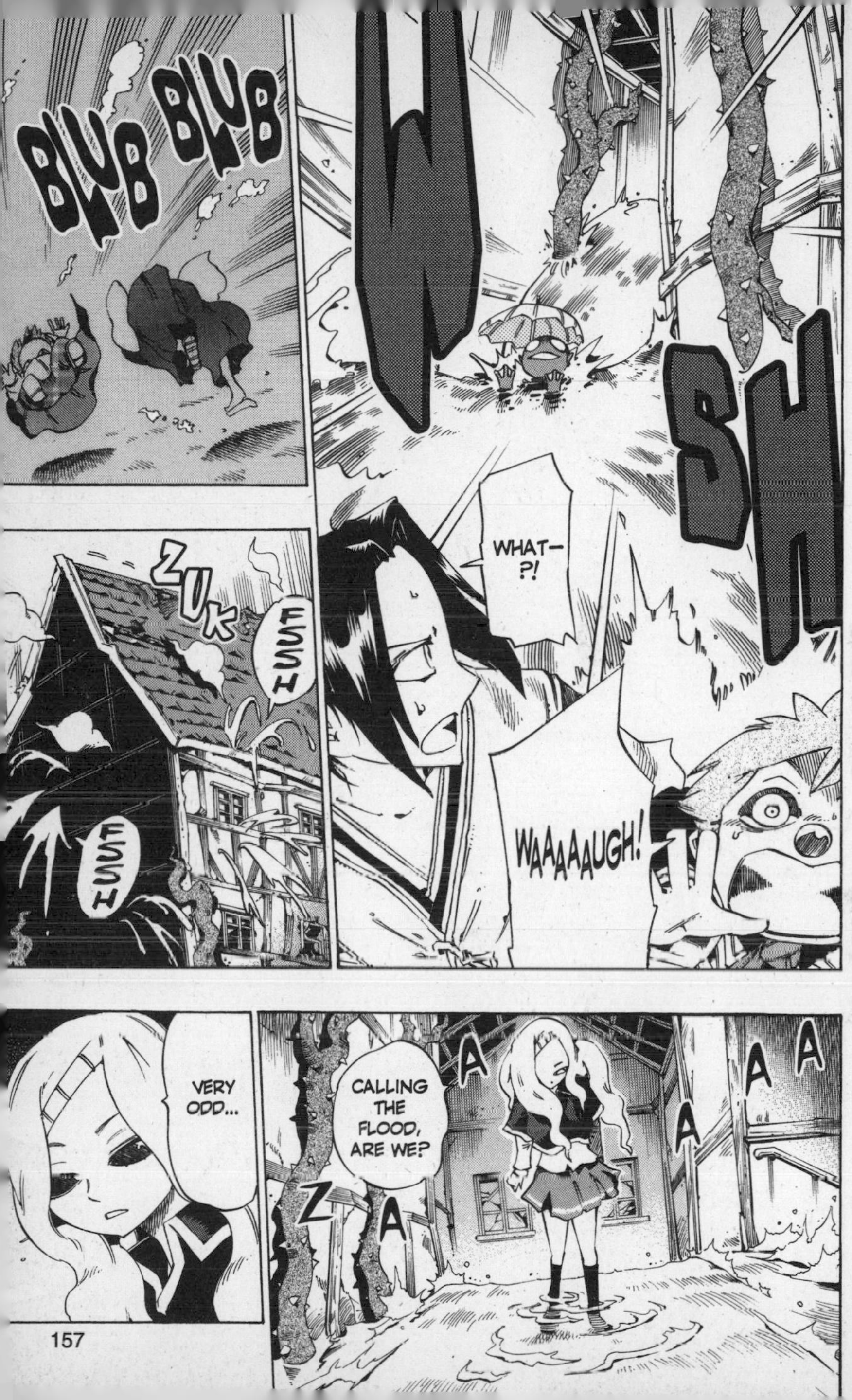
SH
W
WHAT— ?!
WAAAAAUGH!
BLUB BLUB
ZUK
FSSH
FSSH
AAAA
CALLING THE FLOOD, ARE WE?
ZA
VERY ODD...

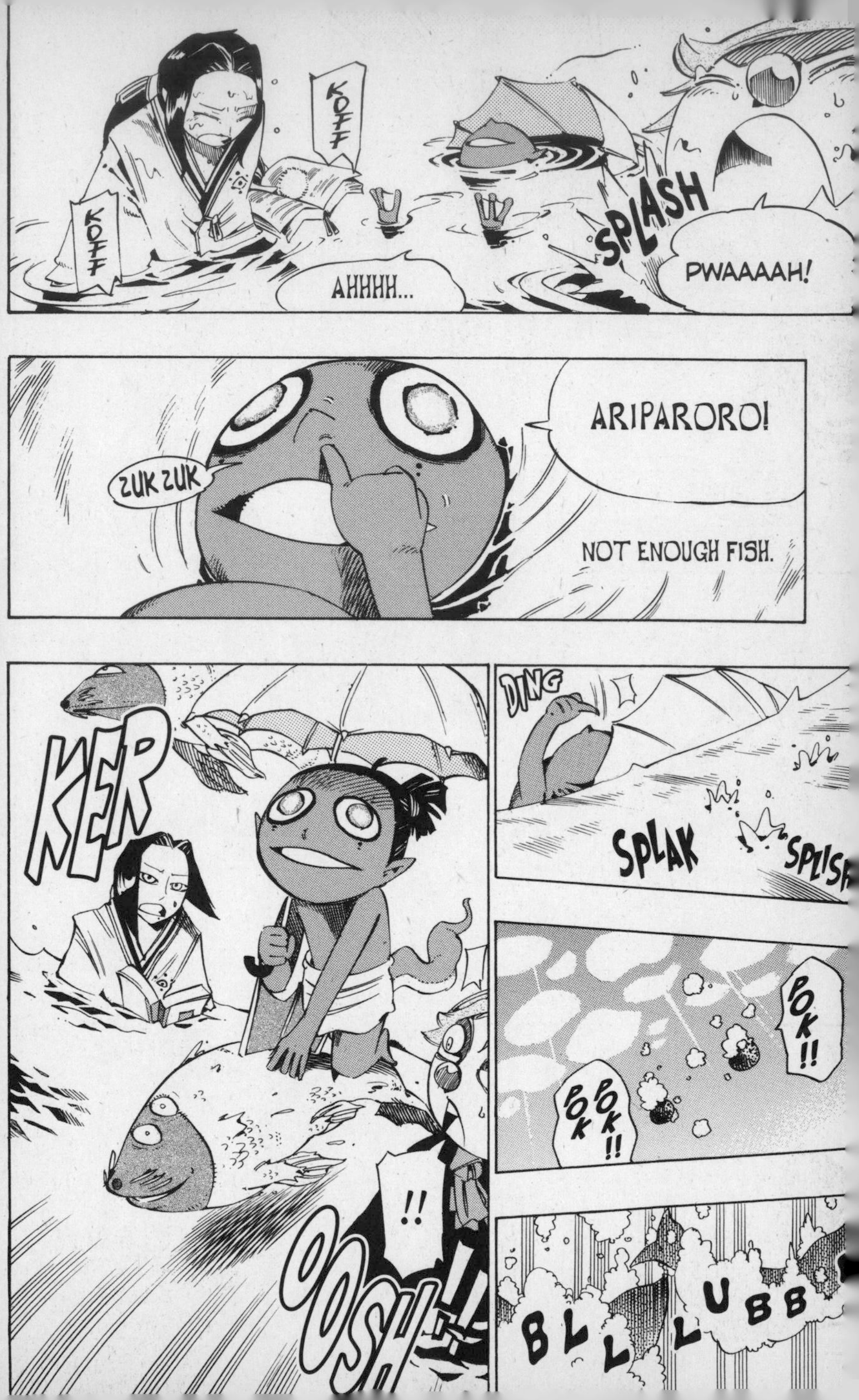
PWAAAAH!
SPLASH
KOFF
AHHHH...
KOFF
ARIPARORO!
NOT ENOUGH FISH.
ZUK ZUK
DING
SPLAK
SPLIS
POK!!
POK POK!!
BLLLUBB
KER
!!
OOSH!!

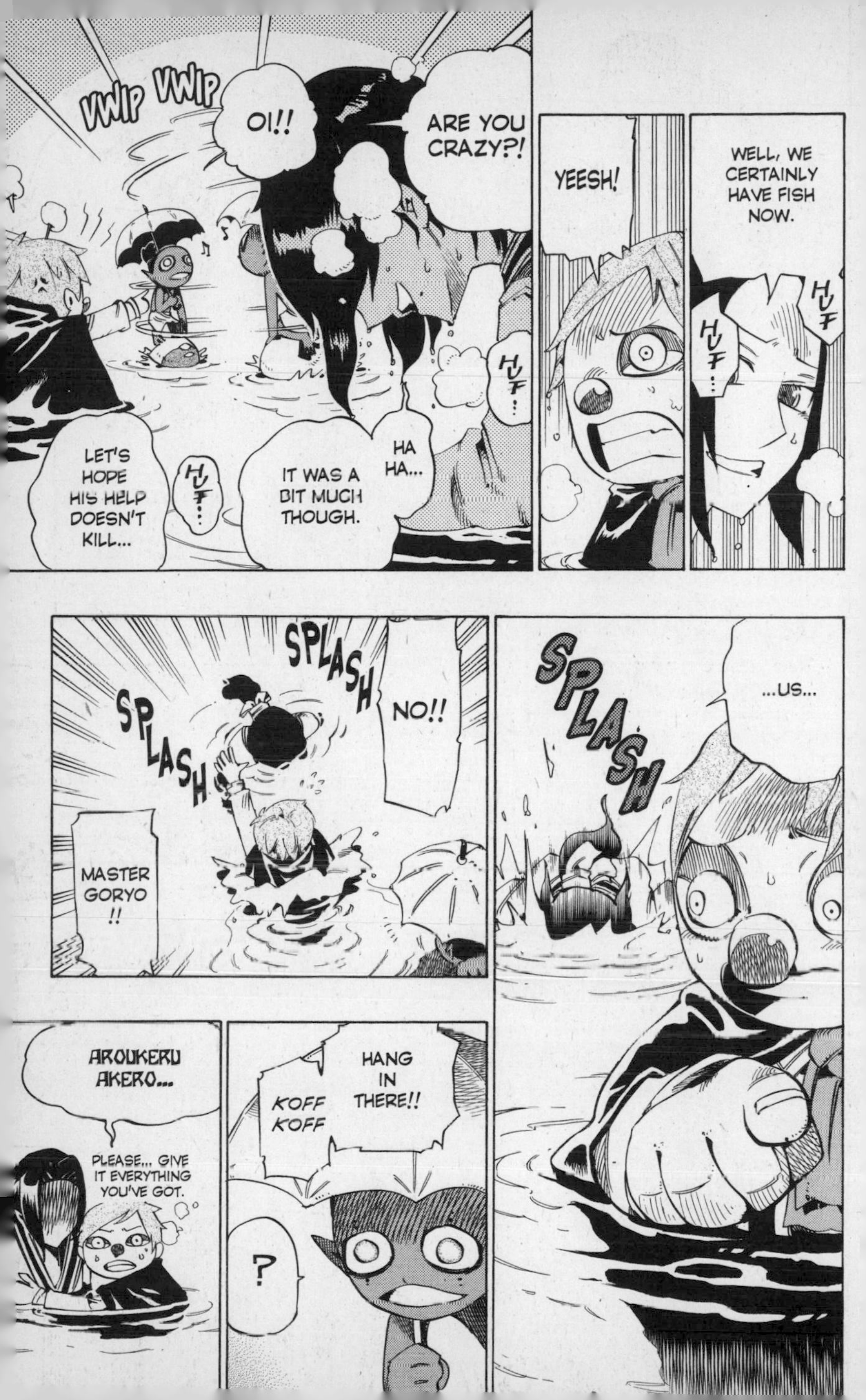
WELL, WE CERTAINLY HAVE FISH NOW.
HUF
HUF...
YEESH!
ARE YOU CRAZY?!
OI!!
VWIP VWIP
HUF...
HA HA...
IT WAS A BIT MUCH THOUGH.
HUF...
LET'S HOPE HIS HELP DOESN'T KILL...
...US...
SPLASH
NO!!
SPLASH
SPLASH
MASTER GORYO !!
HANG IN THERE!!
KOFF KOFF
?
AROUKERU AKERO...
PLEASE... GIVE IT EVERYTHING YOU'VE GOT.

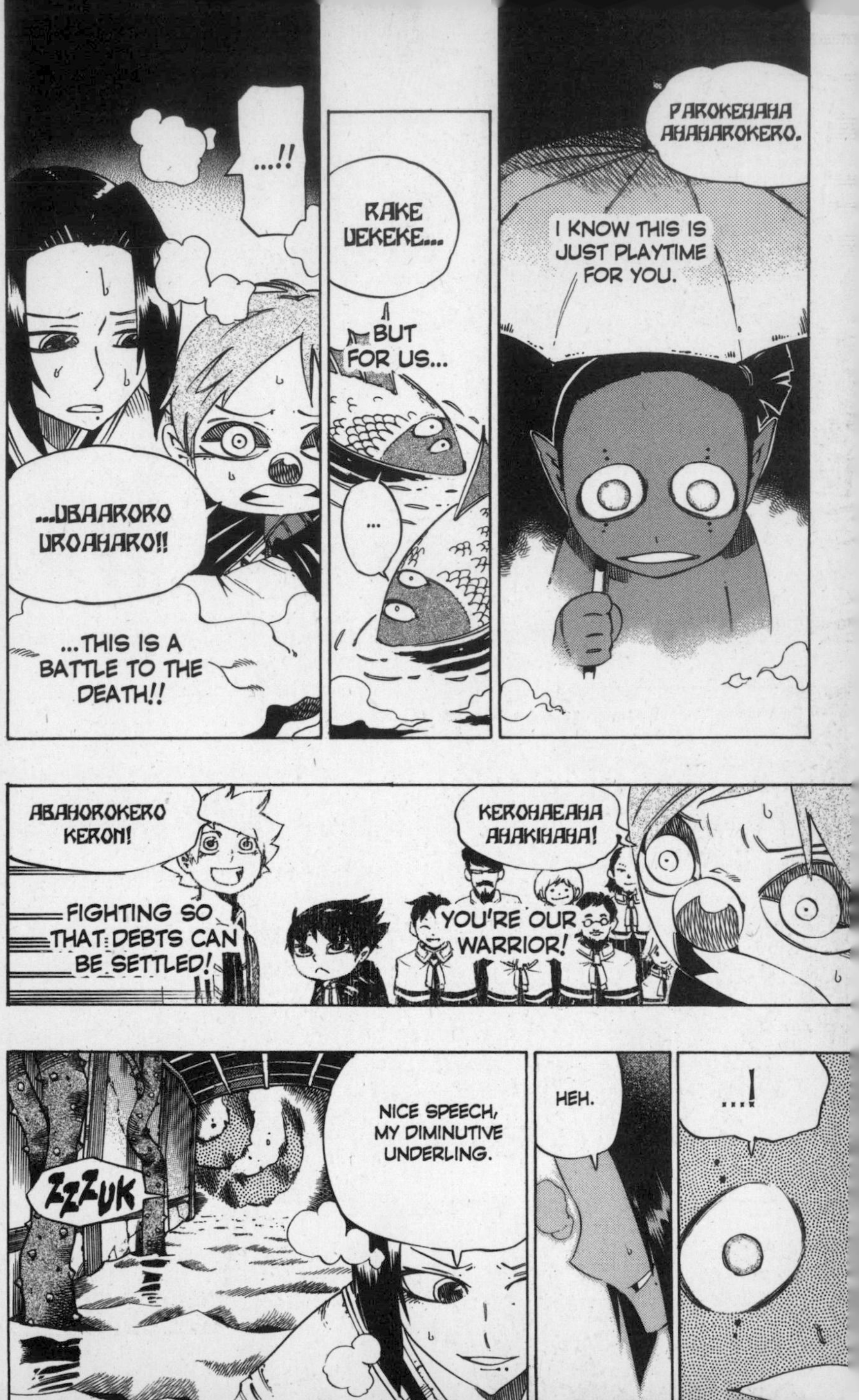
PAROKEHAHA AHAHAROKERO.
I KNOW THIS IS JUST PLAYTIME FOR YOU.
RAKE UEKEKE...
BUT FOR US...
...
...!!
...UBAARORO UROAHARO!!
...THIS IS A BATTLE TO THE DEATH!!
KEROHAEAHA AHAKIHAHA!
YOU'RE OUR WARRIOR!
ABAHOROKERO KERON!
FIGHTING SO THAT DEBTS CAN BE SETTLED!
...!
HEH.
NICE SPEECH, MY DIMINUTIVE UNDERLING.
ZZZUK

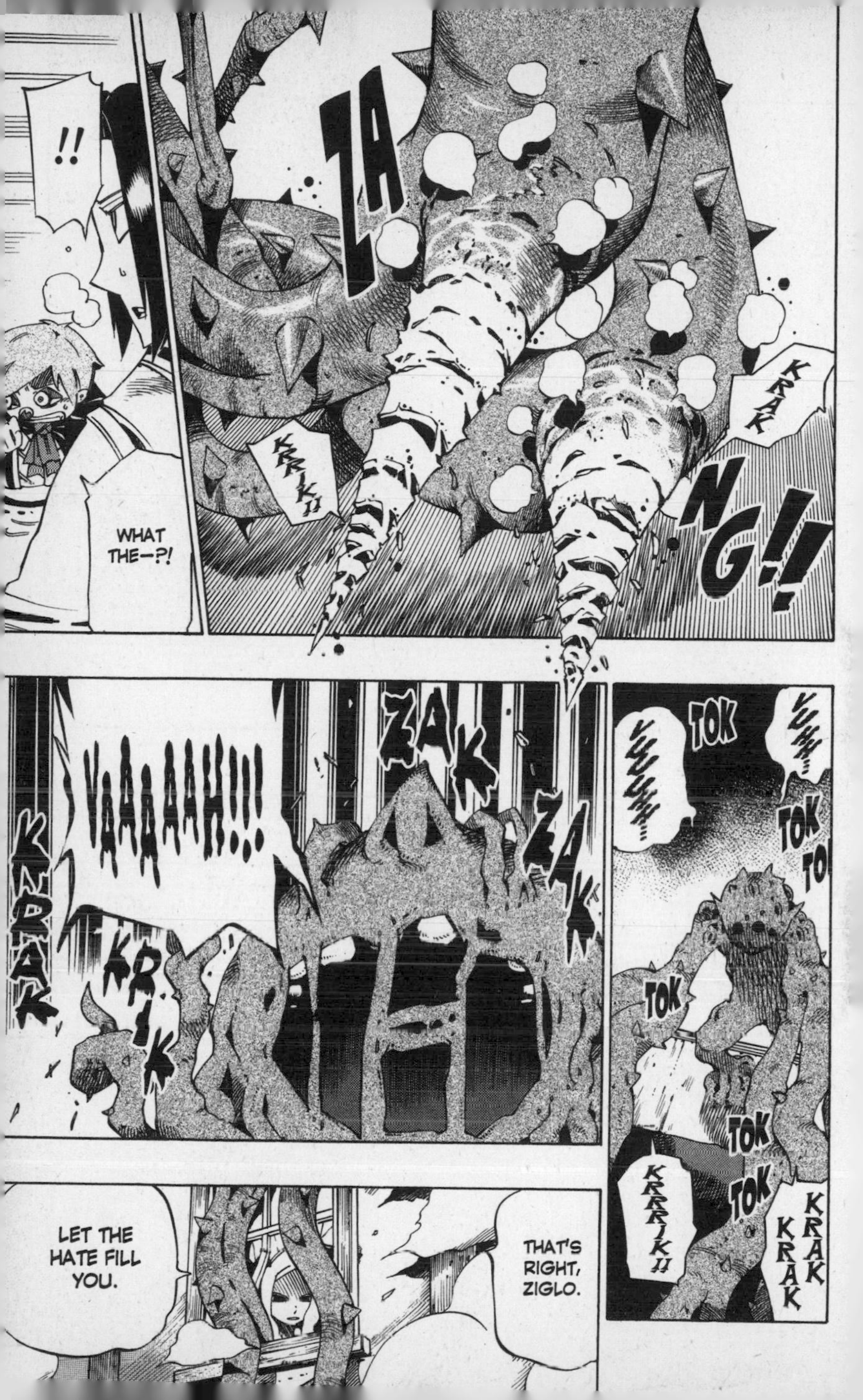
ZA
KRAK
NG!!
KRRIK!!
!!
WHAT THE--?!
VUUH...
TOK
VUUUUH...
TOK
TOK
TO
TOK
TOK
TOK
KRRRIK!!
KRAK
KRAK
ZAK
ZAK
ZAK
VAAAAAH!!!
KRRIK
KRRAK
THAT'S RIGHT, ZIGLO.
LET THE HATE FILL YOU.

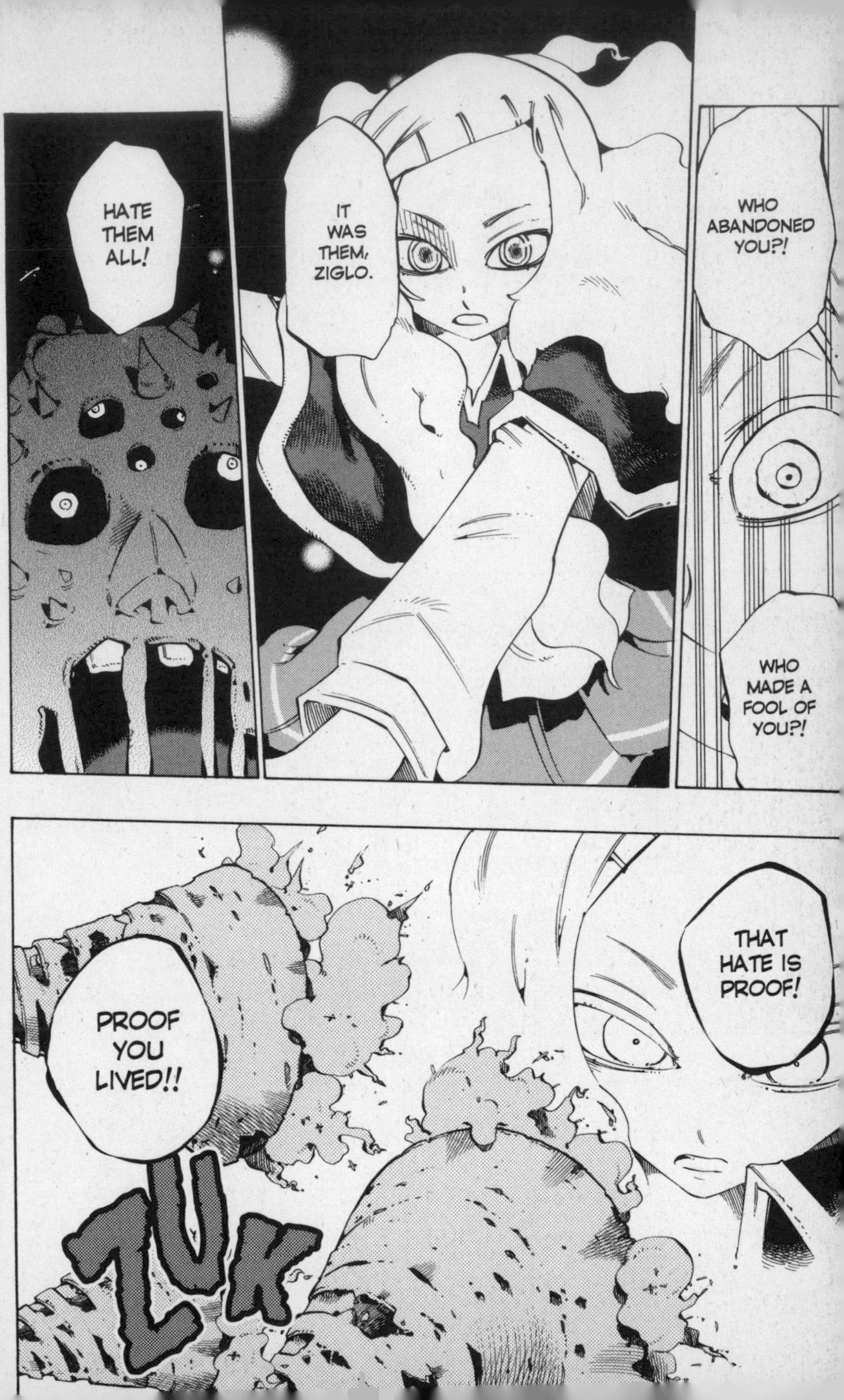
WHO ABANDONED YOU?!
WHO MADE A FOOL OF YOU?!
IT WAS THEM, ZIGLO.
HATE THEM ALL!
THAT HATE IS PROOF!
PROOF YOU LIVED!!
ZUK

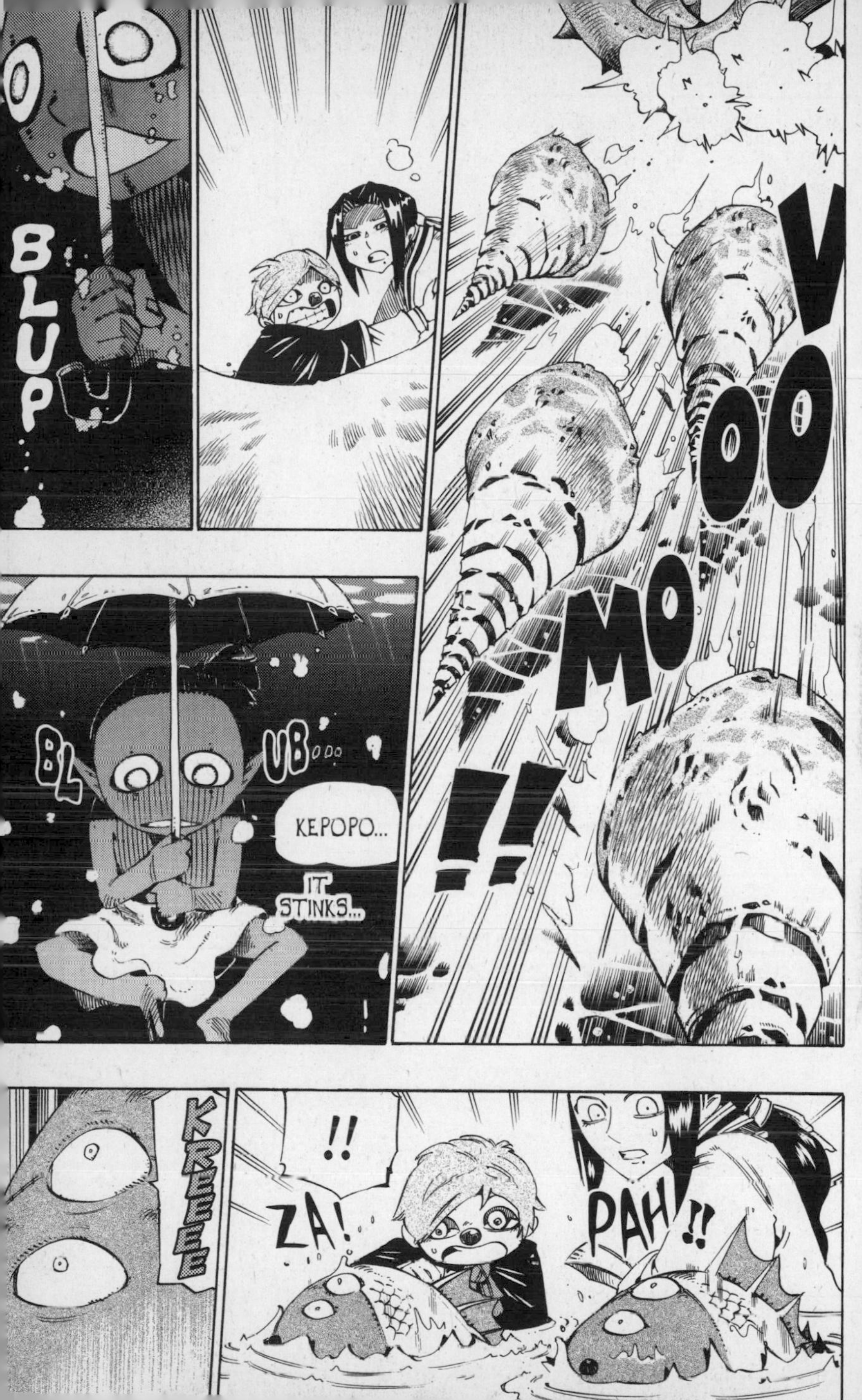
VOOOOM!!
BLUP...
BLUB
KEPOPO...
IT STINKS...
!
!!
ZA!
PAH!!
KREEEE

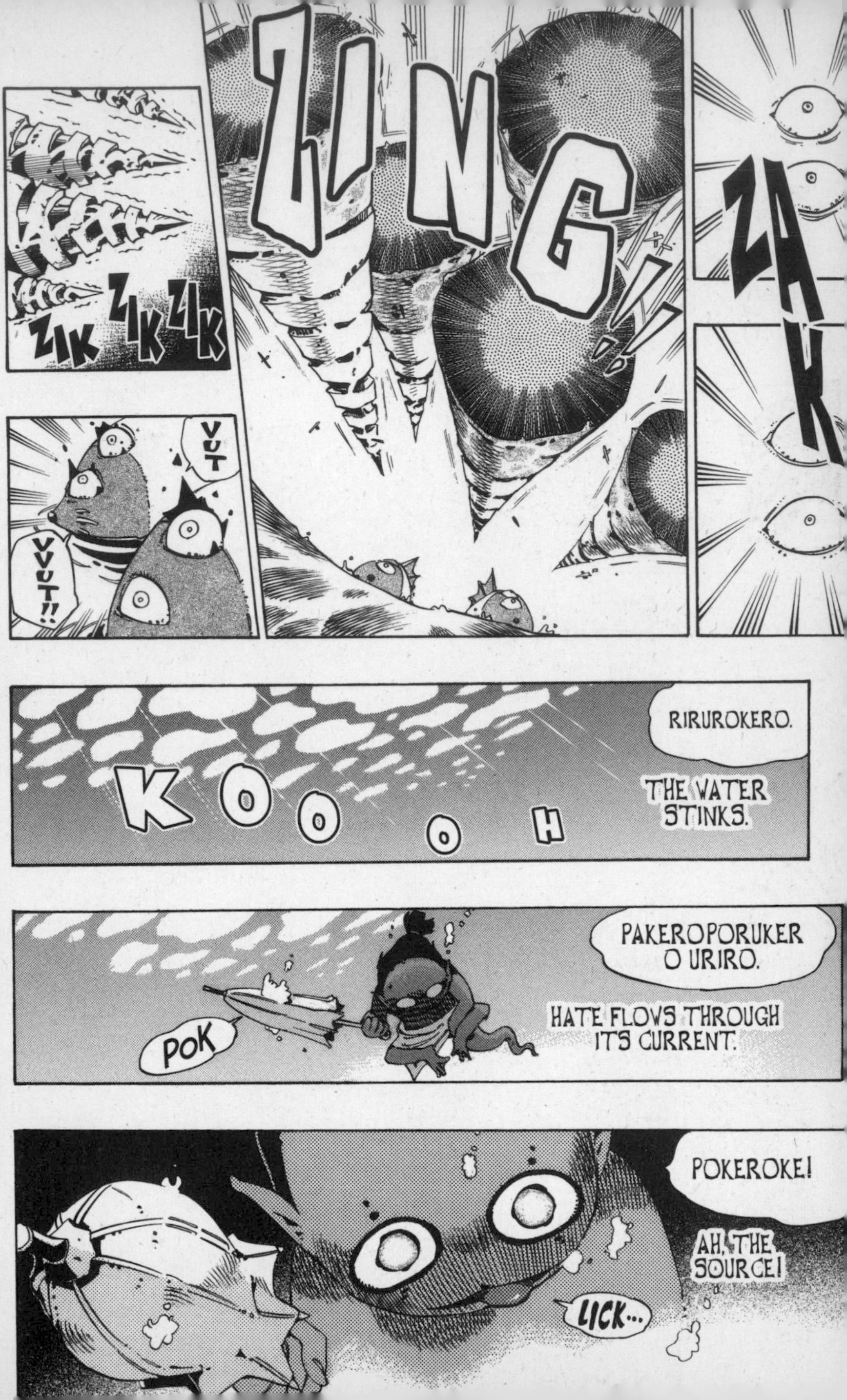
ZAK
ZING!!
ZIK ZIK ZIK
VUT
VVUT!!
RIRUROKERO.
THE WATER STINKS.
KOOOH
PAKEROPORUKER O URIRO.
HATE FLOWS THROUGH ITS CURRENT.
POK
POKEROKE!
AH, THE SOURCE!
LICK...

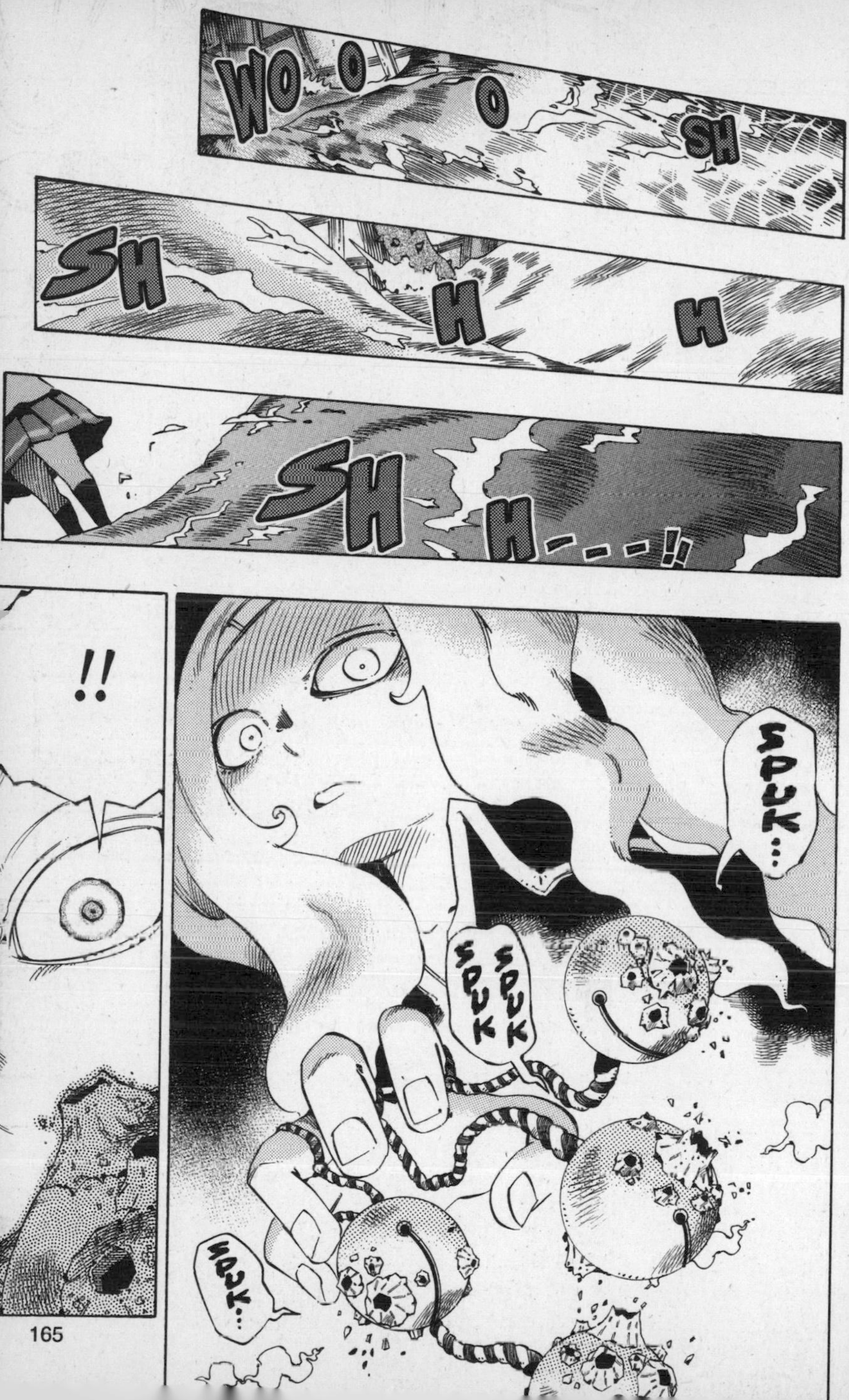

WOOOOSH
SHHH
SHHH...!!
SPUK...
SPUK SPUK
SPUK...
!!

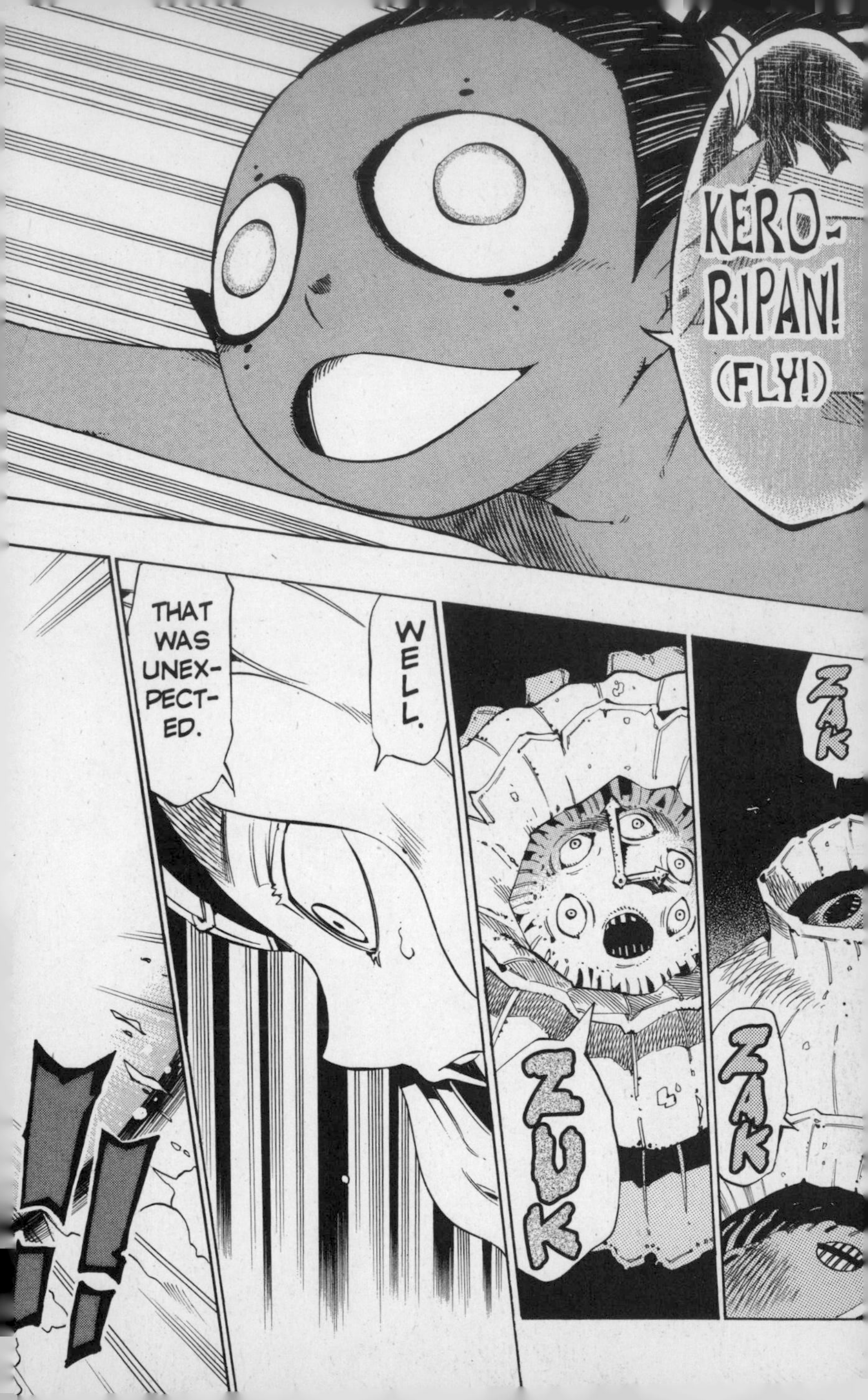
KERO-RIPAN!
(FLY!)
ZAK
ZAK
ZUK
WELL.
THAT WAS UNEXPECTED.
!!

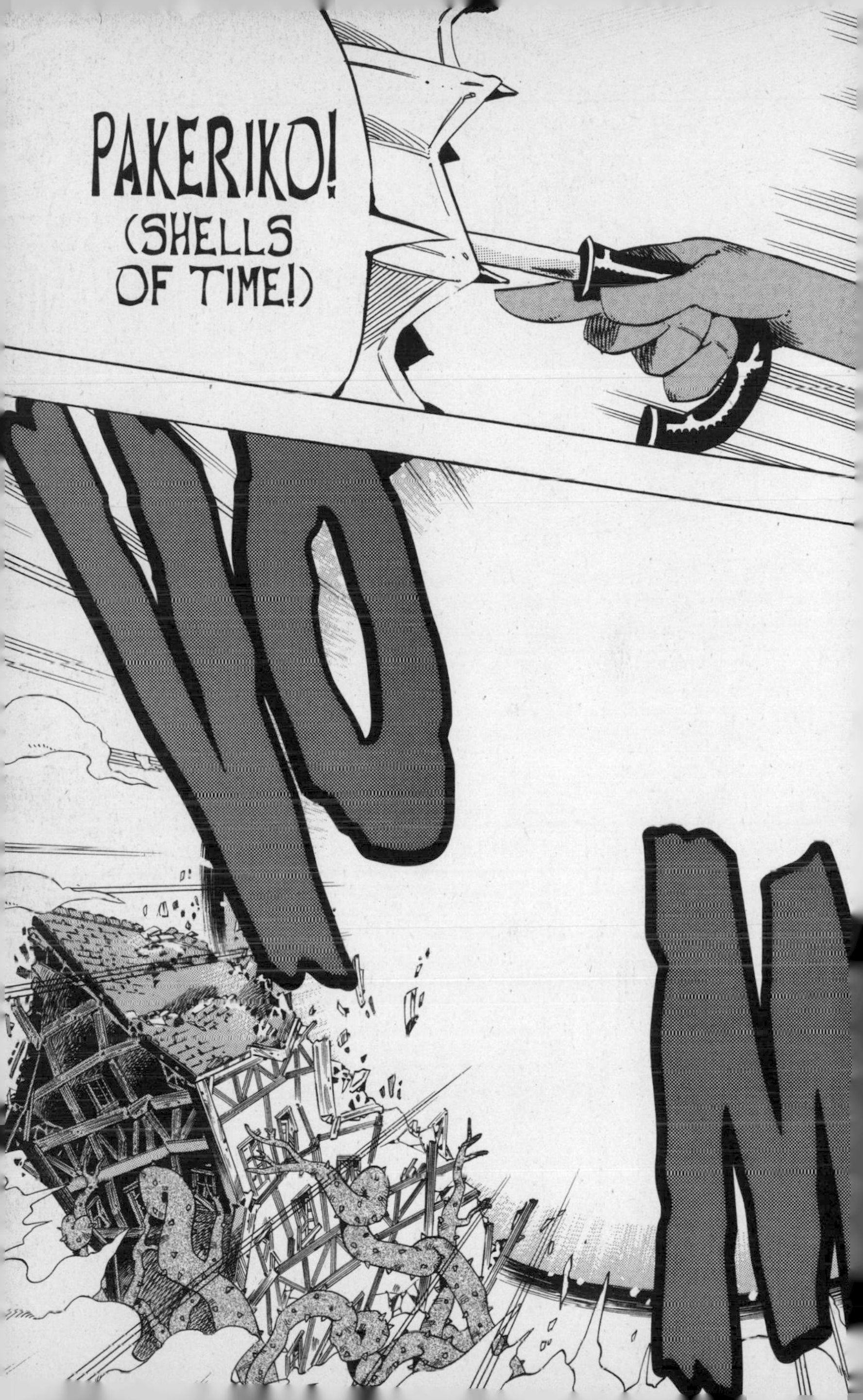
PAKERIKO! (SHELLS OF TIME!)
WOM

Muhyo & Roji's
Bureau of Supernatural Investigation
BSI

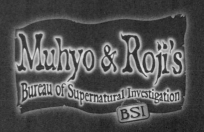

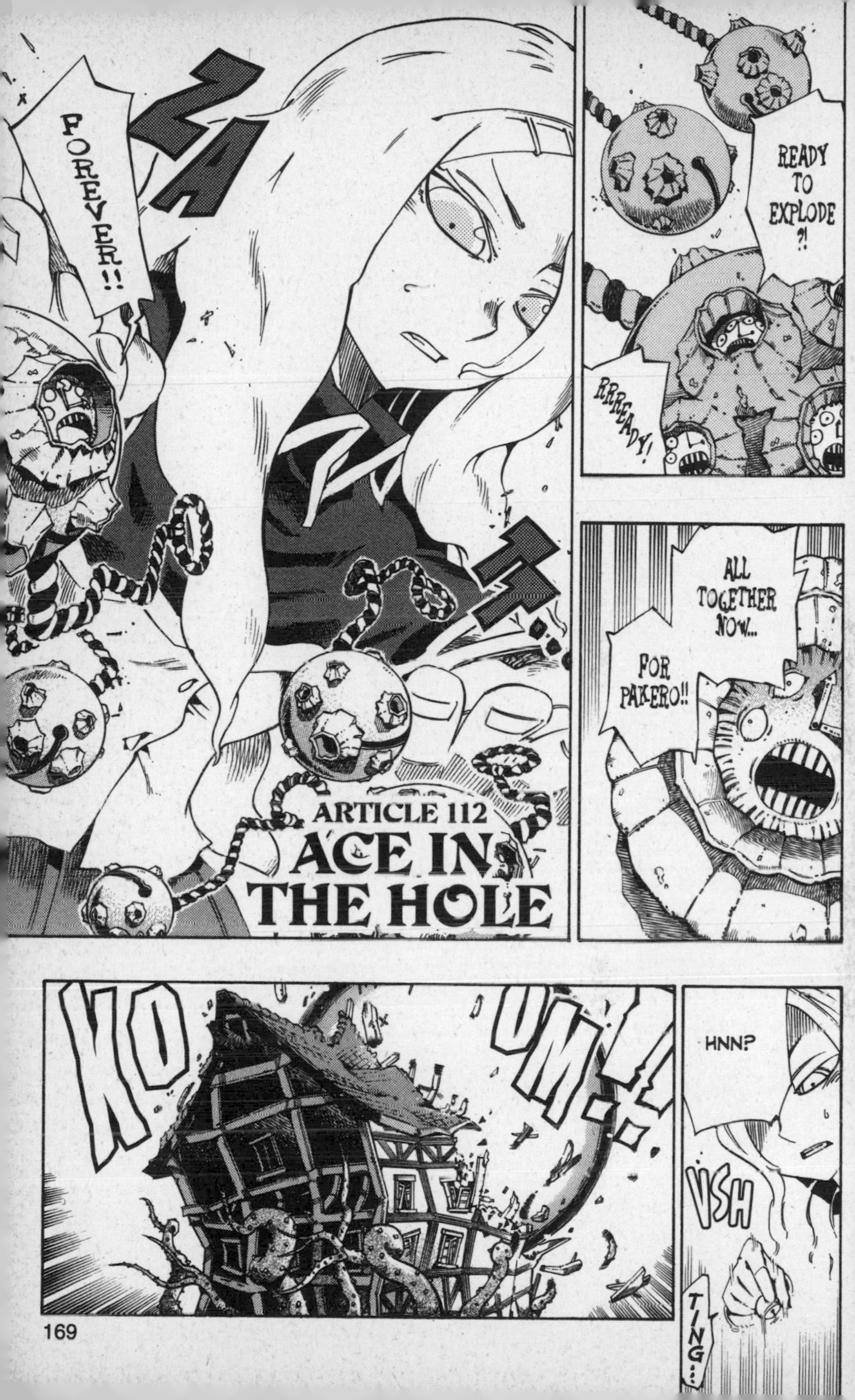
READY TO EXPLODE ?!
RRREADY!
ALL TOGETHER NOW...
FOR PAKERO!!
FOREVER!!
ZA
TT
ARTICLE 112
ACE IN THE HOLE
HNN?
VSH
TING...
KO
UM!!

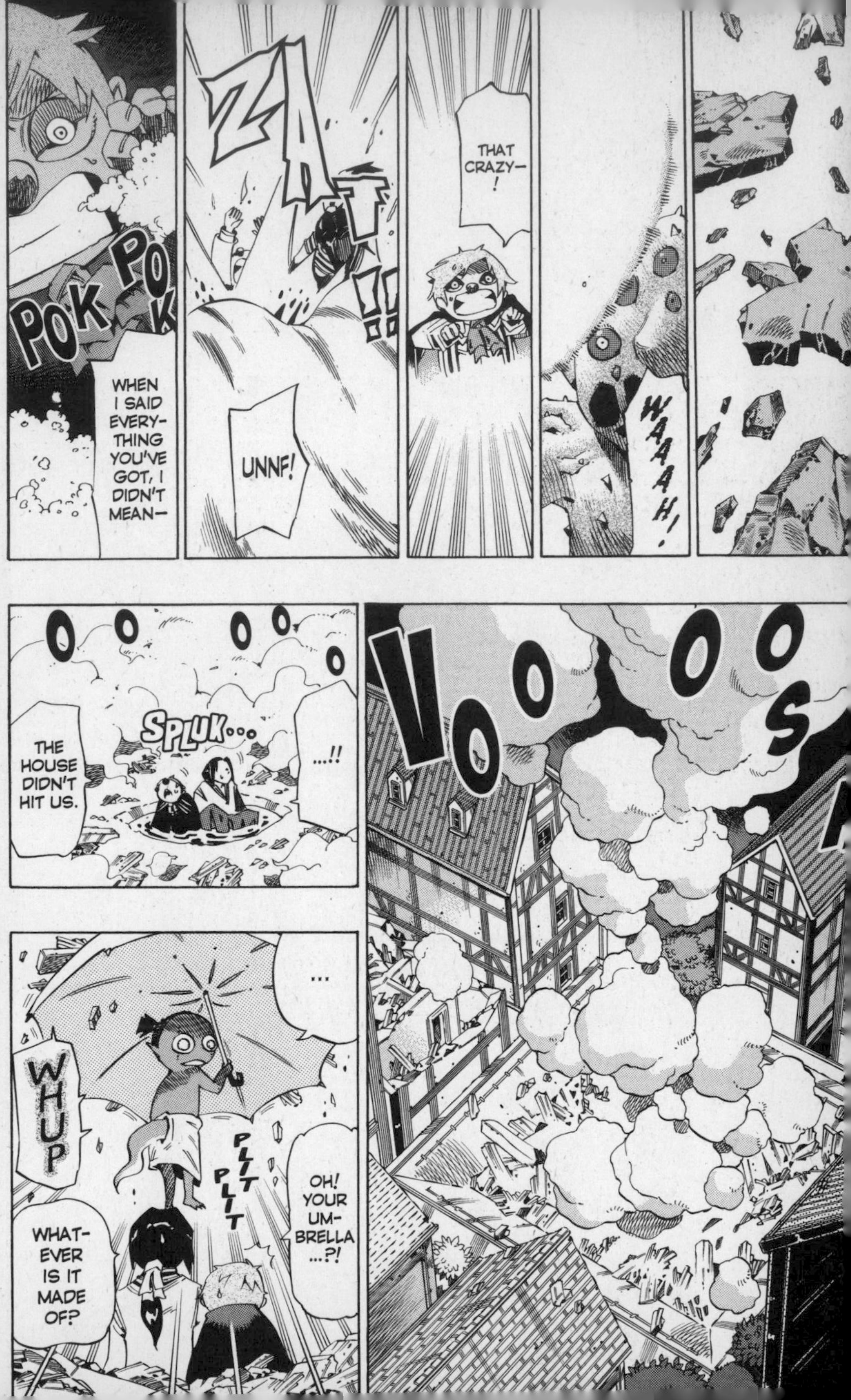
WAAAAH!
THAT CRAZY—!
ZAT!!
UNNF!
POK POK
WHEN I SAID EVERYTHING YOU'VE GOT, I DIDN'T MEAN—
VOOOOOS
OOOOOO
...!!
SPLUK...
THE HOUSE DIDN'T HIT US.
...
OH! YOUR UMBRELLA ...?!
PLIT PLIT
WHUP
WHATEVER IS IT MADE OF?

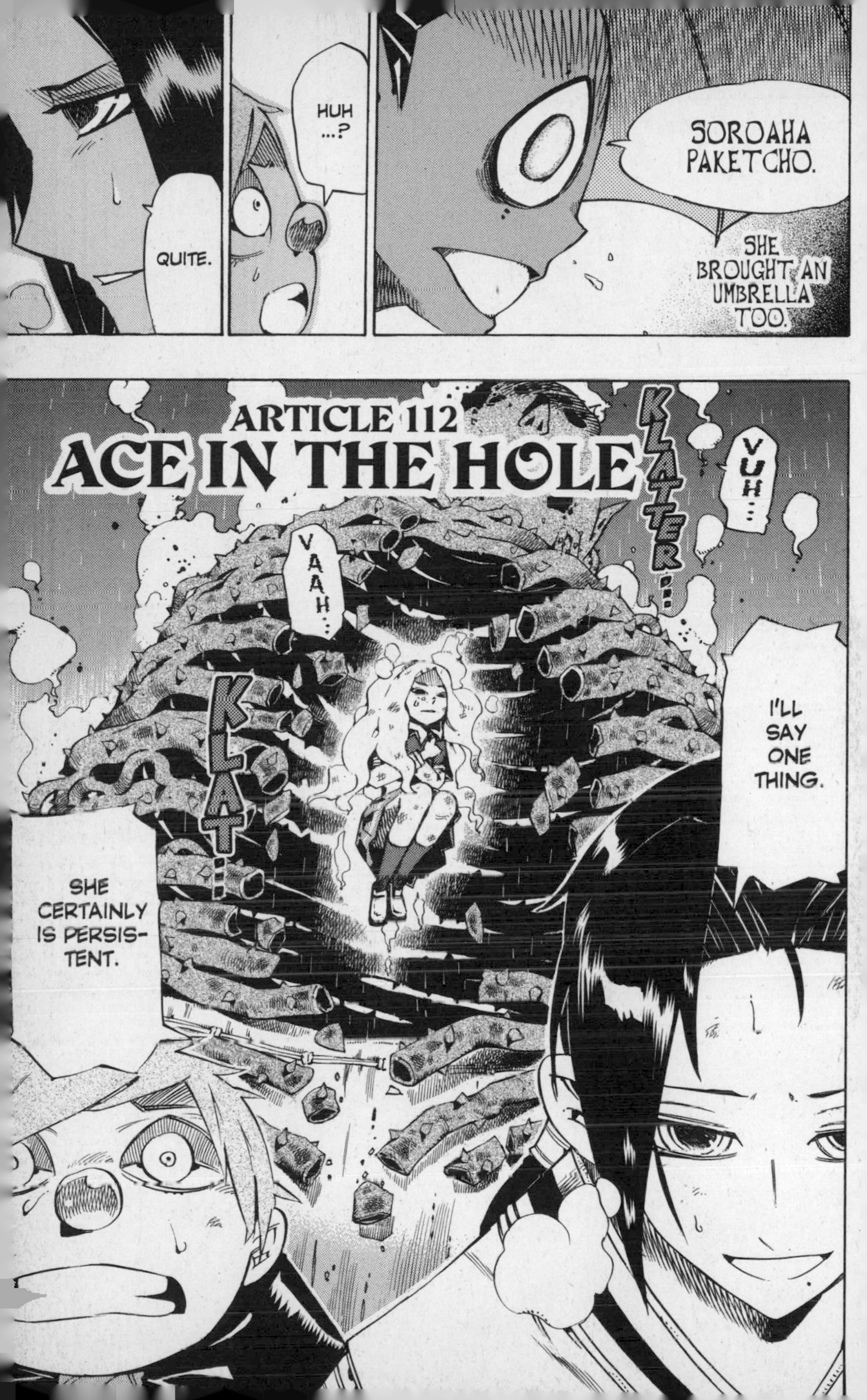
SOROAHA PAKETCHO.
SHE BROUGHT AN UMBRELLA TOO.
HUH ...?
QUITE.
ARTICLE 112
ACE IN THE HOLE
VUH...
KLATTER...
VAAH...
KLAT...
I'LL SAY ONE THING.
SHE CERTAINLY IS PERSIS-TENT.

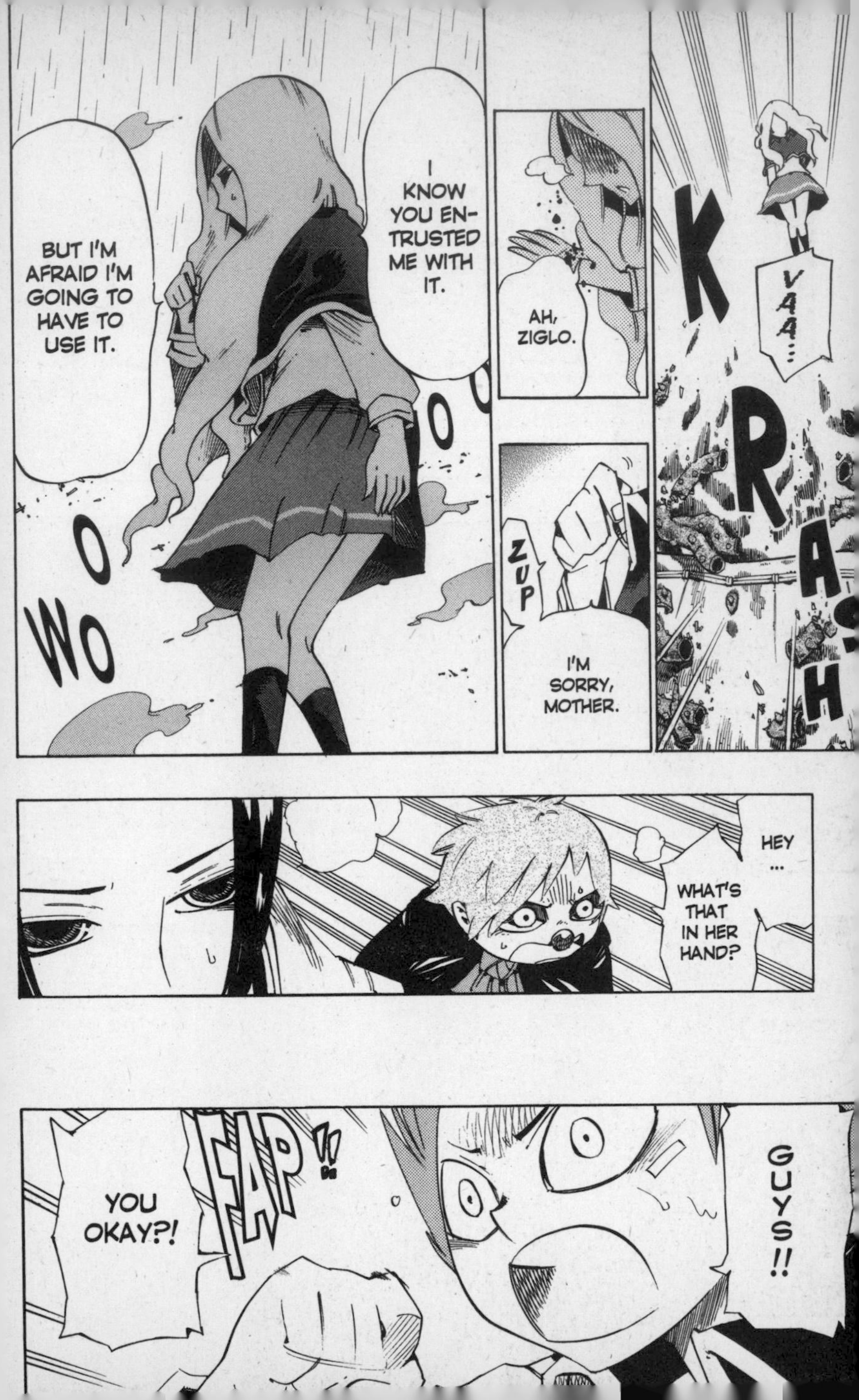
VAA...
KRASH
AH, ZIGLO.
ZUP
I'M SORRY, MOTHER.
WOOOO
I KNOW YOU ENTRUSTED ME WITH IT.
BUT I'M AFRAID I'M GOING TO HAVE TO USE IT.
HEY ...
WHAT'S THAT IN HER HAND?
GUYS!!
FAP!!
YOU OKAY?!

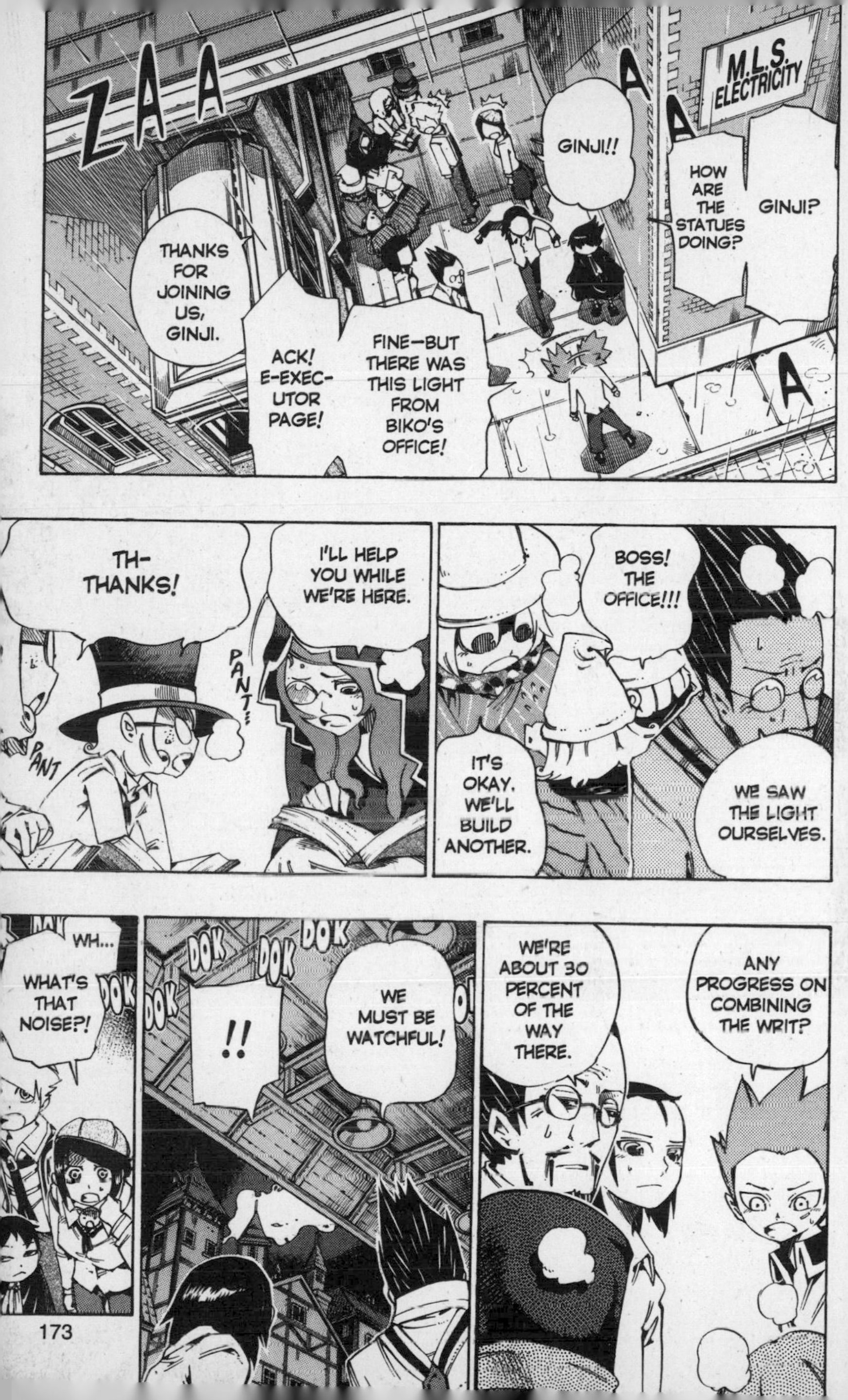
M.L.S. ELECTRICITY
ZAA A A A A
HOW ARE THE STATUES DOING? GINJI?
GINJI!!
FINE—BUT THERE WAS THIS LIGHT FROM BIKO'S OFFICE!
ACK! E-EXECUTOR PAGE!
THANKS FOR JOINING US, GINJI.
BOSS! THE OFFICE!!!
WE SAW THE LIGHT OURSELVES.
IT'S OKAY. WE'LL BUILD ANOTHER.
I'LL HELP YOU WHILE WE'RE HERE.
PANT
TH-THANKS!
PANT
ANY PROGRESS ON COMBINING THE WRIT?
WE'RE ABOUT 30 PERCENT OF THE WAY THERE.
DOK DOK DOK DOK DOK
WE MUST BE WATCHFUL!
!!
WH... WHAT'S THAT NOISE?!

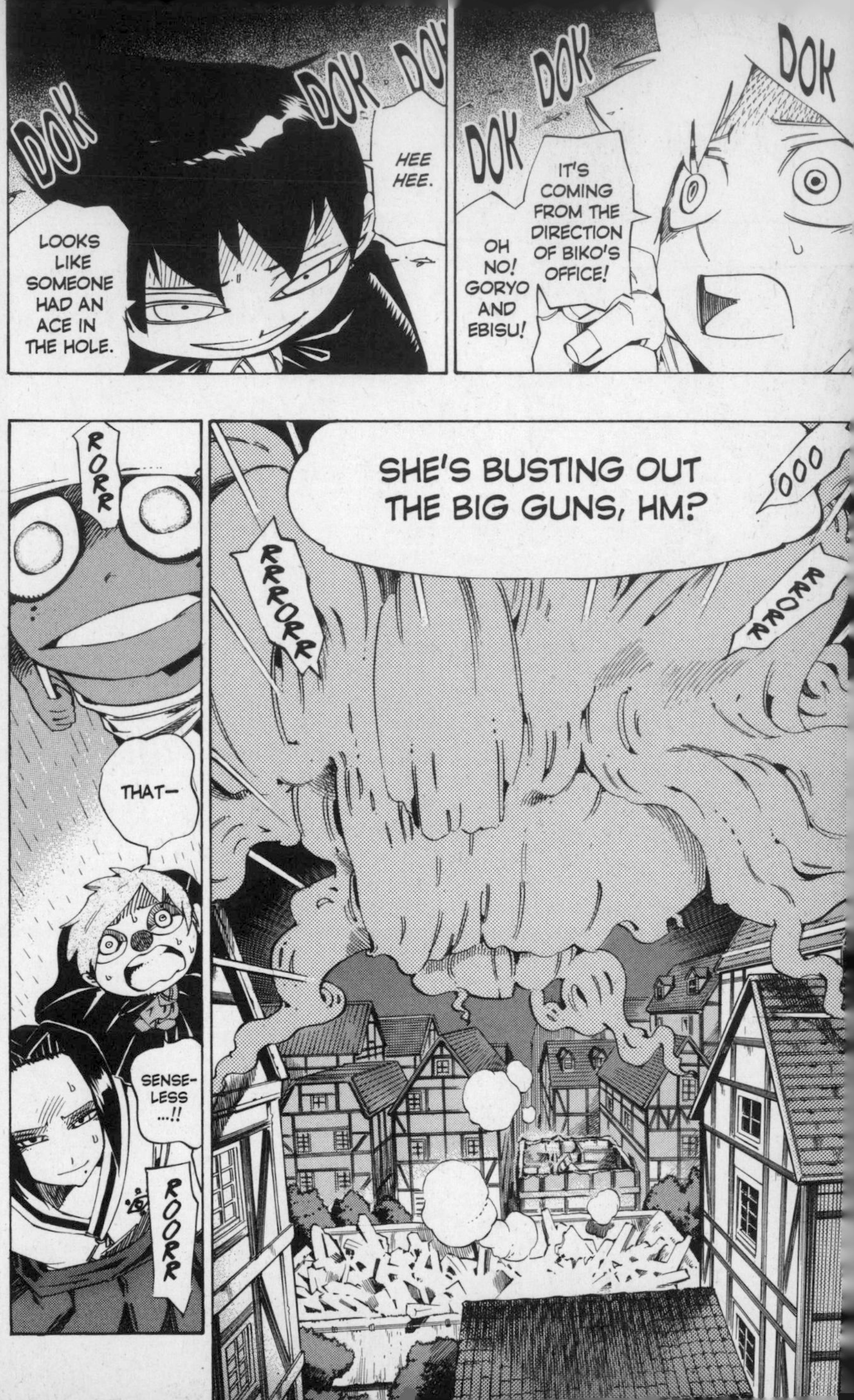
DOK
DOK
DOK
IT'S COMING FROM THE DIRECTION OF BIKO'S OFFICE!
OH NO! GORYO AND EBISU!
DOK
DOK
DOK
HEE HEE.
LOOKS LIKE SOMEONE HAD AN ACE IN THE HOLE.
SHE'S BUSTING OUT THE BIG GUNS, HM?
OOO
RRORR
RRRORR
RORR
THAT—
SENSE-LESS ...!!
ROORR

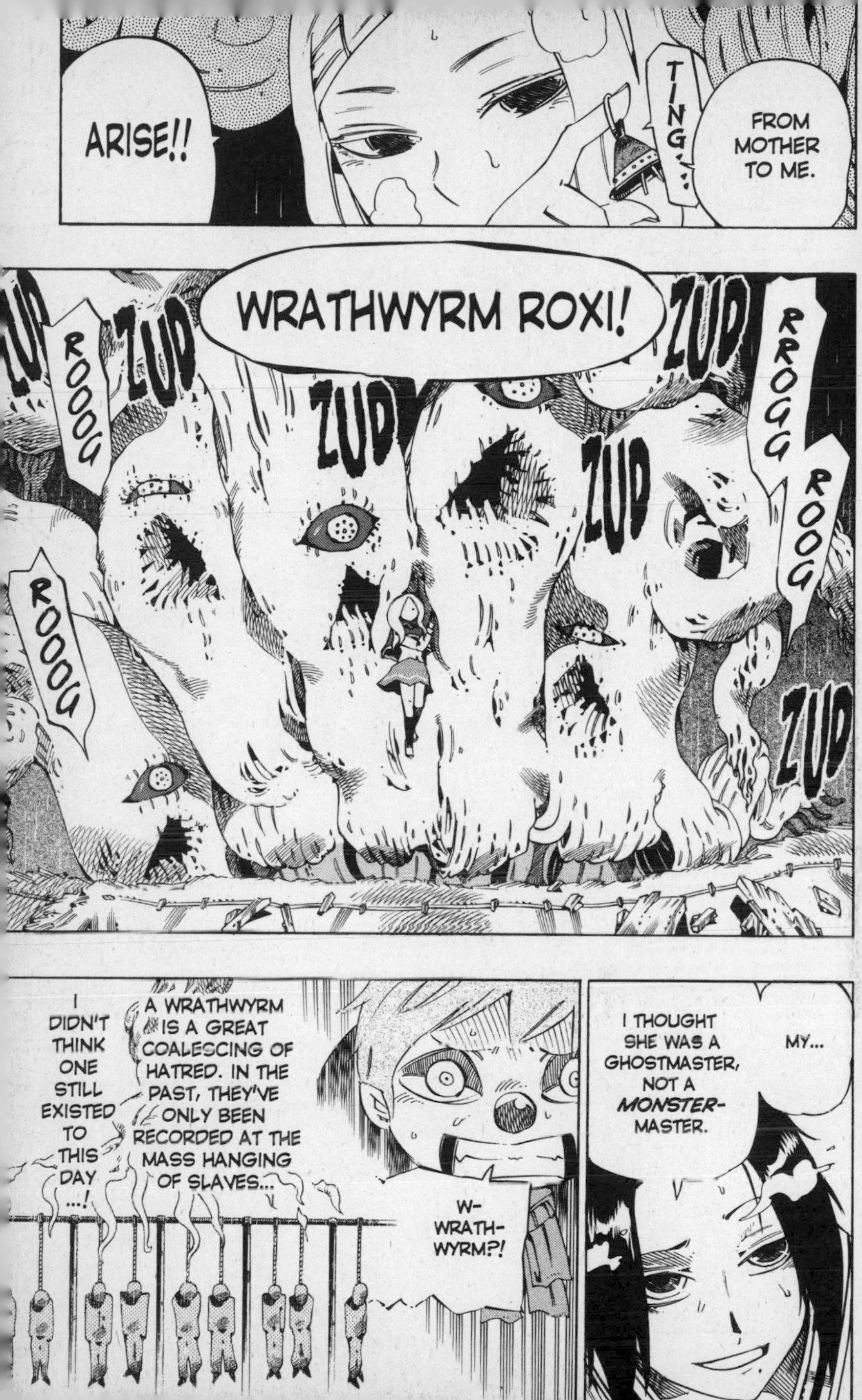
FROM MOTHER TO ME.
TING...
ARISE!!
ZUD
RROGG
WRATHWYRM ROXI!
ZUD
ZUD
ZUD
ROOOG
ZUD
ROOOOG
ZUD
ROOOOG
ZUD
MY...
I THOUGHT SHE WAS A GHOSTMASTER, NOT A *MONSTER*-MASTER.
W-WRATH-WYRM?!
A WRATHWYRM IS A GREAT COALESCING OF HATRED. IN THE PAST, THEY'VE ONLY BEEN RECORDED AT THE MASS HANGING OF SLAVES...
I DIDN'T THINK ONE STILL EXISTED TO THIS DAY...!

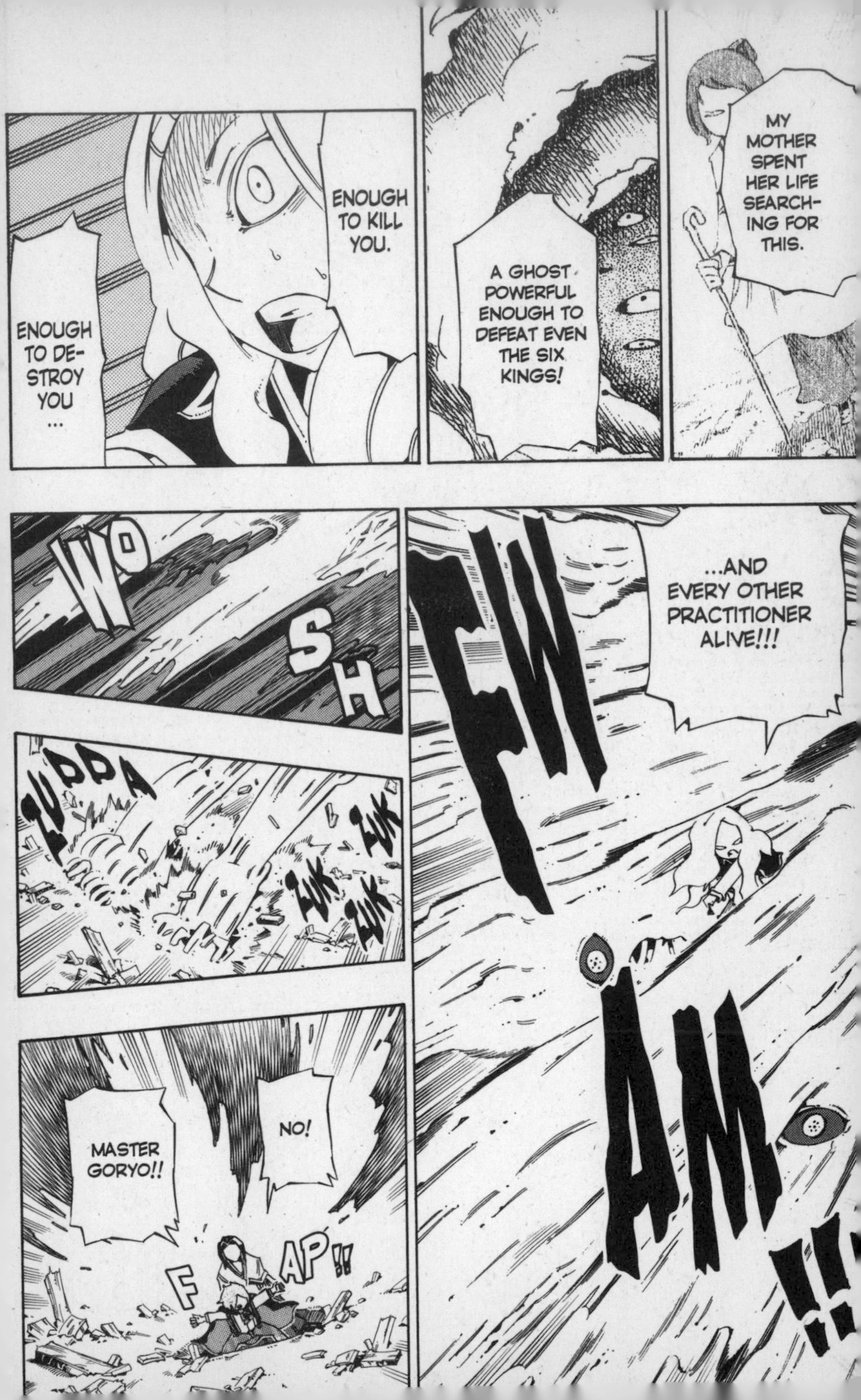
MY MOTHER SPENT HER LIFE SEARCHING FOR THIS.
A GHOST POWERFUL ENOUGH TO DEFEAT EVEN THE SIX KINGS!
ENOUGH TO KILL YOU.
ENOUGH TO DESTROY YOU...
...AND EVERY OTHER PRACTITIONER ALIVE!!!
FWAM!!!
WOSH
ZUPPA
ZUK
ZUK
ZUK
ZUK
NO!
MASTER GORYO!!
FAP!!

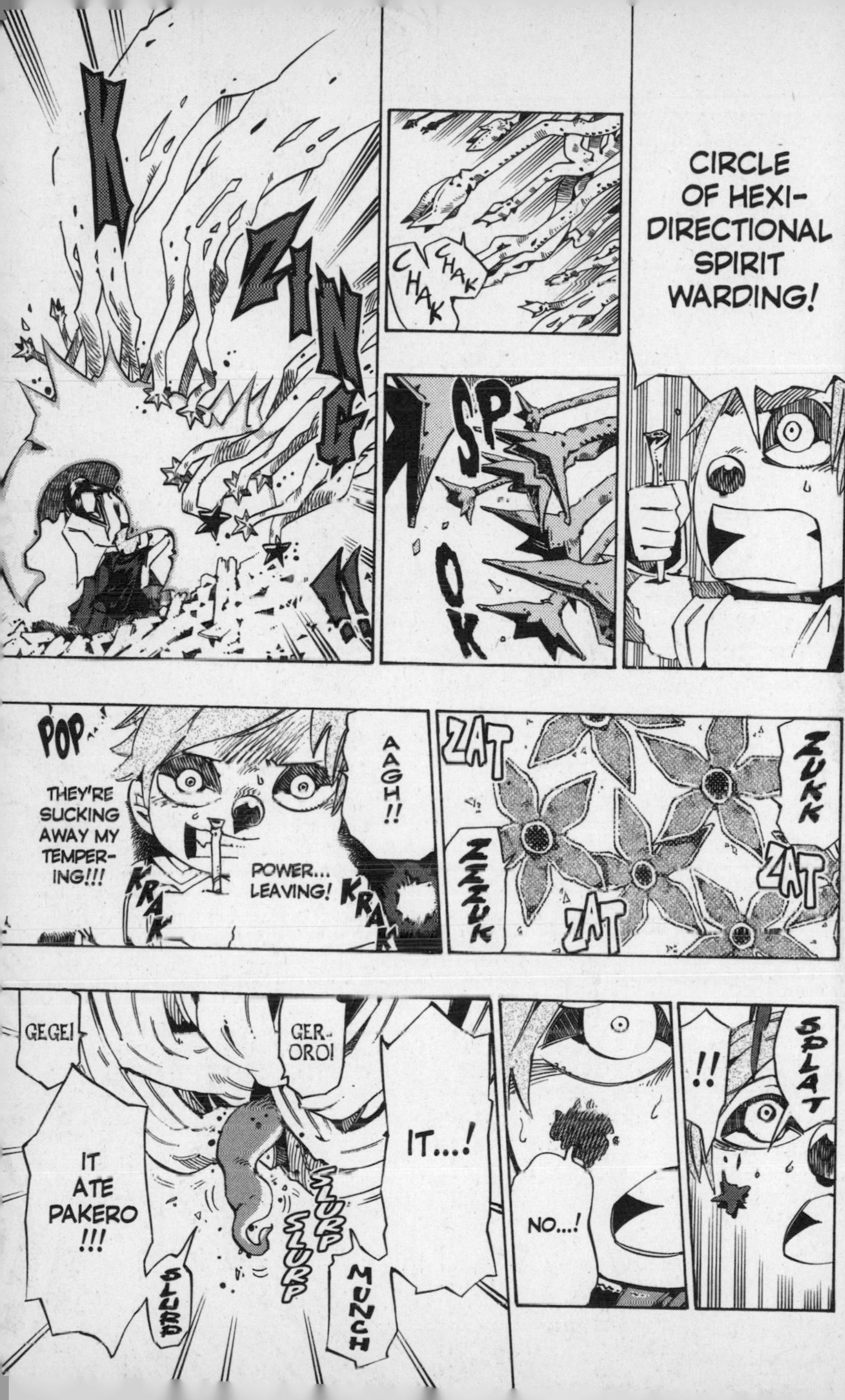

CIRCLE OF HEXI-DIRECTIONAL SPIRIT WARDING!
CHAK CHAK
SPOK
KZING
ZUKK
ZAT
ZAT
ZIZZUK
ZAT
AAGH!!
POWER... LEAVING!
KRAK
KRAK
POP
THEY'RE SUCKING AWAY MY TEMPER-ING!!!
!!
SPLAT
NO...!
IT...!
GER-OROI
GEGEI
IT ATE PAKERO!!!
SLURP
SLURP
MUNCH
SLURP

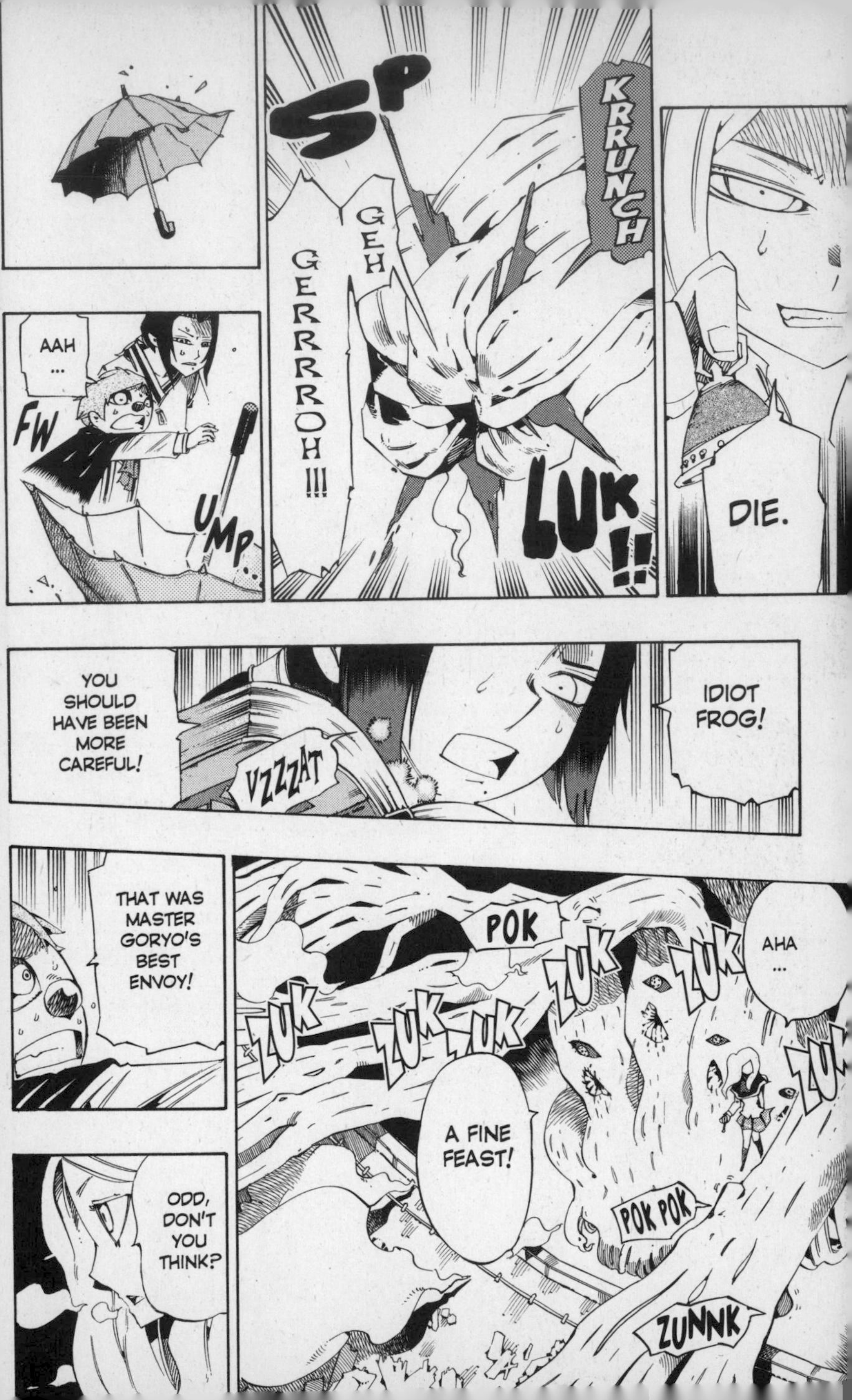
DIE.
KRRUNCH
SP
GEH
GERRRROH!!!
LUK!!
AAH ...
FW
UMP...
IDIOT FROG!
VZZZAT
YOU SHOULD HAVE BEEN MORE CAREFUL!
AHA ...
ZUK
POK
ZUK
ZUK
ZUK
ZUK
ZUK
A FINE FEAST!
POK POK
ZUNNK
THAT WAS MASTER GORYO'S BEST ENVOY!
ODD, DON'T YOU THINK?

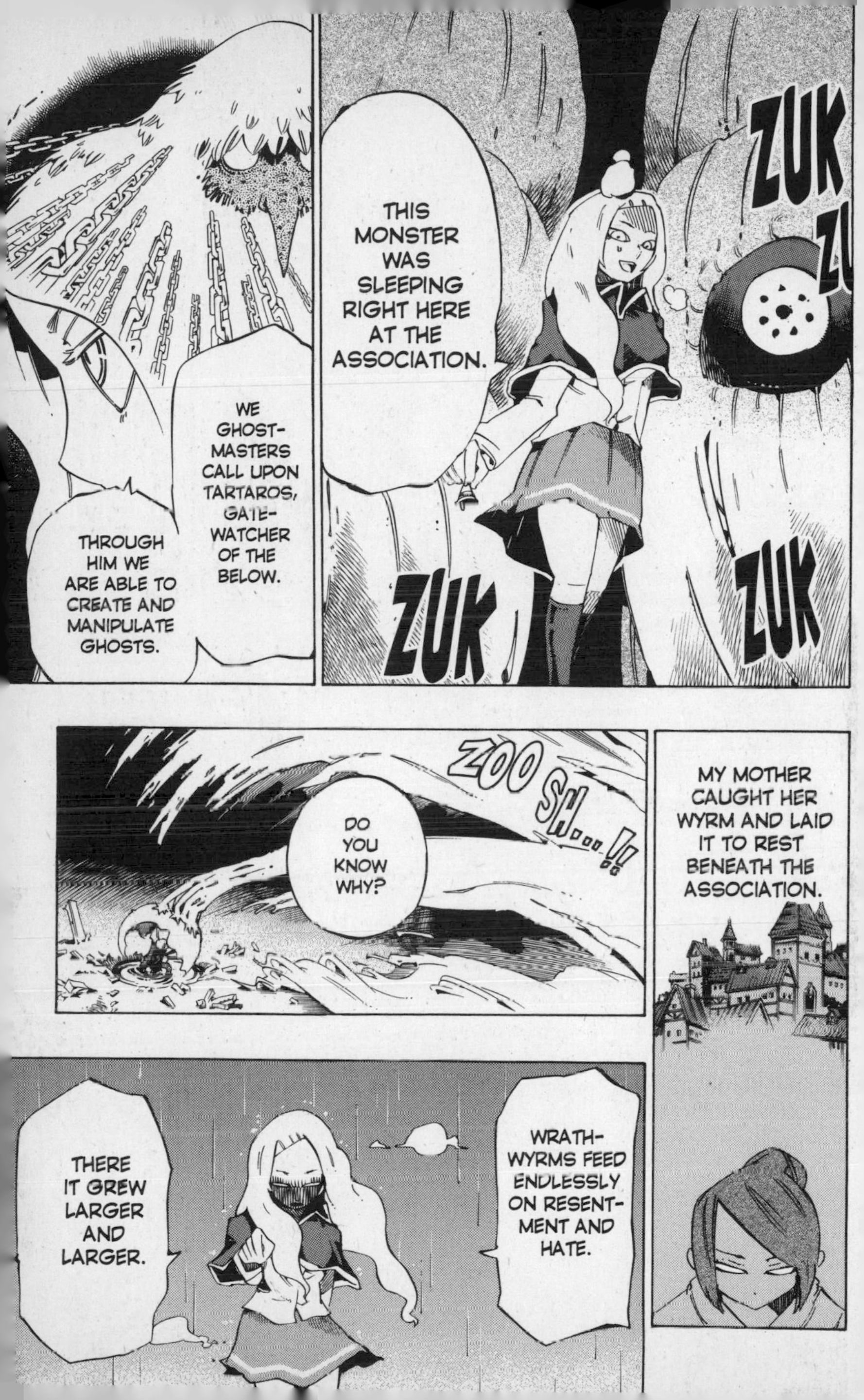
ZUK ZU
THIS MONSTER WAS SLEEPING RIGHT HERE AT THE ASSOCIATION.
ZUK
ZUK
WE GHOST-MASTERS CALL UPON TARTAROS, GATE-WATCHER OF THE BELOW.
THROUGH HIM WE ARE ABLE TO CREATE AND MANIPULATE GHOSTS.
MY MOTHER CAUGHT HER WYRM AND LAID IT TO REST BENEATH THE ASSOCIATION.
ZOOSH...!!
DO YOU KNOW WHY?
WRATH-WYRMS FEED ENDLESSLY ON RESENT-MENT AND HATE.
THERE IT GREW LARGER AND LARGER.

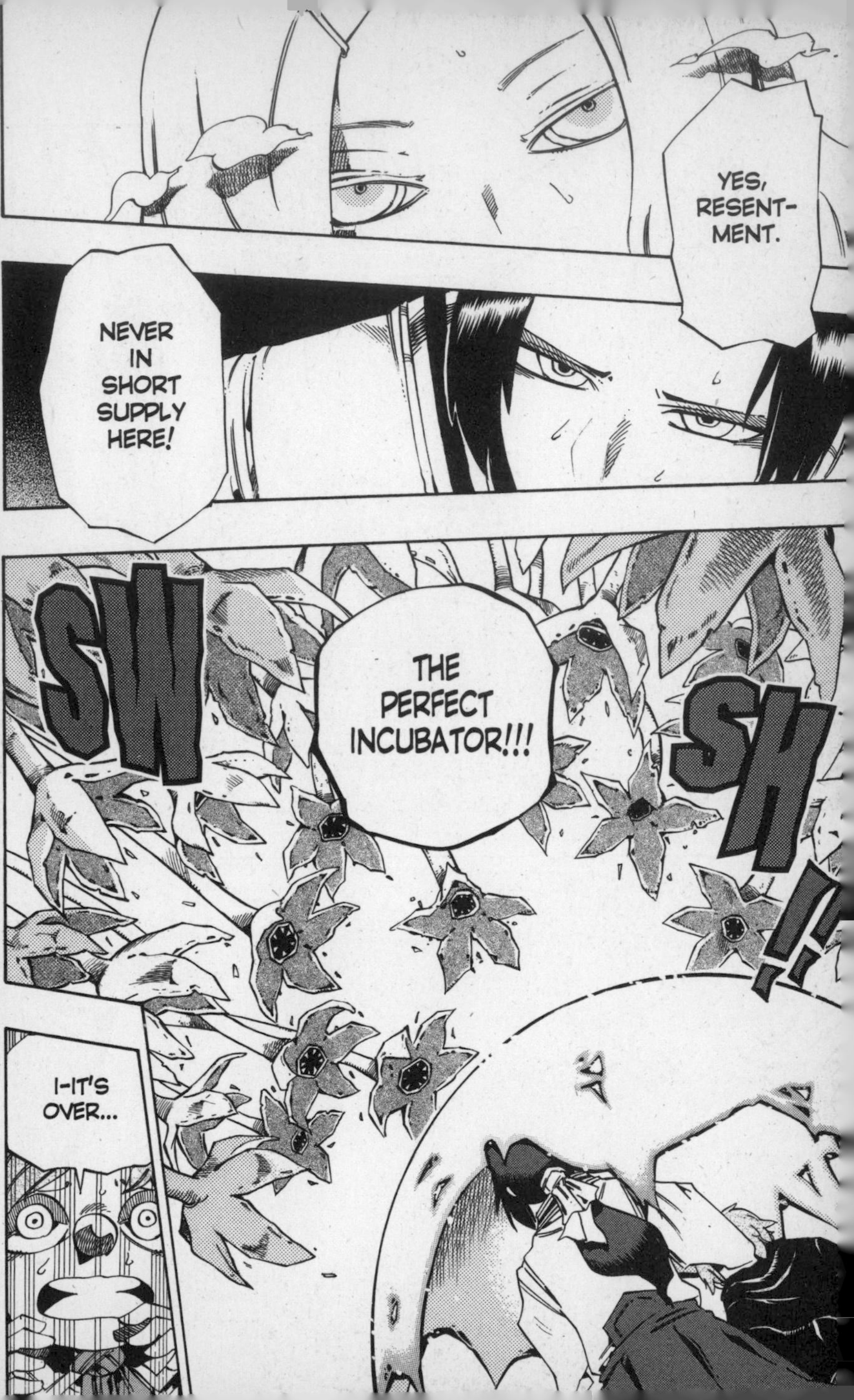
YES, RESENT-MENT.
NEVER IN SHORT SUPPLY HERE!
SH
THE PERFECT INCUBATOR!!!
SW
SH!!
I-IT'S OVER...

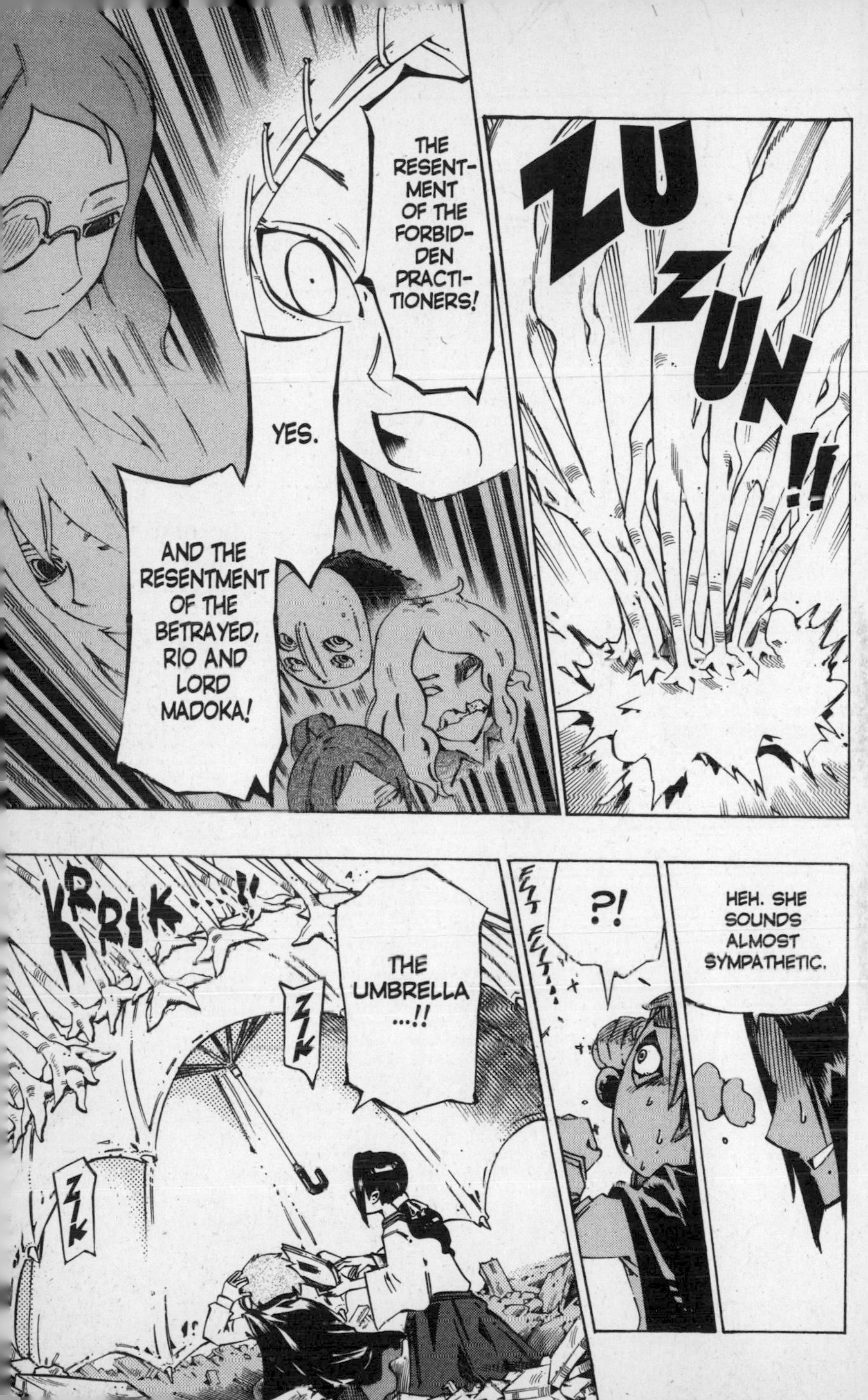
ZUZUN!!
THE RESENTMENT OF THE FORBIDDEN PRACTITIONERS!
YES.
AND THE RESENTMENT OF THE BETRAYED, RIO AND LORD MADOKA!
HEH. SHE SOUNDS ALMOST SYMPATHETIC.
?!
THE UMBRELLA...!!
KRRIK...!!
ZIK
ZIK

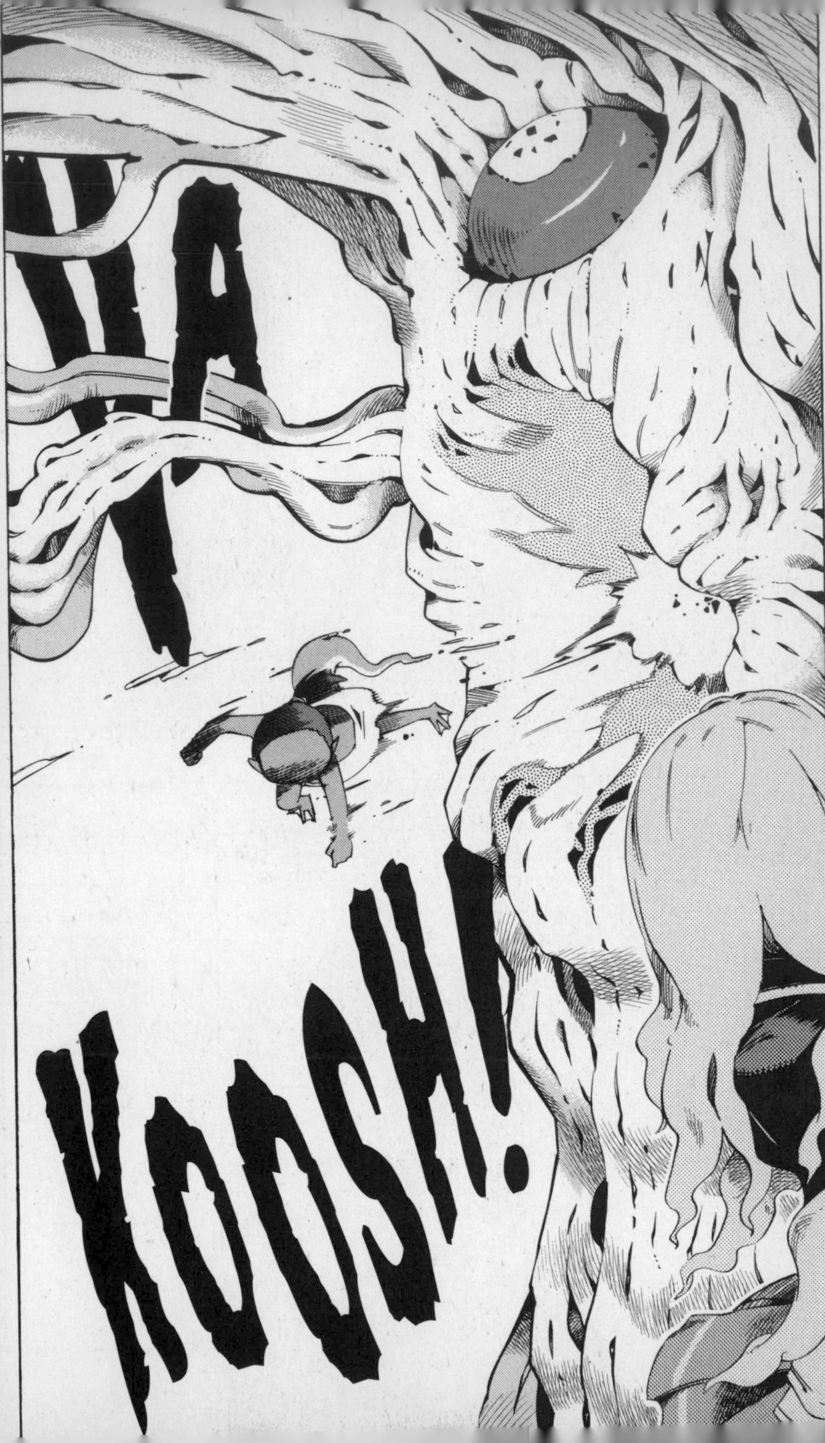
WA
KRASH!

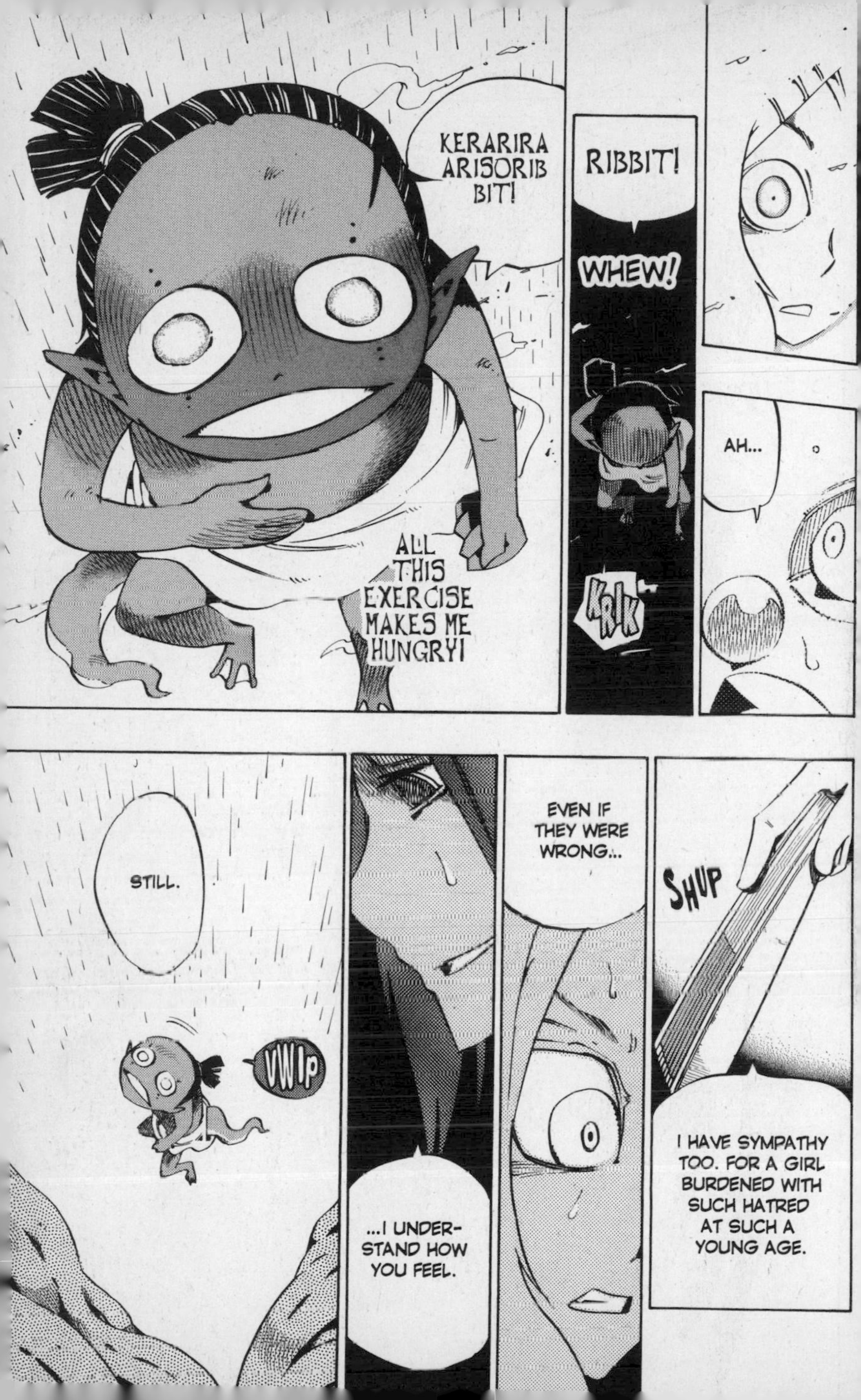
AH...
RIBBIT!
WHEW!
KRIK
KERARIRA ARISORIB BIT!
ALL THIS EXERCISE MAKES ME HUNGRY!
SHUP
I HAVE SYMPATHY TOO. FOR A GIRL BURDENED WITH SUCH HATRED AT SUCH A YOUNG AGE.
EVEN IF THEY WERE WRONG...
...I UNDERSTAND HOW YOU FEEL.
STILL.
VWIP

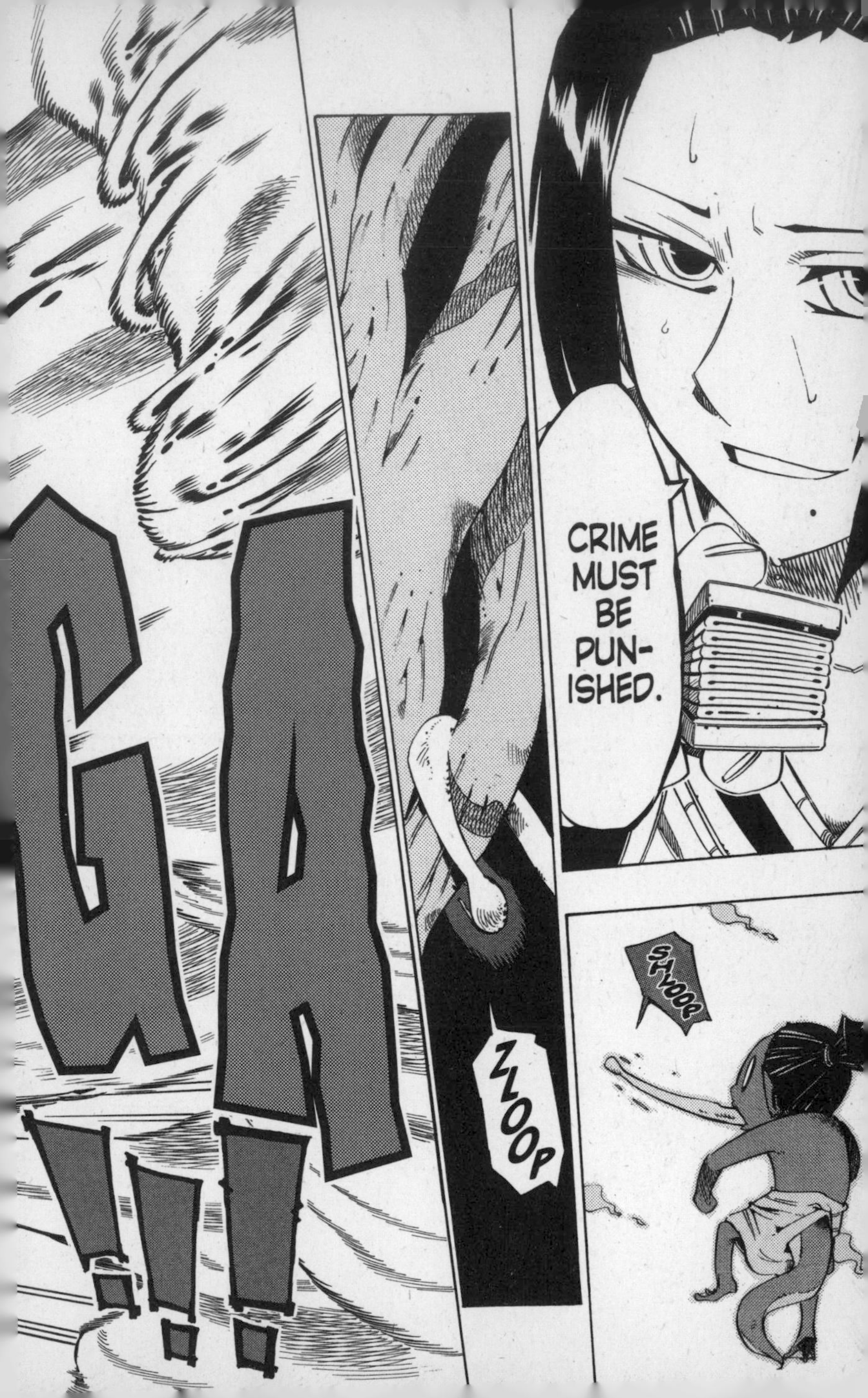
CRIME MUST BE PUN-ISHED.
SHYOOP
ZLOOP
GA!!!

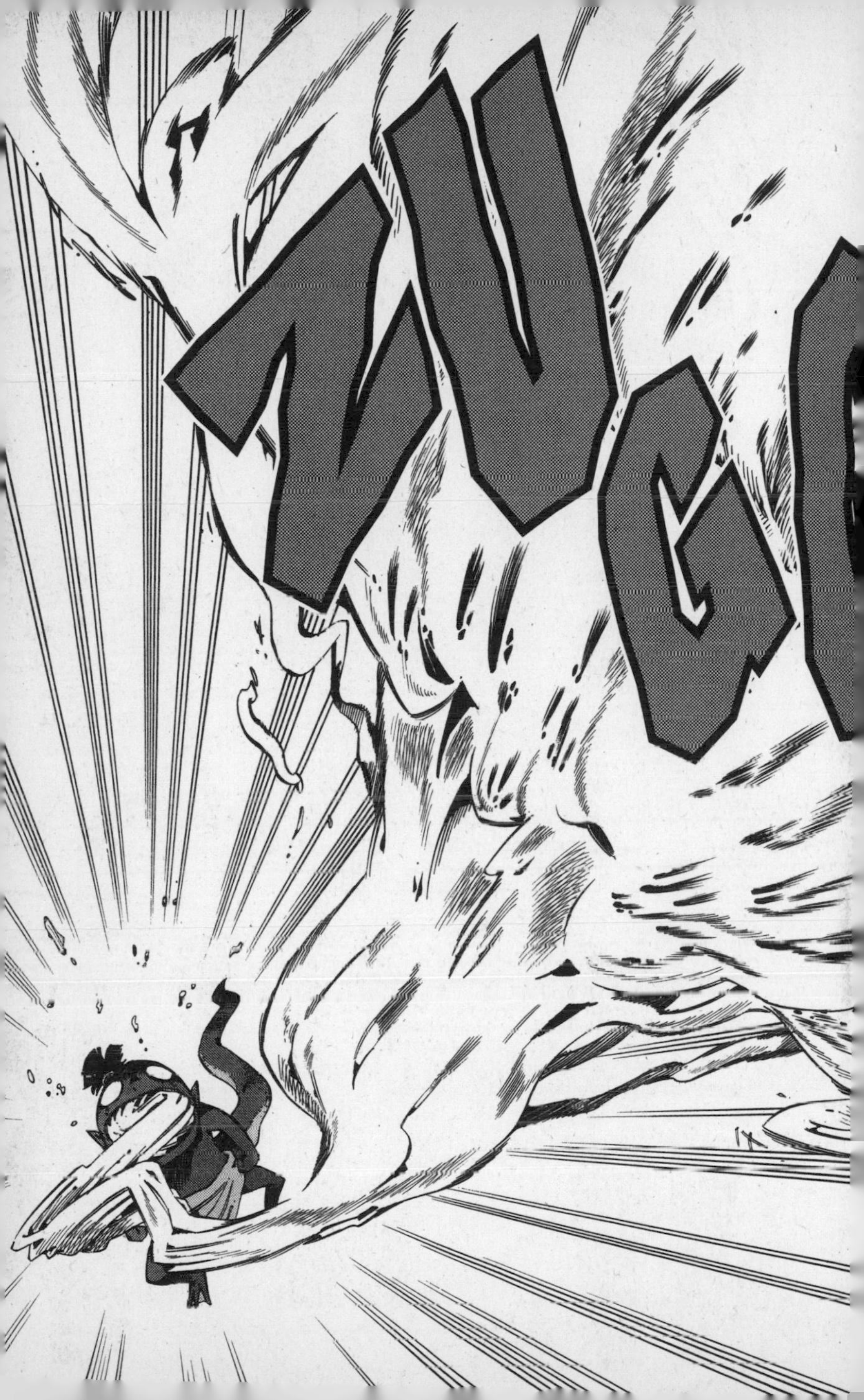
ZUG

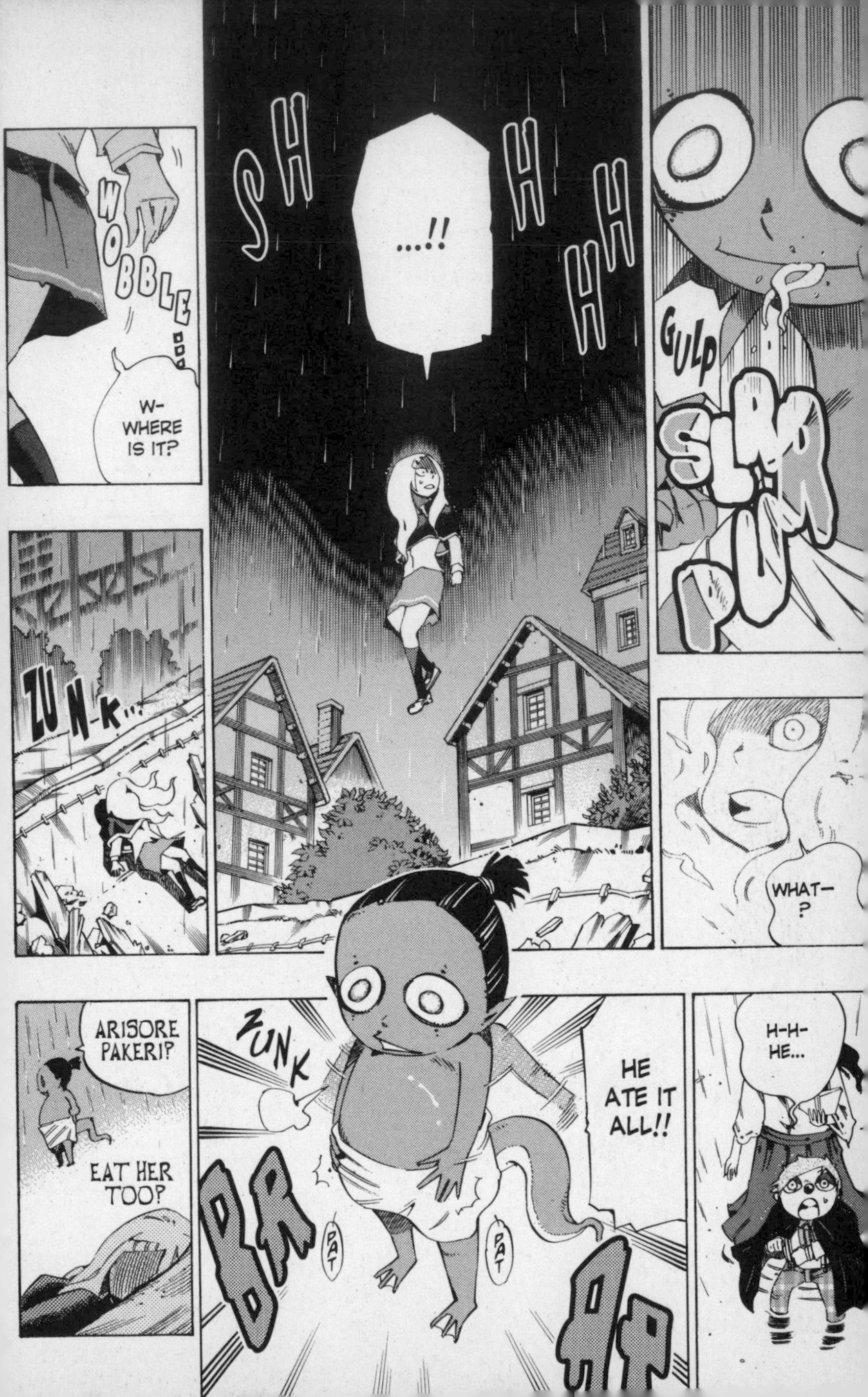
GULP
SLURP
WHAT—?
SH
...!!
HHHH
WOBBLE...
W-WHERE IS IT?
ZUN-K...
H-H-HE...
HE ATE IT ALL!!
ZUNK
PAT
PAT
BRAP
ARISORE PAKERI?
EAT HER TOO?

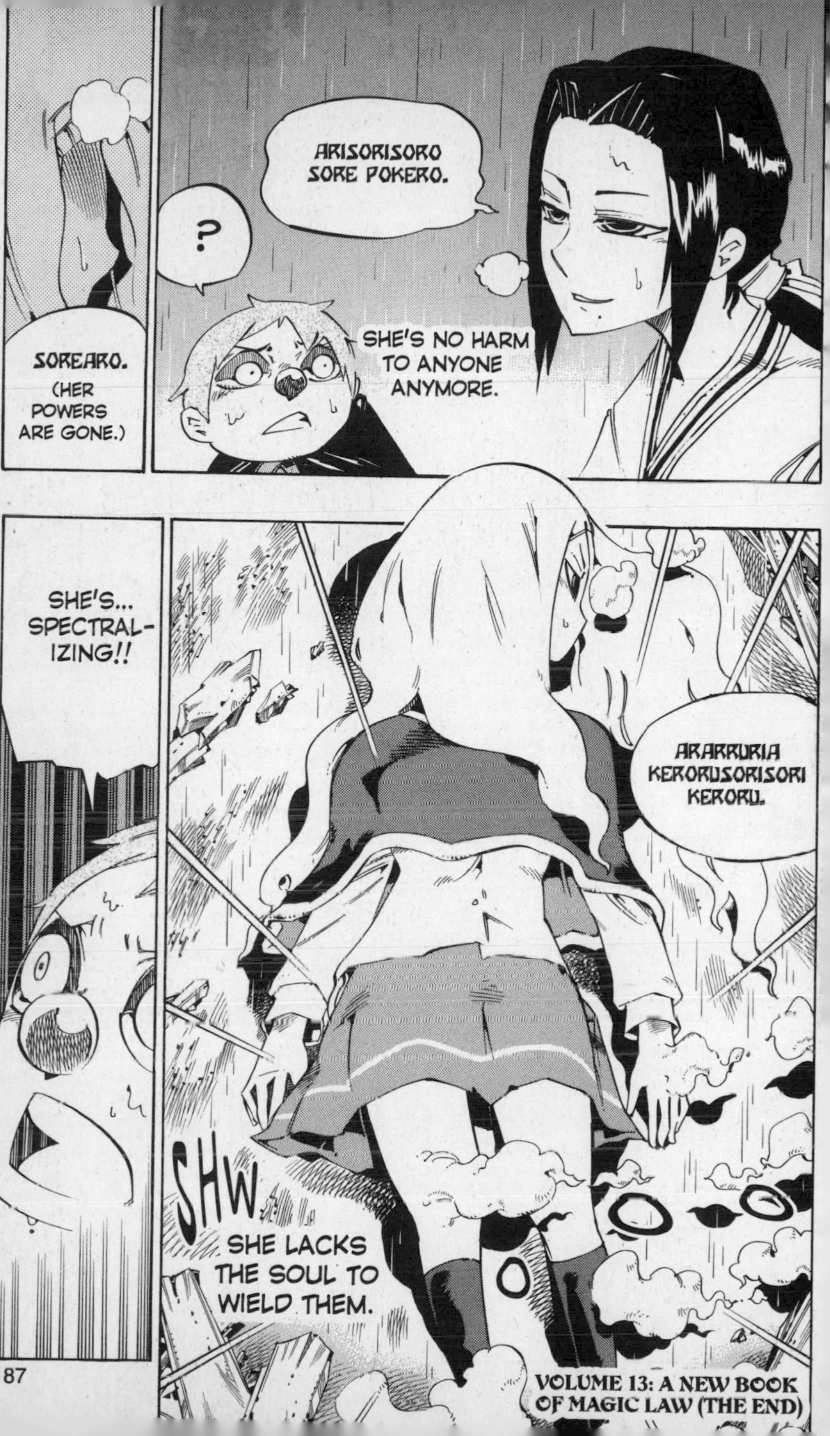
ARISORISORO SORE POKERO.
?
SHE'S NO HARM TO ANYONE ANYMORE.
SOREARO.
(HER POWERS ARE GONE.)
ARARRURIA KERORUSORISORI KERORU.
SHW
SHE LACKS THE SOUL TO WIELD THEM.
SHE'S... SPECTRAL-IZING!!
VOLUME 13: A NEW BOOK OF MAGIC LAW (THE END)

In The Next Volume...

This Kid's not someone you discount... especially when he's a Cortlaw!

Available December 2009!

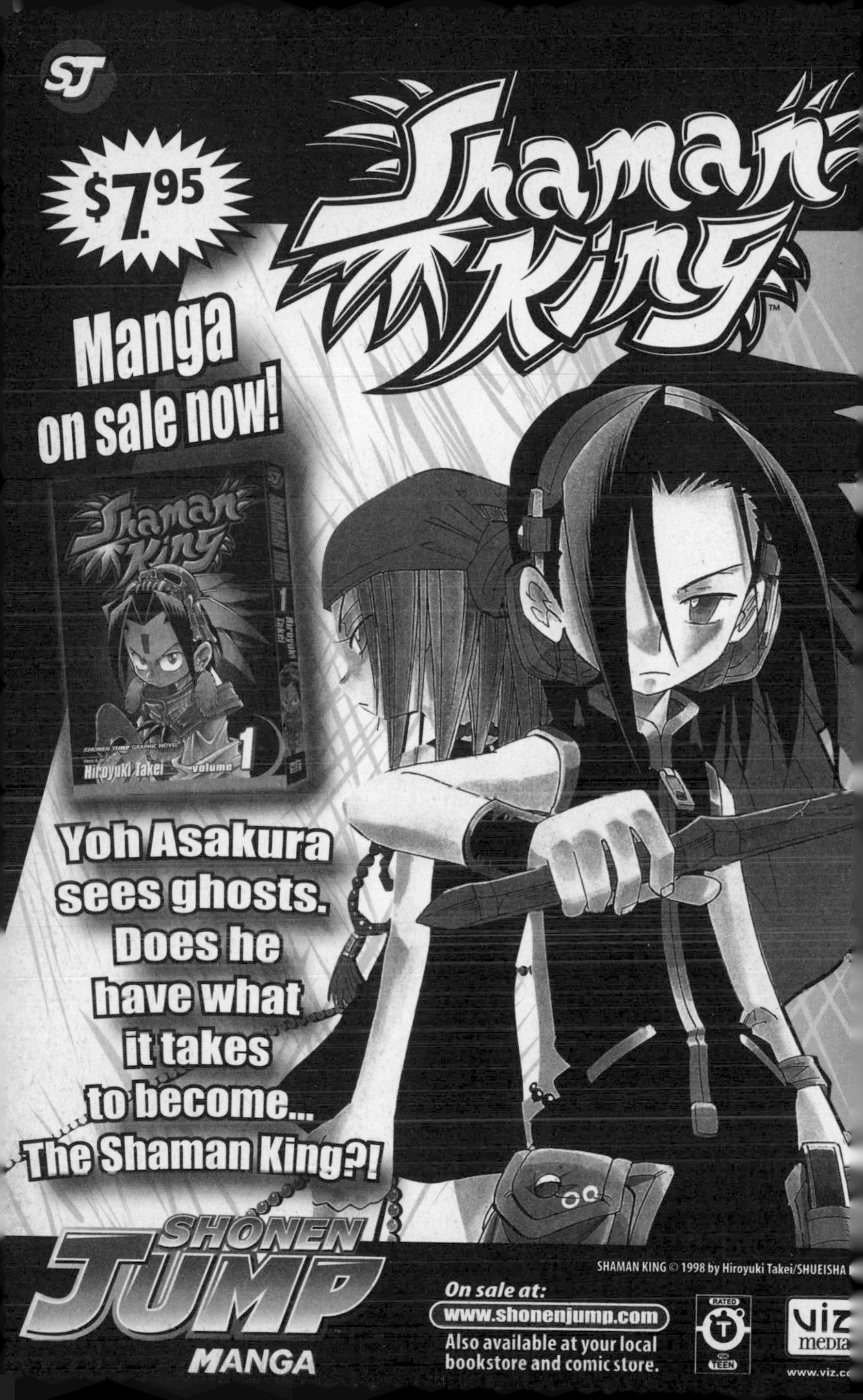
SJ
$7.95
Shaman King™
Manga on sale now!
Shaman King
1
Hiroyuki Takei
SHONEN JUMP GRAPHIC NOVEL
Hiroyuki Takei
volume 1
Yoh Asakura sees ghosts. Does he have what it takes to become... The Shaman King?!
SHONEN JUMP
MANGA
SHAMAN KING © 1998 by Hiroyuki Takei/SHUEISHA
On sale at:
www.shonenjump.com
Also available at your local bookstore and comic store.
RATED T FOR TEEN
viz media

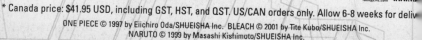